To Richard
Best wishes ~
Dorothy Ogilvie

For Richard,
A good history student—
with best regards,

Taylor Pensoneau

mber 24, 1997

GOVERNOR RICHARD OGILVIE

GOVERNOR

RICHARD OGILVIE

In the Interest of the State

Taylor Pensoneau . . . .

Southern Illinois University Press
Carbondale and Edwardsville

00 99 98 97   4 3 2 1

Library of Congress Cataloging-in-Publication Data

Pensoneau, Taylor.
    Governor Richard Ogilvie : in the interest of
the state / Taylor Pensoneau.
        p. cm.
    Includes bibliographical references and index.
    1. Ogilvie, Richard B. 2. Governors—Illinois—Biography.
3. Illinois—Politics and government—1951–   I. Title.
F546.4.O38P46   1997
977.3′043—DC21   97-3816
    ISBN 0-8093-2148-3 (alk. paper)   CIP

Frontispiece: Richard B. Ogilvie.
Courtesy of the Illinois State Historical Library.

For my wife, Elizabeth,
and Jared, Jennifer, Terry, and Travis

Contents

Preface . . . . *ix*

1. Turning Points: 1944 and 1969 1

2. Inauguration and Transition:
   The Early Days of Ogilvie's Governorship 11

3. A Political Career on the Line 29

4. From Sheriff to Cook County Board President 38

5. The Accardo Case: Taking on the Big Tuna 59

6. The 1968 Campaign and Vote 65

7. Bourbons in the Senate, Scandal in the High Court 82

8. Proposed, Debated, Passed: The State Income Tax 95

9. More Ogilvie Coups 108

10. The Constitutional Convention: A Triumph amid Setbacks . 119

11. War on Polluters 145

12. Campus Riots and the Guard 160

13. Winning Control of the Budget 171

14. Ogilvie in Person and in the Press 188

15. Prisons, Highways, and Other Ventures 209

16. Dorothy Ogilvie 226

17. Powell's Cash and Racetracks: Public Anger Boils 234

18. Political Death 247

19. Afterward 261

Notes 271

Select Bibliography 285

Index 287

Illustrations following page 94

Preface

A few weeks before the end of 1972, I stood alone on a frosty evening at Meigs Field in Chicago waiting for a flight that would take me home to Springfield. Staring at Lake Michigan from the terminal, I failed to notice an individual who rather suddenly had approached and was standing by my side. When I did turn my head, I found myself facing Governor Richard Ogilvie. Having covered the administration of Ogilvie as the Illinois political writer for the *St. Louis Post-Dispatch*, I had become well acquainted with the governor. When he learned that I was heading for Springfield as he was, he convinced me to join him on his flight aboard a state airplane. This came at a time when he was a lame-duck governor, having just lost a bid for reelection.

As we soared over the dark, flat Illinois prairie, we chatted informally about his four years in office, rehashing in particular the far-reaching governmental revision that he had choreographed to a backdrop of riots, political scandals, and other turbulence. We pretty much agreed, and I think the word was his, that his period in the Illinois capital was a "wild" one. I remember telling him that I'd bet the Ogilvie era would make a book some day, when it was possible to look back and digest it all. I do not recall his reply, and it was not a subject I dwelled upon.

Not until 1993. I had just coauthored a book on former governor Dan Walker of Illinois, the individual who brought the Ogilvie governorship to an end. After the Walker book hit the bookstores, several friends and colleagues strongly suggested to me that an Ogilvie book also was in order. As many of them saw it, there was no better governor in a more tempestuous era in modern Illinois history than Ogilvie, a man whose life revolved around an especially gritty sense of leadership. Continued ignoring of Ogilvie by political biographers, they felt, was a grave omission.

Consequently, in the spring of 1994, I undertook the writing of this book after obtaining the cooperation of Mrs. Richard Ogilvie and Elizabeth Simer, the Ogilvies' daughter. The many hours I spent interviewing them and working with them to gather background materials for the book were most warm and rewarding. Overall, more than eighty interviews were conducted for the book.

With few exceptions, those questioned were overly generous with their time. Special thanks also must be accorded certain other persons for assistance on this project. They include Janice Petterchak, the former director of the Illinois State Historical Library; Mary Michals, curator of the audio-visual collection at the historical library; Christine Henderson, reference librarian at the Illinois State Library; and Judy Stephenson, reference librarian at the United States Army Armor School Library at Fort Knox in Kentucky.

The Illinois State Historical Library at Springfield is a repository of many documents tied to Governor Ogilvie and his administration. The Ogilvie papers consist of 126 cubic feet of materials dating for the most part from 1969 through 1972, the years of his governorship. The collection contains papers of and relating to the governor, Dorothy Ogilvie, and the key members of Ogilvie's staff. Much of the governor's file contains correspondence regarding agencies under Ogilvie, reports by department heads, and Ogilvie's appointment books and schedules. Mrs. Ogilvie's file features her speeches and correspondence on two projects to which she devoted considerable time, restoration of the Governor's Mansion and care of the mentally retarded. The files of the governor's aides are quite informative and contain some of the most reflective material on the administration. Assistants contributing to the collection include Brian Whalen, John Dailey, William Hanley, Jay Bryant, and Fred Bird. The single most uniform and consistent record of the administration well may be Bird's file of chronologically arranged press releases, starting with ones during Ogilvie's campaign for governor and running through his final day in office.

I also want to note that some material in this book was drawn from my earlier book, *Dan Walker: The Glory and the Tragedy*. And a much more extensive resource for this book was the collection of my personal notes from my coverage of the Ogilvie administration, an indispensable reference.

The Ogilvie era was an exciting time to be reporting on Illinois government and politics, and I was fortunate to have had the opportunity to be part of the Illinois Statehouse press corps in those days. Readers of this book may have little trouble recognizing the writing style of a journalist. In addition, the book does not follow a rigidly chronological format. Some segments are presented out of chronological sequence in an effort to make the story as readable as possible. The Ogilvie story is a very interesting one. If it does not read that way, it is the fault of the author.

GOVERNOR RICHARD OGILVIE

Turning Points: 1944 and 1969

1944

Nineteen forty-four. The things people remember about that year. It was the one and only time the Cardinals and the Browns, the two professional baseball teams from St. Louis, ever met in the World Series. Naturally, the Cards won. The mighty Army backfield tandem of Doc Blanchard and Glenn Davis, Mr. Inside and Mr. Outside, coasted through opposing linemen in black-and-white newsreels. And Americans swayed across the land to the Andrews Sisters' "Rum and Coca-Cola," which came close to becoming a national theme song.

When thoughts turn to the images of Yanks fighting and bleeding and dying on the battlefields of the European and the Pacific theaters, "Rum and Coca-Cola" always seems to be playing in the background, somehow making the terror of it all go down smoother. They came from all over to fight in World War II, and for every American in uniform, life never would be the same. Many did not return home. Others made it back torn and scarred—some broken for good and an equal number more determined than ever to still make something out of the rest of their lives. For a few, their taste of battle would leave them bathed in glory.

Nineteen forty-four. The year that the war dealt a trump card for many. It could occur so quickly, in a flash. A thousand times a day, every day, including December 13, 1944. That was the day life changed violently in a split second for a spunky kid who had dropped out of Yale University to enlist in the army at the age of nineteen.

By the time he arrived in France late in October 1944, the Allies were moving steadily across that war-ravaged country, pushing the Germans back to their own border and toward their eventual surrender in early 1945. But the action was still hot and heavy in those waning days of 1944, and Dick Ogilvie, the erstwhile Eli, was in the middle of it, right where he wanted to be. A thirst for military life was in Ogilvie's blood. He had yearned to go to West Point or, failing that, to the Virginia Military Institute. But poor eyesight barred him from both places. Keeping him out of uniform, though, was another matter.

The final days of 1944 were pivotal ones in what was known as the European theater. By then, the young man from Yale had become Sergeant Ogilvie, a tank commander in Company B of the army's 781st Tank Battalion. His unit, which had been activated less than two years before at Fort Knox in Kentucky, had a motto, "Duty Before Self." It could not have been more appropriate for the guys in the tanks.

The truth of the matter was that many soldiers shied away from duty in the hundreds of thousands of tanks that rumbled, clanking and growling, across the landscapes of World War II. Being confined in a cramped armored box without windows for lengthy spells could cause a soldier to lose his bearings. Limited visibility was just part of the problem, though. The tankers lived in morbid fear of hearing, through the whine and clatter of their machine, that earsplitting clang from a round that could mean the destruction of their vehicle and death for its occupants. Tank duty was not for the fainthearted.

Getting a taste of combat was a long time coming for the 781st battalion. While other units were going overseas, the 781st seemed mired at Fort Knox, where it spent long days and nights testing tanks and other equipment in the countryside. Contact with the Germans still was nearly two months away when the officers and men of the battalion, their stomachs filled with Red Cross doughnuts and coffee, set sail for Europe in mid-October 1944. They would reach Marseilles by the end of that month, but much of the unit's necessary supplies would not. So the 781st would remain at the French port for a month, while the tedious job of reoutfitting was carried out, before finally departing by truck and rail for the battlefront up north.

Even that expedition appeared to be as slow as molasses. According to a history of the battalion, "engineers stopped the train to drop into a brasserie for a cognac or visit a friend along the way." However, "the French were probably no less surprised by tanks so massive that they fell through flat cars in the middle of tunnels and by marksmen who practiced from moving boxcars with tommy guns."[1]

At last, on December 7, the 781st moved into the heat of battle as part of the Seventh United States Army—which was fighting its way toward the Rhine River, the last western defense line of Germany. From that point until the end of the war, Ogilvie's battalion engaged in one fierce encounter after another, many on German soil against enemy soldiers trying desperately to stave off defeat.

The hours that Ogilvie faced German fire, though, were short-numbered. He was commanding a Sherman tank on December 13 in a battle for Bitche, a Nazi-held town in the Vosges Mountains of northeastern France, very close to Germany.[2] The assault on Bitche, the first engagement for Ogilvie's unit, was no easy undertaking. Bitche was one of the most heavily fortified places on the Maginot Line, which ironically had been built by France to protect its frontier against Germany.

While Ogilvie was attempting to herd some German prisoners back to American lines for questioning on that fateful December day, he came under heavy bombardment. At one point, he opened the turret of his tank to see for himself what was happening. He was standing on the floor of the tank, his head exposed above the rim of the hatch.

Suddenly, for Ogilvie, combat in the war was over. Shrapnel from a German shell exploding by his tank slammed into his mouth, leaving him dazed and temporarily blinded. Later, he would compare the impact to being hit with a sledgehammer. He didn't remember much else. The shell fragment that tore into his lower face knocked out many of his teeth before passing through the back of his mouth and lodging in the rear of his neck. Ogilvie's jaw was demolished. His right eye regained its vision fairly quickly, but he remained blinded in his left eye for several days. Ogilvie's jaw and face were so badly maimed that a tracheotomy was performed on him at a field hospital, allowing him to breathe through his throat. For the next several months, this was how he would breathe.

The next seven months Ogilvie spent in hospitals, first in Europe and then in the United States at Valley Forge General Hospital in Pennsylvania. The army had a plastic surgery center at Valley Forge, and it was there that doctors painstakingly reassembled the face of the young tank commander. The task was not easy. Ogilvie's jaw was damaged so severely that doctors put it in a plaster cast at first instead of just wiring it together with wire and rubber bands. That came later. For a time during this ordeal, Ogilvie had in his mouth what he dubbed "a metallic thing" for easier acceptance of drugs. This contributed greatly to the distortion of his face. Etched into his memory were the reactions of those who saw his face.

For a while, depression dominated Ogilvie's life. His weight plummeted from 200 pounds to 140. His badly cut lips needed repairing; he had shreds of shrapnel buried in other parts of his body. And in his mind, the operations seemed never ending. But only so much could be done. He was never to regain feeling in his lower lip, and one side of his mouth lacked a gum. Permanent damage to the left side of his face made smiling in a normal fashion nearly impossible.

When Ogilvie was honorably released from the army on July 21, 1945, his discharge certificate noted that he had a disability. But his spirits were on the rise, and one thing was for sure. Richard Buell Ogilvie was dead set against becoming a permanent casualty of World War II. Before entering the army, Ogilvie wanted to be a history teacher and football coach. However, he had changed his mind during the hospital days, deciding to become a lawyer instead. So, he figured, finish at Yale first and then go on to law school.

When he entered the service, his parents lived in New York. By the time of his release, they had moved back to Illinois, a state where Ogilvie had spent part of his childhood. Well then, why not Illinois as the place to study law? Illinois, with that great big city of Chicago, certainly had to be rich in opportunities for lawyers, he thought. This was one tank commander focusing on the future, and Illinois just might be a good bet.

1969

Two-and-a-half decades after his brush with death in World War II, Richard Ogilvie had every reason to believe he had moved wisely in pinning his hopes for success in life on Illinois.

In September 1962, *Life* magazine included Ogilvie, a Chicago attorney, among the "red-hot hundred" in the publication's "Take-over Generation"—the future movers and shakers in the United States.[3] Ogilvie, thirty-nine years old at the time, was pictured right along with playwright Edward Albee, novelist John Updike, Metropolitan Opera soprano Leontyne Price, an assortment of young business tycoons and obviously up-and-coming politicians, people like John Lindsay, Frank Church, Thomas Eagleton, and Mark Hatfield. *Life* was duly impressed that Ogilvie had taken on the Chicago underworld, including the prosecution of mobster Tony Accardo, as a special assistant to the United States attorney general from 1958 to 1961. The magazine also noted that Ogilvie was the Republican candidate for sheriff of Cook County in 1962.

Ogilvie made the editors of *Life* look good. He won the sheriff's contest, then the top office of Cook County in 1966, and still another post in 1968, the governorship of Illinois—the crown jewel of state politics. Ogilvie almost made it appear easy. His rise in only six years from sheriff of the state's largest county to governor happened in a fashion so smooth and almost predictable that one could be forgiven for feeling that Ogilvie ascended to the governor's office in Springfield matter-of-factly.

Very little drama attended his rise to the top. Outwardly, the man did not have charisma, or more bluntly, he lacked political sex appeal. Never pretended to have it, never would.

Actually, *Life* magazine had noticed Ogilvie prior to 1962. In 1959, *Life* ran an intriguing picture of Ogilvie with a spread on organized crime.[4] The photo shows him, bundled in an overcoat, standing alone on a wintry night by a one-time gambling joint in the Chicago suburb of Niles. His face is fixed in a determined stare that seems to be daring somebody unseen to draw on him. The slice of uncolored cityscape in the background is bleak and darn near haunting. It could have been a shot out of one of those big-city detective movies in the 1940s. The caption under the picture says simply that Ogilvie "gave up good law partnership to hunt hoods." A real tough guy this Ogilvie.

This was the only image, that of a tough guy, which many Illinoisans held of Ogilvie when he became the thirty-fifth governor of their state. He had emerged politically as a law-and-order advocate during a tempestuous period in which the nation was beset violently by domestic upheaval and opposition to a war in Vietnam in which Americans were dying. Ogilvie was truly, some argued, a tough guy in the proverbial right place at the right time.

As Ogilvie took the oath of office on January 13, 1969, the only expectation or hope of many in Illinois was that the new governor could keep a lid on things, make sure the streets were safe for law-abiding folks.

The decade of the 1960s, a cauldron of dissension unlike any other period in modern American history, was nearing an end. The forces unleashed during the decade—the political activism and an erupting social consciousness—had to be dealt with in Illinois and elsewhere. Reeling from the 1960s and uncertain of what lay in store in the 1970s, Illinois was dangerously adrift in a sea of turmoil that begged for leadership. And so along came Ogilvie, riding into the breach.

When Ogilvie raised his right hand in the Illinois State Armory in Springfield to receive the oath of office from Chief Justice Roy J. Solfisburg Jr. of the Illinois Supreme Court, the state was getting its first Republican governor since William G. Stratton, who left office in 1961. In the eight years between Stratton and Ogilvie, the governor's chair had been occupied by two Democrats, handsome Otto Kerner and the genial Samuel Shapiro. They had been live-and-let-live individuals, hardly exponents of a strong governorship. After Kerner and Shapiro, Ogilvie would give a rude awakening.

Propelled by Ogilvie, Illinois government would undergo radical change. More than a boat rocker, Ogilvie would give the government the hard kick in the pants needed to make it responsive, really responsive, to the glaring needs and concerns of the citizenry. Modern Illinois government came of age under Ogilvie—so much so that little deviation from the course set by Ogilvie would be visible through the rest of the twentieth century.

And it all happened so rapidly. Ogilvie only had four years at the helm. When he sought reelection as governor in 1972, he was beaten by his Democratic challenger, Chicago lawyer Dan Walker, one of the most dynamic campaigners to come down the political pike in Illinois.

After his defeat, Ogilvie passed quickly from the state scene, returning to Chicago where he successfully mixed the practice of law and business dealings until his death in 1988. To many of those he had governed, Ogilvie was out of mind the day after he left the Capitol in Springfield. Anyway, few had gotten a close look at the man when he was governor. All that may have been remembered was that Ogilvie led Illinois in a painful period of turmoil, in an era when turmoil also plagued the rest of the nation.

Nobody could have predicted all of the things that came to a head in Illinois during the Ogilvie years. Fortunately, the stalwart Ogilvie neither hesitated nor flinched at doing what he knew had to be done to keep his state afloat during these years, though some of his actions were unpopular and politically disastrous.

Yet in the days following his reelection defeat, Ogilvie was the beneficiary of kind words from sources not always forthcoming with compliments. "In one term," wrote Mike Royko, then a hard-boiled columnist for the old *Chicago Daily News*, Ogilvie "built one of the nation's finest state governments." Moreover, added Royko, "the calm Scotsman" thought that he could retain the governorship because of his "honest approach and excellent performance." But "the voters weren't buying it. . . . the best man in Illinois government, maybe the best governor in the country, didn't make it."[5] Not long afterward, an editorial in the rival *Chicago Tribune* agreed that Ogilvie had accomplished something rare in bringing "political courage to the governor's chair."[6]

For their part, political scientists, historians, and others suspected that it might be a long time before the likes of a Richard Ogilvie would be seen in Illinois again. They were to lament that, as his successors approached the job so much more animated, Ogilvie was being relegated far too quickly to the dustbin of Illinois history. That was unfortunate, they felt, because the Ogilvie story is a good one.

Roots

The governor was not the first in his family to be seriously hurt in combat. Reuben M. Spivey, the great-grandfather of Ogilvie on his father's side, lost an arm from a wound that he received while serving with the Confederate Army at the bloody Battle of Shiloh in 1862.[7]

Revelations about Reuben Spivey's life indicate he was a true forefather of

Dick Ogilvie. After the Civil War, Spivey went to Kansas, where he established a reputation during a long career with the Santa Fe railroad as a law-and-order advocate fighting cattle town desperadoes. Spivey crammed more into his years on earth than numerous other men combined. No wonder *Santa Fe Magazine* called him "a grand old man" in a 1914 feature, written when Spivey was pushing seventy years of age.[8]

Born and raised in Alabama of Scottish-English parentage, Spivey was a military academy cadet in his home state who put on the uniform of the Confederacy when federal troops burned his school. Serving with the Thirty-fifth Alabama Volunteers, he saw action in numerous battles besides Shiloh, including engagements in Georgia and Mississippi. In 1864, he was commissioned a captain of his company. Nobody mistook Spivey for anything but a military man the rest of his life.

A pioneer in the building of the Santa Fe, Spivey was for a time a land commissioner for the railroad, a job that involved a lot of surveying and appraisal work. Later, he was the company's immigration agent, another key assignment in that the Santa Fe wanted to spur migration to Kansas to trigger economic development along the railroad. It was during these years that he helped put Newton and Dodge City on the map, two Kansas towns linked to the Santa Fe. Spivey was the first mayor of Newton, which in the days leading up to its incorporation was a haven for gamblers and bawdy women who preyed on the cowpunchers driving cattle up the Chisholm Trail. Under the leadership of Spivey, though, law-abiding folks got the upper hand in Newton, especially after Spivey succeeded in isolating the vice dens in a tenderloin. Too, Spivey was an incorporator of Dodge City, which was as notorious for wickedness as Newton before it also was tamed.

Spivey later lived for many years in Topeka with his wife, Lina Owens, who ironically was a daughter of a Union Army colonel in the Civil War. They raised two sons and two daughters, one of whom, Alta, married a lanky fellow named Ralph Ogilvie. He was a son of an immigrant to the United States from Scotland. Unfortunately, the marriage of Alta and Ralph ended in divorce, and it fell to her to bring up their only child, a son born in 1898 named Kenneth Spivey Ogilvie.

Brought up in the Kansas City area, Kenneth Ogilvie made one move early in life that was certainly characteristic of the men in his family. He tried to enlist in the military during World War I but was turned down because he was not old enough to become a doughboy. As it happened, Kenneth Ogilvie would spend his life not at army posts but in the insurance industry. His career, in which he handled various executive roles in the indemnity business, eventually would take him and his family across the country. However, Kansas City remained his base in his early years in the industry.

It was at an agency in his hometown that he met Edna Mae Buell, a sprightly Kansas City woman four years younger than him who was holding down her "first real job" at the place. Matters between them progressed, leading to an exchange of vows on February 11, 1922, a marriage that would last more than half a century.

Tall and thin, Kenneth Ogilvie had a courtly manner about him that was visible in many ways, such as in his insistence on formal dinners with his family on those occasions when his demanding business schedule permitted him to be home. He was not, all recognized, a kisser of babies. Tim Thoelecke, a Chicago insurance man close to the Ogilvies after they came to Chicago, recalled Kenneth as "having a typical European male type of attitude. He'd put on a coat and tie to go out to get the mail. He was a very proud man." Yet, Thoelecke added, "the thing that really stood out about Ken and Edna was their modesty."[9]

In Thoelecke's mind, Edna Ogilvie was "an early version of Barbara Bush—the kind of warm, wonderful person that everybody wanted for a mother." Edna was not lacking in strong-mindedness, but she also had a sense of humor, a knack for good-natured banter. Unlike many young women at that time, she also had a love of sports that went back to her tennis playing days while in high school. Later on, Edna shared with her husband a passion for golf, a devotion to the sport that would be picked up by the couple's two sons.

The oldest was Richard Buell. He was born on February 22, 1923, the birthday of George Washington, in Kansas City, Missouri. Edna Mae Ogilvie remembered that little Richard was "a big baby, a twelve-pounder, but also, I thought, the prettiest baby I ever saw." Richard's brother, Robert Spivey, came along two years afterward.

Because Kenneth Ogilvie spent so much time on the road in his professional life, Edna was instrumental by most accounts in the rearing of the two boys. Her colleague for many years in this undertaking was Nellie, a black nanny who was a fifth member of the family for all practical purposes. Edna and Nellie were a team in housekeeping, sharing kitchen and other duties. Reportedly, both were darn good cooks.

Even the disciplining of the Ogilvie sons was shared by their mother and Nellie. To little Dick, slender and patient Nellie was an early authority figure in his life. Decades later, when Dick married Dorothy, Nellie was the only person outside of the immediate families at the small ceremony.

Being able to afford a nanny was a sign to many acquaintances that Kenneth Ogilvie was an up-and-coming young man. Although never regarded as noticeably rich, Kenneth and Edna would maintain a conspicuously comfortable lifestyle throughout their many decades together. There were times, though, when money got tight. One such time came during the family's New York years when Edna and Kenneth moved out of their house and into a less-expensive apartment so that the dollars would be available to send Dick to Yale.

Upper middle-class. That's what the Ogilvie family was. Or better yet, make it Midwest upper middle-class. There was a difference, of course.

Many of Dick Ogilvie's earliest memories lay in the big house, so typically midwestern, that his parents bought in the 1920s on East 65th Street in Kansas City. It had bedrooms upstairs and down. The front bedroom on the upper floor was Nellie's. Dick and Bob shared the large bedroom at the rear of that floor, the bedroom with the porch off it.

By the start of the 1930s, the country had plunged into the beginning of the Great Depression, and Kenneth Ogilvie had been moved from Kansas City to Chicago by Norwich Union, the British insurance company employing him at the time. The Ogilvie family and Nellie settled in Evanston, the university city north of Chicago.

The move brought Edna to her mother's home state. Elizabeth Dorothy Davis Buell was born in 1869 in or near Jerseyville, Illinois, daughter of a Union Army infantryman, Haston Davis, and his wife, Margaret Bealer. About the time of Elizabeth's tenth birthday, her parents moved from Illinois to the Kansas City area in a covered wagon.

For Elizabeth Davis, her life centered in Kansas City for years. Here she grew to adulthood, married Thomas J. Buell, and, in 1902, gave birth to their daughter, Edna Mae.

The life span of Edna Buell paralleled most of the years of the twentieth century. When she died in a North Carolina nursing home early in the 1990s a few days shy of her ninetieth birthday, she had outlived her husband and her son, the governor.

Many American families have their legends. An often-repeated story about the Ogilvie family, which intimates swore to be true, was that Edna Ogilvie's dark hair began to turn white quickly after she was notified that Dick was wounded in action. No further word on her son's situation was received for a matter of weeks. During this period of anguish for the normally unflappable Edna, her hair grew white.

When Dick Ogilvie left Yale to enter the service, his family was in the thick of its New York hiatus for six or so years from Chicago. By the time he got out of uniform, Dick was back in Evanston, along with his family, a move like the others tied to the father's career in insurance.

High school days for Richard Ogilvie were spent with the class of 1940 at Port Chester Senior High School, in Port Chester on New York's Long Island Sound. A look through the 1940 edition of *The Peningian*, the high school yearbook, reveals more than a little diversity in Richard's activities. Ogilvie played football for three years for the Port Chester Rams, just as he was briefly on the football team at Yale before getting injured. Proud of his days as a grid jock, Ogilvie often went out of his way to make sure they were mentioned in features on him later in life. But Ogilvie was a lot of other things in high school. He had a leading role in a comedy staged by the senior play committee. He himself was chairman of the senior prom committee. As a member of the yearbook staff, he was responsible for coming up with "senior personals." He was even part of the school's mixed chorus, although individuals who knew him best insisted Ogilvie could not carry a tune.

On the other side of the continent at that exact time, a dirt-poor kid named Daniel Walker became the valedictorian of the class of 1940 at San Diego High School. Ending up in Illinois was then the furthest thing from Walker's mind—no more to be believed than if somebody had told Walker he'd be running for governor of Illinois one day against another high school senior in 1940, Dick Ogilvie, living three thousand miles away in New York.

Inauguration and Transition: The Early Days of Ogilvie's Governorship

The Inauguration

A lot of the festivities marking the inauguration of a new governor of Illinois have the trappings of New Orleans's celebration of Mardi Gras—one dance after another, private parties, sometimes even marching bands. Nothing about his inaugural could have been sweeter for Ogilvie, though, than the concert by the Chicago Symphony Orchestra in its ornate old home on Michigan Avenue, architect D. H. Burnham's classical Orchestra Hall. The high and mighty of Chicago society graced this occasion, and the eyes of many of those assembled were turned often toward the box occupied by Ogilvie and his wife Dorothy.

Really, it couldn't have gotten much better for Ogilvie. Little if anything on this evening seemed out of his reach. If a fellow ever had an inkling of what it might be like sitting on a throne in Illinois, this was the time. Arthur Fiedler, the maestro of the Boston Pops, was a guest conductor of the CSO that night. He had orchestrated a special program for the occasion.

The part that Ogilvie enjoyed most, which would have been surprising to many seated in the four-story-high auditorium, was the orchestra's rendition of "Mack the Knife." The popular recording by Bobby Darin was Ogilvie's favorite song. And Ogilvie had no idea he would hear the tune at the concert.[1] It was a warm touch, just one of the many things going his way at the beginning of his governorship in 1969.

New governors in Illinois normally start off with a reservoir of goodwill, with the hatchet of partisan strife buried for a period of time known as the governor's honeymoon. For most governors, the honeymoon is too short; for a few, it never ends. The tone of press coverage can also affect the length of the grace period in which a fledgling administration finds itself. Since Ogilvie's meteoric political rise was accompanied by favorable media reporting and editorial page backing, Ogilvie could cautiously count the press as a plus, at least at the beginning.

Other factors also appeared at first glance positive for him. Ogilvie's capture of the governorship was the climax of a strong comeback by the Republican Party in the Prairie State in the 1960s. For most of that decade, the Grand Old Party had stood in sad shape in Illinois, unlike the two previous decades, when the balance of political power usually favored the GOP. The election of 1964 was the nadir for the Republicans. After the wreckage from Barry Goldwater's presidential candidacy was sorted out, the Republicans were left with only one real source of power in state government—their continued control of the Illinois Senate.

Of course, this was nothing at which to snicker. The GOP majority in the Senate, dominated by one of the greatest collections of Bourbons in Illinois political annals, was led by a fiery strongman, W. Russell Arrington. This political bantam rooster from Evanston almost single-handedly assured a still potent Republican presence in Springfield during the party's darkest hours of the 1960s. It fell to Arrington to hold it together for the GOP while the party regrouped to capture standing in other areas of Illinois government. Was the GOP on a political mission? If so, it achieved a great deal in the four years following the Goldwater debacle.

As Ogilvie sat serenely that inaugural evening listening to the CSO play "Mack the Knife," he knew his party was back in the catbird seat in Illinois politics. In addition to the Republican lock on the Illinois Senate, the House of Representatives had come under GOP control in the 1966 election. Any governor with a long wish list for the General Assembly, like Ogilvie, naturally warmed at the sight of his party in control of both chambers of the legislature. On top of that, having a guy like Arrington still running the Senate, a person Ogilvie truly liked and admired, made it all seem almost too good to be true.

The 1968 election also put an old Ogilvie friend, Bill Scott, in the state attorney general's office, another situation that should have augured well for the Ogilvie governorship. The two went back to their days together at Chicago-Kent College of Law. Dick and Dorothy Ogilvie, as a young married couple, had no closer acquaintances than Bill Scott and his wife Dorothy, who lived in an apartment on Chicago's Surf Street right across from the Ogilvies' apartment.

Another Ogilvie friend, Republican Charles Percy, won election to the United States Senate from Illinois in 1966. This meant that both of the state's seats in the Senate (the other was held by Everett McKinley Dirksen) were in GOP hands when Ogilvie became Illinois chief executive, not a bad sign for an ambitious governor wanting help from Washington.

One thing that Ogilvie did not have going for him was a lieutenant governor from the Republican Party. Illinois voters did something in the 1968 election

they had not done before. They elected a Republican governor and, as lieutenant governor, a popular Democratic state senator, Paul Simon. Having an odd
couple like this at the top of Illinois government, if not a serious political glitch
for Ogilvie, necessarily created an awkward predicament.

Democrats also held three of the other statewide offices at the start of the
Ogilvie administration. He'd especially have to keep a watchful eye on Treasurer Adlai E. Stevenson III, whose father, the late Adlai Ewing Stevenson, had
been governor of Illinois and the unsuccessful Democratic candidate for president in 1952 and 1956. The state auditor of public accounts was Democrat
Michael Howlett, who politically could not be taken for granted either. The
third Democrat was the crafty, to some persons legendary, secretary of state,
Paul Powell. Ogilvie did not view Powell, from little Vienna in deep southern
Illinois, as a political threat, but Ogilvie had heard enough about Powell to be
sure that he would find him fascinating. Ogilvie was not likely to lose sleep over
his relations with these other political heavy hitters, ever mindful as he was
that he had won two Cook County offices, sheriff and county board president,
over the opposition of Mayor Richard J. Daley of Chicago and his fabled Democratic machine. After Daley, Ogilvie found it tough to imagine any other Democrat in Illinois that he could not handle.

Anyway, Ogilvie was one of those people in public life who sincerely
thought that one's political fortune, or fate, was tied to performance in office.
His belief that he had done a good job in the two county posts was certainly
buttressed by the widespread acclaim accorded him during those years. He was
not viewing the governorship any differently, just as a broader playing field with
a range of problems and challenges wider in scope than he previously had encountered. Sure, gutsy decisions would be required, but that was nothing new
for the former tank commander.

Even that night in Orchestra Hall in Chicago, while those around him were
content to revel in his success, Ogilvie could not keep his mind from racing
ahead to his game plan for Springfield. His objectives were hardly a secret. He
had made many promises in his campaign, a number of which he repeated in
his inaugural address.

One concerned the organization of state government itself. He reiterated to
the some 5,500 persons on hand in the State Armory for the inauguration that
he would push the revamping of Illinois government because it had "to be
sharpened to become the agent for constructive change instead of the custo-
dian of an accumulation of separate and unresponsive agencies and programs."[2]

No idle boast, this was crucial to Ogilvie's design for his governorship. Without shaking up or restructuring many agencies and creating more than a few

new ones, Ogilvie could not get government to respond meaningfully, he was certain, to the multitude of unmet challenges facing the state. Should Ogilvie pull it off, Illinois government might be getting its biggest overhaul since the World War I–era governor Frank Lowden secured enactment, shortly after taking office, of the *Civil Administrative Code of 1917*, one of the most important pieces of legislation ever passed by the General Assembly.

Through that act, drafted under Lowden, both a Republican and a reformer, numerous obsolete or controversial state agencies were abolished and others were reorganized into nine departments, each run by a director reporting to the governor—a move that more centralized matters under the power of the governor. Stressing that only a radical revision like that would permit Illinois government to react efficiently to the rapid economic and social changes of that period, Lowden's success in this area made Illinois a leader in the state government reform movement and won Lowden something rare, national recognition for an Illinois governor. Indeed, Lowden achieved so much in his one term as governor (he refused to run for a second term) that he would become a serious if unsuccessful contender for his party's nomination for president.

Ogilvie's awareness of Governor Lowden was extensive, and numerous parallels between the two would become evident.

Along with governmental reform, Lowden's other main goal was the convening of a state constitutional convention. He succeeded here, too. First the legislature in 1917 and then the electorate in 1918 approved the calling of a convention to propose a revision of the antiquated Illinois Constitution of 1870. However, the new charter drawn by that convention was rejected by voters.

Interestingly, on November 5, 1968, the day of Ogilvie's election as governor, the voters also approved a call for another constitutional convention, the first since the ill-fated one back in Lowden's time. The work of this convention, intended to recommend another replacement for the 1870 constitution, would transpire during Ogilvie's days in office. Recognizing that the proceeding presented a rare opening for constructive changes as well as pitfalls for the state and his governorship, Ogilvie knew that delicacy was needed in dealing with what everybody would simply call "Con Con."

Ogilvie took note of that in his inaugural address, saying that "in the days ahead, we have one special and immense opportunity. And that is to create a new constitution that will help us achieve present and future goals. The constitutional convention can write a new document that will live and grow, and will provide a rational basis for fair taxation and fiscal responsibility. No other task before us will demand such a moratorium on partisanship and such an exercise in citizen involvement."[3]

It was uncanny, the issues that Ogilvie and Lowden had in common. Although close to a half century separated their terms of office, both had to contend with racial flare-ups. Lowden was forced to use troops to deter violence and maintain order when blacks who had come to Illinois because of a shortage of labor were attacked by mobs at Chicago and East St. Louis. Ogilvie, too, would have to mobilize the Illinois National Guard to prevent violence triggered by racial unrest. When taking office, Ogilvie was aware that the first anniversary of the assassination of Martin Luther King Jr. was only a few months away, an occasion that easily could provoke violent protests by angry blacks in Chicago and other places.

Cairo, a small town at the southern tip of Illinois, was a tinderbox of racial tension staring the new Ogilvie administration in the face. And then there was East St. Louis. The increasingly African-American city along the Mississippi River in southwestern Illinois had become a national symbol of urban decay. Few persons expected East St. Louis, a Democratic stronghold, to get priority attention from a Republican governor from Chicago, but new governor Ogilvie had a few special cards in his hand that he intended to play in regard to East St. Louis. If he were successful, a measure of economic revival might result.

Ogilvie could not have been more aware that the long-festering injustices of racial discrimination had finally come home to roost in the years of his political progression. So many in his party, though, were indifferent to the pleadings of blacks and other minorities for change, for a fairer shot at sharing in the American dream. The lopsided support for Democrats especially by black voters gave practical Republicans reason to look away from blacks, many cold-eyed analysts certainly felt. Ogilvie could not and would not, and he sought to dispel any thought to the contrary by delving into the ticklish race issue early in his inaugural speech.

"The black man, the youth, the philosopher who protest are demanding change, and they confront our conscience the way slavery, the sweatshops and other hypocrisy of earlier times stirred Americans," said Ogilvie. To which, he added, "I am deeply conscious of the demands on the office of governor to serve with equal devotion the hopes of Cairo and Chicago, of young and old, of black and white."[4]

No goal of his governorship, he stressed, was more urgent than "to mobilize the full force of this state government against poverty and ignorance." They were, in the words of the new governor, "the twin scourges of our society . . . the roots of crime and of the decay of our cities."

Ogilvie did not duck major issues of the day in his inaugural address. At least not many. As events later would confirm, Ogilvie used the speech as a blueprint for what he had in mind for Illinois. His listeners among the notables in the Armory that day got a preview of what was in store for the state under the new man at the helm. Ogilvie had made it clear in his campaign for governor that he stood for change, but campaign rhetoric is one thing and the dignified status of an inaugural speech is another.

The rapid acceleration of the environmental movement in many parts of the United States had not exactly taken hold in Illinois, but Ogilvie declared on the day he took office that this was going to change. Pledging to "preserve and restore our natural resources," Ogilvie said that "we are seemingly at war not only with ourselves, but also with nature." People have the power to destroy nature, he lamented, "and we have already done this to an alarming degree. This process must be stopped—and in fact, rolled back."

He meant it, as despoilers of Illinois air and water would discover. He was just as serious in signaling his determination to convert Illinois's prisons and mental hospitals from "dead-end streets" into "means to repair and renew human lives."

The segment of the address that got the heaviest media play in many places was Ogilvie's appeal for an end to the historic split between Chicago and the rest of the state. Ogilvie minced no words over a matter glossed over by so many other Illinois politicians through the years as "just fiction." To Ogilvie, the traditional mistrust between Chicago and downstate had to be recognized for what it was, a dichotomy that "has cost us dearly in wasted bitterness and squandered effort." A remedy, he said, was for the leaders of Illinois to "discipline ourselves so that we can work effectively with all sections of the state, to avoid bickering our way into stalemate." After all, the new governor reasoned, no single region of Illinois "can stand apart from the rest."

One subject, but hardly a minor one, that Ogilvie ignored in his inaugural address was the state's fiscal mess. A few days before the inauguration of Ogilvie, outgoing Governor Shapiro warned in his last message to the General Assembly that Illinois "will live from crisis to crisis" unless a solution was found to the state's severe revenue problems.[5] Repairing the situation could not be put off, Shapiro added, an admonition he knew to be both on target and now safe for him to say since this political hot potato no longer was in his hands.

Ogilvie realized full well that he had to come up with additional dollars, an awful lot of them, if he was to carry out all those plans for the state and its citizens mapped out in his inaugural address. But he was postponing straight talk on state finances for a few more weeks. He'd let the good feeling of being governor of Illinois sink in a bit more before getting down to brass tacks on the money crunch. First, he would spell out the seriousness of the problem.

Then, he'd have to reveal how he intended to deal with it. Whatever he tried to do, political risks would be entailed.

Nevertheless, Ogilvie being Ogilvie, the revenue crisis would be tackled head-on at the start of his term of office. He would pursue the course of action he felt necessary—and let the chips fall where they may.

The Transition

If a new governor ever started out in office like a world-class sprinter shooting off the starting blocks, it was Richard Ogilvie. For a world as stodgy as Illinois government, the pace of the first months under Ogilvie was furious. Nothing like it had been seen in the years before Ogilvie or in the era that followed him.

Appropriately enough, Ogilvie's first executive order, issued about two weeks after he took office, dealt with crime. Under the order, Ogilvie upgraded a Shapiro creation, the Governor's Committee on Criminal Justice, into the Illinois Law Enforcement Commission and designated it the official state planning agency for law enforcement and juvenile delinquency prevention, a broad task.[6] This was a logical first step for a governor who mainly had built his reputation as a crime fighter and who still was called, even after becoming governor, Sheriff Ogilvie by some persons.

A few weeks later, in a special message to the legislature, Ogilvie went deeper into the crime issue. Arguing that his state had a violent crime record so bad that "our citizens are three times as likely to become victims of violent crime as residents of any of our neighboring states," the governor called for the restructuring of the state agencies "concerned with this fundamental problem in a free society." The General Assembly was asked by Ogilvie to approve legislation setting up two new major agencies, the Department of Law Enforcement and the Department of Corrections.[7] The lawmakers would give him both of them.

The new corrections agency would revamp the Illinois penal system, bringing under one administrative roof the running of the prisons for adult offenders and the supervision of the training schools and camps for troubled youths. More than that was involved, though. Ogilvie sought to greatly increase emphasis in the penal facilities on offender rehabilitation programs, both inside and outside prison walls, in an effort to break what he called "the present cycle of arrest, incarceration and release which in a majority of cases is repeated over and over again." Nothing short of a "whole new philosophical framework for our corrections effort at every level" was ordered by Ogilvie. Remedial education, vocational training, individual and group therapy, and job counseling were to receive much higher priority. Old-line penologists might not like it, but Ogilvie intended to more humanize the status of inmates. To carry all this out, Ogilvie would place the new corrections agency under the direction of Peter Bensinger, a Yale graduate and former Chicago businessman in his early thirties, the type of "new look" individual Ogilvie had promised to bring into state government to reenergize it.

At the heart of Ogilvie's new law enforcement department was the Illinois State Police, the ranks of which Ogilvie wanted to increase by two hundred troopers in each of his first two years in office. However, much more publicity was given to the General Assembly's approval of the governor's request for inclusion in the law enforcement agency of a new operation, the Illinois Bureau of Investigation. Everybody called it the "Little FBI," including Ogilvie. He said that the IBI's chief task was to fight organized crime, just like he had once done, and that he expected to staff the unit with the same kind of men found in the Federal Bureau of Investigation. To some, setting up the IBI reflected a bit too much of what they perceived as Ogilvie's police-state tendencies. Before too long, the IBI would be generating other concerns as it sought to establish its niche in gung ho fashion.

Less than a month after taking office, Ogilvie issued the second executive order of his administration. It represented an early step by Ogilvie to address one of the most painfully visible crises in the state, the racially tinged deterioration of the core of Illinois's larger cities. The order created the Governor's Office of Human Resources, which Ogilvie intended, in his words, to be "a major social policy arm" of his administration.[8] In announcing the news at an urban affairs conference at the University of Illinois at Chicago Circle, the governor told the gathering that "the task we are beginning has no equal in importance or complexity in state government. This office—with the assistance of all possible public and private agencies—must evolve broad new approaches to problems of employment, job training, education, welfare and housing."

Ogilvie tapped what looked like a good choice for executive director, A. Donald Bourgeois, a black lawyer. Tall and adroit, but also amiable, Bourgeois had the marks of a class act. He was a native of Chicago and had spent much of his life there. Before joining Ogilvie, though, Bourgeois lived in St. Louis, where he had become prominent in city affairs as director of the St. Louis Model City Agency, a federal program coordinating efforts to rebuild target neighborhoods in decaying parts of the city. The St. Louis experience was important because Bourgeois's duties would include serving as a consultant to

Ogilvie on East St. Louis–area problems. In his campaign, Ogilvie pledged to have a member of his staff employed full-time combating the joblessness and fiscal chaos of East St. Louis. Since Bourgeois had to worry about the whole state, he presumably would help to find someone for the liaison role with East St. Louis.

Smooth though he was, Bourgeois got the message early on that mounting a statewide assault on urban poverty was easier said than done. Achieving cohesion between civil rights and other urban groups in Illinois was a formidable task, he found out. By the end of September 1969, eight months after joining Ogilvie with much fanfare, Bourgeois departed to teach at Ohio State University.

An early casualty of the administration? Yes and no. As he left, Bourgeois had in his hand a letter from Ogilvie in which the governor told Bourgeois that his "energy and enthusiasm have inspired many in and out of government to join the fight to solve the problems of people in our cities."[9] After exiting, Bourgeois also would receive a state consulting contract to tide him over, a practice not uncommon in Illinois government.

Few faced a tougher assignment than Bourgeois at the start of the Ogilvie governorship. His task was to find a path out of what more and more people were seeing as a bottomless pit of human degradation. The naming of Bourgeois may have been little more than a token gesture in the eyes of some, but Ogilvie himself certainly recognized that the buttressing of law and order demanded corresponding attention to the horrid conditions spawning so much of the activity that even then was terrorizing Illinoisans. Anyway, the gates on this issue had been opened wide before Ogilvie became governor.

Illinois was part of a nation immersed in a social revolution. Ogilvie's entrance into the governorship, of course, followed the presidency of Lyndon Johnson and his push through Congress of the most liberal domestic legislative program since President Franklin D. Roosevelt's New Deal in the Great Depression. Illinois, like the other states, was caught up in carrying out the Johnson legacy: the Civil Rights Act of 1964, Medicare, federal aid to education, the War on Poverty, and so much of the rest that Johnson got in place before he was politically drowned by the Vietnam War.

In those early salad days of the Ogilvie administration, though, most of the initiatives were in areas in which he and his team felt quite if not most comfortable. Ogilvie called on the legislature, again with success, to create a Department of Local Government Affairs to marshal maximum assistance to municipalities. He put at its head a former respected mayor of Peoria, Robert J.

Lehnhausen. Ogilvie also sought to curtail or restrict the great limitations on local governments in Illinois that limited their taxing or borrowing powers, their regulation of businesses, the kinds of services they could provide, and even the salaries they could pay their employees.

The governor, a recent graduate of the top post of Cook County government, considered himself the number one and probably most knowledgeable advocate of local government modernization in Springfield. He personally had chafed under the restrictive yoke of the state's stringent statutory barriers that stifled the local governing initiatives so obviously necessary on numerous issues. Put simply, Ogilvie wanted legislative approval for a wide range of bills designed, he said, "to begin the freeing of our cities."[10]

Before the first spring of Ogilvie's term was out, he also launched a major offensive to obtain revenue for extensive upgrading of the Illinois road system. Ogilvie's program, which he adopted just about verbatim from a recommendation of the Illinois Highway Study Commission, called for a big hike in the state gasoline tax and in road-related license and registration fees to permit an attack on the deterioration of many of the state's roads—a condition Ogilvie had observed firsthand in the 1968 campaign when he had first traversed many downstate highways. Here too, the Republican-dominated General Assembly gave the new governor his wish, including his request for creation of a state highway trust authority empowered to issue $2 billion in bonds to finance an emergency program of highway construction. Proceeds from the bonds were to be used to update 5,000 miles of impaired roads, widen 1,500 narrow bridges, and build 1,950 miles of new supplemental freeways.

The real bombshell of his first months in office still would be his plan for addressing the state's pressing need for new revenue in general, not just for highways. Nothing in his early days in Springfield was absorbing more time for Ogilvie and his top assistants than their covert strategy sessions on this issue. When they went public with their plan, most other topics on the Ogilvie agenda would be pushed back to the inside pages of the newspapers. The import of their decision was that heavy.

But in those early days of the administration, the matter was hush-hush. The Ogilvie crowd wanted the public spotlight to focus on the furious pace of the new man in the driver's seat, on the energetic atmosphere that Ogilvie was generating.

One thing noticeable in the new look of the Ogilvie administration was the young age of so many of the top people on the governor's staff. To old governmental hands in Illinois, Ogilvie's crew was a kiddie corps. Brian Whalen, the individual regarded as Ogilvie's chief of staff, was only twenty-nine years old when he went from Chicago to Springfield with Ogilvie. Not many of the others were over thirty. Hardly any had gray hair.

However, one who did was the person tapped by Ogilvie to direct the formal transition of Illinois government from Shapiro to Ogilvie—George E. Mahin. Only a few hours after Ogilvie's victory, word surfaced that Mahin would be joining the team. Signs of what lay in store appeared unmistakable because of Mahin's track record. Going back to the 1930s, the silver-haired Mahin had worked with various groups acutely interested in government but not part of it, like the Taxpayers' Federation of Illinois. In the eleven years before he hooked up with Ogilvie, Mahin had been executive director of the Chicago-based Better Government Association, a role in which he became an anathema to much of Illinois's political establishment.

Under Mahin's leadership, the privately financed BGA engaged in an all-out war on government corruption. Since Democrats dominated public offices in Chicago, the most frequent targets of the BGA in its home area were naturally Democrats. Nevertheless, the BGA could not shake the charge of Mayor Daley and other leading Democrats that it was a de facto arm of the Republican Party. No doubt this claim was fueled by the evidently cozy relationship in the 1960s between the BGA and the Republican reformer in the Cook County offices of sheriff, and then county board president, Richard Ogilvie.

In fact, Mahin joining Ogilvie was only part of this particular picture. Ogilvie also wasted no time after his election in asking Roswell T. Spencer to join the administration. Spencer had been the chief investigator for the BGA. A former FBI agent, Spencer was the Democrat who lost to Ogilvie in the 1962 election for Cook County sheriff.

As it turned out, Mahin would move from the transition assignment to director of the Illinois Department of Revenue. Spencer would manage the department's investigation division.

There was more. The legal adviser to the BGA, Chicago attorney and Ogilvie friend Jeremiah Marsh, was named special counsel to the new governor, a position that would permit Marsh to function with Whalen at the top of Ogilvie's staff. In truth, Marsh wrote the transition plan used by Ogilvie, a chore Marsh carried out privately in the summer and early fall of 1968 so that matters could move swiftly if Ogilvie won the election.[11]

Mahin, though, was the out-front director of the transition, and it was the quick identification of Mahin with the Ogilvie governorship that triggered anxiety in Springfield as the entrenched bureaucracy there awaited the arrival of Ogilvie. An early rumor was that Mahin would serve as a general troubleshooter for Ogilvie, an assignment that could lead Mahin into investigations of the internal operations of other state agencies. Perhaps, it was suspected, Mahin might have at his disposal some of the FBI agents reportedly being recruited by Ogilvie for service in his regime.

Mahin was not feared in governmental circles because he had made a name for himself opposing graft in officialdom. Numerous investigative operations were set up to protect the public from crooks in government. The difference with the BGA was that it got results. Furthermore, to do so, the association's small staff often had to go to extraordinary lengths. When a public figure suspected of wrongdoing was asked for an interview by a BGA investigator, it usually signified the culmination of an intensive inquiry into that person's activities. Files on the person—public ones and others not as easily obtained—already had been scrutinized. Moreover, the target probably had been trailed on certain days, and the BGA operative may have been crouched outside the subject's window at night.

The BGA had tackled big cases of finagling by politicians that federal or state agencies would not touch. There also were many little cases, and some not too difficult, like the discovery of the Chicago street employees who had unfortunately picked the basement of the BGA building in the city for their sleeping hideout during working hours.[12]

The organization, funded by tax-exempt donations from companies and individuals, had been established in 1923 to increase voter participation in Chicago elections and to serve as a nonpartisan guide to better government. The aggressiveness in exposing corruption materialized during the executive directorship of Mahin.

An irony was the extent to which enemies of the BGA overestimated the resources of the small staff of the association. The few outsiders privy to the BGA's inside workings regarded it as a shoestring operation providing unbridled opportunity for a handful of professional crusaders skilled in the tactics of old-fashioned gumshoes. More than anything else, the success in sleuthing separated the BGA from most of the other private better-government groups in the land. In addition, most BGA investigations in those days were carried out in cooperation with a newspaper, a smart way to proceed, in that publicity on the outcome of the inquiries was assured. When the BGA went at it alone, a press conference usually was called to announce the findings.

Predictably, the BGA was either loved or despised. When the critics sounded off, Mahin routinely was the target. To the end, BGA detractors were convinced that Mahin was the main perpetrator behind the 1965 bugging of a Springfield hotel room in which three lobbyists discussed payments to legislators for votes. Mahin never admitted such a role, but later publication of excerpts from the tape recordings indicated that some legislators were on the take. The public reaction was little short of sensational.

For each nemesis, though, there were many more who saw Mahin, an active-duty navy officer in World War II, as a symbol of clean government. Getting Mahin on board so soon, Ogilvie reasoned, would be a portent of his, Ogilvie's, priorities. Of course, the departure of Mahin did deprive the BGA of a leader with the capability to make life miserable for any elected official, including Ogilvie. Consequently, from Ogilvie's point of view, some observers noted, several purposes could be served by picking Mahin. (As a footnote, James F. McCaffrey, the BGA operative in Springfield, a crackerjack sleuth himself, joined his mentor Mahin in the state revenue agency as an investigator during Ogilvie's third year in office.)

As it was, Mahin's star in the Ogilvie galaxy burned brightest at the start. After the excitement of Ogilvie's transition into office had ebbed, Mahin found himself saddled with the drudgery of running the department responsible for collecting each year many of the billions of dollars necessary to run the machinery and programs of state government. Like a good old soldier, he discharged his duty in commendable fashion. Yet Mahin was eclipsed by a number of the much younger players on the Ogilvie team.

No better example could be found than John W. McCarter Jr. McCarter, an Ivy Leaguer like the governor, with every bit the look of the all-American boy, was Ogilvie's point man for revolutionizing the state budget process, a formidable undertaking in which the executive branch of government supplanted the General Assembly in the driver's seat of budget making. By pulling off this upset, the thirty-year-old McCarter quickly ensured his standing among the best and brightest of the Ogilvie world.

Youthful. Vigorous. Clean-cut. Words often used in the beginning to describe most members of Ogilvie's staff. The fresh character of his aides, in contrast to the mundanity of the Kerner and Shapiro staffs, was an early hallmark of the Ogilvie governorship. Few doubted that Ogilvie had a knack for attracting into public life good men (women staffers were few and far between in those years). Furthermore, Ogilvie gave each of his assistants broad responsibilities and plenty of latitude to carry out his assignments. Most performed like gangbusters from the start, a contributing factor without question to the impressive early record of the administration.

Later on, Ogilvie's staff was to increasingly generate resentment from others on the scene. Not all of it was bred by jealousy. Genuine concern was felt

by many that the stronger individuals on the staff coalesced too obviously into
a palace guard overly protective of Ogilvie, so much so that political damage
resulted.

Back to the initial days of Ogilvie's term, the fact that his team hit the gubernatorial beach feet first and running hard was not by chance. The takeover of
the Statehouse followed almost step by step the transition plan drafted by
Marsh, a document covering everything from the recruitment of personnel for
key spots to the organization of the governor's office itself (which was pat-
terned to a great extent on the makeup of the White House under President
John F. Kennedy).[13] The transition strategy even included a way for Governor-
elect Ogilvie to gracefully exit his Cook County post without causing unnecessary headaches.

While the details of the transition plan would have made dry reading for
most persons, the thinking behind it was summed up succinctly in a quotation
on the cover of the transition document. The quote from Richard Nixon had
appeared in the *Wall Street Journal* a few days before November 5, 1968, the day
he was elected president: "Between November 6 and January 1, that is the time
to get going and get it done. . . . The decisions made between November 5
and the time of the inauguration will probably be the most important decisions
that the new President will make insofar as determining the success of his Administration over the next four years. Because if he makes poor decisions with
regard to selection of his Cabinet, with regard to his budget, with regard to
these basic points [issues] that some of you have raised, it's going to be very
hard to correct them."

Perusal afterward of the files on Ogilvie's transition into office reveal the
participation almost from the word go of virtually all of the individuals who
were to fill the key positions that would make or break the Ogilvie governorship. McCarter, who at the time was an officer of a Chicago management consultant firm, had to be coaxed by Ogilvie to become a permanent part of the
administration. This was not necessary with most of the rest.

The formal transition team under Mahin included Marion Oglesby, William
S. Hanley, and William F. Cellini Jr. The twenty-six-year-old Oglesby had been
an administrative aide to Speaker Ralph T. Smith of the Illinois House. Hanley
was a University of Chicago law school graduate who coordinated much of the
research used in formulating Ogilvie's policy proposals in the gubernatorial
campaign. He was twenty-nine. Cellini, thirty-four, was the commissioner of
streets and public improvements in Springfield, an elective post.

Hanley would go on to serve as Ogilvie's legislative counsel. Oglesby also
would be involved in the governor's legislative relations, one of a number of

hats he would wear on the governor's staff. Cellini would move from the transition role to director of the Department of Public Works and Buildings under Ogilvie. Cellini then would become the state's first secretary of transportation when his department became the main component of the new and wide-ranging Illinois Department of Transportation that went into operation at the beginning of 1972, the result of another Ogilvie initiative.

John P. Dailey, who had been a top assistant to the Illinois Senate GOP leadership and who would join the Ogilvie staff to help deal with legislative and other matters, worked with Marsh on the writing of the transition plan. Dailey was then twenty-six.

As for others providing input into the transition document, one needed to look no further than to Thomas Drennan. A onetime Chicago reporter who had jumped into the public relations business, Drennan was an important part and parcel of the political career of Richard Ogilvie from the start. Ogilvie had relied on the political instincts of Drennan in his advancement from office to office; the hand of Drennan was always visible.

In the race for governor, Drennan was overall director of communications for Ogilvie. When Ogilvie won, some thought Drennan might accompany Ogilvie to Springfield as his press secretary, a post governors matter-of-factly fill with former newspersons. Drennan wasn't interested in that, though. In fact, the first personal staff appointment made by Ogilvie after his election was that of press secretary. The job went to Joseph D. Mathewson, a former newspaper and television reporter who had worked in the campaign.

No, Drennan did not want to go on the state payroll, preferring to remain in the private sector. Yet, his quick access to Ogilvie when Drennan wanted it, or Ogilvie requested it, was recognized by all. Nobody was ever surprised at the sudden appearance of Drennan in Chicago or Springfield whenever a reporter was nosing into a sticky situation possibly brewing.

If anybody could claim to go as far back politically with Ogilvie as Drennan, it was Donald Perkins. He was the president of the Jewel Companies and a tireless raiser of political funds for Ogilvie, who was his neighbor when Perkins lived in the Chicago suburb of Northfield. During the contest for governor, Perkins was campaign finance director for Ogilvie. After Ogilvie became governor, Perkins chaired a panel of business and professional persons set up to advise the governor on state government problem solving. Before that, in the transition period, Perkins was named to head a personnel recruitment committee designed to find candidates for policy-making positions in the new administration.

Hardly necessary to say, the aspect of the Ogilvie victory that many of his supporters found most appealing was the prospect of jobs for Republicans long starved for patronage at the state level in Illinois. Ogilvie had shown great proficiency in moving members of his party onto the public payrolls under his wing in Cook County. The same was widely expected of him with state government. But Ogilvie knew he would have to move cautiously in this area. Research revealed that the governor's office was not what it once was in terms of patronage.

When Ogilvie was elected, there were about 98,000 employees in all state agencies. Of these, roughly 57,000 worked in the then nineteen departments under the direct control of the governor.[14] However, many of these were civil service employees subject to discharge or demotion only "for cause" under the Illinois Personnel Code. Outside of major policy positions, such as directors and assistant directors of state agencies, a good number of the spots left for political appointment were those of highway maintenance workers or unskilled positions in state institutions.

Still, Democrats had no doubt that Ogilvie would find ways to place his people in state government, just as every other governor had done. Ogilvie would be no different in regard to patronage than his predecessors, Ogilvie's political foes predicted. And, of course, they were right.

The importance of moving as many of the right people as possible into state jobs happened to be one of the subjects covered when Ogilvie, members of his staff, and Ogilvie-appointed chiefs of state agencies put their heads together for several days at a retreat in eastern Illinois about four weeks after the governor's inauguration.

Whalen carefully spelled out the ground rules for placing an individual in a department. Seeking to allay fears that the agencies would become dumps for political hacks, Whalen told the department directors that "there is no reason" for the governor's patronage operation to be "at cross purposes with the programs of your departments." The governor's personnel or patronage team, said Whalen, "is just as concerned with placing people who can do the job as every director here."[15]

If a disagreement ensued over the hiring of a person sent by the governor's office, Whalen added, "there should be a free, frank discussion between the department head and the personnel team. If in fact there is a real and legitimate problem over the placing of one individual, then other approaches are in order."

Nevertheless, the message was clear. None of the speakers at the get-together put it more bluntly than Mahin, whom many on hand thought would be the last person to advocate patronage. "This may sound strange coming from me, but . . . it takes troops to win victories at elections," Mahin declared. "This means that jobs have to be provided for county chairmen, [for] some of their foot soldiers downstate, [and] for the ward committeemen and township committeemen in Cook County." The governor needed, Mahin concluded, "a winning political organization."[16]

Mahin also informed most of those present for the first time that he indeed had been given, as speculation held he would, major responsibility for protecting the administration from scandal and embarrassment. This would be handled, Mahin advised the other directors, through a new operation in the revenue department, the Division of Internal Security and Fraud Investigation. The top echelon of this unit, Mahin noted, would be comprised of investigators with past ties to the FBI or Internal Revenue Service. Assuring the collection of every penny of tax revenue due the state would be a main duty of the division. But Mahin also underscored the division's intent to conduct within the administration surveillance and to use other techniques of snoopers so as to ferret out or, at the least, "try to be on top of every scandal before it happens." "By that," Mahin explained, "I mean to be on top of it in-house, and by in-house I mean we wrap it up, action is taken and that action is publicized or not publicized as the Governor wishes."

Mahin also utilized this occasion to urge in the strongest terms that each agency itself retain a "top flight security officer" as a first step to counter internal malfeasance. This last suggestion came as a surprise to Ogilvie, who was present. So, when bringing it up, Mahin said he wanted "the Governor to listen very closely to this because I haven't had a chance to talk to him about it."

While a few in the audience squirmed in their seats at Mahin's remarks, others addressing the gathering were not as somber as Mahin. McCarter presented what seemed like a college lecture on fiscal policy, and Oglesby and several others delved into the intricacies of dealing with the legislature and the bill-passing process—a mysterious ritual to those directors not familiar with the Statehouse. A few of the speakers even bantered a little because, after all, this was not intended to be a heavy-handed event. The gathering was held in the forty-room mansion on the handsomely landscaped grounds of Allerton Park west of Monticello. This secluded conference center, under the stewardship of the University of Illinois, provided a much more relaxed atmosphere for the Ogilvie folks than Springfield or Chicago.

Sam Gove, a political science professor at the University of Illinois who suggested and organized the affair, said it was intended to "give the new administration a chance to get its bearings."[17] Ogilvie himself, in his welcoming comments, labeled the conference a pioneering endeavor designed to let everyone on his "government management team" get to know each other. As the governor, a former gridder, put it: "This is sort of a pre-game huddle before we get out on the field."[18]

Sam Gove, the person behind the conference, was not just a passive observer. Gove had been asked to assist in the Ogilvie transition, which he did. Other governors also asked Gove to get involved in important developments, and he invariably came through. Hardly a run-of-the-mill academic, Gove had gone far beyond his peers in bridging the gulf from a campus to the real political world.

Knowing all the governors did not mean that Gove was fond of each. Ogilvie he certainly liked. Even more meaningful for Gove, he believed that Ogilvie was showing many of the traits of a great governor from the start. Developments down the road would only further convince Gove that Ogilvie was in a league of his own. Several Ogilvie assistants had suggested to Gove that he ought to consider being the historian of the administration. By the time of the rendezvous at Allerton Park, Gove was giving it some thought.

A Political Career on the Line

While just about everybody was reasonably sure it was coming, shock waves still were inevitable when Governor Ogilvie really did it. On April 1, 1969, the April Fools' Day of his first year in office, Ogilvie asked the General Assembly to approve the imposition of a state income tax. For years, no subject had received a colder shoulder from his predecessors.

None of the ventures by Governor Ogilvie would have near the impact of this one—on the governor himself, on legislators reluctant to go along with him, and on taxpayers not the least bit enthused at the thought of possibly having to ante up. Ogilvie was pictured by numerous friends and foes alike as a person engaged in the act of committing political suicide. Because his public career held so much promise, his supporters lamented, it was a shame. Even the man's detractors allowed that he was that rare officeholder with the gumption to take an action that had to be done, unpopular as it was.

Some political historians were quick to equate Ogilvie's decision to seek an income tax with the pardon of three Chicago Haymarket Square bombing anarchists in 1893 by liberal German-born governor John Peter Altgeld, a move early in Altgeld's governorship that undermined his popularity and led to his defeat when he sought reelection to a second term in 1896.

Ogilvie had no illusion about the great political risk involved in his income tax offensive. He was just as certain that the landmark governorship he envisioned would be a pipe dream without a massive infusion of new money into the Illinois treasury. Overcoming the state's fiscal jam, he believed, was the key to whether Illinois would sink or swim under his leadership. Without the income tax, he concluded, there would be no swimming.

In his campaign for governor, Ogilvie did not tell voters that, if elected, he would try to impose a state income tax on them. To the contrary, he left many questioners with an impression that he was not convinced at all of the need for such a levy. Consequently, a lot of folks, Republicans included, felt betrayed when Ogilvie came out for the tax in less than three months after taking office. Reporters' attempts to pin down the timing of Ogilvie's decision to pursue an income tax got only ambiguous answers at the time. However, years later, certain individuals with whom Ogilvie frankly discussed Illinois finances in the days following his election acknowledged coming away with the clear idea that he'd be going for an income tax in either his first or second year in office.

John McCarter, who would be a major player in bringing a state income tax to Illinois, twice was asked by Ogilvie after his election to become Illinois finance director and to set up the state's first real budget bureau. But McCarter, a former White House Fellow, had just been elected a partner in Booz, Allen & Hamilton, a Chicago management consulting firm, and he rebuffed Ogilvie both times. Then McCarter had second thoughts. Realizing that not many thirty-year-olds have an opportunity to run a budget program for a state the size of Illinois, he changed his mind and asked Ogilvie to count him in.

"Even before I accepted the job with Ogilvie," McCarter recalled, "the income tax was talked about. He was saying from the start that if the numbers confirmed the need for an income tax he'd go for it. I had no doubt that there would be an income tax in his first year in office or next. Not one bit of doubt."[1]

Since the call for a state income tax would register highly on the Richter scale gauging public policy upheavals, Ogilvie knew that as much of an effort as possible at damage control had to be made. A foundation had to be laid.

On the one hand, Ogilvie and his top aides were meeting covertly, often at night and at other odd times, putting together a much juicier fiscal program for Illinois, which was dependent for its success on approval of an income tax. The task was consuming much of the early time in office of the Ogilvie team, but it was carried out with a Los Alamos mentality because the Ogilvie men did not want to reveal their call for the income tax until the governor's first formal budget presentation on April 1. As far as the public knew, the Ogilvie administration was focusing in its first months in office on matters being promoted in the open, like reform of the Illinois penal system.

On the other hand, steps had to be taken to condition the public for the income tax bombshell coming April Fools' Day. For it to just appear out of the blue was unthinkable. The punch to taxpayers had to be telegraphed. The governor's legal counsel, Jerry Marsh, remembered that "there was a series of actions taken through January and February and March that were to lay the groundwork for the bitter pill which came on April 1."[2]

The most attention-getting move came February 5, when Ogilvie made his first appearance before the General Assembly to personally present a special legislative message on fiscal matters. Members of the House and Senate, sitting in a joint session, heard the new governor spell out in a most forceful fashion the quagmire of Illinois's finances. Most present anticipated that Ogilvie would order fiscal restraint by the state, which he did, but the message was much more severe than that.

Declaring that he had assumed captaincy of a state teetering "on the brink of bankruptcy," Ogilvie stated that he had no alternative but to seek increased revenue for Illinois.[3] He said he would "submit legislation to this end," but he did not specify what he had in mind, such as whether he would seek a sales tax hike or chase a state income tax. The costs of state government, Ogilvie stressed, were simply out of control. "Empires have been built within this government," the governor charged. "Inefficient procedures have developed in many areas, so that simple tasks are being performed at costs far above the cost for the same tasks in industry; overlapping and uselessly duplicated procedures are widespread."

The governor also implied criticism of the public, saying that the state's fiscal incapability was linked to people who "have called for public services far exceeding the present management capability of the state government and far exceeding the state's revenues." Solution of the state's financial plight, Ogilvie went on, would require "understanding from our local communities" and "support and leadership from both parties and from all concerned citizens." In the meantime, Ogilvie said that, in an effort to "assure the solvency of the state," he was mandating an austerity program eliminating many state jobs, freezing virtually all capital improvement spending, and requiring a 10 percent cash saving by each department director in his current appropriation.

In presenting this dark picture, Ogilvie played it to the hilt. The sedate tone and unvarnished language of the message were characteristic of his unembellished manner. No small talk, no mincing of words. Just the facts as he saw them.

Few of his subsequent appearances before the General Assembly would be as memorable. This was assured by the final line of the fiscal message, which became in the eyes of many the theme of his governorship. The words were: "I propose to manage this state government as it has never been managed before."

George A. Ranney Jr. coined that phrase, just as he authored most of the fiscal message.[4] He wrote it barely two weeks after going to work for Ogilvie as the administration's number-two budget person under McCarter, a friend of Ranney who asked George to sign on.

A member of a family prominent in both society and the steel industry in Chicago, Ranney was an interesting addition to the Ogilvie entourage. University of Chicago law school graduate, twenty-eight years old, and a moderate or even liberal GOPer, what one might have labeled in those days a Ripon Society Republican. An active supporter of the civil rights movement, Ranney had turned his conviction into action in 1964 by heading south to teach summer school at black Tougaloo College in Mississippi.

Ranney also had a big hand in the drafting of the income tax legislation. In point of fact, Ranney recommended Charles W. Davis, chief counsel to the IRS during Truman's presidency, to design the income tax bill. Davis was by 1969 the senior tax partner at the Chicago law firm of Hopkins & Sutter, and the Ogilvie administration contracted with the firm to get the services of Davis.

Actually, the legislature already had the income tax issue on its agenda before Ogilvie's bill was submitted. A measure introduced by Representative Clyde L. Choate of Anna, the assistant Democratic minority leader in the House, proposed imposition of a 2 percent flat-rate income levy on individuals and a 5 percent tax on corporations. However, a bill from Choate was one thing and a measure from the new governor, whose party led both branches of the General Assembly, was another.

Legislative uneasiness on this subject was evident in those early days of 1969. The prospect that the long-deferred decision on a state income tax seemed finally at hand was unsettling. Reluctance to consider the income tax, though, might lead to another unpopular road, an increase in the state sales tax. With Illinois facing one of its worst general fund crises since World War II, many of the state's power blocs felt that the only feasible choice other than an income tax was a hike in the sales levy, which then was five cents on a dollar.

Income tax proponents, including numerous organizations, believed that an unfair tax structure had emerged in Illinois. The sales levy, which was providing about thirty-six cents of each dollar the state was receiving, was regarded as regressive and discriminatory against low-income persons because they were forced to pay a large proportion of their money for food, clothing, and the other goods covered by the sales tax. The sales tax was adopted in the Depression when the state property tax was discontinued. But the sales levy was not approved before the Illinois Supreme Court held in 1932 that a state graduated income tax was unconstitutional. By the time Ogilvie was in office, though, there was wide agreement that a flat-rate income levy would be valid under the Illinois Constitution.

The momentum for enactment of an income tax also was aided by the report of the Governor's Revenue Study Committee, named by former governor Shapiro in 1968. The panel, headed by Simeon E. Leland, a dean emeritus of Northwestern University, recommended the imposition of a flat-rate income levy for individuals and corporations, with the rate to be determined by state needs. Another committee recommendation was that a temporary hike of one or more cents in the sales tax might be necessary to tide the state over financially until the validity of an income tax was tested and confirmed legally and the machinery established for its administration and collection.

As April 1 was approaching, Democrats in the legislature warned that they intended to oppose any fixed-rate income tax that hit individuals the same as corporations. Insisting that the same level of taxation for both was not equitable, they pointed to the bill already introduced by Choate as the kind of income tax measure they would consider. As for many legislators from Ogilvie's party, they were hardly anxious to entertain any income tax bill at all.

Also around were people like Paul Simon. The lieutenant governor, a Democrat, was opposed to an income tax without corresponding reductions in some other levies. For example, Simon contended that the state would receive more than $300 million in new revenue annually if it eliminated the sales tax on food and reduced the then-existing personal property tax by half while adopting Choate's income tax proposal.

Among many nonpartisan observers, the most common guess in the final days before April 1 was that Ogilvie would request imposition of a flat-rate income levy of from 2 to 3 percent on individuals and corporations. They could not see the governor asking for a bigger chunk than that the first time around. They guessed wrong.

Ogilvie proposed a fixed-rate tax of 4 percent on the incomes of individuals and corporations when he went before the legislators. He called also for new or higher taxes on tobacco products, alcoholic beverages, rented equipment, and certain consumer services. He refrained from seeking a sales tax hike. Still, he went on record in favor of the most drastic tax increase program by an Illinois chief executive in years.

This was one time the enthusiasm that customarily accompanies a personal appearance by a governor before the General Assembly was absent—even on the GOP side of the aisle. Ogilvie was ushered out of the House chamber to lackadaisical applause. A number of Democrats did not even get out of their seats. The dismal mood in the Statehouse was magnified by hundreds of state employees who slowly filed in picket lines through corridors of the elegant old Capitol as Ogilvie delivered his budget message. They marched in protest against what they termed the low pay and inadequate working conditions of most Illinois state employees.

In one move at the last minute to build support for his tax proposal, Ogilvie met at the Governor's Mansion the night before his budget presentation with newspaper executives from throughout the state. Newspaper types, especially editorial writers, often were among the first to endorse increased taxes. Nevertheless, some walked away from the mansion muttering about the unexpected severity of the rate of Ogilvie's proposed income tax.

More significant was the cool reaction of Republican senators when they were notified in a caucus the morning of April 1 about the governor's tax plan. The caucus climate, in the words of one of the solons, was "quite chilly, as if many realized that 4 percent tax was too big a bite to take at one time." He added, "Too many of us got elected campaigning against the type of proposal the governor presented. If no compromise is found, his tax request will go down."[5]

In his budget message to the lawmakers, Ogilvie cautioned that the levy on incomes could no longer be put off in Illinois.[6] Proclaiming that "nothing else will suffice," the governor insisted that the tax represented the only recourse for providing money to close a gap of more than $1 billion between necessary state spending and the revenue available to finance it. "The responsibilities of state government can be ignored no longer," said Ogilvie. "We can delay no longer unless we would risk the consequences of the economic and social chaos that threatens our immediate future."

As expected, a variety of new and extended programs were to be covered by the income tax–bolstered budget that the governor proposed for fiscal year 1970, the new state financial period beginning July 1, 1969. He called for record expenditures of $4,447,500,000 in the approaching fiscal year, a figure that—while seeming large at the time—was picayunish compared to the annual state budgets of $30 billion or so only several decades afterward.

The importance of Ogilvie's proposed income tax was that it was expected to produce $1,083,000,000 the first year, almost one-fourth of his intended expenditures in fiscal 1970. He wanted the levy to go into effect August 1 and for revenue from it to start reaching the state coffer by September or October of 1969.

One of the first things Ogilvie wanted covered by the new tax dollars was a $100-per-pupil increase in state aid to education to guarantee every public school district a minimum of $500 per pupil each year instead of $400.

In a potentially more controversial proposal, Ogilvie recommended that $32 million in state grants be distributed in the coming fiscal year to private and parochial schools in Illinois. The governor asserted that the state could not afford a financial collapse of many private school systems, but numerous persons involved in the church-state separation issue saw Ogilvie opening up a can of worms on the issue known as "parochiaid." Nevertheless, the governor insisted that his proposal in this ticklish area was "based upon legal advice that the state can properly make distributions to students attending these schools, even if it cannot give them direct financial assistance."

Ogilvie also asked for grants totaling $14 million to private Illinois colleges in order to "help them achieve higher standards of quality." Direct grants were requested by the governor for cities and local governments. He earmarked for this purpose about $135 million, roughly an eighth of the projected yield from the first year of the proposed income tax. This recommendation flowed from Ogilvie's pledge to devise a program for sharing some state revenue with financially hard-pressed Illinois cities.

The governor's proposed budget also fulfilled his promise to replace the state's traditional system of budgeting for two years at a time with annual budgeting. "We no longer can project or plan our outlays 30 months into the future," he had said earlier.[7]

Public education (higher as well as elementary and secondary) along with highways were ticketed for the greatest amounts under Ogilvie's budget. Another big spending item, public assistance, was also getting a major share of the pie. Estimated public aid expenses of $758,100,000 in fiscal 1970 would be $137,300,000 above the comparable figure for the fiscal period then ending, Ogilvie noted.

As the dust settled from Ogilvie's initial budget presentation, the governor stood out more than ever as the man of the hour in Illinois public life. Downstate especially, where many residents had viewed the new Illinois chief executive as mainly a law-and-order fellow, a lot of people were taking a much closer look at Ogilvie.

Was he really a Republican? Is this what he meant when he said he intended to manage the state "as it has never been managed before?" After all, standardbearers of the party were not exactly identified back then with big-time tax and spending programs, with initiatives seemingly every other day leading to larger government. Such matters were usually in the domain of Democrats. The behavior of Ogilvie was suddenly responsible for some serious rethinking about state politics. Amid the scratching of heads and theorizing, though, there were those who refused to let the subject get overcomplicated.

Maurice W. Scott, executive director of the Taxpayers' Federation of Illinois, simply credited Ogilvie with "lots of guts" in striving to meet the state's fiscal problems by proposing an income tax.[8]

It also was not difficult to see that Ogilvie, in trying to get an income tax passed as early as possible in his term, was picking the most politically safe time to do so. He did not face reelection until 1972. Too, more than a few persons believed that the governor may have called for a higher income tax rate than expected in an attempt to establish a bargaining position for the political battle certain to follow on his proposal. Judging by the reaction of GOP senators and representatives to the Ogilvie income tax, some Democratic votes almost certainly would be required if an income tax measure of any substance were to pass by the end of that legislative session. Thus, the Democrats appeared to be in a good position to negotiate for what they wanted in the levy.

Still, responsibility for the push for the tax in the General Assembly would fall to the Republican leadership in each chamber, a reality that spawned an ironic exchange when Ogilvie met with GOP legislative leaders to inform them of his definite intent to seek passage of an income tax.

"What fool in the Legislature," asked Senate Republican leader W. Russell Arrington, "do you think you are going to get to sponsor the bill?"

"You, Russ," replied the governor.

Following a moment of silence, Arrington reminded everybody present that he had strongly opposed a state income tax throughout his legislative career. Then, looking at Ogilvie, Arrington added, "But, if in your judgment, Governor, it's that time, then I'll sponsor it."[9]

Later, after Ogilvie had made public his desire for an income tax, Arrington would tell listeners that he intended "to live up to my responsibility as a legislative leader. We may have to resolve ourselves into a position to do things we may not want to do."

Arrington would need every bit of his prowess as a legislative strongman to prevail on this issue, which went against the grain of so many with a voice in the matter. Arrington would have his hands full running interference on the income tax for Richard Ogilvie, the person holding the seat that Arrington himself had fancied.

Once under way, the fight to enact the income tax dominated Illinois political news coverage in 1969, which was no small doing. That was the year the General Assembly, by going along with almost all of Ogilvie's reorganization proposals, helped change the face of Illinois government. It also was a year of extraordinary extracurricular activity in the public realm, not all of it planned: Immersion of the Illinois Supreme Court in scandal. Election of delegates to the Illinois Constitutional Convention. Even charges of fraud at the apple-pie Illinois State Fair.

For that matter, the final year of the 1960s provided a fitting windup everywhere to that whirlwind decade. On July 20, 1969, American astronaut Neil Armstrong set foot on the moon, the first time any man or woman had walked on its surface (as far as was known). The short trek by Armstrong was the high point of the *Apollo 11* manned mission to the moon, an event that captured the attention of the world. Several days before the lunar landing, the national media was focused on Chappaquiddick Island, off the Massachusetts coast, where a car driven by Senator Edward (Ted) Kennedy plunged off a bridge, resulting in the drowning of a young woman passenger. Her death effectively dashed Kennedy's hopes at the time of reaching the White House. It was also in 1969 that the nation was shocked by the ghastly, ritualistic murders in Los Angeles of actress Sharon Tate and four of her jet-setter friends by the perverse countercultural family of ex-convict Charles Manson.

Woodstock, or as it was properly called, the Woodstock Music and Art Festival, was another happening in 1969. Some 400,000 young persons were drawn to the rock music festival in New York, which actually was quite a few miles away from the village of Woodstock. Woodstock was the everlasting Eden of hippiedom to many, the zenith of communality. Others would not forget the mud and the stink, and the sight of nude flower children frolicking in ponds.

Come 1994, twenty-five years later, Illinoisans joined the rest of the nation in celebrating again the success of the *Apollo 11* mission as well as other things in 1969 that people cared to remember. A repeat of Woodstock was even promoted.

The income tax of Governor Ogilvie was the political story of the year in Illinois in 1969. But 1994 passed without anybody bringing it up. Just the same, it was the political story of the year in 1969. It really was.

From Sheriff to Cook County Board President

Decades *after* Ogilvie's governorship, Brian Whalen could not resist now and then sitting back in his office at Navistar International Transportation Corporation in Chicago's NBC Tower to reflect on his years as Ogilvie's right-hand man.

From start to finish of Ogilvie's political career, all ten years of it, Whalen was his top administrative assistant. He kept the machinery of the governor's office well oiled, and his hand was in everything from policy matters to logistics. He was the gatekeeper to Ogilvie's inner sanctum. People in the administration knew him as the chief of staff for the governor. In the outside world, Whalen was accorded the lofty title of deputy governor, which was quite impressive to governmental groupies, if for no other reason than the fact of Whalen's age, twenty-nine.

After Ogilvie's election, Whalen accompanied his boss on a visit to Springfield to work out details for the transition to the governor's office. Landing in the capital, Ogilvie and Whalen were met by state troopers anxious to attend to the transportation and other needs of the governor-elect. As Ogilvie and Whalen were being chauffeured into the heart of the city, Ogilvie turned to his young aide, smiled ever so slightly, and quietly asked, "Do you think we can get used to this?" Whalen answered with a nod and a smile of his own.[1] What was there to say? After all, it was a question that only someone like Whalen would fully appreciate, certainly more so than the hundreds of other persons just then latching onto Ogilvie's political star.

The first time Whalen met Ogilvie, the future governor was sitting alone in his campaign office. The year was 1962, and Ogilvie was the Republican candidate for sheriff of Cook County. Ogilvie's campaign office was situated in the old LaSalle Hotel in downtown Chicago, and Whalen happened to be spending time in the LaSalle that year while working on another political campaign. One day Whalen decided to break the ice and seek out Ogilvie.

"I had made up my mind to go and meet him, and to offer to help him where I could," related Whalen. "I found him sitting by himself in his campaign office in the hotel. I just walked in and introduced myself." Although expecting only a brief round of small talk, Whalen ended up conversing with Ogilvie for two hours.[2]

Afterward, Whalen felt that Ogilvie "had shown more depth to me than any public official or candidate I'd encountered. When I left him that first time, I really believed he would win the sheriff's race and that, before he was done, he'd be elected governor of Illinois. I told that to some of my friends, and they thought I was crazy."

Unlike many men and women in public office or running for it, Ogilvie actually listened as much as he talked. Probing Whalen about his background, Ogilvie learned a lot about the fresh-faced young man who had stopped to say hello: Whalen had obtained a Jesuit education, first at Loyola Academy on Chicago's north side and then at Loyola University in the city, where Whalen majored in social science. Whalen was a grandson of Dr. Charles Whalen, a former Chicago health commissioner, lawyer, and writer as well as a personal physician to more than one Chicago mayor. Dr. Whalen also was a Democrat, though Brian's father, an early promoter of the automatic laundry machine business, was not. He influenced his son to become a Republican, and so he was, even before he started to shave.

In 1952, at the Republican National Convention in the International Amphitheater in Chicago, twelve-year-old Brian Whalen paraded around hoisting a sign promoting the nomination of Senator Robert A. Taft of Ohio for president because Whalen "had decided on my own that Taft was a political leader I could believe in."[3] However, the convention nominated General Dwight David Eisenhower for president instead.

While at Loyola University, Whalen had organized a young Republicans' club. During the 1960 presidential race, Whalen campaigned for Vice President Richard Nixon at the Loyola campus, a Catholic school with a strong student backing for Senator John F. Kennedy of Massachusetts, a Catholic and Democrat. Whalen, a year later, was elected president of the Illinois Young Republican Federation, and in 1962, he led the Midwest College Republican Federation.

It was in 1962 that Whalen was hired as one member of a team of young field coordinators for the reelection campaign of Republican senator Everett McKinley Dirksen of Illinois. The lineup of the team would prove to have some later recognizable names. There was a young James S. Brady, of the south central Illinois railroad town of Centralia. He subsequently became known to the world when, as presidential press secretary, he was seriously wounded during an assassination attempt in 1981 on Ronald Reagan. Another was Tom Corcoran, an Ottawa farm boy and University of Notre Dame graduate, who would later run the State of Illinois office in Washington during Ogilvie's governorship and then serve in Congress. Two of the others were Alan Drazek, another Loyola University graduate who would serve as state personnel director under Ogilvie, and Perry Roberts, assistant director of the Illinois Department of Conservation in the Ogilvie administration.

Following the initial meeting with Ogilvie, Whalen interrupted his toiling for Senator Dirksen to organize some college support groups for Ogilvie. On election night, Whalen was with the Ogilvie campaign crew at the LaSalle.

When Ogilvie entered the race for sheriff, the conventional thinking had him as a long shot. The Daley machine had carried its candidate for sheriff by a big 320,000-vote margin four years earlier. Most people figured that, for the GOP to win the sheriff's office or any other Cook County post, a voter revolt of some significance had to occur. Nevertheless, Whalen recollected, Ogilvie "sure seemed to have incredible self-assurance" for a first-time Republican candidate against Daley's vaunted organization. Also, Whalen noted, "Ogilvie as a candidate was always in the newspapers, it seemed." That was nothing to sneer at.[4]

Ogilvie was already looked upon as a bona fide good guy by the Chicago press before he got into the sheriff's race, thanks to his hoodlum-chasing days as a special assistant to the United States attorney general in Chicago. Ogilvie's standing with Chicago newspapers also was not hurt by the infamous West Side bloc's opposition to his nomination for sheriff. The West Side bloc was the popular name for a political faction centered around a gang of Chicago legislators who were elected as Republicans but in reality had much closer ties to the Daley machine and, in the case of some in the bloc, to the underworld. To media types, the West Side bloc was nefarious.

Good guy Ogilvie also happened to be running for an office that had a poor image, an office overloaded with Democratic hacks poorly trained for professional law enforcement. Worse than that, Ogilvie charged in the campaign, some on the sheriff's payroll were crooks protective of the crime syndicate. A look at many county sheriff offices around the state showed that this was not unusual, regardless of whether the sheriff was a Democrat or Republican. Illinois had many a sheriff of Nottingham. As a result, the Ogilvie candidacy for sheriff was a natural for support from the press, civic organizations, and other groups often turned off by the normal run of office seekers.

This was not to say that Ogilvie did not have a respected Democratic opponent, because he did. Former FBI man Roswell Spencer was the chief investigator then for Cook County State's Attorney Daniel P. Ward, later chief justice of the Illinois Supreme Court. Spencer, though not a flamboyant type, had solid credentials in law enforcement.

Another consideration in the sheriff's race was that Ogilvie was no political neophyte. He had been a Republican activist going back to his law school days at Kent, where he and fellow student and chum, Bill Scott, worked hard to energize the Cook County Young Republican movement. Also, in the 1950s, the social life of newlyweds Dick and Dorothy Ogilvie revolved around the GOP. The young attorney and his bride gave unbridled devotion to the causes and activities of the party.

"Back in those years, our early years together," Dorothy Ogilvie later reminisced, "it seemed like all our free time was spent on the party. Wherever we were, we put in time ringing doorbells, urging people to vote, doing whatever we could for Republican candidates. It was just such an important part of our life."[5]

By the time his hat was in the ring for sheriff, Ogilvie had gone far beyond pushing doorbells. The candidate was showing that he could attract people to his political banner, that he could motivate persons with differing backgrounds to commit time, energy, and even dollars to the furtherance of his political ambition. Because of the mulligan-stew nature of Chicago life and politics, success in public life was pretty much limited to those who could forge alliances out of the melange of incongruous groups making up what was then the nation's second biggest city. Democrats did a superb job of this in Chicago through much of the twentieth century, especially in the twenty-one years that Richard J. Daley was mayor. Before Ogilvie's bid for sheriff, Daley was well on his way toward revamping his city and machine, the former to what he felt best for it and the latter to his own political taste. If there was a better-known political leader in the country, only the occupant of the White House qualified.

Yet, by 1962, signs were appearing that Ogilvie, a seemingly small political potato and an untested Republican at that, was succeeding in lining up a team cogent enough to get Daley's attention.

It had long ago become axiomatic in major Illinois political success stories for the official to have a former reporter, normally a political writer, at his or her side. Ogilvie had his already in place in 1962 in Tom Drennan, known back in his newspaper days as a hard-boiled digger covering Chicago government and politics. Drennan was a real McCoy in the Ogilvie campaign, a guy who brought a healthy dose of practical political perspective to the undertaking, because Drennan truly understood the workings of the Daley machine—and had proven it. Since leaving the *Chicago Sun-Times* in 1954 to open his public relations firm, he had shown he could do very well in handling candidates running against Richard Daley.

After the 1960 election, Drennan had been hired by a group of Republicans in Cook County to try to revitalize the party. Not long thereafter, at a luncheon, Drennan was introduced to Ogilvie, who had returned to the private practice of law after the Accardo prosecution. The first time the two talked, Drennan recounted, "Ogilvie mentioned that he was thinking of going for sheriff. I told him he'd better look out, especially if he won, because most sheriffs ended up disgraced."[6]

Nevertheless, after making up his mind to run, Ogilvie retained Drennan's firm, Chicago Public Relations, for somewhere around $1,000 a month. It was the start of an association between the two of them that would be beneficial for both. However, in their first outing together in 1962, Drennan had a notion that Ogilvie needed him more than he needed Ogilvie.

Years later, Drennan minced no words about that. "I can tell you," said Drennan, "I ran the campaign for sheriff. He [Ogilvie] didn't really know how to run a campaign, and neither did anybody else right around him. I was the only one who did."[7]

If Drennan had any qualm about Ogilvie running for sheriff, it paled in comparison to the anxiety of Don Perkins, Ogilvie's neighbor and golfing pal in Northfield. Perkins was stunned to hear one night, while the two men and their wives were playing bridge, that Ogilvie was leaving his law firm to seek election as sheriff. "I looked at him and told him it was a dumb thing to do," related Perkins. "I said, 'Dick, you are short, fat and ugly. You can't succeed in politics.' But, he insisted he had decided to do it."[8]

Pressing Ogilvie about the wisdom of this decision, Perkins asked his friend where he thought his quest might lead. Perkins never forgot Ogilvie's reply. "Dick told me that he just would like to see how far he could go with this new direction in his life." At that moment, said Perkins, "I realized what a sacrifice and expression of his idealism it was for him to run for sheriff." But, added Perkins, "I still thought he was nuts to do it."

Oh yes, another ramification of Ogilvie's political ambition was broached during the bridge game that evening in 1961. Money. Perkins told Ogilvie that he did not have the dollars to go for sheriff, which was true. Well, countered Ogilvie, would Perkins help raise funds? Perkins said he would, just as he agreed to do so for each of Ogilvie's political campaigns to follow.

The first contributions came quickly. Perkins, a rising young executive with Jewel Tea Company (later Jewel Companies, Incorporated), immediately informed Jewel president George L. Clements of what Ogilvie was up to. "George replied to me that he thought that was good," said Perkins. "Hearing that from George, I replied to him, 'Good, how much will you give?' "[9] The result was a contribution of $100 or so from Clements, which likely was Ogilvie's first political donation. Perkins right away doubled the amount with a check of his own. In the end, a relatively modest sum of about $45,000 was raised for Ogilvie's race for sheriff, Perkins estimated.

As for soliciting votes, Ogilvie's team depended on the support of Chicago suburbanites like Perkins. But Ogilvie would also have to establish at least a measure of political footing in the city itself, a tricky challenge for a suburban Republican. That was where a person like Louis J. Kasper entered the picture. Kasper had taken a liking to Ogilvie in the late 1940s when Kasper, like Ogilvie, joined the Young Republican ranks of Cook County. The two found they had a lot to talk about. A year younger than Ogilvie, Kasper had survived many dangerous skirmishes as an army reconnaissance sergeant after landing in Normandy as part of the D-Day invasion. When Ogilvie went after the sheriff's job, Kasper was there for him. At the time, Kasper was the acting GOP committeeman for the north side ward covering the Logan Square community, where Kasper operated a tavern and restaurant, the Dugout. He maintained a political office on Milwaukee Avenue, a place in which he often huddled with Ogilvie.

In the months before the election, Kasper made sure that "my part of Chicago got to know Ogilvie. We had signs all over and organized rallies. I drove him around it seemed like everywhere. We got to be very close friends."[10]

After Ogilvie became sheriff, Kasper served as his chief bailiff, a post in which Kasper supervised about every function of the office except for the police department. Kasper, whose parents came to Chicago from Poland, was not Ogilvie's only link to the city's huge Polish community. Another was Edmund J. Kucharski, the GOP leader of the Thirteenth Ward in southwest Chicago who became the undersheriff of Cook, the number-two person in the office, when Ogilvie was sheriff. Ogilvie was quite adept at lining up allies like Kucharski and Kasper in other big ethnic groups in Chicago. This was important since Ogilvie himself, as a white Protestant with mainly English-Scottish ancestral roots, was representative of one of the unquestionably smaller ethnic bodies in the city.

For a Republican seeking a Cook County office, Ogilvie certainly got around in the city. Most GOP contenders were not seen very much in the polka halls of Bucktown, the living rooms of liberal lakefront independents, the Avondale neighborhood, Rogers Park, or the bungalow belt working-class residential sections. Some Republican candidates did not even make it to the stretches of comfortable homes at certain edges of the city, about the only places where real Republicans resided to any extent in the city. Sheriff-aspirant Ogilvie was an exception, though, as he gained uncommon insight into many of the political wards—the layout of which was used by a lot of people, along with the location of Catholic parishes, as a way to get around in Chicago.

Even though the GOP county candidates in Cook were clobbered in the elections of 1954 and 1958, Hayes Robertson, the county Republican chairman, predicted victory by every nominee on the party's ticket in the county in the 1962 election. His forecast was based partly on the expected strong showing of Senator Dirksen at the head of the GOP ticket over his Democratic opponent, Congressman Sidney R. Yates of Chicago. He hoped this would have a coattail effect on lesser-known Republican contenders.

As for the Democrats, there were signs they were worried. Mayor Daley exhorted his troops to take nothing for granted by "reading the riot act" at closed meetings of Democratic ward and suburban Cook township committeemen.[11] Keenly aware that a taxpayers' revolt was brewing in Chicago, Daley departed from custom to point out several days before the election that the 1963 budget for the city would reverse a long upward trend. Word even surfaced that some GOP ward committeemen in the city, not known for doing much for their party's ticket most years, were eyeing the election quite seriously this time. A few were even said to have placed wagers on their candidates.

So, did the election produce a major political eruption? Well, not enough of one to bring down the roof. As widely expected, Illinois voters on November 6, 1962, returned Dirksen to the Senate for a new six-year term. Republicans also captured control of two state offices from Democrats in something of a surprise. Evanston resident William J. Scott, the same Bill Scott close to Ogilvie, was elected state treasurer. Ray Page, who coached the Springfield High School Senators to the state basketball championship in 1959, came out of nowhere politically to win the then-elective office of state superintendent of public instruction.

However, in Cook County, members of the GOP ticket went down to defeat, with one exception. Ogilvie. Out of the nearly 1.9 million votes cast in the sheriff's race, Ogilvie received 964,001 and Spencer 931,680. As expected, Spencer beat Ogilvie in the city of Chicago, 759,869 to 600,515. But Spencer's plurality of 159,354 in the city was wiped out by Ogilvie's showing in the rest of Cook County, where he clobbered Spencer, 363,486 to 171,811—a lopsided margin for Ogilvie of 191,675. Regardless of the spread, Ogilvie's victory was a huge one, both for himself and for his job-starved party in Cook. It was a significant breakthrough.

Ogilvie was tired but jubilant as he awaited with his wife the arrival of Dirksen in the wee hours of the morning after the election at a gathering of Republican workers in downtown Chicago. "Dick," Dirksen observed to Ogilvie after the Senator showed up, "do you realize you have made it possible for me to walk into the Cook County sheriff's office and meet a friend for the first time in my political career?" Dirksen then showed his appreciation for this turn of events by clapping Ogilvie quite hard on the back for photographers. One picture taker who missed the slap asked Dirksen to "hit him like that again." As Dirksen was about to oblige, Ogilvie suddenly piped up, "Never mind that. You guys aren't going to send me into office with a dislocated shoulder."[12]

Ogilvie then moved to get through the crowd, but stopped when someone was heard to ask, "Sheriff, are you going to wear a gun?" Breaking into one of the broadest grins anybody could remember seeing on his face, Ogilvie replied, "I can only say one thing. I know definitely I'm not going to wear two of them."

Later, those around him in his days as sheriff could not recall him carrying even one gun. He didn't trade his suits for a uniform either. But he was the sheriff of Cook County all right. Without a doubt. Few officeholders at any level got more boffo reviews than Sheriff Ogilvie. To believe the raves that seemed to come from every direction, one might have thought that Ogilvie walked on water.

In the view of the Chicago Crime Commission, Ogilvie's performance produced the "greatest four years" in the history of the sheriff's office. When his four-year term was ending, the *Chicago Daily News* mused that "since 1962 he has conducted the office of Cook county sheriff without a blemish to his personal reputation." However, Ogilvie's record as sheriff did have one good-sized blemish, a personnel blunder that would haunt him politically. At least one bad apple had sneaked into the barrel.

On the other hand, Ogilvie took over an office that was swamped by poor personnel, an office that was a veritable political refuse pile. A house cleaning was in order, as was more revamping if Ogilvie was to achieve his goal to make a model operation out of the office, one of the biggest of its kind in the country. Some three thousand jobs were controlled by the sheriff's office, and the occupants of many of those positions knew they were doomed anyway when Ogilvie got elected. For starters, a civil service system was instituted for the sheriff's police department, a primary part of the office. Up to then, the hiring and promotion of members of the sheriff's police force were tied to political sponsorship.

Written examinations were established for applicants for the police force. The door was opened for recruits to go through Chicago's police training academy, which provided them with top-notch instruction and a better understanding of what it took to have a productive working relationship with the Chicago police and other law enforcement agencies. Ogilvie also successfully enlisted help from the prestigious police administration school at Michigan State University in his reorganization of the sheriff's corps of cops.

In what was apparently his first major foray into Springfield, Ogilvie convinced the General Assembly to approve legislation specifically enabling the Cook County sheriff's office to implement a merit program for its police that governed job standards as well as job security. Without it, Ogilvie's overhaul would have floundered. Actually, Ogilvie's legislative request was at first rebuffed by the lawmakers. But they relented and gave him what he wanted after Ogilvie took his case for the merit legislation to publishers and editors in Chicago and obtained their support for his plan. Going to the press was a tactic often utilized by Ogilvie to gain added leverage in political fights. Under the merit code, the sheriff's office set up a board for dealing with disciplinary actions and other personnel problems, another stride in moving toward a professional police force.

All of the steps taken to modernize the sheriff's law officers were insisted upon ahead of time by Arthur J. Bilek, the person named by Ogilvie to be the chief of the sheriff's police. Bilek, who had worked his way up from patrolman to acting training director with the Chicago Police Department, grew to know and respect Ogilvie when Ogilvie was fighting the syndicate in Chicago for the United States attorney general. He would take charge of the sheriff's police, Bilek told Ogilvie, only if the force were "totally free of political control, involvement or interference" and if there were "no corruption of any kind tolerated, no agreements or control by vice elements."[13] Ogilvie readily agreed in saying, "Art, I wouldn't have asked you to take this job if that wasn't what I wanted."

Six years later, when Ogilvie was running for governor, Bilek would tell Willard Hansen, editor of The News-Gazette at Champaign-Urbana, that Ogilvie as sheriff "never reneged one iota on any of the pledges he made. I worked without interference or control. Some on the force had to be dismissed, and he tolerated no corruption of any kind."

Bilek, who would chair Ogilvie's Illinois Law Enforcement Commission, was quick to point out that in Ogilvie's initial year as sheriff not even fifty requests for assistance came to the sheriff's police from suburban towns in Cook County, a sure sign of how the sheriff's crew was regarded. In Ogilvie's last year as sheriff, Bilek added, that number had jumped to more than one thousand.

More striking to the public, though, were the roughly 1,800 vice raids carried out by Bilek's force while Ogilvie was sheriff. Dens of illegal activity, safe in the pre-Ogilvie years from bother by the sheriff's men, were hit again and again—

just like Ogilvie's great-grandfather Reuben Spivey made life miserable for vice lords in the Kansas cattle town country in the previous century.

Insiders were struck by several things as Ogilvie sought to carry out his campaign pledge to "smash the syndicate." He went extra miles to cultivate a more cooperative relationship between the intelligence personnel in his office and those of the Chicago police and the state police. Too, nobody could remember seeing the Cook sheriff's crew as fired up as it was under Ogilvie. To Bilek, Ogilvie "inspired tremendous dedication." One year, he noted, the sheriff's police amassed thirty thousand hours of overtime work in the county's unincorporated areas, "overtime for which they never were compensated in money or time."

Still, while earning respect for law enforcement was the bottom line in the sheriff's office under Ogilvie, political considerations were not ignored. Along with the police force, the office of the sheriff was an umbrella for a wide gamut of responsibilities in places ranging from the court system to the Cook County Jail—which was housed in a dreary complex that reminded some of a Spanish fortress, in the Pilsen neighborhood of Chicago. Many citizens did not know it, but running the jail was the sheriff's baby. Patronage jobs still were around at the jail and in certain other areas under the sheriff, and Ogilvie and his men made sure they were filled with Republicans or political friends. After all, those in the highest echelon of the sheriff's office who were not top GOP officials seemed to be in a minority.

Whalen was one in the minority. Early in Ogilvie's first year as sheriff, Ogilvie asked Whalen to leave his job with a foundation in Chicago and join him. Whalen did so, going to work as Ogilvie's administrative assistant, the formal beginning of their working days together. Whalen recalled, "He wanted me to deal with the civilian side because he was pretty much surrounded by cops and he needed somebody like me to handle a lot of matters not pertaining to only cops. I was really just a kid at the time."[14]

Kid or not, Whalen found himself sitting with Sheriff Ogilvie in the colossal City Hall–County Building, a granite neoclassical structure occupying an entire block in downtown Chicago. For all practical purposes, the whole place was a fiefdom of Mayor Daley, whose office was on the fifth floor of the city hall section. With the arrival in the building of Ogilvie, though, Daley had a fly in the ointment.

Another top man in the sheriff's office was chief bailiff Louis Kasper. Administering much of the sheriff's office meant heady days for Kasper. He became the Republican committeeman for the Thirty-fifth Ward while Ogilvie was sheriff and the proverbial man to see in the sheriff's office. The ranks of bailiffs and some other jobs beneath the sheriff were well populated by political appointees anointed by persons like Kasper or his friend and fellow GOP ward leader, Kucharski, the undersheriff.

Still, even the political appointees were closely screened to keep out bums and anybody else who might become an embarrassment to Ogilvie. This was the rule in the hiring of all hands in the office, from the top on down. For no other reason than that, the case of Richard Cain was as surprising as it was bizarre. Former Chicago policeman Cain was the chief investigator for Ogilvie in his first years as sheriff. But Ogilvie dismissed Cain after it became clear that he also was a consort of the underworld.

Cain's stay with the sheriff's office ended with his conviction in the Circuit Court of Cook County late in 1964 on charges of conspiring to commit perjury in connection with a burglary. Two other members of the sheriff's investigative unit also were convicted of the charges. Their indictment grew out of a burglary in 1963 of $240,000 in drugs from a warehouse in the Chicago suburb of Melrose Park. Cain and the other defendants were alleged to have protected the burglars. The convictions were reversed in 1967 by the Illinois Supreme Court on grounds that the three men did not have a fair trial before an impartial jury.

In 1968, one month before the electorate went to the polls to vote in the governor's race, Cain was convicted in federal district court in Chicago with four other men for bank robbery conspiracy. Cain went to prison that time. The conviction of the five stemmed from the robbery of $43,000 from a bank in another Chicago suburb, Franklin Park, in 1963. Cain was accused of arranging a private lie detector test, while working for Ogilvie, to help gangsters ferret out a stool pigeon among the robbers. The test reportedly was ordered by William (Willie Potatoes) Daddano, a crime chief in the Chicago suburbs who was among those convicted with Cain.

Cain's conviction, so close to the 1968 election, was seized upon by Governor Shapiro as a good reason for not putting Ogilvie into the governor's chair. Of course, this was not the first time the Cain matter had been raised against Ogilvie. Whenever it came up, Ogilvie had a stock reply. It generally went as follows: "I can only repeat what I have said again and again. I fired Cain when he went wrong, just as I fired others during my administration of the sheriff's office who failed to measure up to the standards of the office."[15] To this, Ogilvie would invariably add that the Chicago Crime Commission as well as other bodies credited him as sheriff with unprecedented reduction of syndicate gambling and other unlawful activities in the suburbs of Chicago.

Nevertheless, innuendoes about the Ogilvie-Cain link seldom took long to surface when a critic sought to really sting Ogilvie, to hit him where it hurt. And Cain did not help to quash interest in himself. Before and after his days in prison, which ended in 1971, Cain was an intimate of exiled Chicago mob boss Sam Giancana. Prior to his federal court conviction, Cain was conspicuous in Mexico as a companion of Giancana and a girlfriend of the mobster, singer Phyllis McGuire. Then in 1973, Cain was murdered by masked killers who blew away his face with a shotgun in a gangland-style slaying in a Chicago sandwich shop. According to police, Cain was thought at the time to be keeping files and tapes on several underworld figures.

Guesswork was rampant on how Cain got into the Ogilvie orbit. One early account had it that a Chicago columnist who knew both Ogilvie and Cain got them together. True or not, Ogilvie had a relationship with Cain going back at least to the period at the end of the 1950s when Ogilvie was a special anticrime assistant in the Chicago area for the United States attorney general. In those days, Ogilvie was investigating racketeer Tony Accardo. Officers from various law enforcement agencies, at Ogilvie's direction, were working undercover on this detail. One officer was Cain and another was FBI agent William F. Roemer Jr., who later would become a well-known author on the Chicago mob.

"I met Cain through Dick [Ogilvie] during that investigation of Accardo," Roemer said years later from his retirement home in Tucson. Roemer said that Cain handled wiretaps during the inquiry, an assignment carried out by Cain "so well that he ingratiated himself with Ogilvie."[16] Several years afterward, Roemer and several others in law enforcement warned Sheriff Ogilvie not to hire Cain. But, Roemer recalled, "Dick told me he was sure he could keep Cain under control." Hiring Cain, Roemer concluded, was "the biggest mistake Ogilvie made in his public career."

However, Louis Kasper did little more than shrug on a June day in 1994 when the name of Richard Cain was brought up while Kasper, then sixty-nine years old and still a GOP wheelhorse in Chicago, lunched at a favorite hangout, Tommy's Chicago Bar & Grill on North Dearborn Street. "So, what's to say about Cain?" questioned Kasper. "It was an unfortunate thing. You can't do it all right every minute of the time. You never can. But, I'll tell you, I respected Richard Ogilvie more than any public official I ever knew."[17]

The memories Kasper preferred to dwell upon were the events that brought accolades to the sheriff's office in its Ogilvie years—not just actions like the closing of syndicate joints, but Ogilvie's use of the office to defuse situations socially explosive. Kasper recalled the targeting by civil rights activists of the racially rigid Chicago suburb of Cicero. The town turned out to be a test ground for Ogilvie in working with the Illinois National Guard to try to maintain law and order.

More than a few on the scene noticed Ogilvie walking the streets of Cicero in a straw hat when he headed a peace-preserving law enforcement contingent in the town during a civil rights march that easily could have ignited violence. Kasper, who was with Ogilvie that day, recalled that others wore protective helmets, but Ogilvie did not because he wanted to underscore his confidence that a riot would not break out.[18] None did. This was the type of thing that Kasper liked to remember. For Kasper, though, memories of Ogilvie went beyond the sheriff's office.

After Ogilvie lost the governorship, Kasper went to Springfield to help Ogilvie move his belongings from the Governor's Mansion to Chicago. "Ogilvie wanted me to do this," said Kasper, "and not the state." In gratitude, Ogilvie gave Kasper several of his suits for assisting him, and Kasper wore the suits for years.

. . . .

In 1959, the Blue Demons of Maine Township High School of Des Plaines won their second straight state baseball championship, which had to be a dream of every red-blooded boy in Illinois. The captain of that 1959 team was senior catcher Ronald Dwight Michaelson, who played every inning of every game that season, including the state finale in which the Blue Demons beat Harrison Tech of Chicago. The day after the championship game, the *Chicago Tribune* featured a picture on the front page of the sports section showing Michaelson tagging out a Harrison base runner trying to steal home. When he saw that picture, Michaelson knew, no matter what the future may hold, he'd already been to the top of the world.

Well, the immediate future for Michaelson involved Wheaton College, where he played more baseball and was graduated in 1963. Two years later, he received a master's degree in political science at Northwestern University. While there, a door opened to his eventual participation on another winning team.

At the end of class one day, the instructor casually mentioned that the United Republican Fund, a fund-raising organization for the state GOP, was looking for students to do research. For free, of course. Michaelson responded, he said, although "for whatever reason possessed me to respond I didn't know." The URF, it turned out, wanted to obtain a fresh picture of the ins and outs of political fund-raising in Cook County. Students were recruited to conduct field interviews for the project, which was being managed by another one of those bright young political science students of the 1960s, Jim Nowlan. One of the people Nowlan asked Michaelson to interview was Sheriff Ogilvie.

Michaelson got access to Ogilvie in his downtown Chicago office, peppered him with the prescribed questions, and then, being an enterprising young chap, Michaelson gently steered Ogilvie on to the subject of political job possibilities.

"Right now," Ogilvie told Michaelson, "the only job I have available is as a guard at the county jail." Michaelson thanked Ogilvie, but said he'd pass.

"I thought you would," remarked Ogilvie. "But, I will keep you in mind in case something comes up." Sure enough, Ogilvie did.[19] Several months later, said Michaelson, he received "a call out of the blue from Brian Whalen, who I didn't know. He said the sheriff recalled the interview with me and that he was putting together a campaign to run for county board president. He said the sheriff wanted to know if I was interested in coming aboard to handle research. Brian wanted to know what I thought. I told him I thought it sounded great." As it turned out, Michaelson really did find the job great. He was one of only a few full-time salaried persons in Ogilvie's campaign office.

A long way before the end of Ogilvie's term as sheriff, few in Chicago politics doubted that Ogilvie was eyeing the presidency of the Board of Cook County Commissioners. Even if he had wanted to, Ogilvie was prohibited from running for a second consecutive term as sheriff by the Illinois Constitution.

To many in the know, the presidency of the Cook County board was one of the three most important public offices in the state. But whereas the holders of the other two offices, governor and mayor of Chicago, were household names, the occupant of the Cook County board post was nearly anonymous outside the county. Few downstaters knew anything at all about the governing board of Illinois's largest county, which consisted of fifteen commissioners, ten elected from the city of Chicago and five from the suburbs. The president of the board, who was elected county-wide, was the chief administrator of the county's government, which employed 17,000 persons and spent more than $400 million annually. These figures were nothing to sneeze at.

Ogilvie's campaign for the board presidency evolved almost naturally out of both the mechanics of his race for sheriff and his record once in that office. Perkins again was the main solicitor of campaign funds, proceeding this time in a more organized fashion and raising in the end close to $100,000.[20] The public relations firm of Drennan was again retained. When the election was over, and Ogilvie had won big, Drennan would view the campaign as "one of the best I was ever connected with."[21] In Drennan's mind, Ogilvie's 1966 campaign was just as satisfying as Drennan's success ten years before in handling the winning race of Benjamin S. Adamowski for state's attorney of Cook County. The triumph of Adamowski, a former Democrat turned Republican, was a major victory for Drennan over the Democratic organization of Richard Daley, who in 1956 was still a somewhat-new mayor of Chicago.

When Ogilvie ran for sheriff, Drennan's sales pitch was that the gangster-fighting Ogilvie was cut from the mold of Eliot Ness, the young federal agent who had led the "Untouchables" in a war against the crime empire of Chicagoan Al Capone. Ness and his crew were called the Untouchables because they were reported to have turned their backs on Capone's bribes. Drennan tried to impart this image of Ogilvie in television commercials prepared for the 1962 campaign.

In my 1994 interview with Drennan, he said he felt that the Ogilvie commercials were effective, even though they may have appeared amateurish compared to the slick political advertising on the tube in later decades. Too, Drennan noted, "it was not yet that expensive to buy a few TV spots" in 1962. In 1966, Drennan depicted Ogilvie as the right person for a tough job. Ogilvie's high rating as sheriff would bolster that theme.

Ogilvie also gained the backing of the *Chicago Tribune* and other newspapers for the county board post. A *Tribune* editorial said he was "unusually well qualified to serve as president" and observed that while the sheriff's office had previously been "the graveyard of ambition for a number of politicians," Ogilvie had "made such a good record there that he obviously deserves advancement." The editorial went on to praise Ogilvie for establishing a merit system for the sheriff's police force and added that he "plans to do the same for other county employees, starting with the huge County hospital, which for years has suffered from the political spoils system."[22]

So there he was. As in 1962, Ogilvie was the right person in the right place at precisely the right time. Taking command of the top job in the government of Cook County was just a logical step-up for the forty-three-year-old Ogilvie.

Not so for Ogilvie's Democratic opponent, Harry H. Semrow, a Chicago businessman and onetime state legislator who had resigned as Chicago postmaster to seek the board presidency. Throughout the campaign, Semrow was dogged by a lingering feeling that the Daley machine might have fielded a stronger candidate in view of the great number of jobs controlled by the county board chief. The bulk of the jobs were held by persons with years of service and fealty to the Democratic Party.

No, a much more dynamic foe than Semrow was needed to derail Ogilvie in the 1966 election season. Timothy P. Sheehan found that out before Semrow. Sheehan, the Republican chairman of Cook County, was not as taken with Ogilvie as many others in the party. Sheehan wanted to deny the sheriff party backing in his bid for nomination for the county board slot. Ogilvie made it clear he would run anyway. The outcome? The GOP elders of Cook not only slated Ogilvie for election to the post but also anointed his choices for certain other spots on the party's county ticket, a sure sign of Ogilvie's emerging stature.

One of the Ogilvie picks, Kucharski, the second in command in the sheriff's office, was endorsed for county treasurer, and Joseph I. Woods got the GOP nod to succeed Ogilvie as sheriff. Kucharski already had shown he could win elections, having captured a Chicago aldermanic seat in 1947 and then several other posts in the next decade, including the office of Cook County recorder of deeds. As for Woods, Ogilvie's support was crucial. Woods had served with the FBI and also with the Ogilvie-aligned Better Government Association as its chief investigator. Ogilvie viewed Woods as a man of integrity who would carry on the sheriff's office war on organized crime.

Woods was one of several individuals tied to Ogilvie who had links to Richard Nixon. Woods's sister Rosemary served as Nixon's secretary, a role that would put her in the White House. Another person in Ogilvie's campaign, Jeb Stuart Magruder, would gain wide notoriety down the line as a result of his heavy involvement in the Watergate scandal that engulfed the Nixon presidency. Magruder labored for various Republican candidates while working in Chicago in the early 1960s for a management consulting company and then Jewel Tea, where he was a management trainee under Ogilvie's close friend Perkins. Having met Ogilvie when he ran for sheriff, Magruder would relate later in an autobiography that Ogilvie had asked him late in 1965 to help in his run for the county board presidency.[23] After numerous breakfast meetings with Ogilvie, Magruder said he agreed to manage the campaign. However, according to Magruder, the Jewel board of directors refused to grant his request for a leave of absence to work on the Ogilvie race. This left Magruder, in his words, frustrated and angry. As a result, he said, he made a major mistake by abruptly leaving his job at Jewel (and the Ogilvie campaign) and taking another position in California. Magruder added that Perkins, by then the president of Jewel, tried to talk Magruder out of leaving, but that he, Magruder, foolishly ignored Perkins.

One who did not lament Magruder's departure was Drennan, who in his characteristically blunt manner said that "it was okay that he wasn't around that long because I didn't think he understood enough about our situation to play a leading role. I knew what had to be done, and I didn't want to have to work around Magruder."[24]

Most Chicagoans who knew Magruder would next hear of him when he fell into disgrace as staff director of the committee working for the reelection of President Nixon in 1972, the discredited committee that financed the break-in at Democratic headquarters at the Watergate complex in Washington. Besides eventually forcing Nixon's resignation from office in 1974, the Watergate mess had a depressing impact on GOP fortunes in many parts of the country.

One was Illinois, where the party—after having already lost the governorship in 1972—went on to lose control of both houses of the General Assembly in the 1974 election. Yet the period of Republican domination in Illinois from 1966 to 1974, even though wild and woolly much of the time, produced the framework for public life in the state for the rest of the century and beyond. To view it as a Republican-coated era of political renaissance, a transition from the medieval to modernness, is not an exaggeration. Too, it was easy to see that the roots of that period were enmeshed in the election in 1966, the one in which Ogilvie pursued and won the top job in Cook County government.

Of course, the Ogilvie race was far from the main event of the 1966 election season in Illinois. That distinction was reserved for the contest in which Republican Charles Percy undertook to oust Democrat Paul H. Douglas from the United States Senate seat that he had held since 1948. Percy, a vigorous and wealthy Chicago industrialist, had been an appealing Republican nominee for governor in 1964. However, the candidacy of Percy, a political moderate, was buried in the GOP debacle of Barry Goldwater's run for the presidency that year. However, Percy was back on the hustings in 1966 with no Goldwater-like baggage on his party's ticket to weigh him down. A lot of people sensed that Senator Douglas, a venerable social liberal, was in trouble.

In just the two years from 1964 to 1966, change in the United States had become rampant. Yet, so much of it was only a forerunner of greater upheaval on the horizon. Underlying concerns and discontent were popping up everywhere, fueled by the growing but no-win war in Vietnam, increasing hostility between blacks and whites, and soaring prices and high interest rates. All of this did not bode well in 1966 for candidates such as the seventy-four-year-old Douglas who were disparagingly placed in the same-tired-old-face category. Douglas, an honorable man, was cast as frail and out of touch, while Percy, forty-seven, a person taught economics by Douglas twenty-five years earlier at the University of Chicago, exuded vitality.

Another issue in the 1966 election, crime and violence, took a lurid and personal turn in the Douglas-Percy race. In September, Percy's twenty-one-year-old daughter Valerie was murdered in the Percy home in the posh Chicago suburb of Kenilworth. The killing of Valerie Percy cemented even further the media focus on her father's contest, leaving in its wake a wave of sympathy for Charles Percy that pretty much doomed any remaining chance of victory by Douglas.

When Illinoisans went to the polls November 8, 1966, a Percy triumph seemed almost a given. The only surprise, albeit a mild one to some, was that he beat Douglas in Cook County as well as downstate.

While the GOP fared well across much of the land in that election, the party did better in few places than Illinois. The Republican majority in the Illinois Senate was easily maintained and control of the Illinois House was recaptured by the GOP. Besides the United States Senate contest, two other statewide races were on the ballot in Illinois. In one, Republican Ray Page was reelected state public instruction superintendent, defeating Donald M. Prince, an Illinois State University professor with a broad background in education. In the other one, Representative Adlai E. Stevenson III, a Chicago Democrat, edged a fellow House member, Republican Harris Rowe of Jacksonville, for Illinois treasurer—an office where the Republican incumbent, William Scott, could not constitutionally succeed himself. In spite of the narrow margin of Stevenson's victory, it was noteworthy in view of the strong Republican tide in the election. The victory automatically thrust Stevenson, a thirty-six-year-old lawyer, into the Democratic spotlight, willing or not.

But the winner in the 1966 balloting who ultimately would exert the greatest impact was Ogilvie, whose name was seldom mentioned in media coverage of the election outside of the Chicago area. Downstate newspapers would inform their readers of rumors of the Beatles splitting up and about actor George Hamilton, a beau of President Johnson's daughter Lynda, taking a pre-induction physical and saying he'd be willing to fight in Vietnam if he was drafted. Or they could read about the reduction to a trickle of the water flowing over Niagara's American Falls to permit firsthand inspection of the bed and rock formations of the cataract. But hardly a word was printed about the fellow elected president of the Cook County board—only the third Republican elected to the position in the last half century.

Ogilvie 1,057,360. Semrow 885,040. Ogilvie by 172,320 votes, a plurality much greater than his 32,321-vote victory margin in his race for sheriff four years earlier. Ogilvie creamed Semrow in suburban Cook County, 455,657 to 177,264 and gave Semrow a heck of a battle in Chicago, where Semrow prevailed, 707,776 to 601,703. For a candidate blessed by the Daley machine, Semrow ran like a weak sister in Chicago.

In the other Cook County races, the GOP did not win as many offices as some observers predicted. Take the contest for county clerk, for example, where the Democratic incumbent, Edward J. Barrett, succeeded in defeating a challenger with a very big name, Earl D. Eisenhower, an Illinois House member and brother of President Eisenhower. On the other hand, the Republican winners did include Kucharski and Woods, which further bolstered the image of Ogilvie.

Facing a throng of excited backers after the election, just as he did in 1962, Ogilvie seemed to be a victor with a broader purpose this time around when he declared that his triumph placed "a great burden upon the shoulders of the Republican Party." Elaborating, he said, "We must assume responsibility for developing, in an orderly manner, the cultural, economic, and social well being of a very complex metropolitan society. This will not be accomplished by replacing Democratic payrollers with Republican payrollers. It can only be accomplished by performance which will fulfill our pledge to end the system of spoils politics which has become synonymous with the Democratic administration."[25]

The day after the election, Ogilvie, looking fresh and spirited even though he had gotten only a few hours sleep after his victory, discussed his own political future. "When I was elected sheriff, they said it was a political burial ground. Now I am elected county [board] president and they say that office is a political burial ground. I like these political burial grounds. They are darn hard jobs. As to my future, I have a great interest in the welfare and future of the Republican Party. I will want to stay in public service wherever that may be."[26]

Drennan and Whalen, and perhaps others close to Ogilvie, had little doubt that Ogilvie already had visions of the governor's office dancing in his head before he had even settled into his new Cook County post. Would he seek the governorship in 1968, the year of the next Illinois gubernatorial election and the midpoint of Ogilvie's four-year term as county board head? "Really, how difficult was it to see?" questioned Whalen. "His political stock had risen very high in the most populous part of the state, and he wanted to obviously advance politically."[27]

As president of the Cook commissioners' board, Ogilvie wasted little time carrying out his campaign proposal for the naming of a so-called Little Hoover Commission to recommend an overhaul of the county's government. The panel, composed of blue-ribbon individuals from different segments of life in the Chicago area, called for many reforms. Some required General Assembly approval and others a green light only from the county board. In addition, a number of the suggested changes could be made by Ogilvie himself through executive action.

Overseeing the work of the "Little Hoover Commission" was Michaelson, who was asked by Ogilvie to join his small staff in the new office. Along with Michaelson, the staff included Whalen, Ogilvie's top assistant, and a lawyer, Alexander White, who would serve as chairman of the Illinois Industrial Commission during Ogilvie's governorship and, after that, as a circuit judge in Cook County. Directing the staff of the "Little Hoover" panel was a logical assignment for Michaelson since a number of the commission's proposals grew out of research done by Michaelson during the Ogilvie campaign. Soon enough, Michaelson saw that one import of the "Little Hoover" group "would be as a major linchpin of Ogilvie's upcoming race for governor."[28]

However, the challenge immediately at hand for Ogilvie was the governing of Cook County. In that world, the existing state of affairs was among threatened species with Ogilvie at the helm, regardless of whether the changes emanated from the "Little Hoover Commission" or Ogilvie himself. Operational savings, resulting partly from a quick streamlining of administrative procedures, were realized in pretty short order. Ogilvie moved to end restrictive bidding on highway building contracts, and he supported efforts to improve county purchasing practices and to up the quality of county electoral activity. He followed through on his pledge to rehabilitate the county's hospital, one of the largest general medical facilities in the United States. As he did with many programs in the sheriff's office, he acted to combat blatantly malodorous political influences in the hospital's bureaucracy. He asked medical professionals to get more involved in areas like advising him on the selection of a medical director.

Just as in his days as sheriff, favorable media coverage accompanied many of Ogilvie's undertakings, such as his push for a Cook County governmental council. This provided a vehicle for Ogilvie-initiated meetings of mayors, village presidents, and numerous other suburban officials, leading to sorely needed cooperative ventures and a personal relationship between Ogilvie and these individuals that could do nothing but help him politically.

Ogilvie's rapid headway in shaking up the government of Cook was all the more noteworthy because Chicago Democrats still controlled ten of the fifteen seats on the board. With that lineup, Ogilvie would have gotten a good grade for just barely holding his own. As board president, he did have veto power, and thus, it was nearly impossible for the commissioners to override an Ogilvie veto. However, savvy observers equated a lot of Ogilvie's success in getting his way to his cordial and productive relationship with George W. Dunne, the Democratic wheelhorse on the board.

At first glance, this may have raised eyebrows because Mayor Daley had few closer political confidants than Dunne, and Ogilvie certainly had done his share of Daley bashing in climbing to the top of Cook County government. It was a safe bet that Ogilvie also would continue to take after Daley, especially when Ogilvie found himself beyond the city limits of Chicago in any race for governor.

After Ogilvie became president of the county board, those looking for political drama or possibly irony found it on the famous fifth floor of the City Hall–County Building, where the new office of Ogilvie was directly across from Daley's office. In the words of Whalen, "We looked at their glass door and they looked at ours. There was not a lot of talk [back and forth]. We certainly were not chummy."[29]

At the same time, Whalen was in a position to see that "people like Ogilvie and Daley and Dunne knew that 80 percent of governing was not political confrontation. . . . to these people, the business of governing was to be carried out in a very serious fashion. And these people knew their business. They had this in common." Ogilvie never assumed, as Whalen put it, that "Daley would show him any political sympathy or quarter." Nor would Ogilvie or Dunne pass on political posturing against each other at board meetings or at other appropriate times.

Out of the public eye, though, what Michaelson witnessed was a far different relationship, a much more respectful one between Ogilvie and Dunne—a former stalwart of his party in the Illinois House who led a very strong Democratic organization in his north side Chicago lakefront ward. Michaelson would not forget Ogilvie frequently commenting to him that "his job was made easier, even though his party was in the minority on the board, by the fact that he really had a good person to work with in George Dunne."[30] Watching the off-the-record interaction between Dunne and Ogilvie left Michaelson fascinated with "the great difference in political life between the things people say publicly, a lot of which they don't mean, and what they say and do in private. It was an important lesson for me in trying to better understand the real workings of the political system."

Michaelson was not the only one learning things in those days. Ogilvie emerged from his stint with the county board as a much more skilled political pragmatist. And Daley, through his friend Dunne, learned that Ogilvie was a political opponent with whom the mayor could deal. That was good for the mayor to know about Ogilvie because, Daley recognized, the man's political ambition well could keep him moving up the ladder.

The Accardo Case:
Taking on the Big Tuna

Throughout his eighty-six years of life, Tony (Big Tuna) Accardo boasted that he never spent a night in prison. The blame for this could not be placed on Richard Ogilvie.

On November 11, 1960, Accardo, a onetime associate of Al Capone, was convicted of income tax fraud in United States District Court in Chicago. One week later, he was sentenced to serve six years for the crime in a federal penitentiary. However, on January 5, 1962, the conviction was reversed by the United States Court of Appeals on a ground that the notorious Accardo was the victim of "prejudicial error" during his nine-week trial before Judge Julius J. Hoffman. A new trial for the wealthy gangster was ordered by the appellate tribunal, provoking sharp criticism from others in the federal judiciary, from the operating director of the Chicago Crime Commission, and from Ogilvie, the special federal attorney who successfully prosecuted the mob leader.

Ogilvie voiced deep disappointment at the reversal, which was understandable. Ogilvie was the leader of a special team of federal lawyers and agents that labored for a nearly two-year period that seemed like an eternity to put together the case against Accardo. Once in court, Ogilvie could not have been a more unflappable prosecutor in convincing a jury of six men and six women that Accardo was guilty of making phony deductions on his income tax forms from 1956 through 1958.

Ogilvie was propelled into public view by the prosecution of Accardo. More than that, though, he came to the attention of people in the best possible light— as a person taking on the nefarious underworld of Chicago. Ogilvie certainly had lived up to that tough-guy picture of him in *Life* in 1959.

The pursuit of Accardo by Ogilvie captured national interest for clear reasons. Accardo was the undisputed boss of the old Capone crime syndicate for twelve or thirteen years, starting in the middle 1940s. In 1956 or 1957, according to Chicagoans who chronicle such occurrences, Accardo voluntarily surrendered his role to Sam Giancana but stayed around as the *consiglieri* to organized crime in the city, meaning a highly respected counselor or adviser. It was difficult, though, to convince gangland buffs around the country that Accardo was not still the czar or mastermind of crime in the Midwest. He well may have been. Without question, in tackling Big Tuna, Ogilvie was going after a big fish. The targeting of Accardo by the Ogilvie squad coincided, and not by accident, with one of those times in Chicago when "the outfit," as the crime syndicate in Chicago was known, was riding high, an era in which gangsterism's influence was detectable in countless aspects of the city's life. The rampage of terror in Chicago three decades earlier, when the murderous Capone was at his peak as the nation's biggest bootlegger, was no more insidious, many persons were convinced.

The end of the 1950s was a heyday for racketeering across the land, from the Florida gambling controlled by Meyer Lansky to the vice empire in the Northeast of the enduring Genovese family. But the pervasiveness of the mob in Chicago was uppermost on the mind of United States Attorney General William Rogers when he and his Justice Department set up a special nationwide group of mostly young lawyers to pursue the prosecution of major figures in organized crime.

Placed in charge of this squad's all-important effort in the Midwest in 1958 was Ogilvie, who had practiced with the Chicago law firm of Lord, Bissell & Brook after getting his degree from Chicago-Kent College of Law in 1949. (From 1954 to 1955, Ogilvie interrupted his private practice of law in Chicago to serve a year as an assistant to the United States attorney.) When he joined the Justice Department's express crime-fighting legal unit, Ogilvie was thirty-five years old and in the process of laying what some of his law associates believed to be a solid foundation for a lucrative practice. This was a pleasing thought to those acquaintances of Dick and Dorothy Ogilvie who knew the couple had strived hard to get ahead financially in the early years of their marriage.

Like many other young marrieds, the Ogilvies realized they were making progress when they found they could live off his earnings at the law firm, where he put in the long and grinding hours common for an aspiring young attorney, and could save a good part of Dorothy's salary from her job at an advertising agency for a down payment on a house.

Not long after the Ogilvies did get their home in Northfield, Don and Phyllis Perkins moved into the neighborhood. The guys got together quickly. The first Saturday Perkins was in his new home, he recollected, "I met this heavyset fellow wearing a T-shirt who was cutting grass. We started talking and discovering things like the fact that we both had gone to Yale. He offered me a drink." Then Perkins added a postscript. "However, it was a beer and not a martini as

Ogilvie would say later in telling people how we first met. He could not afford to offer a martini in those days."[1]

In throwing himself into the federal war on crime, Ogilvie was postponing the time of his highly likely admission to the ranks of Chicago attorneys making big bucks. Many expected that to happen, but it would be down the road, perhaps a long way down the road for Ogilvie.

So, after eight years of marriage, and with daughter Elizabeth—the only child she and Dick would have—turning three years old, Dorothy Ogilvie found herself caught up in her husband's radical change of professional direction. At the same time, she understood that her husband was driven by an inner force compelling him to seek out challenges avoided by others. She realized that her husband had a side to him that could not be satisfied by the mundane practice of law. She not only was aware of this, she was proud of it.

Although admitting that she "did not know I was marrying a crusader," Dorothy Ogilvie left no doubt years later that "it certainly turned out to be fine with me. I thought it was very important for him to do the things he was doing. He just had so little tolerance for corruption in life. He just felt somebody had to step forward and do something to clean things up."[2]

After Ogilvie went to work directing the Chicago part of the Justice Department's new drive to put top gangsters behind bars, little time passed before Accardo became a target. Following several months of preliminary investigation, Ogilvie and an associate in the prosecuting effort, William Carey, began to call witnesses before a special grand jury early in 1959. The going was not easy. Federal agents had tried for some time to nail Accardo for tax evasion but without success.

Even after Ogilvie appeared on the scene, agents snooped for months before Ogilvie and Carey discovered an opening that would lead to the grand jury's indictment of Accardo for alleged tax fraud. The path was not all that complicated. On his tax forms covering 1956 through 1958, Accardo had deducted the costs of operation and depreciation of his sports car because he claimed he used it in his business as a salesman for Premium Beer Sales, from which he reported drawing an annual salary of $65,000. Many legitimate salespersons took such a deduction. But the government agents reporting to Ogilvie could not find anybody who had seen Accardo selling beer while tooling around in his Mercedes-Benz auto. Many tavern keepers were interviewed, but none remembered buying beer from the mob boss. Consequently, Ogilvie and his crew decided to snare Accardo with his own tax dodge. If he did not really work as a beer salesman, they surmised, his deductions for the car expenses were improper.

In Accardo's trial, Ogilvie, Carey, and Walter Cummings, another one of the special federal prosecutors, argued that the defendant never actually sold beer in the three years in question and that the pay he purported to receive for doing so was only a ruse—a ploy to deter investigation of his true income from syndicate activities. Accardo tax returns from 1940 to 1955, showing $1,200,000 in income from mob gambling joints, were offered in evidence by the government to demonstrate what the prosecutors charged was the reason for Accardo's switch to the reporting of fictitious income from the selling of beer. Those tax returns were accepted as evidence by Judge Hoffman. Ironically, the tax deductions which tripped up Accardo only added up to $3,992, a paltry sum for a fellow living in the splendid manner that he did. His stone mansion in suburban River Forest was valued at the time at $500,000. The place had twenty-two rooms and gold-plated plumbing. Accardo's fleet of expensive cars was taken as another sign of his obvious affluence.

This was not bad for a fellow with a very modest beginning: Born in Chicago's Little Italy. A son of a shoemaker. Only a sixth-grade education. Yet as a sullen but hot-tempered street thug in the 1920s, Accardo had caught the eye of Capone. Soon Accardo was a figure garnering respect in the underworld, serving as a bodyguard for Capone and handling sundry other tasks with impressive dispatch. Former FBI man Roemer, many Chicago mob buffs, and others would claim that Accardo was among the triggermen in the 1929 St. Valentine's Day massacre in a North Clark Street garage in Chicago, a bloodbath in which Capone gang members blasted away with submachine guns and other weapons at members of a rival bootleg crowd headed by George (Bugs) Moran. Seven men died in the hail of bullets, a slaughter that shocked the nation and did much to color Chicago as a gangster-ridden city. No one was convicted in the slayings.

After Capone went to prison for income tax evasion in 1931, direction of the crime syndicate was in the hands of Frank (The Enforcer) Nitti and Paul (The Waiter) Ricca—individuals who used Accardo as a front man, so said the Chicago Crime Commission. Then after Nitti committed suicide in 1943 while under indictment and Ricca went to prison the next year for attempted extortion of the movie industry, Accardo took over. His reign would earn him depiction at a hearing of the United States Senate Rackets Committee as the "godfather of Chicago organized crime . . . a legend in his own time, the heir to Al Capone."[3]

Of course, gangland tradition decreed that mobsters like Accardo had to have a nickname, a practice that made them seem more human, more in the vein of those almost likable Damon Runyon characters. To the crime-following public, Accardo was Big Tuna, an outgrowth of his fishing trips. However, many of his colleagues referred to him as "Joe Batters," an acknowledgment of his skills as a syndicate enforcer. Call him Big Tuna, Joe Batters, or whatever, Accardo was a dangerous quarry, even for a hunter with the resources of the federal government behind him.

Dorothy Ogilvie may have professed years afterward to "not recall ever being afraid in those days," but some of her Northfield neighbors were skittish. One, admittedly, was Perkins. To hear him talk, the neighborhood had "to face the fact that he [Ogilvie] was doing a very risky thing because the mob had to be pretty unhappy with him. I said at the time I was going to put up a neon sign in the neighborhood making it quite clear which was the Ogilvie house."[4]

Ogilvie was hardly a lone ranger in the Accardo prosecution. He had carte blanche to tap law enforcement agencies across the board for information and to seek and get investigative assistance from numerous Treasury and FBI personnel as well as others, all of which he did. Bill Roemer and another FBI agent, John Roberts, handled a lot of the legwork by their organization in the Accardo investigation. Generally speaking, Roemer was a spark plug of the FBI's effort against organized crime in Chicago for two decades, beginning with his assignment in 1957 to the agency's Top Hoodlum Program in the Windy City. In Roemer's mind, Accardo remained the "man" in the Chicago family of La Cosa Nostra for many decades after World War II.[5]

As for the conviction of Accardo, though, Ogilvie got the lion's share of the credit. Well before the jury found Accardo guilty, some were picturing the case as a personal confrontation between this very serious federal attorney, a previously unknown fellow who had suffered a severe facial wound in World War II, and the up-to-then invincible Accardo, a man who got to stay home during the war because his draft board found him "morally unfit" for military service.

Ogilvie still got featured billing when the United States Court of Appeals, in a split decision, nullified Accardo's conviction, ruling that trial judge Hoffman should not have admitted into evidence the gangster's income tax returns from 1940 to 1955 and, in addition, that Hoffman had given insufficient instructions to jurors to ignore publicity deemed prejudicial to Accardo that appeared in Chicago newspapers during his trial. The reversal of the Accardo conviction at the start of 1962, Ogilvie declared, redoubled his resolve to get elected sheriff of Cook County that year. "The story of the Chicago crime syndicate," said Ogilvie, "is personified in the life of Accardo, which explodes the myth that crime does not pay—at least in Cook County."[6]

Court ruling or no court ruling, Ogilvie wanted the world to know, as he saw it, that Accardo had "used a lifetime of crime to amass a fortune and power which enabled him to live in a manner that only a few can achieve. His activities have left a trail of violence and murder and have included gambling, vice and every other type of illegal activity." Accardo's rise to the top of the syndicate, Ogilvie concluded, "had to be the result of a criminal-political alliance which gave him immunity from prosecution—immunity broken only by our prosecution."

On October 3, 1962, a little more than a month before Ogilvie's election as sheriff, Accardo was acquitted by a federal court jury in his second trial on the income tax fraud charge. After the jury returned the not-guilty verdict, Accardo's customarily expressionless face broke into a wide smile, and he pronounced that he was "very happy." A bit later, he was on his way to his mansion in River Forest for a victory celebration. Accardo had survived the effort led by that tenacious government lawyer whom Accardo and his crowd found so repugnant. But, as for Ogilvie himself, he really had not lost. Without the Accardo case, Ogilvie might have had little chance of making it to the sheriff's office. Without the record he built as sheriff, Ogilvie's eventual capture of the governorship would have been far less likely.

Ogilvie was neither the first nor last Illinois governor in modern times with experience as a prosecutor. Dwight H. Green, the state's chief executive from 1941 to 1949, spent the first part of the 1930s in the office of the United States attorney in Chicago, first as an assistant and then as the head man. Although Eliot Ness and his Untouchables reaped most of the credit for bringing down Capone, Green had prepared the income tax evasion case on which Capone was indicted, and Green handled much of the load in presenting the evidence against Capone to a jury.

Governor Kerner, who was in office during most of the 1960s, had been appointed United States attorney in Chicago not long after his release from active duty in the Second World War. The man who served as governor from 1977 to 1991, James Thompson, had resigned as the United States attorney in Chicago to run for Illinois's highest office. Thompson had a remarkable run as a federal prosecutor. While he held the post, scores of public officials and their associates were indicted on various charges of official corruption. Thompson's best-known action occurred when he sent former governor Kerner to prison in the early 1970s for allegedly illegal activities connected to lucrative racing stock manipulations while he was governor.

Even Governor Shapiro, the individual Ogilvie had to beat to become governor, was a member of the prosecutors' club. In 1936, one Samuel Harvey Shapiro, a twenty-nine-year-old lawyer, had been elected state's attorney of Kankakee County. He must have been a popular fellow, since he was the only Democrat holding a county office in Kankakee back then.

The 1968 Campaign and Vote

The Ogilvie Campaign

The story of the 1968 election in Illinois could not have been more aptly illustrated than by the movement of two campaign trains that rumbled through the state that year, one carrying the Republican state candidates and the other a major Democratic contender.

Without a glitch. That's the way the GOP train tour went, a four-day excursion shortly before the November election in which Ogilvie and others on his party's state ticket whistle-stopped in one of their last appeals for votes. Enthusiastic crowds of supporters awaited the train at most places, bolstering the impression that the election was looking good for Republicans.

However, the rails were not as kind to Democrat William G. Clark, the attorney general of Illinois, when he undertook a train trip in early August to boost his underdog campaign for a seat in the United States Senate. Clark faced powerful incumbent Everett McKinley Dirksen, the Republican floor leader in the Senate. Near the end of the first day of Clark's rail tour of downstate Illinois, those on board lurched in their seats as the train suddenly jolted and then screeched toward an unscheduled halt not long after a rally in Minonk in Woodford County. The train, it turned out, had rammed into a truck at a remote rural crossing, killing the driver of the vehicle. To put it mildly, the tragic accident dampened the tour, giving frustrated Illinois Democrats one more reason for griping that nothing was breaking right for them in 1968.

Two weeks later in August, the state's Democrats would face more severe consternation over seeing their party torn apart at its national convention in Chicago. The Democratic mecca, Chicago, was under siege, literally. With the whole world watching, the Illinoisans asked, what chance did the party's candidates have in the upcoming election? After the smoke from the convention cleared, and all the raging Vietnam War protesters, the Chicago police, the National Guardsmen, and the federal troops had gone back to where they came from, not even the most ardent Democrats had any doubt that the party was in a deep hole going into the last two months of the election campaign.

Not too many Americans survived 1968 without their lives or souls altered, even shattered, by the incredible events occurring so frequently that they almost became commonplace: The Tet Offensive in Vietnam. The capture of the *USS Pueblo* by North Korea. President Johnson's revelation that he would not run for reelection. The violent deaths of Martin Luther King Jr. and Bobby Kennedy. The list went on and on, all in addition to the calamitous Democratic National Convention. Finally, as the year wound down, came the election that ended Democratic control of the White House and cost the party dearly in many other places, including Illinois.

Richard Ogilvie could not have run for governor under more favorable conditions. He did not waltz into the top Illinois office; few do. But it was not a case of Ogilvie having to claw and scratch against all odds either. Ogilvie's Democratic opponent was the incumbent in the office, but few persons viewed Sam Shapiro as the most formidable candidate in the Democrats' stable for trying to keep the governorship in the party's hands.

Hardly anybody who met Shapiro personally during his long public career disliked him, but he had built little standing with the bulk of the state's populace. When voters went to the polls on November 5, 1968, the short, stocky attorney from Kankakee had been governor less than six months, and he was not an elected one at that. During the more than seven years that Shapiro was lieutenant governor prior to becoming governor, he was viewed as a good-natured but reserved official who avoided the spotlight. He was pretty much of a behind-the-scenes fellow, which was par for the course for an Illinois "light governor," as the lieutenant governor is often called in the state. Yet, while many outside government had little impression of him, the man addressed as "Mr. Sam" was better known by rank-and-file state employees than most of the other major Illinois officeholders. Years after he was gone from Springfield, memories lingered of Shapiro—a person with a perpetual smile—conversing with state workers at a third-floor lunch stand in the Statehouse or seeming to always be accessible to visitors in his spacious, uncluttered office behind the Senate chamber.

When the sixty-one-year-old Shapiro was inaugurated as governor on May 21, 1968, in an unpretentious ceremony, many felt the most newsworthy aspect of the occasion was *Tribune* correspondent Robert P. Howard's disclosure that Shapiro had been born in Estonia—a fact that made him not only the state's second Jewish governor but also the second born abroad. Waggers in the Statehouse were quite surprised at learning of Shapiro's foreign birth because they assumed they knew everything about the bigwigs in the building.

The kickoff for Shapiro's career in the Statehouse was the 1946 election, which sent the World War II navy officer to Springfield as a state representative. In the fourteen years that he served in the House, Shapiro won recognition in particular for his efforts to improve the lot of patients in the state's mental health hospitals. However, most important politically, many observers believed, was Shapiro's refusal in 1959 to support downstate Democratic leader Paul Powell for speaker of the House. Instead, Shapiro was one of only several downstaters that remained loyal to Mayor Daley's choice for speaker, Joseph L. DeLaCour of Chicago. Although Powell won the fight for speaker, Shapiro's stand was thought to be a factor a year later when Daley and other party bosses slated Shapiro as the lieutenant governor candidate on a ticket headed by Otto Kerner for governor. Kerner and Shapiro were victorious in 1960 and then again in 1964 when both were reelected to their offices.

Shapiro moved into the governor's chair after Kerner resigned to accept appointment as a judge of the United States Court of Appeals in Chicago. Before that, though, Kerner had announced that he would not run in 1968 for election to a third term, and the Daley-led Democratic hierarchy had decreed the slating of Shapiro for the party's nomination for governor. This was intended to discourage other Democrats from seeking the party's gubernatorial nomination in the primary election in June of 1968. It worked. Shapiro had no primary opposition.

Nevertheless, suspicion was strong in political circles that Shapiro would be a weak candidate, especially in view of the availability of bigger names— Illinois Treasurer Adlai E. Stevenson III for one and quite possibly R. Sargent Shriver for another. Shriver, head of the federal government's antipoverty program, was the husband of one of the sisters of the late President John Kennedy. Shriver had lived in Chicago when he ran the Merchandise Mart in the city for the Kennedy family. But a Democratic glamour ticket, as some envisioned a slate headed by Stevenson or Shriver, was not to be. Shapiro was Daley's pick for the governor's slot, and since Daley was the boss, that was that.

Ogilvie's road to his party's nomination for governor was not as easy as Shapiro's. Three persons ran against Ogilvie for the Republican nomination for governor, and one of them, John Henry Altorfer, posed a serious threat to Ogilvie. The other two, former Governor William G. Stratton and lawyer S. Thomas Sutton of Wayne, did not. Stratton clearly was long past his political prime. Sutton's candidacy was a narrow one based on his outspoken opposition to racial integration.

Altorfer, a wealthy Peoria industrialist several years older than Ogilvie, was another matter. He was the unsuccessful Republican candidate for lieutenant governor in 1964. Like Ogilvie, he was a combat veteran of World War II. Un-like Ogilvie, Altorfer was handsome; his visage fit Hollywood's idea of how a governor should look.

Not many individuals thought that Altorfer would beat Ogilvie, but Ogilvie could ill afford to spare any effort in the primary campaign. First, the fact that Altorfer was a respected downstater would alone virtually assure him of a de-cent percentage of the primary vote in traditionally Republican regions of Illinois. Also in Altorfer's favor—Ogilvie was largely unknown to a great num-ber of downstate Republicans. It was true that many of the GOP county chair-men had lined up behind Ogilvie because they saw him as an emerging Repub-lican strongman who had proven that he could match the Democrats in political muscle. But Republicans in those days did not follow the wishes of party leaders like many Democrats did.

Another problem for Ogilvie was closer to home. In the event he became governor, he would leave the Cook County board presidency halfway through his four-year term, meaning the Democratic majority on the board would elect one of its own to serve as interim president until the next regularly scheduled election. An upshot would be a premature end to the Ogilvie effort to revamp Cook County government, including the movement of as many Republicans as possible into county jobs.

Consequently, Ogilvie's candidacy for governor created a quandary for Re-publicans in the Chicago area, according to James (Pate) Philip, then a freshman Republican state representative from Elmhurst. An Ogilvie victory would "leave the [Republican] party in Cook pretty high and dry," noted Philip, who twenty-five years later presided over the Illinois Senate as its president.[1]

This concern was addressed more graphically by Tim Sheehan, still GOP chairman of Cook County and no admirer of Ogilvie, when he announced his support for Altorfer. In a memorandum to Republican township and ward com-mitteemen in the county, Sheehan cautioned that, even though "most of you have signed a petition pledging support" to Ogilvie, every Republican jobholder in the county was "in the ridiculous position of having to work to put himself out of a job because, if Mr. Ogilvie is elected governor, the Democrats take over the county and would discharge our Republican jobholders."[2]

Too, Ogilvie interestingly was a target of sniping from some old hands in Illinois Republicanism—a number of them with conspicuous ties or allegiance to Senator Dirksen, who they regarded as the titular lord of the state GOP. To these old guarders, Ogilvie was still in 1968 a bit of an upstart trying to move up the political ladder too rapidly.

Nevertheless, Ogilvie, acutely aware that timing can be everything in politics, had made up his mind well beforehand that 1968 was the year to go for governor. At least for him. Strike while the iron is hot, he believed. Capitalize on his image as a winner while he truly was riding high. As for those questioning his candidacy or its timing, he could only reply that he was the Republican with the best chance of capturing the governor's office in 1968. Ogilvie entertained little doubt that he would outdistance any primary opponent in campaign expenditures, public exposure, and newspaper endorsements as well as in party organization backing, especially by his own tightly disciplined GOP group in Cook. The county GOP functioned for the most part with little or no input from many of the older established Republican leaders like Sheehan. On every one of these subjects, Ogilvie's confidence of prevailing was justified.

Ogilvie also was aided by another development in the primary campaign, a growing realization by many close to the situation that Ogilvie's solid grasp of governmental workings and issues was not shared by Altorfer. To be fair, Altorfer supporters promoted him as an individual who had matured in business instead of politics. In his campaign, Altorfer was proposing various programs that he viewed as applying a businessman's approach to the problems of state government. But as for the operation of government, the knowledge of Altorfer was shallow.

This became evident on many occasions, such as during the primary contest when Altorfer was interviewed by Mike Lawrence, a government affairs reporter for the *Times-Democrat* in Davenport, Iowa (later the *Quad-City Times*), which covered Illinois politics closely. With Altorfer during the interview was Lambert Engdahl, a Monmouth car dealer, member of the GOP State Central Committee, and an Altorfer backer. Lawrence said that "Altorfer was certainly good looking and affable and appeared to be a success in business," but the writer added that "it grew clear during the interview he knew very little about state government—even though he had been the Republican candidate for lieutenant governor in 1964." Consequently, Lawrence related, "Engdahl called me aside after the interview and asked me as a personal favor to take it easy on his candidate. Lambert had been a wonderful source for me, and I really liked the old guy. But I told him I could not oblige."[3]

Many of the reporters covering that campaign were struck by the Ogilvie team's overall self-assurance, which manifested itself into an almost cocky attitude among some of the younger workers. One person far from jaunty, though, was Thomas Drennan, who in 1968 had been retained to help Ogilvie get elected to another office.

Back in 1968, not all people in politics swore by the polls, as seemed to be the case later on. However, when Drennan was a reporter for the old *Chicago Times*, he was a director of the newspaper's straw polling on candidates. Out of that experience, Drennan said, he came "to believe that honest polls could detect what people were thinking and what might happen." As a result, he never hesitated to engage in polling, in the 1968 campaign or any other one. As for his canvassing on the 1968 primary, the results showed Drennan that, in his words, "Ogilvie had a tough election, rougher than many around him thought." After thinking about it, he decided not to fully convey that finding to Ogilvie or Perkins, who was playing his usual role as the Ogilvie campaign finance chairman.[4]

Joseph L. Harris, who left his position as a political columnist for the old *Illinois State Journal* in Springfield to join the Altorfer campaign as a paid assistant, always felt that Altorfer well might have beaten Ogilvie if either state senator Arthur R. Gottschalk of the Chicago suburb of Flossmoor or former Cook County state's attorney Benjamin Adamowski had carried out an announced or perceived intent to seek the Republican nomination for governor. But neither one did, and both ended up backing Altorfer.

"I could never forget sitting in Altorfer's living room in Peoria and hearing him say how great it was that they had dropped out and were supporting him," Harris said. "I thought it was terrible." Harris reasoned that if Gottschalk or Adamowski, or both, had run in the primary "the Republican vote in Chicago and the suburbs would have been split much more and that certainly could have given it to Altorfer."[5]

After the primary, Harris as well as others in the Altorfer camp campaigned for Ogilvie's election. Furthermore, Harris would conclude not too many years later that "the best person won that primary race because Ogilvie went on to become a good governor while, in looking back, I am not really sure Altorfer could have handled all the things that happened in the years that followed."

Still, the results of the primary on June 11 revealed that Harris may not have been wrong in contending Ogilvie was fortunate to have the field in Cook County pretty much to himself. Ogilvie ran up a huge lead on Altorfer in the county, 163,332 votes to 65,698, a plurality of 97,634. In the rest of Illinois, lumped together under the label "downstate," Altorfer whipped Ogilvie by 50,811 votes, as the Peorian got 223,206 to 172,395 for Ogilvie. Thus, Ogilvie outscored Altorfer statewide, 335,727 to 288,904, giving Ogilvie a winning vote margin of 46,823. Stratton received 50,041 votes, about 75 percent of them downstate, and Sutton 31,925 votes, of which 17,803 came in Cook.[6]

Except for Ogilvie's perhaps narrower-than-anticipated victory margin, the primary voting pattern went about as expected. The result in Cook spoke for itself. As for the rest of Illinois, the outcome of Ogilvie versus Altorfer produced interesting but hardly radical currents.

In the mainly GOP counties surrounding Cook, the so-called collar counties, Ogilvie ran a bit more sluggish than many predicted. In counties with large Republican turnouts, like DuPage, Lake, and Will, Ogilvie did not prevail by eye-catching numbers. Of course, in DuPage, the foremost GOP stronghold in the state, Ogilvie was opposed by the county's veteran Republican chairman, Elmer J. Hoffman, and numerous other party old liners. Altorfer even captured one collar county, Kane.

On the other hand, Ogilvie carried thirty-eight counties in addition to Cook—and twenty-nine were in largely Democratic southern and south central Illinois, a sign that the normally small groups of GOP voters in those areas preferred a law-and-order fellow from distant Chicago to a more traditional downstate Republican, Altorfer. True to form, though, most of the largely Republican counties between central Illinois and the Chicago area, the eternal breadbasket of the Illinois GOP, went for Altorfer. One, Altorfer's home county of Peoria, supported him by a lopsided nine-to-one margin.

Ogilvie strategists could not help but notice that their candidate fared quite poorly against Altorfer in Sangamon, the home of Springfield, and in a number of the counties bordering Sangamon, such as Morgan, Logan, and Macon. In Macon, the GOP county chairman, Harry (Skinny) Taylor of Decatur, head of the Republican County Chairmen's Association, was a campaign manager for Altorfer. Springfield and Sangamon County were another story. Here, the credit for Altorfer's strong showing was greatly attributed to his backing by the personable William Cellini, the elected public works commissioner of Springfield. It was no accident that, on the heels of the primary, the Ogilvie camp sought and obtained the assistance of Cellini for the general election campaign.

Ogilvie also quickly extended an olive branch to other Republicans who had not supported him in the primary. One not asked to smoke a peace pipe was Tim Sheehan, whom the Ogilvie people viewed as an implacable foe. Knowing he was facing the ax, Sheehan relinquished the party chairmanship of Cook County to Ogilvie ally Kucharski. However, for a party in which many adherents seemed to enjoy fighting with each other more than against Democrats, the GOP appeared amazingly united behind Ogilvie as he turned his attention full-blown to the last obstacle between himself and the governorship, Shapiro.

All along, from the June primary to the November general election, Ogilvie was depicted as the front-runner in his race with Shapiro, partly because so many smelled a Republican trend in the air in 1968. Nevertheless, getting a fix on the extent to which Ogilvie may have been leading Shapiro was difficult.

As important as the gubernatorial contest was, other features of the Illinois election scene also occupied people's minds. At that juncture, Illinois was still very much a bellwether state in presidential balloting because only once in the twentieth century had Illinois not cast its electoral votes for the winning candidate in a presidential election. That occurred in 1916 when Republican Charles Evans Hughes won the state's electoral votes over Democrat Woodrow Wilson.

In the early going, Richard Nixon, the Republican nominee for president in 1968, appeared to have a sizable lead in Illinois over his Democratic opponent, Vice President Hubert H. Humphrey. But in the last stage of the campaign, Humphrey was viewed as gaining ground, in part because of the feeling by many analysts that Humphrey was benefiting from the eleventh-hour defection of some of the Illinois support for third-party presidential candidate George C. Wallace of Alabama. Nixon did hang on to carry Illinois in his victorious bid for the presidency. Even so, Democratic leaders held out hope to the last minute that Humphrey's defeat in the state would not necessarily mean the loss of the governorship. They pointed to a tendency of numerous Illinois voters to split their ticket, often voting for the presidential candidate of one party and the nominee for governor of the other. In addition, the Daley factor, which surfaced in every major Illinois election in the 1960s, might cut more ways than one.

Ogilvie still was running throughout the state in 1968, as he had earlier in the decade in Cook County, as an angry-man type who first sought elective office to fight what he termed the abuses of Daley's machine. Ogilvie was equating his quest for the governorship with an attempt to eliminate machine politics in Springfield, a euphemistic reference to the standard GOP line that Democratic governors were puppets of the Chicago mayor. However, some thought that playing the Daley card could backfire for Ogilvie, primarily as a result of the mayor's heavily debated role in the Democratic National Convention in Chicago. There were, of course, critics, including Democrats, of Daley's handling of demonstrators, critics who said they would vent their protest by voting against Shapiro. On the other side of the coin, though, were those who believed that Shapiro might benefit from non-Democrats' new and favorable opinion of Daley. These voters supported the protest crackdown actions taken by the mayor during the convention.

As in the primary campaign, Ogilvie revealed not one iota of doubt, publicly or in private, that he would beat Shapiro. Campaign press secretary Joe Mathewson found Ogilvie so sure of victory that he asked Mathewson a month before the election to accompany him to Springfield as his press secretary when he became governor. To Mathewson, Ogilvie was "one very calm guy" in control of a campaign that "was in many ways one for the textbooks."[7]

Mathewson, who had met Ogilvie four years before when both were members of the Winnetka Presbyterian Church, did not have to sell Ogilvie to a Chicago press. It had long seemed enamored with Ogilvie. Thus, Mathewson could invest much of his energy into a crash effort to better acquaint the downstate press with his candidate. To get this done, Mathewson spent considerable time at Ogilvie's side during the general election campaign, accompanying him on board the campaign bus or motor home. While the vehicle traveled between major stops, Mathewson and Ogilvie employed a little routine that permitted many in the downstate media to get to know them. Mathewson, formerly a Chicago writer for the *Wall Street Journal* and a reporter for WBBM television in Chicago, described it in the following words: "When we were en route in the bus, I'd get on a phone that was installed in the bus and line up radio reporters and small town editors for interviews with Dick. When I had one on the line, I'd turn the phone over to Dick while telling him the name of the reporter he was going to talk to. Through these one-on-one situations, we were able to build a lot of rapport with the press away from Chicago. After these conversations, the reporters could see that Ogilvie was for real, that he was very down to earth with them, something the Chicago press knew for a long time."

Frequently, as Ogilvie conversed with an interviewer from his moving bus, the discussion got around to the particular highway that the vehicle was bumping over at the time. Following law and order, roads may have been the biggest issue of the campaign, at least downstate. Ogilvie clearly intended to use the poor condition of thousands of miles of old, narrow highways winding through the state to help catapult him into the governor's seat.

However, law and order, or the alleged absence of it, got attention first, just as it did on the national political scene in 1968.

In Illinois, debate raged on about the role of the National Guard, about the extent of state efforts to combat organized crime, and about administration of the Illinois penal system—all to a backdrop of soaring crime rates, riots, and disorderly protest demonstrations. Ogilvie and others on the GOP state ticket charged everywhere that lack of respect for the law, above all else, discredited the state's Democratic leadership. By way of his speeches, television advertisements, and any other means he could find, Ogilvie tried to convey a basic campaign contention that Illinoisans soon would not be able to safely walk many big-city streets without a fresh approach to law and order. To underscore that he meant to provide this new approach, Ogilvie proposed sweeping revisions in just about every program in Illinois related to the maintenance of a lawful society, initiatives that in many cases would strengthen the hand of the state.

There was just no hotter issue in 1968. Literally. May 1, Law Day, was proof of it. That was the day Ogilvie and his campaign's salaried research director, Chicago lawyer Bill Hanley, ventured south to spell out to a dinner gathering at an Urbana country club the principal planks in Ogilvie's law enforcement improvement program. All was going well as everybody finished the meal and prepared to hear Ogilvie deliver what was being billed as a major campaign address. But as political campaigners are the first to know, things seldom go as planned.

Right before Ogilvie was to start his talk, recounted Hanley, "we suddenly were all asked to get out of the place, to go outside. As we retreated out of the building, we saw smoke in a hall. A fire had erupted in the kitchen, and it would soon engulf the entire country club. So there we stood, Richard Ogilvie, myself and the others, watching the site of his big Law Day speech burn to the ground. One news photographer managed to get a picture of Ogilvie standing and smoking his pipe as he watched the conflagration. It was quite a sight."[8]

As the flames ebbed, it hit Ogilvie that since the speech had already been released in Chicago for publication he had an obligation, in his mind at least, to still give it. So Ogilvie and some of the others at the scene of the fire hastily skedaddled over to the Champaign County Courthouse, where Ogilvie delivered the address word for word.

Later, during the fall campaign, Shapiro stepped up his counterattack on the law-and-order issue, claiming that Ogilvie appeared hell-bent on turning Illinois into a police state in which the primary responsibility for law enforcement would be taken away from local officials. Taking on the Republican national ticket as well as Ogilvie in an appearance before the Illinois Municipal League in Peoria, Shapiro was sharply critical of "those who want the people to believe that what this country needs is a good five-cent billy club at the state and national levels." That, added the governor, "makes no sense and makes a farce of local responsibility."[9]

Of course, Ogilvie tackled other issues in the campaign. Whether the problem was inadequate state aid to education, government waste, pollution, a shortage of recreational facilities, urban slums, or whatnot, Ogilvie had a proposed remedy—many times sculpted at the desk of Hanley over in Drennan's public relations office in a building, the Chicago Temple, that stretched above the Loop.

A great number of Ogilvie's position papers on the less-than-sexy issues even made it into print because this was 1968, a time when the focal points of high-level Illinois political contests did not yet revolve so completely around primarily negative thirty-second broadcast commercials.

Still, for those expecting the race for governor to be a gentlemanly affair, since neither contestant was a political firebrand, the windup was feisty and more than a tad nasty. Near the campaign's end, Ogilvie and Shapiro were accusing each other of distortions and character assassination.

Taking off the gloves, as he put it, Shapiro resurrected, with bells ringing, Ogilvie's entanglement with Richard Cain, the cop and hoodlum who ran investigations for Sheriff Ogilvie. The Cain episode should have been sufficient to finish the public career of Ogilvie or any other official, Shapiro insisted. Ogilvie really took umbrage at a Democratic campaign pamphlet distributed in the final weeks, "Myth of Ogilvie—Mark of Cain." During a debate late in the campaign at a Chicago television station—a confrontation that ended without a handshake—the governor repeatedly pressed Ogilvie about Cain. Ogilvie shot back that Shapiro had no room to talk because being a Democrat automatically put him under obligation to Democratic leaders in Chicago's infamous First Ward. These leaders reportedly associated with mobsters. On it went, back and forth.

To Ogilvie campaign insiders, though, another development could have been more damaging than the revival of the old Cain controversy. Beginning in 1967 and continuing through much of 1968, innuendos circulated that Ogilvie was a target of a tax fraud investigation by the Internal Revenue Service. While nothing more specific spewed out of the rumor mill, the thought of even a possibility that Ogilvie might be hit by an IRS action in an election year triggered great discomfort among those around him. The reality of the matter was that contributions to Ogilvie's 1966 race for Cook County board president were being scrutinized by the IRS as part of a widespread inquiry into allegedly illegal tax deductions based on reputed political donations.

Ogilvie turned to his attorney friend Jerry Marsh, then still in private practice, to represent him during this proceeding. As it worked out, Marsh fielded questions from IRS agents and provided other information necessary to show that Ogilvie was unaware of any improper tax deductions linked to his political contributions. The investigation, at least the segment concerning Ogilvie, would come, in the words of Marsh, "to nothing because, as far as myself and others involved in the situation could determine, Ogilvie was as clean as could be imagined."[10] No such deductions were ever identified.

The Ogilvie inner circle was sure that its man was fingered for inclusion in the IRS investigation by one or more of those Republicans who did not want

Ogilvie to be the party's nominee for governor, but this was never substantiated. One could have made a safe bet, though, that the suspected informants would not have won any popularity contest at the regular Sunday morning strategy huddles of the Ogilvie campaign brain trust. On hand for these sessions, frequently in Ogilvie's home, were the candidate himself, Drennan, Perkins, at times Kucharski (after he became GOP chairman of Cook), sometimes Whalen (who was essentially running the Cook board president's office in the absence of his boss), and one other individual, James H. Mack.

The managership of the campaign was shared, more or less, by Drennan and Mack, a fellow Irish Catholic. Drennan was obviously more visible, as he pushed the communications and policy goal buttons intended to sell Ogilvie to the public. Mack's role was not as out front. He directed scheduling and the other logistics of the campaign as well as its organization from the top to the regional leaders and on down. He was the campaign's chief machinist, a role for which he had received training as a field operative in the Great Lakes states for the Goldwater campaign in 1964. Following the 1964 election, Mack went to work handling government relations for Chicago-based Illinois Tool Works. To serve the Ogilvie campaign, Mack was given a paid leave of absence from Illinois Tool by its head, Harold Byron Smith Sr., an Ogilvie supporter.

Support for Ogilvie by the Illinois business world could not be overstated. Donald Perkins was more aware than any other person that corporate and individual checks from business interests comprised a large amount of the roughly $2,500,000 that, in Perkins's memory, was raised for Ogilvie's race for governor.[11] Cash contributions were not uncommon either, often being handed to Ogilvie himself. When that happened, Perkins said, "Dick gave me the money and I'd put it in the bank." During Ogilvie's run for reelection as governor four years later, Perkins noted, the campaign refused to accept cash or corporate checks because of questions raised about fund-raising for President Nixon.

The 1968 campaign was one where financing was not the problem it would be for many Illinois candidates in the decades after Ogilvie. At the start of Ogilvie's first race for governor, Perkins later pointed out, "Dick and I agreed that we would not be in debt at the end of the campaign, win or lose." And, said Perkins, "we were not."

One precaution taken by Perkins to keep the campaign out of the red, as he phrased it, was "to stay on guard to keep the spending requests by Drennan under control." Of course, Perkins tacked on, "I recognized that Drennan wanted to win so badly." For two individuals so close to Ogilvie, Perkins and Drennan never became bosom buddies. Yet, while the two came from different social worlds, Perkins felt that Drennan respected him because "I produced money," and Perkins said that Drennan had his respect because "Drennan was one damn good political adviser who understood voters in the way I liked to know grocery consumers."

Still, while nobody would argue that Drennan had a good nose for determining what was on voters' minds, the bottom-line chore of bringing out Ogilvie voters in 1968 fell pretty much on the shoulders of Mack and his campaign organization. Mack would go on to direct Ogilvie's campaign in 1972, which would seem like a world apart from 1968 because of radical changes on the Illinois political scene and in view of the different demands involved in trying to again sell Ogilvie to the public. But in 1968, "the focus of our organizational effort," Mack specified, "was to just get out our vote."[12]

All the signs in the world could point to a Republican tide in 1968, but GOP leaders with their feet on the ground knew not to breathe easy in Illinois until the ballots in the November 5 general election were cast and counted. Historically, Illinois Republicans were more prone to late campaign overconfidence than Democrats, a trait that had proven costly to the GOP. Victor L. Smith, a soft-spoken Robinson newspaper publisher who was Republican state chairman, liked to say that a political contest was similar to a horse race in that "you don't want your horse too far ahead at first."[13] Smith believed that for once the Republican effort had peaked in Illinois not too soon but at the right moment, several weeks after the turbulent Democratic convention. However, plenty of time remained for a GOP backslide, prompting Smith and other Republicans who had been around the horn to caution against any letup.

No one had noticed the Daley people waving any white flag, meaning that they would be actively trying to turn out the usual massive Democratic vote that had earned the Daley machine such renown. America had no other political organization to rival the proficiency of Daley's in exchanging favors and patronage for votes. Daley's army of precinct captains, its infantrymen, were still every bit as effective under the city's first Mayor Daley as in the earlier heydays of the machine under Democratic bosses with names like Patrick Nash and Jacob Arvey.

Too, Ogilvie partisans had to admit that Shapiro was displaying surprising spunk in the campaign's final weeks, in sharp contrast to his prior lackluster effort. If it were true, as some surmised, that a candidate for governor could be helped or hurt by the caliber of the nominee for lieutenant governor, then that also could be a fly in Ogilvie's soup. Shapiro's running mate was state senator Paul Simon from Troy in Madison County, a good-government crusader quite popular downstate. The Republican candidate for lieutenant governor was a tall, dapper businessman from Winnetka who never had held elective office, Robert A. Dwyer. The candidacy of Simon was noticeably underscored by the *St. Louis Post-Dispatch* when it endorsed him and Shapiro. As the liberal *Post-Dispatch* viewed it, Illinois voters had a choice between two Democrats with a "progressive and humanitarian record" and a pair of Republicans, Ogilvie and Dwyer, "seeking office on the basis of slick and costly public relations campaigns."[14]

Chicago's American, which had observed Ogilvie much more closely than newspapers away from Chicago, saw the governor's race differently. The *American* editorialized for the election of Ogilvie, stating he was the best choice to tackle "the obsolescence of state government," which that newspaper called "the great challenge" facing Illinois. Throughout his public career, the *American* declared, "Ogilvie has shown a rocklike sincerity of purpose that sets him well apart from the usual run of politicians. He has the driving tenacity needed to change governmental habits and systems whose nature is to resist change."[15] The *American* editorial, typical of others in support of Ogilvie, assessed the candidate precisely, to Drennan's satisfaction. Now, if just a majority of Illinois's voters viewed Ogilvie in this mode.

As the Ogilvie entourage congregated in Chicago's Bismarck Hotel on November 5, 1968, not everybody displayed their boss's aplomb. With the lead in the gubernatorial contest seesawing, thanks to the haphazard reporting of returns, the evening became "one long night with more than enough suspense," Brian Whalen recalled. Several times, supporters tallying the available results thought they were on the verge of being able to tell Ogilvie he could claim victory. But they hesitated because they knew some returns from key Democratic areas in Chicago were being held out, a routine tactic of the Daley gang.

On the other hand, Ogilvie strategists had quietly and successfully implored officials in suburban Cicero, where the GOP organization was strong, to withhold for as many hours as necessary their reporting of votes. Thus, a bloc of Republican votes would be held in reserve to offset, if needed, the intentionally delayed Democratic returns.[16] In sum, the tallies from a number of precincts in Cook County, some Democrat and others Republican, had yet to be included in the county's vote count in the first hours of the morning after the election.

When this situation came to the attention of certain individuals elsewhere in the country who were anxiously awaiting the final vote in Illinois, the natural assumption was that the unreported votes in Cook County were Democratic. One of these people was a brusque New York bond attorney, John Mitchell, Richard Nixon's law partner and campaign manager. Nixon would never forget the role of Illinois in the 1960 presidential election, when his defeat was ensured by John Kennedy's extremely narrow victory in Illinois—a result that many Republicans swore to their dying day occurred because of vote stealing by Democrats in Chicago. Smelling a case of déjà vu, a tense Mitchell placed a call to the Ogilvie headquarters a few hours after midnight of election day and found himself talking to Jim Mack. At that point, Mack was much more relaxed than he had been a short while earlier because it had become certain, finally, that Ogilvie had won.

Mincing no words, Mitchell expressed concern to Mack that the Nixonites knew a number of precincts "were still out" in Cook, precincts with enough potential votes to threaten the still seemingly tenuous Nixon lead in Illinois. Maybe the FBI should be brought in, suggested Mitchell. However, this time around, Mack assured Mitchell, "You don't have to worry because half of those votes still out are ours."[17]

The Vote

Three weeks after the general election of 1968, on a gloomy day close to Thanksgiving, the lame-duck governor of Illinois was still not his old cheery self as he poured coffee for a handful of reporters he had invited to breakfast. They were scribes from the Statehouse pressroom who had covered Governor Shapiro's race with Richard B. Ogilvie. Shapiro did not know that these writers were really rather excited that Ogilvie had won because it meant fresh faces— always good for the news business—would be arriving in Springfield to guide state government. But on this day, when the mood in the Governor's Mansion was as dismal as the weather, the reporters feigned sympathy for the husky little man who reluctantly agreed to discuss the vote that ended his brief hold on the governorship.[18]

In the end, Shapiro's Republican challenger prevailed by 127,794 votes, as Ogilvie received 2,307,295 to 2,179,501 for Shapiro. Translated, Ogilvie won with 51.2 percent of the vote. Shapiro's percentage was 48.4, while the remaining tiny fraction went to Edward C. Gross, the candidate for governor of the Socialist Labor Party.[19]

The breakdown of the vote showed that much of it was standard for a state-wide Illinois race. Ogilvie carried the GOP collar counties around Cook and the rest of the state by a margin big enough to counter Shapiro's predictable capture of Cook with its large Chicago vote. Little surprise here. However, the stunner was the victory by Shapiro's running mate, Paul Simon, in the race for lieutenant governor. That result created a situation in which the electorate for the first time had picked the lieutenant governor candidate of one party to serve with a governor from the other major party. For Shapiro, that had to be the real zinger in his defeat.

As far as Shapiro's race with Ogilvie went, the Chicago Democratic organization provided Shapiro with a plurality of votes in Cook County that should have dispelled speculation in some corners that the machine might be lackadaisical in its support of the Democratic state ticket. Shapiro's vote total in Cook was 1,218,617, a healthy margin of 169,657 over the 1,048,960 for Ogilvie. But as for the rest of Illinois, Ogilvie topped the governor 1,258,335 to 960,884, a difference of 297,451 votes. Beyond Cook, Shapiro carried only eighteen counties—mainly in central and southern Illinois—while the other eighty-three ended up in Ogilvie's pocket.

For the record, Ogilvie almost overcame Shapiro's 169,657-vote lead in Cook by the 152,468-vote margin alone that Ogilvie amassed in the counties collaring Cook—DuPage, Lake, Kane, McHenry, and Will, places where the growing population was greatly inflated by incoming families leaving Chicago and, more often than not, their loyalty to the city's Democratic machine. Consequently, in order for Ogilvie to wrap up the election, he only had to whip Shapiro throughout the remaining part of Illinois by a little more than 17,000 votes. This he did with plenty to spare. Ogilvie readily held his own in traditional GOP terrain downstate, and Shapiro ran poorer than expected in a number of downstate counties that routinely went Democratic. The downstate counties Shapiro carried included only a handful with a sizable vote, namely his home county of Kankakee, Peoria, and neighboring Tazewell, Macon, and St. Clair. Shapiro could or even should have made a killing in St. Clair, a heavily populated county with an East St. Louis–based Democratic machine of its own. St. Clair only went for Shapiro, though, by 52,037 to 43,152. In the densely inhabited neighboring county of Madison, home of another powerful old-line Democratic organization, the outcome was even more disappointing for Shapiro. He lost it by 373 votes, as Ogilvie garnered 48,429 in Madison to 48,056 for Shapiro.

Madison and St. Clair. To some analysts, one had to look no further for keys to Shapiro's defeat. While Shapiro won St. Clair by 8,885 votes, another Democrat, Governor Kerner took St. Clair in 1964 by 31,544 votes. Kerner swept Madison in 1964 by 20,856 votes.

In the 1968 election, Simon demolished the Republican candidate for lieutenant governor, Bob Dwyer, by a 23,583-vote margin in St. Clair and by 26,674 votes in Madison, the home county of Simon. A profound disparity between the showings of Shapiro and Simon in those two counties led many observers to suspect that more had to be involved than the fact that Simon was a well-liked figure on the "East Side," the St. Louis newspaper name for nearby Madison and St. Clair Counties. Some conjecture about Shapiro's lag even figured that he might have been a target of anti-Jewish sentiment.[20] Another possible factor, at least in Madison, was that the leader of the downstate Ogilvie campaign was a resident of the county, Illinois House Speaker Ralph Smith of Alton.

All in all, Simon carried thirty-three counties in comparison to Shapiro's nineteen. Simon was a winner in fifteen counties that Shapiro lost. The governor carried only one county that Simon lost, Kankakee. Yet in most of the counties that Shapiro and Simon both carried, including Cook, Simon prevailed by the greater margin.

At that long-ago breakfast for certain reporters at the Governor's Mansion in 1968, the governor asked his guests for any final thoughts on his unsuccessful race. They discussed several factors: that it was not unusual in Illinois for a lieutenant governor candidate to run ahead of the party's gubernatorial nominee; that Shapiro had not run with a winning presidential candidate at the head of the party's ticket; and that Shapiro was the target of most of the GOP campaign criticism in the state, including the barbs depicting him as a toady of the Daley machine. Simon was not subject to any such charges. Also, they reminded the governor that Simon was opposed by probably the least-known of the major candidates on either party's state ticket.

For his part, Shapiro said he could not ignore the mixed bag of winners in the statewide contests. Besides Ogilvie, Republican victors included Dirksen as expected; Justin Taft, a Rochester farmer, who won the clerkship of the Illinois Supreme Court; and William Scott in the race for attorney general. Joining Simon in the Democratic win column were two others who bucked the GOP tide, Paul Powell and Mike Howlett. Powell was reelected secretary of state, and Chicagoan Howlett was returned as state auditor of public accounts. Both veteran politicians still had some of their biggest news-making days down the road.

As for Shapiro, the days of headlines were over. He would return to Kankakee, from where he could commute to the Chicago law firm where he worked. Shapiro was still practicing law when he was found dead in his house in Kankakee one morning in 1987. In the years before he died, Shapiro would surface in the Capitol now and then, occasionally in regard to some ceremonial task of government that he was asked to handle. The sandwich stand in the Statehouse where he once shared hot dogs and soft drinks with state workers was gone. However, that hardly prevented Shapiro, again his chirpy self, from mingling with the old familiar faces.

Bourbons in the Senate, Scandal in the High Court

Arrington and the Bourbons

No way could Ogilvie's push in 1969 for enactment of the state income tax *not* ignite political drama. Too much was at stake, and besides, the cast of players with a big say in the matter was dominated by strong-willed and even explosive characters. More than a few of them were found in the most exclusive political club in the state, the old-guard Republican majority in the Illinois Senate. The General Assembly's upper chamber had been a Republican stronghold through the decades since the Depression. Moreover, in 1969, the public careers of some of the Senate GOP Bourbons still in the saddle dated back to the Depression.

A year or two later, a combination of age, the stepped-up pace in the legislature, and exasperation would take a toll on a good number of the Bourbons. However, in the first year of the Seventy-sixth General Assembly, 1969, the Senate's Republican majority—with its lopsided advantage, thirty-eight to nineteen—over the Democrats reigned.

Even in the mid-1960s, when Democrats were in control, except in the Senate, the tightly knit contingent of GOP senators still managed to have its voice heard on issues. That also happened to be the period when the image of the General Assembly was soiled by an unpleasant episode, the disclosure in 1965 of those tape-recorded discussions of lobbyists on purported payments to legislators for votes. None other than the old guard came to the rescue. Its leader, W. Russell Arrington, forcefully whipped the Senate into a model of operating efficiency, one designed to prove that the legislature still could play a very full role in government.

As Arrington molded the Republicans into a cohesive battalion, Governors Kerner and Shapiro found themselves having to compromise on most of their programs. If they didn't, GOP versions were passed. The Bourbons may have been criticized for being recalcitrant on civil rights and other hot issues surfacing in the 1960s, but nobody argued that any interests were better served than those protected by the old guard—financial institutions, insurance firms and other big businesses, public education, agriculture, and strict interpretation of the Illinois Constitution. The Bourbons could attack with almost puritanical zeal subjects they frowned on. Extension of legalized gambling beyond horse racing was one. Another was the multiplication of social welfare programs, a favorite goal of the Chicago Democrats. New or increased taxes were not on the Bourbons' agenda either, meaning that Arrington faced a tough chore in selling his men on Ogilvie's income tax. (In 1969, only one woman held a seat in the Illinois Senate, Democrat Esther Saperstein of Chicago.)

Arrington was far from the only featured performer in the General Assembly's passage of the income tax. Mayor Daley's influence hung heavily over the Democrats in both chambers of the legislature, and he could only relish the call by Ogilvie for a levy the mayor obviously wanted. Over in the House, the Republican speaker, Ralph Smith, would have to put votes for the income tax on the board. And southern Illinoisan Clyde Choate, a key cog in the Democratic leadership team in the House, would certainly get his due before any income tax legislation was sent to Ogilvie.

Wrenching votes for the income levy out of the Senate Bourbons, though, had to be the least-desirable assignment for those seeking the tax. Daley would dictate in the end a vote for the tax by a large number of Senate Democrats, but that would have been meaningless without significant support for the levy in the overwhelmingly GOP majority. So the onus was on Arrington.

W. Russell Arrington had commandeered a huge role on the state government scene. *Commandeered* was hardly an exaggeration because Arrington seemed to do everything forcibly. Moving ahead with all the delicacy of that proverbial bull in a china shop, Arrington was the majordomo behind the General Assembly's progression from a part-time institution to one functioning almost full-time. For that, he would be praised and condemned. Success in the world of Illinois government and politics seldom came to persons with small egos, but Arrington's critics insisted that he set a new standard in self-esteem. And that was one of the nicer things they said about Arrington. *Arrogant* and *overbearing,* not to mention *ruthless*—those were adjectives attributed to Arrington by some of those on his side in addition to Democrats and other unfortunate souls who got in his way. At the least, Arrington clearly was a man driven to seize the same success in politics that he had achieved in private life, where he had used his law practice and business dealings to make himself a wealthy person.

Maybe, just maybe, Arrington's thirst for prominence was rooted in his humble beginning. Not many who squared off with Arrington in his heyday realized that the high-powered Republican lawmaker from genteel Evanston on Lake Michigan was an Irish miner's son born in one of those Democratic coal towns in downstate Illinois, Gillespie. Before Arrington moved to the Chicago area in 1930, the year he received a law degree from the University of Illinois, his family lived in rough and tough East St. Louis. The law practice that he opened in Chicago prospered in spite of the Depression. He also became a business associate of W. Clement Stone, a colorful individual with a genius for making money. Stone and Arrington hit the jackpot with Combined Insurance Company of America. Stone founded and headed the firm, which sold personal accident and health policies, and Arrington was its general counsel, vice president, and secretary. The two men also were major backers of the Alberto-Culver Company, a hair products business. With money to burn, both Stone and Arrington became philanthropists and civic leaders. They had their hands in politics, too. Stone became a financial angel for Republicans, while Arrington went the elective office route.

By the time Ogilvie got to Springfield, Arrington was a Capitol veteran. He won a seat in the Illinois House in 1944, the year Ogilvie was wounded in World War II, and served in the lower chamber until winning his Senate seat in 1954. A decade later, Arrington replaced fellow Republican Arthur J. Bidwill of River Forest as the Senate's majority leader, then known as the president pro tempore. Not until the Illinois Constitution of 1970 was in place did the leader of the majority party in the Senate preside over the chamber with the title of president. Prior to that, the Senate's presiding officer was the lieutenant governor, and the majority leader only wielded the gavel when the lieutenant governor was absent or acting as governor. Whether the lieutenant governor was on the podium or not, though, the Senate was run from Arrington's red leather chair on the east side of the old chamber. From the time he became the GOP leader until his party's loss of the Senate majority in the 1970 election, Arrington led the Senate. Arrington may have been called the president pro tem, but he was the Senate's potentate in every sense of the word.

Arrington bossed the Senate in a no-holds-barred manner. It was fascinating the way he stood by his little desk, one hand on his hip and the other holding a long cigar, and willed the room to silence with nothing more than a nod of his head or a brusque word or two. One minute Arrington was Dr. Jekyll, warm and even facetious. Moments later, he'd be Mr. Hyde, firing a torrent of invectives at the hapless Democrats across the aisle and their easygoing leader, Senator Thomas (Art) McGloon of Chicago. But just as Arrington's volcanic personality permeated the hours the Senate was in session, the changes in the Illinois legislative process wrought by Arrington also were obvious to one and all, including Democrats like Paul Simon.

As a state senator and then lieutenant governor, Simon was a target of more than one Arrington tongue-lashing. But those may have seemed mild in comparison to the put-down Simon absorbed when he became lieutenant governor. Use of the spacious, well-appointed office behind the Senate chamber that Shapiro had occupied as lieutenant governor was denied Simon by Arrington, who used it for his own office. For at least the first two years of his term as lieutenant governor, Simon had to operate out of a much smaller enclosure behind the chamber, a glorified broom closet that hardly befitted the second highest elected official in Illinois. Everybody assumed that Arrington had usurped Simon's rightful office, but Simon himself would say years later that "Arrington had the jurisdiction to determine that matter." Still, Simon would add, the office flap did represent "a power play by Arrington, a man to whom things like big offices, big cars and diamond rings meant a lot."[1] Having said that, Simon never wavered from his view that Arrington did more than any other person in modern Illinois political life to "upgrade the legislative process."

Annual sessions. Legislative staffing. Higher pay for lawmakers. General Assembly oversight of the propriety of state spending. And not the least of all, escorting Governor Ogilvie's programs through the legislative labyrinth. Arrington was behind all of this.

Arrington's astute grasp of the complexities of state finances gave him a leg up in his ascension to power. He had served as chairman of the Illinois Legislative Audit Commission since its creation in the 1950s and received much of the credit for the panel's success in uncovering misuses of state funds. Spurring the legislature to involvement in almost everything seemed to be Arrington's credo. For that to happen, the General Assembly had to switch from its traditional six-month sessions every other year to annual meetings, a transition that would propel Illinois toward a virtually full-time legislature.

To be truthful, one of the last things a lot of folks wanted, and their number included numerous legislators and more than one governor, was for the General Assembly to be in Springfield more often. The idea scared those who viewed less government as best government. They were gratified when Illinois voters rejected annual sessions in a 1964 referendum. But as the 1960s progressed, an increased push was on from many quarters to get the General Assembly more involved in the daily functioning of Illinois government and, by implication, in the day-to-day doings of average citizens. Ogilvie himself went into the governor's office advocating annual sessions.

On this subject, as with so many things, Arrington had taken matters into his own hands. At the insistence of Arrington, the legislature broke new ground by moving on its own volition to follow its regular six-month session in 1967 with a unique follow-up session in the fall of that year. Then again in 1968, it reconvened the two chambers. Normally, the General Assembly ended its constitutionally mandated biennial session beginning early in each odd-numbered year by adjourning *sine die*—without specifying any date for reconvening. If any sessions were held in between, they were called by the governor.

The upshot of this trend was that the General Assembly would sit in session every year. Any remaining doubt of it was eliminated by the Constitution of 1970, which decreed—unlike the previous charter—that the legislature convene every year.

More frequent sessions and deeper involvement in seemingly every issue facing Illinoisans triggered a much bigger workload for the senators and representatives. Without increased staffing, many worried, they might get lost on their new fast track. But Arrington had covered that base too—that is, Arrington and Sam Gove. Gove, the University of Illinois political science professor who had assisted Ogilvie's transition into the governorship, had pioneered a legislative staff internship program earlier in the 1960s that ushered a cadre of bright young men and women into the halls of the Capitol. In the early years, these young people were known as Ford Foundation Fellows because of the foundation's financial support for the program. Many of them would later find prominent roles in either government or the private sector. Some would win elective office, like Jim Edgar, a Gove intern out of Eastern Illinois University who would eventually become Illinois secretary of state and then governor.

Once in Springfield, a number of Gove's interns worked for Arrington. Those who did not get assigned to Arrington still were beneficiaries of his strong championing of top-notch staffing for the General Assembly. Richard W. Carlson, a onetime Illinois lottery director who first set foot in Springfield in 1969 as a Gove intern, saw it simply enough. Carlson viewed Gove as "the father of Illinois legislative staffing" and Arrington as "the one who actually implemented it."[2]

Whether on the Senate floor or striding toward the pressroom, Arrington seldom was seen in the Statehouse without one or more of his interns or other young staffers trailing him. These staffers became another one of his trademarks, yet a number of veteran legislators were not enthralled by the almost overnight presence of these fresh-faced scholarly kids—the upstarts. Arrington even had the audacity to rotate the interns in and out of Senate GOP caucuses, those most sacrosanct of gatherings. It was not true that Arrington spent every waking hour with his young assistants, as some critics asserted, but it was true that Arrington at times covered out of his own pocket the Springfield lodging bills for a few of the aides who were starved for cash.

It was also true that on days when the General Assembly was in session, not one of those youthful staffers would dare be late for Arrington's strategy breakfast each morning at a back table in the State House Inn, a short walk from the Capitol. They congregated at seven o'clock sharp, and by the time breakfast was over an hour later, each individual had his marching orders for the day. The breakfasts also were intended to bring Arrington up to snuff on the latest gossip connected with state government. Not even the most far-fetched rumor was deemed unworthy of his attention. As much as anything, Arrington wanted the lowdown on what his own Republican senators were thinking, a desire that prompted a bit of subterfuge on his part.

In a 1994 interview, Carlson remembered that "when the General Assembly was in session, he [Arrington] would send out the young staff people to mingle in the bars and other gathering spots at night and listen to what the Republican senators were talking about. Their gripes, their concerns, things like that. We were his eyes and ears. Then, the next morning, we had to tell him at breakfast what we had heard. He wanted to know everything the guys were talking about. Of course, he had a photographic memory, which meant he recorded every tidbit he was told. Later, in caucus, our senators couldn't believe that Arrington knew all about their concerns. They didn't know we were reporting back to him on what we had heard in the bars the night before."[3]

Legislative aides were sprouting up all over the place in those days, but the ones working for the Senate Republicans under the tutelage of Arrington were the most esteemed. No wonder Ogilvie tried to choose as many of the Arrington proteges as he could. Two that always come to mind are John Dailey, who as an Ogilvie assistant seemed to have his fingers in everything, and Tom Corcoran, who was dispatched by Ogilvie to direct the state's office in Washington, an assignment that laid groundwork for his later election to Congress from northern Illinois.

Few Arrington staff members symbolize better than Richard Edward Dunn the qualities that Arrington sought in the members of his young crew. Dick Dunn grew up in Bloomington, son of a prominent attorney, Richard T. Dunn. After arriving in Springfield as a Gove intern and landing with Arrington, Dunn soon found himself serving as an Arrington point man on state budgetary reform. Dunn left Springfield for a time to pursue a doctorate in political science at the University of Illinois, but he returned to Arrington's staff. His boss later picked him to direct the staff in what turned out to be the twilight period of the Arrington era.

One striking trait of Dunn and other Arrington disciples was their abhorrence of governmental corruption. None was more of a straight arrow than Dunn, whose strict moral upbringing ruled out any tolerance for the underside dealings that so often had given Illinois government a black eye. Anyone who knew Dunn should not have been surprised to learn that it was he who tipped off federal authorities in Chicago to a bribery scheme. Cement industry officials were bribing a number of Illinois legislators to support passage of a bill to hike the load limit for ready-mix trucks on state roads. An investigation of the scheme—which did lead to approval of a measure that was subsequently vetoed by Ogilvie in 1972—resulted in highly publicized indictments and a federal trial in Chicago in 1976 for eight individuals, including six sitting or former lawmakers, on charges of complicity in the bribery activity linked to what became known as the "cement bill" case. Six defendants were found guilty, including a former speaker of the Illinois House, Republican Jack Walker of Lansing.

Dunn's whistle-blowing, hardly a common occurrence in Illinois politics, would have been an even more extraordinary move if his legislative tutor had been any person besides Arrington. Not to be forgotten, the Arrington mystique was fed by an unpredictability that could confound even his own political crowd. It may or may not have been lost on Dunn and others that Arrington had pledged late in 1971 at age sixty-five that the following year would be his last in the legislature. Arrington, who had suffered a stroke earlier, planned to concentrate his remaining lawmaking days on seeking passage of ethics legislation covering public officials.

Arrington had found himself in strange political waters long before Ogilvie prevailed upon him to help pass the income tax. In 1967, onlookers were mildly surprised when Arrington introduced and successfully pushed legislation requiring Illinoisans to obtain a firearm owner's identification card from the state before buying or possessing guns or ammunition. Although the legislation was submitted with the backing of the Illinois State Rifle Association, the Chicago Crime Commission, and other groups, opposition was very strong in parts of the state that were rural, conservative, and largely Republican.

However, this early attempt at gun control was not the most explosive topic before the General Assembly in 1967. That honor went by far to the open-housing initiative—legislation to help minorities obtain housing in white neighborhoods. Arrington launched an eleventh-hour initiative that was little short of astounding. The Senate Republicans were notorious for ensuring that fair-housing legislation never made it to the floor. Several such measures were passed in 1967 by the House, but these bills—along with those submitted by Senate Democrats—could not get around the brick wall of the Senate's Registration and Miscellany Committee. This panel was dominated by implacable foes of open housing, starting with the chairman, Republican lawyer Frank Ozinga of Evergreen Park. Few Illinois legislative committees gained the notoriety that this one did in 1967 in bottling up one open-housing bill after another. Ozinga's committee was fronting, of course, for the bulk of the GOP crew in the Senate, which just did not want any of these measures to reach the Senate floor.

Thus, imagine the amazement when Arrington, two weeks before the end of the spring session, vigorously sought approval of open-occupancy legislation. His bill was not a world-beater. It would have outlawed racial discrimination in the sale or rental of any real estate or housing accommodation, but the measure would not have covered owner-occupied homes or owner-occupied apartment buildings containing ten or fewer units. Still, the mere idea of such a bill from the leader of Senate Republicans was mind-boggling.

To boot, Arrington was the same fellow who one day during his legislative prime found himself suddenly staring at a state policeman's car, which had pulled alongside his sleek black Cadillac (with the "Number 1" legislative license plate). No wonder. The young Arrington aide driving the senator's car was zipping along toward Springfield at more than ninety miles per hour at the behest of his boss.

Arrington, surprised that any state cop would have the nerve to pursue him, noticed that the trooper was black. Even more surprising, the officer, using a loudspeaker, warned, "Slow down, senator, for your own safety." Flushing with anger, Arrington quickly snapped to his driver, "If you slow down, there'll be a race riot." The Cadillac did not slow down, and the trooper gave up.[4]

When Arrington made his move on open housing, the only race riot that might have ensued would have involved his own Republican senators—all white men who, with an exception or two, were dead set against the measure. Yet Arrington gambled successfully on an unorthodox procedure to get his version of a fair-housing proposal out of a Senate committee, the one on public welfare instead of the registration-miscellany panel. One enraged Republican senator, Chicagoan John J. Lanigan, compared Arrington's scheming to "the tactics used at Pearl Harbor." "Unfortunately," Lanigan added, "they are the tactics of my own leader."[5]

Optimism among open-occupancy advocates that Arrington's effort might pay off was soon extinguished in a five-hour caucus of the GOP senators. Be-

hind closed doors, individuals who rarely questioned Arrington's leadership reminded him in no uncertain terms that he stood virtually alone in support of
open housing. They told him that any persistence on his part to gain their backing would only put his leadership position in jeopardy. On the Senate floor, the
GOP contingent then prevailed in a vote to not accept the public welfare committee's favorable recommendation on Arrington's bill. Just two Republicans
joined Arrington in voting with the Democratic minority to support the committee's decision.

Afterward, an unusually subdued Arrington slumped in his office, alone
with his secretary, Denysia Bastas, and this writer and commented that "it's a
social problem that forced me to do what I did." Although conceding he did not
know whether legislation could eliminate racial discrimination in housing, he
insisted that his legislative approach would have been "a reasonable beginning
to determine if the solution could be through law."[6] To most on the scene, the
upshot of the drama was the revelation that Arrington could only push his
people so far. The memory of it was still quite vivid two years later when Arrington got behind Ogilvie's income tax.

That Arrington did not suffer defeat easily was a major reason, some suspected, for the lack of a follow-up on his once purported intention to run for
governor in 1968. Donald Tolva, a young Chicago attorney and another Ford
Foundation Fellow who reached Arrington's staff in the 1960s, sensed this to be
the case. Tolva became close to Arrington, close enough to detect that in spite
of the continuing rumors about Arrington's gubernatorial ambition, "Russ was
uncharacteristically unsure of himself on this one, not sure that he could win
and not sure how he would handle defeat."[7]

Before the 1968 campaign season, Tolva and John Dailey were with Arrington in his law office when Cook County Board President Ogilvie paid a memorable visit. Tolva would not forget Ogilvie sinking into the soft couch in the
office and being informed by the diminutive senator sitting at his desk that he,
Arrington, definitely would not be running for governor. "This was a meeting
to clear the air," recalled Tolva, "because it was assumed that Ogilvie wanted
to run for governor, but probably would not have done so if Arrington had
intended to run. So, Arrington was giving Ogilvie an open door to go for governor."

Historically, this may have been the beginning of Arrington's seemingly ongoing obeisance to Ogilvie's wishes, a pattern most noticeable with Arrington's
introduction in 1969 of Senate Bill 1150, the measure proposing the state income
tax. Also listed as sponsors of the bill were two assistant Republican leaders in
the Senate, William C. Harris and Robert Coulson, and a Democrat, James P.

Loukas of Chicago, an individual destined to become the governor's political ally and eventually assistant director of the Illinois Department of Financial Institutions in the Ogilvie administration.

If there ever was a legislative spark plug, it was Harris. First, though, a word or two on Coulson. Upon reflection, Coulson may have been almost too good to be true. A Lake countian, lawyer Coulson was a graduate of both Dartmouth and the University of Chicago, and he had been an OSS officer in India and China in World War II. Before reaching the Illinois Senate, he was mayor of Waukegan and a member of the Illinois House. By 1969, few in the upper chamber commanded more respect than Coulson because of his legislative creativity, open mind toward compromise, and dignified composure. When he passed from the scene a few years later, all agreed that a class act was gone.

Not only did Coulson not toot his own horn, but as Harris would observe in a bit of an understatement, "Bob was not as excitable as Russ or myself."[8] Arrington turned to Harris instead of the more reserved Coulson to serve as the Senate floor manager for rounding up votes for the income tax. What about Bill Harris? He was a life insurance agent in Pontiac who found politics to be a good outlet for the abundance of energetic enthusiasm that he brought to life. For Harris, the apex of a twenty-two-year career in the General Assembly came in 1973 when he became the first senator formally elected president of the Illinois Senate. After retiring from the Senate at the end of 1976, Harris proceeded to serve as the state commissioner of banks and trust companies through 1990.

Harris's public life was not all roses. He entered the 1969 legislative session on a sour note, having been the unsuccessful GOP candidate for state auditor in the 1968 election. Nevertheless, Harris was well liked by most Senate Democrats as well as by his fellow Republicans. He could, and would, successfully arm twist for the income tax on both sides of the aisle. As Harris darted to and fro on the issue in 1969, the chunky redhead with an old-fashioned 1950s crew cut was a self-admitted "set of legs" for Arrington.

Like Arrington and almost every other Illinois legislator in the power-broker league, Harris had a handle on state finances. Harris was the last of the potent chairmen of the freewheeling Illinois Budgetary Commission. Of course, the commission was to go the way of the dodo bird when Governor Ogilvie moved quickly and forcefully to make the executive branch the clear-cut king in the Illinois budget-setting process. Because Harris was so well aware of the debits and credits on the state's ledgers, he knew Ogilvie was right in claiming that Illinois was "on the brink of bankruptcy." Harris also was almost fanatical in his personal opposition to state indebtedness, whether incurred through the issuance of bonds for capital construction or through other means of borrowing. Harris even went so far as to try to insist that highways be built on a pay-as-you-go basis. Consequently, he agreed to do his part, which was plenty, to secure the income tax.

In the fight to pass the levy, the Senate was the battleground, literally. Nearly two months passed from the first reading of SB 1150 in the upper chamber to its passage by the Senate on June 27. Three days later, on the scheduled windup day of the session, the House approved the measure. The following day Ogilvie signed it. Both the House action and Ogilvie's approval seemed almost anticlimactic. The arguments and emotions over the issue were spent while the income tax bill was in the Senate. By the time the Senate finally rendered its verdict on SB 1150, everybody involved felt exhausted, including some of the reporters in the Statehouse who had breathlessly followed the deliberation of the matter day after day.

Besides, with all due respect to the significance of the income tax, a few of the scribes and others in the Capitol were finding their attention sidetracked in the waning hours of June 1969 toward a seething scandal brewing among the justices of the Illinois Supreme Court, those dark-robed figures of high authority closeted in their judicial temple just east of the Capitol.

Scandal in the Wind

For the longest time before June 1969, Sherman Skolnick's mission was a fool's errand. Nobody savvy would get caught dead giving the time of day to Skolnick, with his wild charges that parts of the Illinois judiciary were rotten with corruption. Try as hard as he could, Chicagoan Skolnick, a self-styled legal researcher and a paraplegic, could not get himself taken seriously. To the established order, he was *persona non grata,* a gadfly recklessly seeking recognition through his repeated assertions of wrongdoing by judges and other public officials. The first to give Skolnick the brush-off were seasoned reporters. He reminded many of them of those old ex-convicts who'd appear in newsrooms, offering to talk for a hefty price about the horrors of imprisonment. Skolnick was not asking for money, though, just for somebody to listen to him.

Enter Ed Pound. Pound stood out like a sore thumb from the day he burst into the Capitol pressroom shortly after Ogilvie's inauguration to man the newly established bureau of the *Alton Evening Telegraph.* More than a few veteran reporters on the Illinois government beat, some old enough to be father of the twenty-five-year-old Pound, immediately disliked him because of a brashness evidenced by his refusal to show even the slightest hint of the awe normally displayed by pressroom newcomers at their sudden access to the state's high and mighty. This kid Pound, many of his new colleagues felt, came in with a chip on his shoulder. They were not all wrong.

The poop sheet on Edward Thomas Pound went as follows: Grew up poor in south suburban St. Louis, son of a railroad worker. Graduated in 1961 from Affton Senior High School, where he played football. Earned spending money during high school days as a carhop at Steak-n-Shake. Went to college briefly, dropped out. Employed as a copyboy at the *St. Louis Post-Dispatch*, where editorial writers urged him to become a reporter. He never forgot helping editorial cartoonist Bill Mauldin move out of the *Post-Dispatch* building when Mauldin left for the *Chicago Sun-Times*. Before the end of 1962, he was well into his first job as a reporter for the *Republican-Register*, a small daily in Mount Carmel, Illinois. By the fall of 1963, he landed with the staff of the larger *Telegraph*, where he became a hell-raising reporter under the guidance of hard-driving *Telegraph* city editor Elmer Broz. After hunting shady politicians and other dubious characters in Madison County, Pound coveted greater quarry and began stalking in the Illinois capital.

In the decades before Pound came to Springfield, the state government certainly had been fertile ground for investigative journalism, involving both reporters stationed in the Statehouse and outsiders who came to the Capitol just to check out suspected malfeasance. However, it was hard to argue that the majority of the newspeople assigned full-time to the big domed building in Springfield were not boat rockers, or at the least not anxious to voluntarily upset anyone's applecart. A cozy live-and-let-live atmosphere was in place with the sometimes evident transgressions of officials ignored by pressroom veterans as long as the principal officeholders and their agents kept the reporters amply supplied with straight news stories. Understandably, the guardians of the status quo got irritably nervous when upstarts like Pound began filtering into the pressroom with increasing frequency in the late 1960s.

When the reportorial gumshoes weren't on the trail of something hot, they did have to cover more mundane developments like everybody else. So, in his first months in Springfield, Pound had to bide his time following the arguments over the income tax and all the governmental changes being pushed by Ogilvie. Boy, that was boring for him. Pound came to the seat of Illinois government to expose corruption. It was his life's vocation. He needed a breakthrough, though, a real score to achieve legitimacy.[9]

That Pound and Skolnick finally made contact was as inevitable as the old boy-meets-girl story. Unlike umpteen other reporters, Pound was interested in Skolnick's insistence that one for sure and possibly more justices of the state's highest court may have been guilty of a conflict of interest when the Illinois

Supreme Court upheld in 1967 a lower court's dismissal of criminal charges against Theodore J. Isaacs, a former state revenue director under his close friend, Governor Kerner.

Pound got a green light from his paper's home office to pursue an inquiry into Skolnick's contention in the early days of June. Working with Pound would be Ande Yakstis from the *Telegraph's* local staff, Pound's partner in numerous disclosures back in Pound's days in Madison County. As they embarked on their latest venture, Pound told Yakstis they were knocking on the door of a really big-time hit, which if true would not have been bad for a fellow such as Pound, who not all that far back was hustling burgers and malts to drive-in restaurant patrons.

Ogilvie in uniform in early 1944, as his army tank battalion awaits assignment to combat duty overseas. The unit was sent to Europe later that year. *Photograph courtesy of Dorothy Ogilvie.*

Cook County Sheriff Ogilvie administers the oath of office in 1963 to a class of recruits for his office. *Photograph courtesy of Dorothy Ogilvie.*

Ogilvie takes a break from the campaign trail during his successful race for governor in 1968. *Photograph courtesy of the Illinois State Historical Library.*

Ogilvie being sworn in as governor of Illinois, January 13, 1969, in the State Armory in Springfield. The oath was administered by Chief Justice Roy J. Solfisburg Jr. of the Illinois Supreme Court. *Photograph courtesy of the Illinois State Historical Library.*

The governor in Washington in 1969 with a group of Illinois Republicans. *Left to right:* Governor Ogilvie, Representative Leslie C. Arends of Melvin, Senator Everett M. Dirksen, Senator Charles H. Percy. *Photograph courtesy of Dorothy Ogilvie.*

The Illinois first family in 1969, Richard and Dorothy Ogilvie with their daughter Elizabeth. *Photograph courtesy of the Illinois State Historical Library.*

Ogilvie addresses a joint session of the Illinois House and Senate in 1971. *Photograph courtesy of Dorothy Ogilvie.*

Senator W. Russell Arrington of Evanston, the fiery Senate Republican leader who helped to push many of Ogilvie's proposals through the General Assembly. *Photograph courtesy of the Illinois State Historical Library.*

The governor chats with reporters (Taylor Pensoneau, facing camera) in his office after a press conference in late 1969. Frequent sessions with Statehouse reporters were a hallmark of Ogilvie's term as governor. *Photograph by Les Sintay, courtesy of United Press International.*

President Nixon and Governor Ogilvie head a caravan through the Illinois State Fair in 1971. *Photograph courtesy of the Illinois State Historical Library.*

The governor chuckles as Representative C. L. McCormick, a Vienna Republican, lampoons Dan Walker, Ogilvie's Democratic opponent in the governor's race, at a rally in southern Illinois in 1972. *Photograph courtesy of Dorothy Ogilvie.*

Charisma isn't everything.

In his bid for re-election as governor, Dick Ogilvie has a problem.

His opponent.

Dan Walker is dashing, handsome and sometimes even charming.

Rumor has it that some people may vote for him solely because they think he has a stunning personality.

Which is unfortunate.

Because Dick Ogilvie offers voters a refreshing alternative to a stunning personality.

Stunning performance.

Take a drink.

As governor, Dick Ogilvie gave Illinois the finest anti-pollution laws in America. For the first time in history, our water is actually getting cleaner.

State aid for people who can't dribble.

You don't have to be a jock (or a genius) to get state aid for college anymore. Under Governor Ogilvie, 100,000 scholarships and loans are available this year.

To qualify, all a needy student has to have are grades good enough to get accepted at college.

For road freaks.

Governor Ogilvie has improved more dangerous roads than any governor in the history of our state. The result is that for the first time in 50 years, the death rate on Illinois highways has gone down.

For speed freaks.

Governor Ogilvie's drug rehabilitation program has been copied by the federal government and studied by 10 foreign countries. Quite simply, it's the finest in the world.

Are you in labor?

Governor Ogilvie signed our first minimum wage law and gave Illinois the biggest workman's compensation increase in history.

More places for lovers to park: More parks.

Governor Ogilvie has acquired over 56,000 acres of new park land. And it's all located near cities. So you don't have to go too far away to get away from it all.

Let my people go to work.

Governor Ogilvie has provided more jobs for minorities than any governor in the state's history.

A helping hand for the helpless.

Under Governor Ogilvie, a program for mentally retarded children was created that the experts say is the finest in America.

Ah, the joys of growing old.

Governor Ogilvie gave senior citizens their first tax break.

Guts.

He saved the state from bankruptcy by risking his political life for a fair state income tax.

The end.

Neal Peirce, author of *The Megastates of America*, ranks Dick Ogilvie as one of the best two governors in America.

Many political experts feel he's the finest governor Illinois ever had.

On November 7th, it's what you think that counts.

And when you make your selection between Walker and Ogilvie, you have a clear cut choice.

You can vote for a great candidate.

Or you can vote for a great governor.

Richard B. Ogilvie for Governor.

A campaign poster for Ogilvie's 1972 re-election bid that sought to turn the governor's perceived lack of charisma into a plus. *Photograph courtesy of the Illinois State Historical Library.*

Governor and Mrs. Ogilvie present Pope Paul VI with an Abraham Lincoln memento during an audience at the Vatican in 1972. *Photograph from Wide World Photos.*

Ogilvie with comedian Bob Hope, at a Gateway Foundation dinner in 1978. After leaving office, Ogilvie devoted much of his time to civic and benevolent undertakings, such as Chicago-based Gateway Foundation's program to combat alcohol and drug addiction. *Photograph courtesy of the Gateway Foundation.*

EIGHT

Proposed, Debated, Passed:
The State Income Tax

*C*ourage. It sure took courage. After Ogilvie decided to propose the income tax, he threw himself into the politically dangerous fight to attain the levy without blinking an eye. Ignoring those who admonished him to wade in cautiously, Ogilvie moved with extraordinary haste to consolidate support for the tax, putting his political life on the line. The man had no finer hour in the view of individuals who foresaw catastrophe without the income tax.

Ogilvie took his case for the levy to wherever he could find an audience. Early on, he knew that backing for the tax already was in place or could be won from many major interests, such as the Illinois Education Association, the Illinois AFL-CIO, the Illinois State Chamber of Commerce, and, quite obviously, the Illinois Agricultural Association. Farmers had no objection to an income tax because they knew it would relieve the pressure for higher property taxes on their lands. Organized labor had complained for years about the state's heavy reliance for revenue on the sales tax, arguing that the sales levy burdened regular wage earners and poorer Illinoisans more disproportionately than would a fairly constructed income tax.

The decision to seek a flat-rate income levy rather than a graduated or progressive type was hashed over thoroughly by the Ogilvie hierarchy prior to the governor's public call for the tax. The nod went to a flat-rate imposition mainly because of the 1870 Illinois Constitution, which had been used earlier in the century as an obstacle to a state graduated income levy. As soon became evident, it was Ogilvie's intent to tax the incomes of both individuals and corporations at the same flat rate of 4 percent that ignited heated debate. Generally speaking, many Democrats had always held that they would only consider support for a flat-rate income tax if individuals were not hit as hard as corporations. Consequently, Senate Democratic leader McGloon groused about the Ogilvie proposal from the start, but not too loudly, because McGloon was Mayor Daley's man. McGloon knew that Daley would be maneuvering with Ogilvie to make a deal for Democratic support for an income tax.

No, the out-and-out Democratic firebrand on the issue was Clyde Choate, the minority whip in the House and a person to whom a number of downstate Democratic legislators showed considerable allegiance. Choate, it could not be forgotten, had introduced his own income tax bill, one that would have taxed corporations at 5 percent of their income and individuals at only 2 percent.

The arising of Choate followed the Senate Revenue Committee's recommendation in early June 1969 that Senate Bill 1150, the income tax bill, be passed. However, the measure escaped the committee only after the rate of the tax was reduced to 3 percent from 4 percent for both corporations and individuals, a step taken on a motion by Arrington, who had given up hope of getting sufficient GOP support for the higher rate sought by Ogilvie. Even with that, some of the Republican committee members who voted "do pass" did so only to keep the bill alive and were not committing themselves to vote for the measure on the Senate floor. Still, by moving SB 1150 to the floor with just under three weeks left in the session's scheduled run, the door was opened to a critical stage in the evolution of the Illinois income tax. Emotional debate and power plays erupted daily.

Nothing more inflamed the situation than the recognition that the 3 percent flat rate for both individuals and corporations represented a deal between the governor and the Chicago mayor that, with this tax rate, they assumably could garner enough support for its passage. The problem was that too many legislators in each party still weren't in step with the big boys on this one. Since rebellion of any kind normally was not likely in the ranks of the Daley-dominated Democrats, a revolt by downstate Democrats in the House quickly took center stage. Led by Choate, they openly charged that Daley had capitulated to Ogilvie on the income tax bill in exchange for Ogilvie's agreement to go along with a Daley-sought measure that would have provided cities and counties with a greater share of the proceeds from the state sales tax. Why, asked the insurgents, did thirty-seven of the forty-one states with an income tax assess individuals and corporations at different rates if that was not the thing to do?

Representative John P. Touhy of Chicago, the Daley Democrat leading his party in the House, a no-nonsense person who usually could keep his troops in formation, tried to insist that the state fiscal crisis left Democrats in both chambers with little choice but to support the 3 percent rate for both corporations and individuals. However, Choate, the person right under Touhy in the House Democratic leadership, countered angrily that "two people in this state [Ogilvie and Daley] are not going to sit down and make an agreement that is supposed to be binding on this Legislature and the people of this state."[1] Choate even went so far as to draft a statement that would have announced his resignation as Democratic whip. Choate was prepared to say, as hard as it was for seasoned observers to believe, that he could no longer accept Daley's leadership on the income tax showdown because the mayor had gone along with the governor's proposal without consulting the entire Democratic leadership team.

Persisting in his defiance of the Ogilvie-Daley deal, Choate launched a filibuster and threatened to tie up the House with parliamentary moves if the protest of the downstate Democrats was not heeded. The warning could not be taken lightly because it appeared that Choate was supported by most of the thirty-five House Democrats from outside Cook County, an important development. The Republican majority in the House, splintered as it was on the income tax question, was not likely to produce enough votes for passage without substantial Democratic help. So besides having their hands full with the Senate Bourbons, proponents of the income tax also had to contend with Choate stirring up dust in the House.

Years later, Ogilvie noted Choate's impact when an interviewer asked him to reflect on his fight for the income tax and on his failure to obtain a levy taxing individuals at the same rate as corporations. Replied Ogilvie: "I ran into the situation where Clyde Choate didn't feel that individuals should pay the same as corporations, sort of a classic Democrat position."[2]

Choate's emergence as a major player in the income tax brouhaha was not the first time that he and Ogilvie found themselves in the same battle theater. On October 25, 1944, only a few days before Sergeant Ogilvie and the 781st Tank Battalion reached Marseilles, a violent clash had occurred in France near the small resort town of Bruyeres. It would change the life of another young American sergeant, Clyde Choate. Choate, a Depression-poor individual from Anna in southern Illinois, saw action in North Africa, Sicily, and Italy as well as in France and was cited for bravery in the fighting at Anzio and in other battles. However, he achieved the ultimate in heroism on that late October day outside Bruyeres.

Choate was the commander of a tank destroyer set ablaze by enemy fire as a German Mark IV tank and a company of Nazi infantry attacked an American infantry position on a wooded hill. After ordering his men to abandon the destroyer, according to an official army narration of the situation, Choate himself "reached comparative safety." But the narrative went on to relate that Choate returned to his burning destroyer "to search for comrades possibly trapped in the vehicle, risking instant death in an explosion which was imminent and braving enemy fire which ripped his jacket and tore the helmet from his head."[3] The report continued:

Completing the search and seeing the tank and its supporting infantry over-running our infantry in their shallow foxholes, he [Choate] secured a ba-zooka and ran after the tank, dodging from tree to tree and passing through the enemy's loose skirmish line. He fired a rocket from a distance of 20 yards, immobilizing the tank but leaving it able to spray the area with cannon and machine-gun fire. Running back to our infantry through vicious fire, he se-cured another rocket, and, advancing against a hail of machine-gun and small arm fire, reached a position 10 yards from the tank. His second shot shattered the turret. With his pistol he killed two of the crew as they emerged from the tank; and then running to the crippled Mark IV while enemy infantry sniped at him, he dropped a grenade inside the tank and completed its de-struction. With their armor gone, the enemy infantry became disorganized and was driven back. Sergeant Choate's great daring in assaulting an enemy tank single-handedly, his determination to follow the vehicle after it had passed his position, and his skill and crushing thoroughness in the attack prevented the enemy from capturing a battalion command post and turned a probable defeat into a tactical success.

For his valor in this encounter, Choate was awarded the Congressional Medal of Honor. He actually learned of it by reading about it in a newspaper, when later he was working as an apprentice railroad brakeman in St. Louis. During President Truman's presentation of the medal to him, Choate remem-bered, "He said that he would rather have it than be president."[4]

Choate's gallantry made him so well regarded in southern Illinois that many in the region compared him to Alvin York, a World War I infantryman from the Tennessee hills, revered as a hero for single-handedly capturing more than 130 Germans in one day. Quite soon, though, Choate the hero became a politi-cian, a very good one. He got elected to the Illinois House in 1946 when he was twenty-six, and in his years in the House, he became adept at horse-trading on behalf of southern Illinois and a bevy of other interests. Urban political sophis-ticates forced to barter with Choate found him more than a little bit countrified, but they had to watch what they said about a genuine American hero. In his last few years in the House, Choate did experience some rough sledding politi-cally. However, in 1969, Choate, still in his prime, was operating as an advocate of the little person.

He meant to ensure that individuals were not taxed at the same rate as cor-porations. So in a two-fisted effort, Choate brought enough lawmakers to his corner by mid-June to cause suspicion that he had Ogilvie and Daley on the ropes. The mighty Daley was the first to cave. He sent word to Springfield that he had a change of mind, that he too would insist on an income tax with a higher levy for corporations than individuals.

This provoked an angry charge by Ogilvie of "political irresponsibility" by Democrats. He insisted that leading constitutional authorities believed that any state income tax adopted under the 1870 state charter had to be a flat-rate tax and uniform for all taxpayers. Vowing not to "recede from that position," the governor served notice that he had "never run from a fight in my life" and that he did not "intend to run away from this one."[5] Extra troubling for Ogilvie, though, was the reality that his fight was still as much with Republican legislators as with the Democrats.

With the end of the session in sight, Arrington had not obtained the necessary votes in the Senate for approval of his SB 1150 with its identical taxation rate of 3 percent for individuals and corporations. Too many of his own Republicans either still refused to vote for any levy on incomes or recognized that Democrats like Choate were making it politically unpalatable to support an income tax without a lower rate for individuals. Very few GOP senators gave a ready thumbs-up to the income tax like Carbondale's John G. Gilbert, a gentlemanly attorney who pointed out that the state and Chicago both sorely needed the levy and that, in his eyes, "any thinking person in the Legislature who was not playing partisan politics or worrying about his own election realized that."[6]

No, Arrington had more Republicans such as the classics-quoting Hudson Ralph Sours of Peoria to deal with. While no way could be found for Arrington to get this Bourbon stalwart to ever vote for the tax, Arrington still had a monumental task in combating the influence of Sours on other GOP senators. John McCarter, Ogilvie's budget director and a lead soldier for the income tax, retained indelible memories of Sours in the Republican Senate caucuses. Ogilvie would dispatch McCarter to the caucuses to answer questions about the pending levy. Even though he knew that Sours and some of his hard-core compatriots "just hated" him, McCarter nevertheless was taken aback by what he called "those wild, wild sessions." Sours was not only "vehemently opposed to the tax," noted McCarter, "people like Hudson Sours were interested in hearing themselves talk. I mean that was his bag. Arrington was very patient with people like that."[7]

McCarter dutifully reported back to Ogilvie on Arrington's forbearance. So much was riding on it. As McCarter recalled, there was a certain number of downstate Republican senators who "in spite of their adamant opposition to the income tax had been cajoled or bullied into support of it or at least, you know, fainthearted support of it by Arrington or Coulson or Bill Harris. As for others, you could see Arrington working this patient strategy of holding people in line by keeping them talking and trying to find some common ground."

The most obvious target of Arrington's persuasive maneuvering was the sizable contingent of Republican senators open-minded enough on the income tax to be moved to vote for it. Some in this group, like John Joseph (Jack) Lanigan, were not part of the old guard, but were Ogilvie-generation Republicans.

Jack Lanigan proved a good case in point. Lanigan was so unlike most of the other state senate Republicans. He was thirty-four at the time, which made him a youngster among GOP senators. He was from Chicago, the city itself, hardly a hotbed of Republican senators. Really, by every rule of thumb, Lanigan should have been a Chicago Democrat. His parents were immigrants from Ireland. His father, John Joseph Lanigan, left the old country while the Irish rebellion was in full sway. Some of the father's pro-rebel activities had caught the eye of the ruling British authorities. Once in Chicago, the senator's father became a devout Democrat, a devotee of Franklin Roosevelt and Harry Truman. This made him typical of thousands of other Irishmen in Chicago. In the 1920s, the elder Lanigan was a streetcar conductor, working for Chicago Surface Lines. Young Jack Lanigan did not hesitate to pass on the stories his dad told about his job. One concerned the multiple role of some streetcars during Prohibition. "When a guy got on the back end of my father's streetcar," related young Jack, "my dad would punch his transfer. Then, certain motormen up front in the car would sell the guy a shot of whiskey from what amounted to a tiny speakeasy being operated right out of the streetcar."[8]

Naturally, the older Lanigan assumed his only son would be a Democrat. Young Jack would undoubtedly become a Democrat like most of the other pupils at St. Adrian's Catholic grammar school or just like little Michael Madigan, a younger Irish kid growing up across South Campbell Avenue from the Lanigans. This was the same Michael Madigan who would become an ironhanded Democratic speaker of the Illinois House decades later. But a Democrat young Jack was not to be. Contrary to most around him, Lanigan felt that the public interest was not always well served by Democratic control of Chicago because it posed "a threat to the necessary two-party system in my part of the world." Also, Lanigan had a crush in college days on a young Lithuanian woman who was an active Republican. The romance did not last, said Lanigan, "but her political influence certainly did."

Lanigan's going to college did fulfill a wish of his father, who very much wanted his son to be "a white collar." In reality, Jack did not need much convincing after the job experiences he had during his student days. At eighteen,

Lanigan became a "station agent" at Chicago's Midway Airport for an airline that was, he recalled, "the only one to my knowledge to fly nonstop from Midway to Gary, Indiana, a trip for which the one-way passenger fare was $2.50." His duties? He described them as follows: "I took reservations, wrote up tickets, filed flight plans, calculated takeoff weights, ordered gasoline for the planes, unloaded the baggage and cargo from the planes, delivered and picked up mail for the flights and, finally, I was the guy who ushered the planes out onto the runway to take off and who ushered them into parking places. I did everything but fly the darn planes." Later, Lanigan quit the airline and went to work for what he said was "an outfit that gassed, oiled and dumped the johns for planes landing at Midway." On occasion, Jack got to service planes carrying celebrities of the magnitude of Gene Autry and Rocky Marciano, moments he could brag about.

Then there were occasions such as the one on an extremely cold night when a Mexican airliner stopped at Midway for servicing. Jack still winced years later when he talked about it. "When we hooked up the 'turd hearse' for draining the on-board toilets, we did not hook it up properly. The connecting hose came off, and I and several others were drenched with you know what. We had to be washed down right there in that freezing Midway hangar. It was a tremendous growing experience, the kind of thing that gave me real incentive to make it through college."

Make it, Lanigan did, graduating from DePaul University in 1959 with a degree in accounting and commerce. Positions with various accounting firms followed, along with a jump into politics. Lanigan met Richard Ogilvie for the first time at a political gathering at Republic Savings and Loan in 1962, during the sheriff's race. When Lanigan made a strong but losing bid for a Chicago aldermanic seat in 1963, Ogilvie, by then sheriff, came into Lanigan's Thirteenth Ward to give him a hand. The next year, Ogilvie and his undersheriff, Thirteenth Ward GOP leader Ed Kucharski, backed Lanigan for an Illinois Senate seat from southwest Chicago. Lanigan also was aided by a strange new breed for his locale, Republicans on the public payroll, thanks to patronage from Sheriff Ogilvie's office. Lanigan won, edging out Democrat Edmund Sweeney by about a thousand votes, a major upset. Without Ogilvie's help, which included personal appearances, the new senator said that he "would not have made it." Lanigan was reelected to the Senate in 1966, beating Sweeney again, this time by some nineteen thousand votes. Appreciative of Ogilvie's continuing support and, even more, of Ogilvie's rejuvenation of the GOP in Cook County, Lanigan was quick to get behind the Ogilvie candidacy for governor.

Nevertheless, Lanigan refused to commit himself to support of the income tax when Ogilvie proposed it, pointing out that "80 percent of the Republican [Senate] members just did not want an income tax of any kind, including Arrington and Harris, the two who had to convince the rest of us to go for it. Yet, at the same time, many of us realized that we had to take some responsibility to support a governor of our own party, even though he was not very popular with the Republican majority after coming out for the income tax. In addition, I for one knew we'd have to pass some kind of tax increase because of our obviously serious budget balancing problems."[9]

Not long after becoming governor, Ogilvie gave Lanigan a little lift by signing a bill that Lanigan had pushed through the General Assembly with surprising speed. The shortly worded measure authorized a brief period of silence each morning in public school classrooms in order to permit, as Lanigan put it, "an opportunity for silent prayer or for silent reflection on the anticipated activities of the day." The legislation, frowned upon by some who saw it as a possible source of mischief in the then-simmering church-state relationship issue, was written by Senate GOP staffer Don Tolva to counter, recalled Tolva, "the success of atheists in preventing prayers in school at the start of the day."[10] Lanigan got the impression that Ogilvie was not very comfortable with his approval of the bill. Lanigan also remembered, though, Ogilvie looking up at the much taller senator after signing the measure in the governor's office and saying with an impish grin, "Well, I hope I'll have a few more important things to sign than this legislation."[11]

Near the end of the legislative session, Ogilvie was not as genial when he summoned Lanigan to the governor's office for a scolding. The governor told Lanigan he was "fit to be tied" after learning that Lanigan was serving as a go-between from McGloon to various GOP senators. These senators privately agreed with the Democratic stance that an income tax with the same rate for corporations and individuals just was not in the cards. Lanigan acknowledged his role and then tried to convince Ogilvie of the political implausibility of the governor's stance. Ogilvie attempted to press his argument that a variable-rate income tax probably would be held invalid under the Illinois Constitution. Lanigan shot back that "this state is so hard up for funds, Governor, that the [Illinois] Supreme Court would find motherhood unconstitutional to get revenue for the state." The meeting ended with neither Ogilvie nor Lanigan happy with the other.[12]

A few days later, with the Senate vote nearing, Lanigan was asked to return to the governor's office for a more cordial chat. Ogilvie apprised him, said Lanigan, that "he [Ogilvie] sensed momentum going with the Democratic plan for different rates, especially with Daley now in favor of it, and that it looked like that was going to be it." Well, if so, replied Lanigan, he would agree to vote for the income tax as would a number of other Republican senators.

Because the ball game was in the Senate, final rounds of hectic maneuvering consumed the hours leading up to the Senate vote the night of June 27. Ogilvie was in the middle of it all, huddling one moment with Marsh, Drennan, and his other top strategists and then retreating behind closed doors with legislative leaders of both parties. At the climactic juncture, the governor parked Arrington, Speaker Smith, and their top lieutenants in his own office, and he installed McGloon and Touhy in the nearby smaller office of Brian Whalen. Ogilvie then shuttled back and forth, from one office to another, again and again, relaying proposals and counterproposals.

By this point, Ogilvie finally had given up on getting an income tax with the same rate for individuals and corporations. He threw in the towel for good after a final overture to Daley to discuss the matter was rebuffed, after McGloon and Touhy refused to bend in face-to-face encounters with the governor, and in what would be the last straw, after Arrington and Smith determined through a final survey—at Ogilvie's request—that there simply were not enough Republican votes to pass a levy with a 3 percent rate for both individuals and corporations. Consequently, out of that last crucial negotiation, on June 27, emerged the compromise legislative package that would impact taxpayers so heavily for decades.

Under the accord, SB 1150 would be amended to impose a levy of 2.5 percent on the adjusted gross income of individuals and a 4 percent tax on the earnings of corporations. With the enactment of such a levy, everybody was reminded, only the sales tax would provide more revenue for the state.

In a further step considered necessary for Chicago Democratic support, the agreement provided for one-twelfth of the revenue to be rebated to local governments in the form of block grants to aid school districts, reduce real estate taxes, or use for other purposes. The compromise package also allowed municipalities and counties to receive an increased share of the proceeds from the five-cent per dollar state sales tax, another sop to Daleyites. Other parts of the revenue-raising deal included a hike in the state levy on gross receipts from the renting or leasing of hotel rooms and increases in the so-called sin taxes, the state levies on cigarettes, beer, and other alcoholic beverages. Another outgrowth of the compromise, quite significant, was a green light for passage of Ogilvie's ambitious program for improving highways. Besides upping the state motor fuel tax and vehicle registration fees, the program featured as its center-piece the establishment of a trust authority empowered to issue $2 billion in bonds to finance road building and repairs.

In all respects, with so many tax hikes coming at one time, the scope of the revenue-generating package could only be described as grandiose. It was no wonder that, even with Ogilvie, Daley, and the most powerful senators in tow, the vote in the upper chamber on the income tax compromise still was shaping up as too close for comfort for the proponents. At the eleventh hour, Ogilvie took it on himself to personally woo two often independent black Democratic senators from Chicago, Richard Newhouse and Charles Chew, and their poten-tially vital votes. Meeting alone with the two men, Ogilvie confided to them that, in exchange for yes votes on the income levy, he would support giving the Illinois Fair Employment Practices Commission the power to initiate investi-gations instead of waiting for complaints. So Chew and Newhouse agreed to vote for the tax.

In the end, SB 1150 passed with a few votes to spare. In spite of Hudson Sours's last-ditch lament to a hushed chamber that he viewed the occasion as "a rather drab day for the people of Illinois," the income tax was approved by the Senate, thirty-five to twenty-one. At least, that was the tally announced after the vote. Later, the *Journal of the Senate* put the vote at thirty-five to twenty-two.[13] Twenty-one Republicans and fourteen Democrats, all of the latter from Chicago, voted for it. Negative votes, according to the journal, were cast by five Democrats, assistant minority leader Alan J. Dixon of Belleville, and the three other downstate Democrats plus Chicagoan Daniel Dougherty, along with seventeen Republicans. Leading the GOP opposition were Sours and other flag bearers for the old guard, people like Karl Berning of Deerfield, Mount Vernon's ultraconservative Paul W. Broyles, Pekin's Egbert B. Groen, and news-paper publisher John W. Carroll of Park Ridge. Up to the last minute, these individuals were warning other GOP conservatives voting for the tax, like Jack Lanigan, that unhappy constituents might not forget them in the 1970 election. When Lanigan in fact did lose his seat in 1970, he had no doubt that a reason for his defeat was his support for the income levy.

Compared to its ordeal in the Senate, SB 1150 was expected to sail through the House, though not without histrionics. Unlike the Senate with its huge GOP majority, Republican control of the House was by a narrower margin, ninety-five to eighty-two. So a lot more Democratic votes were available for the income levy in the lower chamber. In addition, GOP opposition to the tax in the House did not appear as fierce.

Numerous unsuccessful attempts were launched in the House to amend or change the already compromised income tax measure. One was a move by Choate to further cut the rate for individuals from 2.5 percent to 2 percent. He contended that the negotiated overall revenue package would give the state a general revenue surplus of more than $200 million by the end of fiscal 1970, which to Choate was "a considerable over-soaking" of taxpayers.[14] The job of rebutting such efforts fell to a young Republican representative who was steering the measure on the House floor. He was soft-spoken Edward Madigan from Lincoln, who suddenly found himself in the limelight, deftly fielding questions on the tax. This same Edward Madigan would go on to earn wide respect as a ten-term congressman from central Illinois and then as secretary of agriculture in the administration of President George Bush.

The House vote on SB 1150 was taken the night of June 30, a few hours before the General Assembly ended the session. The bill passed, ninety-one to seventy-three, with sixty-nine Republicans and twenty-two Democrats in support and twenty-five Republicans and forty-eight Democrats, including Choate, opposing it. (A handful of House members either voted present or were not recorded as voting.) Even with the bill in its compromise form, with the lower tax rate for individuals, many downstate House Democrats fought the levy to the end. A bit of Democratic sleight of hand also was evident with the vote itself. Numerous Democrats signaled yes on the electronic tallying board while the voting was in progress but switched to no just before the final count was recorded when it became obvious that their votes were not needed for passage. Thus, the recorded vote made it look as if backing for the income tax in the House came primarily from Republicans. This was only the start of the predictable effort by Democrats to avoid blame later.

When Ogilvie right away signed the bill July 1, he invited the Democratic legislative leaders to join their GOP counterparts at the ceremony in his office. The Democrats did not show up. Noting the Democrats' absence, Ogilvie suggested that "strong public recognition should be given to the Republican leadership . . . for the adoption of a revenue program to meet the needs of the state." And then he added pointedly, "Credit is also due to the Democratic leadership of both houses for participation in the agreement which led to passage of the revenue program."[15] Later, when asked by the press whom Illinoisans should blame for the income tax, Ogilvie averred that there was "no matter of blame involved." Instead, the governor expressed trust that "the people will accept the verdict of their duly elected representatives."[16]

The legislature did take one firm step to soften public anger over the income levy by voting to submit to the electorate in 1970 a proposed state constitutional amendment that would eliminate the hated personal property tax on individuals. Needless to say, the amendment was ratified by voters.

As for the new income tax, its validity was challenged in several suits filed immediately. As Ogilvie feared, the plaintiffs argued that the different rates for individuals and corporations violated the Illinois Constitution. These suits were rebuffed by the Illinois Supreme Court. Implementation of the tax proceeded.

With the start of its collection, resentment of the levy magnified. The indignation was aimed largely at Ogilvie—some of it within earshot, from boos at the Illinois State Fair to insults as he made the gubernatorial rounds. To his credit, Ogilvie, while maintaining publicly that the tax was a truly bipartisan one, confessed that the levy had damaged his image. Whalen would not forget one lunch at the Illini Country Club in Springfield when Ogilvie, certain the tax would pass, told his youthful aide, "I am now the most unpopular person in Illinois. It will be a tough road on this, but we'll do our best."[17]

Many others with access to Ogilvie claimed to have heard the same sentiment from him. But the governor almost always added that Illinoisans would be forgiving once they saw all the improvements that the tax would make possible. John McCarter diagnosed quite accurately the challenge facing Ogilvie's crew when he underscored the "enormous burden" facing the administration in "trying to do things in the course of the next several years to show how the [income tax] dollars were being productively spent . . . to live down the reputation of Richard Ogilvie [as] being the governor who passed the income tax."[18] Even insiders like McCarter were not aware, though, of the extent of the political damage to Ogilvie.

Years later, Jerry Marsh disclosed that Tom Drennan took polls in the spring of 1969, apparently unknown even to Ogilvie, that revealed the political abyss in which the tax proposal placed Ogilvie. After being a "pretty popular governor in March," related Marsh, Drennan found Ogilvie's approval rating to have plummeted like a lead balloon following his April 1 call for the tax. Yet Marsh noted that Drennan's advice in regard to the income tax had been that "we do exactly what we did. Do it right, do it early, and work like hell to recover."[19]

After all, Marsh contended in looking back, had Ogilvie bypassed the income tax issue, the results would have been so disastrous for the state that "your ability to lead, your reputation for effective leadership would have become so severely limited that you then would have had another kind of problem." To Marsh, Ogilvie exhibited no stronger qualities as governor than in his drive for the income levy. It reflected Ogilvie's commitment to "do the right thing." In

Marsh's mind, Ogilvie's insistence on doing "the right thing" was "a repeated decision and attitude throughout the Ogilvie administration that came right from the Governor, and made a big difference. It was what kept those splendid people that he recruited . . . it was the rewarding experience of working for him . . . it was the concern with substance. It was just doing the right thing."

Whether or not Ogilvie's push for the income tax did indeed bring him his finest hour, as Marsh and others seemed to feel, no doubt existed about the mark that the levy left on almost every person that had any connection with its passage—be it Marsh or McCarter or even Clifford B. Latherow. Latherow was one of the Republican pillars of the Illinois Senate in 1969, a straight-shooting farmer from Hancock County who was very hesitant, for a politician, to seek any recognition for himself. Thus, one had to wonder what Latherow might have thought if he could have read the *Chicago Tribune* obituary on his death in 1994. Senator Latherow, wrote the newspaper, "helped establish his courage by voting for the highly unpopular income tax sponsored by Gov. Richard B. Ogilvie."[20]

More Ogilvie Coups

So far, so good. No, more than that. The governorship of Richard Ogilvie was the talk of the town. In just six months in office, Ogilvie had already tasted victory on enough of his bulging agenda to guarantee his brand on Illinois government.

Bill Harris told Ogilvie, after he had signed the income tax bill, that the just-concluded session of the General Assembly was "absolutely astounding" in regard to "the many serious issues that were dealt with constructively." To find anything comparable legislatively, Senator Harris swore, one would have to go back more than half a century.[1]

"Ogilvie Pushed Through Most of His Big Program," declared the *Post-Dispatch*. "Ogilvie Gains National Attention," blared *Chicago Today* in another headline. Given that most governors covet the national spotlight, Ogilvie press secretary Fred Bird wanted to make certain that his boss saw the piece in *Today*. Written by political editor Norton Kay, the analysis led off stating that Ogilvie's "first 6 months in office have made him a national political figure." Passage of the income tax, Kay wrote, "will label him nationally as a 'responsible' leader—one willing to put the welfare of his state ahead of political expediency." Getting to the heart of things, Kay painted Ogilvie as a possible running mate for President Nixon in 1972. Or Ogilvie might be a contender himself for the White House in 1976. Of course, the latter speculation assumed Ogilvie would be re-elected governor in 1972. Through it all, conjectured Kay, "national Republican leaders and national political reporters—who help make or break candidacies—will be watching Ogilvie." But, added Kay, Ogilvie "certainly ranks ahead of many of his potential rivals at this time," including the native Illinoisan and former movie actor serving as governor of California, Ronald Reagan.[2]

Bird handed the Kay piece to Ogilvie as he left the Statehouse to join Mrs. Ogilvie for lunch at the Governor's Mansion. The day was agreeably warm, not the scorcher that Springfield is known for in July, and the governor could afford for the moment to let himself bask in the realization that an extraordinary number of things were going his way. Ogilvie often lunched with Dorothy at the mansion when he was in Springfield. On summer days like this one, they frequently were joined by their teenaged daughter Elizabeth, Ogilvie's "Tin

Lizzie" as he called her during the days when she wore braces on her teeth. This was also one of those luncheons to which Jim Hickey was invited.

Hickey, curator of the Abraham Lincoln collection at the Illinois State Historical Library, was helping to carry out a rather covert assignment for Dick and Dorothy Ogilvie. He was privately conducting research and mapping strategy at the Ogilvies' direction for the restoration of the Governor's Mansion.[3] The mansion, built in the 1850s on a knoll at the south edge of downtown Springfield, suffered chronic structural problems by the time the Ogilvie family moved into the place—windows that wouldn't shut, weak floors in need of shoring. And there were incidents like Elizabeth putting a foot through bathroom floor tiles. These problems convinced the governor and first lady that overhaul of the mansion could be delayed no longer.

As he sat at lunch on this July day with his wife, his daughter, and Hickey, the governor still was turning over in his mind all that had occurred in his first General Assembly session. Besides the income levy and the other tax hikes, legislators had given the green light for Ogilvie's reorganization of the penal system and for the revamping of the state's law enforcement activities. Legislators also okayed Ogilvie's new Department of Local Government Affairs as well as Ogilvie's request for a record increase in state aid to public education and the sprawling highway building program. Little argument could be made with one newspaper's conclusion that, while GOP traditionalists watched in disbelief, Ogilvie won approval of programs so large in their concepts and costs that "the Governor's Democratic predecessors look like pikers."[4]

Yet as satisfying as it was to reflect on these developments, Ogilvie entertained no idea of relaxing. He had miles to go in his reshaping of Illinois government, much to be accomplished to justify his massive tax-and-spend policies. The momentum for governmental reform was infecting the whole scene, bringing into play other proven or intended good-government types. Ogilvie knew that he had to stay ahead in the movement he was generating. Others— like Paul Simon—would be trying to steal Ogilvie's thunder wherever they could. Yes, even Ogilvie's long-standing friend and Republican colleague, Attorney General Bill Scott, was clearly attempting to establish himself as the premier Illinois official in the war against pollution, a hot-ticket subject. Ogilvie recognized that he would have to try to not let that happen.

By any measure, there certainly was no shortage of Ogilvie initiatives. Back in May, he made front-page news by revealing a plan to move more than seven thousand elderly persons in state mental hospitals to private nursing homes and sheltered-care facilities. He allowed that the shift made sense fiscally because care in state hospitals required more tax funds than supervision in licensed private places. The governor also justified the move on compassionate grounds, saying that these were not individuals seriously sick but people institutionalized "simply because they have no where else to go." Moving out the elderly would go far to combat what Ogilvie called "the hated poor farm image" of the state hospital system.[5]

Ogilvie also had been following up on his campaign promise to work for the selection of Illinois as the site for a second major airport for the St. Louis metropolitan area. He proved his intent by naming a special transportation counsel to supervise all state actions to land the airport in Illinois. He knew an airport would be a great economic stimulator for East St. Louis and much of southern Illinois. So he picked John E. Robson, a Chicago attorney and former undersecretary of the U.S. Department of Transportation, to be his special counsel on the new St. Louis airport project. In stressing that Robson would function within his immediate purview, Ogilvie was making it clear that he had "decided to personally call the shots on this matter," according to an aide.[6]

As for East St. Louis, Ogilvie already had played one of those special cards he had been holding for the poverty-wracked city. At his request, the General Assembly passed bipartisan legislation authorizing an experimental junior college in East St. Louis focusing on vocational and technical training. Called the State Community College, it would be quite unique. No local tax would be imposed for its operation, and the school would serve the only junior college district in Illinois created specifically by state law and governed directly by the Illinois Junior College Board. High unemployment and certain other problems peculiar to East St. Louis demanded creation of the facility on an emergency basis, Ogilvie recognized. Yet, he realized, as did others, that the local tax base just could not provide the necessary dollars for it.

At this point, Ogilvie had sat in elective office for seven straight years. He attributed his rise to governor to sticking to certain fundamental tenets for success in public life. One was to never lose control or the appearance of leadership in any situation within his reach, be it riot prevention as Cook County sheriff or any part of public policy susceptible to the broad authority of the governor's office. He abhorred buck-passing anyway. While aware of the danger in getting out too far ahead of his flock, Ogilvie never wanted anyone to doubt that he was the person behind the steering wheel.

Because Ogilvie remained in heart and mind a political realist with both feet on the ground, he did not have to be reminded that the plaudits now coming his way could turn to raspberries overnight. For proof, Ogilvie had to look only at the fickleness of the political columnists, the ones finding him to be presidential timber one week and then hardly fit to be a dogcatcher a month later.

Calling it ephemeral would not cover it. Take Norton Kay. Here he was picturing Ogilvie as a national political figure in 1969, and three years later, he would be scurrying to defeat Ogilvie as the press aide to Dan Walker, Ogilvie's Democratic opponent in the 1972 governor's race.

Ogilvie's situation seemed stable midway through 1969. Yet the pot never stopped boiling, not even outside his own office. Ogilvie and his office crew could have done without the black and white supporters of the Cairo United Front who enlivened the dog days of summer with noisy demonstrations on the governor's doorstep. Pressing for a meeting with Ogilvie to push their campaign for emergency aid for the racially troubled city, United Front leaders engaged in sit-ins at Ogilvie's outer office. Their followers, including a number of nuns, chanted and shouted in the hall outside his office. More than once, demonstrators were arrested on charges of disorderly conduct. Undaunted, they pledged to continue pressuring Ogilvie to act on one or more of the United Front's recommendations. Although put off by tactics of the United Front, Ogilvie had not ignored Cairo. He had met with clergy concerned about racial hostility in the town, and he had ordered more state troopers to the Cairo area. Ogilvie also sought repeal of an old Illinois law permitting the formation of vigilante groups after critics alleged that a Cairo vigilante organization known as the White Hats had been set up to keep blacks "in line."

Some of the difficulties looming elsewhere for Ogilvie were more controllable than Cairo. Several weeks before the end of the General Assembly session, Ogilvie got wind of an inquiry by the *Chicago Tribune* and Better Government Association into possible wrongdoing on contracts at the Illinois State Fair. Without hesitation, the governor set the machinery in motion for the state police and also federal agents to probe into the matter. In so doing, Ogilvie precluded his administration from any accusation of negligence in case the investigation proved fruitful, which it did.

In all honesty, the Illinois State Fair was a ready-made situation for Ogilvie to turn to his advantage while striking a blow for good government. Ogilvie of course knew the working of the BGA inside out. Moreover, the governor's top person on administration internal security, state revenue director George Mahin, ran the BGA before joining Ogilvie. After the BGA-*Tribune* survey uncovered telltale signs of contract fraud, Ogilvie received a request from his new fair manager, Jacksonville broadcasting executive Raymond W. Phipps, for an investigator to assist Phipps in clarifying certain aspects of the fair's operation. Ogilvie relayed the request to Mahin, who ordered Curtis Marsh, a former FBI agent, to aid Phipps. Shortly afterward, Marsh predictably determined that goings-on at the fair merited a full-blown investigation, an undertaking that soon included the state police and later representatives of the IRS and other federal agents.

Choreographed by Ogilvie, the investigation was in high gear as the 1969 fair went through its ten-day August run in Springfield. When it ended, the governor took the investigation public, charging that the annual exposition with its great agricultural exhibits, dazzling midway, and star performers was also "a grab bag for shady operators with political connections."[7] In the last several years, Ogilvie contended, the state had lost more than $500,000 in revenue from alleged mismanagement at the fair, including irregularities in the handling of concession contracts. Early the following year, as a result of the investigation, a grand jury in Sangamon County indicted the former fair manager, Franklin H. Rust, and others on charges of official misconduct in connection with the leasing of space at the fair. However, Rust, former Governor Kerner's choice to run the fair during most of the 1960s, was acquitted of the charges.

The fair scandal had more than one connotation for Ogilvie. The way he handled the matter, especially by directing the investigation, embellished his reputation as a stand-up individual against governmental corruption. At the same time, the messiness at the fair was one of the first—although hardly the most far-reaching—in a string of unsavory situations that tarnished the character of Illinois government during Ogilvie's years in office. The period when Ogilvie sat in the governor's chair coincided, as it turned out, with a dark era in Illinois public life, years in which officialdom was rocked by one scandal after another. Their frequency would leave Illinoisans dismayed and then angered at both the ethical decay of government in their state and the moral failings of those entrusted to run government.

It was a time of great trouble. Nothing more symbolized it than the downfall of Otto Kerner. Kerner went to prison following his years as governor after he was found guilty in a criminal trial of federal tax evasion and other charges stemming from ignominious racing track stock deals while he was governor. He was hardly alone, though. During the administrations of Ogilvie and his successor, Dan Walker, a seemingly endless parade of officials from all levels in the state were herded into court on charges of malfeasance. According to a report by the U.S. Department of Justice, Illinois was way ahead of other states from 1970 through 1976 in the number of state and local officials convicted on federal charges of accepting bribes, engaging in extortion, and other offenses. To be fair, Ogilvie could point out as could Walker that these individuals were not from their administrations. For the record, Ogilvie had no ties whatsoever to the well-known figures or the chicanery, no links to the crooks and their cronies. Walker ran for governor as an alternative to all of the underhanded stuff—which made even more ironic his own imprisonment in the years after he was the Illinois chief executive on federal financial felony charges unrelated to his governorship.

Other chapters in this troubled era could not be stage-managed by Ogilvie like the investigation of the State Fair. Furthermore, the imbroglio at the fair soon was eclipsed by the disclosures that brought disrepute to the Illinois Supreme Court in the summer of 1969. Even though the justices of the high court were elected to their seats in partisan contests, an aura of sanctimony enveloped the panel and its deliberations, shielding the court from the scrutiny routinely applied to the executive and legislative branches of Illinois government. In view of that, pundits could not hide their surprise at the fast pace of the court's discomposure after Ed Pound and Ande Yakstis broke a story in the *Alton Telegraph* in June 1969 that could not be ignored.

Following up on information supplied by Sherman Skolnick, the *Telegraph* disclosed that Justice Ray I. Klingbiel of Moline may have been guilty of a conflict of interest for accepting stock in Chicago's Civic Center Bank and Trust Company in 1966—before he wrote an opinion in favor of Theodore Isaacs, an officer and general counsel for the bank. The gist of the story was that Klingbiel received the stock, composed of one hundred shares valued at the time at $2,000, through an intermediary, Robert M. Perbohner, a member of the Illinois Commerce Commission. Klingbiel, a Republican, allegedly got the stock from Perbohner, a Rockford resident and fellow Republican, shortly after Isaacs transferred it to Perbohner. Although Klingbiel was reported to have received the stock in 1966, the transfer of it was not registered until late in 1968 when, based on files in the office of the Cook County recorder, the shares were transferred to two grandchildren of Klingbiel in the care of the justice. In the meantime, the Illinois Supreme Court opinion on Isaacs written by Klingbiel was handed down in 1967. The opinion upheld an earlier lower-court action dismissing charges against Isaacs of collusion and conspiracy over irregularities in state purchasing. The allegations, returned by a Sangamon grand jury in 1964, grew out of a disclosure that Isaacs owned part of a Chicago firm that sold more than $1 million in envelopes to the state during Otto Kerner's first term as governor. Isaacs, a Chicago attorney, was the state revenue director during most of Kerner's first term and a political confidant of the governor.

The *Telegraph's* revelation of Klingbiel's tie to the bank stock ignited a fast-moving scenario. Pound achieved the statewide journalistic splash he so desired, the first of many for the young investigative reporter. The big Chicago daily papers grudgingly tipped their hats to the *Telegraph*, which was part of the downstate Illinois newspaper world that the Chicagoans liked to label the pygmy press. Another offshoot was that Skolnick was finally on the map. Many still considered him more than a little eccentric, but reporters no longer gave him the brush-off.

Few episodes of Illinois political impropriety would have more of a David and Goliath angle than this one. Skolnick, crippled from an attack of polio when he was a child, forced to spend most of his time in a wheelchair, was facing in the Illinois Supreme Court an adversary as formidable for him as was the biblical Philistine giant for David. Earlier, Skolnick had failed to recover through the Illinois courts an inheritance from his parents that a broker had lost through poor investing. At that point, Skolnick had vowed to devote his energies to helping others fight for fair treatment in a judicial system that Skolnick believed to be fraught with incompetent and dishonest judges. During the 1960s, Skolnick buried himself in a library of used law books that he had accumulated. He thus became as knowledgeable about the law as many persons with formal legal training. When notoriety came his way, the press called him a legal researcher. However, Skolnick preferred to be known as a "court critic." Others unhappy with the courts volunteered to help Skolnick, leading to the formation of the Illinois Citizens' Committee to Clean Up the Courts, a loose umbrella organization for Skolnick and his band.

In Illinois, cases in which the conduct of public officials is challenged seldom are resolved overnight. The Illinois Supreme Court situation would prove to be an exception. A special committee of the Illinois House was established immediately to investigate the background of judicial actions throughout the state, including the possibility that improper circumstances may have clouded the state high court's ruling on Isaacs in 1967. Through petition filing and daily give-and-take with the media, Skolnick and his committee were demanding a thorough investigation of the Isaacs ruling. Numerous reporters joined in the questioning, and new information was surfacing almost every day, including the discovery that Chief Justice Roy J. Solfisburg Jr. also had acquired Civic Center Bank stock when the Isaacs matter was coming before the court.

It would turn out, though, that the Illinois Supreme Court itself took the most decisive action when it created, through an order of its own, a special commission of five lawyers to look specifically into the integrity of the Isaacs ruling. Heading the panel was Frank Greenberg, president of the Chicago Bar Association. Also serving was Henry L. Pitts, president of the Illinois State Bar Association. At first, the commission drew skepticism that its inquiry would be little more than perfunctory. But that suspicion evaporated after the panel conducted a public hearing in Chicago in July 1969 on the matter. In spite of a bizarre twist or two at the hearing, none of the observers at the crowded proceeding at Chicago's Civic Center went away with an impression that the commission was engaging in a whitewash. Quite the opposite, it seemed obvious that the hearing could not have been much more damaging for Solfisburg and Klingbiel.

In less than a month, a professional staff retained by the commission turned up considerable information about the two justices' receipt of stock—before the Isaacs opinion was delivered—in the Civic Center Bank and Trust. Plowing ahead in a manner that sometimes left tempers frayed, attorneys for the commission sought to show that the two jurists both received their shares under unusual circumstances and attempted to conceal their holdings from the public. Moreover, the commission staff, headed by Chicago attorney John Paul Stevens, who later would become a justice of the U.S. Supreme Court, endeavored to confirm that Isaacs, an organizer of the bank, was connected with the shares that reached Klingbiel and Solfisburg. Although these matters already had been asserted in media disclosures, the hearing still brought out or underlined facets of the justices' stock deals not fully known previously. For instance, it was substantiated that the late Robert Dolph of Aurora played a role, along with Perbohner, in funneling stock to Klingbiel and Dolph's friend Solfisburg. Like Perbohner, Dolph was serving on the commerce commission at the time of his death in 1968.

At the hearing, Klingbiel admitted that he had not told the truth about his receipt of the bank stock, especially in contending earlier to reporters and another Illinois Supreme Court justice, Thomas E. Kluczynski, that he bought the shares. Instead, Klingbiel testified that he received his stock free as a contribution from Perbohner and Dolph for the justice's successful campaign to retain his seat on the court in the November 1966 election. He conceded in his testimony that the election was held before he received the stock. Although conflicting statements had circulated on the financing of Klingbiel's stock, the air was cleared when the commission was informed of bank files showing that Isaacs paid $2,087 in October 1966 for the shares that eventually went to Klingbiel. After Isaacs paid for the stock, it was issued in the name of Perbohner. Insisting at the hearing that he thought his shares were purchased by Perbohner, Klingbiel lamented before leaving the witness stand that "had I known in any way that Isaacs had anything to do with the passing of the stock to me, I would not have participated in the Isaacs decision." Added Klingbiel, "This is a sad affair for me, after 68 years of age."[8]

Stevens utilized testimony of a former employee of the bank to show that instructions for the issuance of Solfisburg's stock came from the office of Isaacs. Solfisburg himself testified that he was approached on the purchase of Civic

Center Bank's stock by Perbohner and Dolph late in 1965, but not until May 1966 did he buy seven hundred shares for $14,000. Solfisburg's shares were issued to an Aurora bank trust that he created at the time. The trust never contained any items except the stock and proceeds from its later sale, testimony revealed. The chief justice began to sell his shares at a profit days after the high court finished its consideration of the Isaacs case. As Solfisburg sold his shares, the certificates were delivered to an Isaacs office in Chicago instead of the bank.

As if the hearing was not animated enough, Skolnick further enlivened the proceeding by openly second-guessing its conduct as he sat in his wheelchair facing the main participants. More than once, Greenberg, who was presiding at the hearing, rebuked Skolnick for trying to make a mockery of the situation. Skolnick refused to supply the commission with material supporting some of his charges against the justices, and he was briefly jailed at one point after a Cook County circuit judge held him in contempt for ignoring a court order to answer certain questions pertinent to the investigation. He was bailed out by a friend, Dick Gregory, the comedian and civil rights activist. Skolnick was reluctant to cooperate with the commission, he maintained, because in his words the panel was "a farcical one that will only end up laundering the whole mess."[9] No Illinois lawyer would jeopardize his future by recommending any strong action against a state supreme court justice, Skolnick argued.

However, the commission demonstrated otherwise by calling for the immediate resignation of Solfisburg and Klingbiel, charging that they were clearly guilty of impropriety in the Illinois Supreme Court's handling of the Isaacs case. The commission underscored that the justices undoubtedly violated Illinois Judicial Conference ethics and declared that the Isaacs affair had so shaken public confidence that it could best be restored by the resignation of the two judges. Within a few days, both complied with the commission's request.

With the two justices' departure in early August, the drama of the scandal was over—ending almost before it began. More than finding itself suddenly shorthanded, the court was down-and-out, the collapse of its majesty coming as quickly as the never-to-be-forgotten crumble in September 1969 of the seemingly invincible Chicago Cubs. The first really explosive chapter of this troubled era would stand out for its compactness, for the dispatch with which the matter was addressed and resolved, as if it were neatly packaged and tied up so as to leave hardly any loose ends. That would not be the case further along in the era.

Actually, a disruption as cataclysmic as the state supreme court upheaval could not help but leave unfinished business, none more insidious than that concerning Isaacs. When former governor Kerner was indicted late in 1971 on a variety of federal charges tied to allegedly illicit transactions involving racing stock, many Illinoisans were stunned. However, few who follow such things were surprised that one of those indicted with Kerner was his pal Isaacs, whom federal officials found to be part and parcel of the stock manipulations that profited both men very handsomely. As was Kerner, Isaacs was convicted and sent to prison in the racetrack stock scandal. Because Kerner had once been so esteemed, many supporters were to angrily point to Isaacs as the cause of Kerner's undoing, an accusation that may or may not have been fair. Hardly arguable, though, was the unique place that Isaacs reserved for himself in the state's political annals. Much more than a historical footnote, the slightly owlish Isaacs had a heavy hand in the demise of a governor and the exit of two state supreme court justices.

While the Illinois Supreme Court's woes unfolded in the summer of 1969, Ogilvie's only reaction publicly was to remove Perbohner from his $23,000-a-year seat on the commerce commission. In an order filed with Secretary of State Paul Powell, the governor said the sixty-nine-year-old Perbohner had to go because of his "incompetency and neglect of duty."[10]

As for the long run, Ogilvie felt that the high court scandal certainly magnified the need for reform in the Illinois judiciary. Ogilvie, like others, saw the upcoming Illinois Constitutional Convention as a golden opportunity to bring about judicial revision. Addressing the convention's opening session on December 8, 1969, Ogilvie recommended urgent consideration of judicial reform in the "light of recent events."[11] Then during convention deliberations in 1970, Ogilvie injected himself into the heated debate over whether to appoint or elect judges. Not surprisingly, Ogilvie pushed for governor-appointed judges. The Illinois Bar Association and a lot of other groups sided with Ogilvie on this, but not Mayor Daley. Ogilvie would not win.

Even so, the new Illinois Constitution coming out of the convention did establish a more forceful disciplinary structure for judges. It was a two-tier setup in which a new body, the Judicial Inquiry Board, was empowered to investigate complaints against judges and, if deemed necessary, file misconduct charges with the Illinois Courts Commission, an adjudicatory panel. The board would not be controlled by judges. The commission, composed entirely of judges, had the power to remove a judge from office or impose other penalties in acting on complaints from the board. Since charges filed by the board with the commission became public, the old days in which judges essentially were allowed to clean their house in private were dead.

The new constitution dictated that seven of the nine members of the Judicial Inquiry Board, to be named by the governor, could not be judges. The governor's seriousness on this matter was illustrated by the caliber of his appointees, people like Richard T. Dunn, Frank Greenberg, Wayne W. Whalen, and Anne Willer. Bloomington lawyer Dunn, best known as a former commanding general in the Illinois National Guard, became the first chairman of the board. Greenberg, a hero to numerous court reform advocates, had chaired the commission that called for the resignations of Solfisburg and Klingbiel. But more than a few judges considered Greenberg an enemy. Ogilvie's naming of Whalen, an attorney, and Hillside's Willer also irritated many in the judiciary because the two had supported a strong judicial discipline system at the Illinois Constitutional Convention. Within a few years, the board had filed enough complaints with the commission, leading to the removal or suspension of a number of judges, to show that the inquiry panel did indeed mean business.

The creation of the Judicial Inquiry Board was what governmental reformers wanted to see throughout the document to be proposed by the constitutional convention. Constitutional change may have been a sexless subject to most residents of Illinois, but for governmental purists the convention presented a unique chance to update the charter that governed them.

Since the convention would be the first of its kind in Illinois in close to a half century, hardly anybody on the state governmental stage knew what to expect. Ogilvie already had been active on some of the issues that prompted the call for the convention. But he also was aware that he would be walking a political tightrope regarding the convention. He could not ignore it, which of course he never intended to do, but at the same time, he sensed that he had to avoid an aggressiveness toward the convention that might be construed as an attempt by the governor to dominate it.

Unless things got out of hand, the convention had great potential for putting a positive spin on Ogilvie's second year as governor. Ogilvie wanted great changes, and he did much to bring this about during his initial year in office. The convention could serve to significantly assist Ogilvie in reaching his goal. It could provide an added bonus for Ogilvie's governorship, which already was off to such a flying start. So far so good.

The Constitutional Convention: A Triumph amid Setbacks

"Con Con"

The Illinois Constitutional Convention of 1970 had a good run. Convention delegates pieced together a new governing charter for the state that was accepted by the voting public, something that had not happened in a hundred years. Aside from ceremonial moments, the working of the convention hardly captivated the imagination of Illinoisans. To most of the state's 11,113,976 souls, "Con Con" was an oblivious exercise. Its image as a toy of political elitists may not have been way off base, but many of the changes in basic governmental powers and duties forged at the convention went far beyond cosmetic. Afterward, those bullish on the convention at its start had no hesitation toasting the result with champagne.

No question, the Illinois Constitutional Convention was an uncommon event. Yet it was pretty dry stuff to a citizenry overwhelmed by the passionate, often violent issues of the 1960s and early 1970s. People remained as divided as ever over the Vietnam War, even though American troops were avoiding major battles with the North Vietnamese and Viet Cong early in 1970 and Nixon was reducing U.S. troops in the conflict from 543,000 to 340,000. The upheaval bred by opposition to the war continued to flood the country, including Illinois where the rampaging of rebellious students across university campuses reached a crescendo in 1970. Rewriting the state's constitution just was not a turn-on, nothing like the civil rights or environmental protection movements or other causes that evoked spirited commitment from great crowds.

Nevertheless, the convention persevered. It was a triumph in perseverance for those who wanted it to happen, and it was a triumph in perseverance for those who carried it out to a successful conclusion. Occurring in the wake of the 1960s, a "slum of a decade" as writer Richard Rovere called it, the convention provided a fresh start for the ensuing decade in Illinois. While the new Constitution of 1970 did not go as far in many areas as some desired, its effect on the whole range of Illinois government, on state fiscal policy, on civil rights, and on other fundamental matters was imposing. "Con Con" also was a story of people, big and small, some of whom would go on to larger roles in Illinois public life while others returned to anonymity. Upon second glance years later, the 116 delegates elected to the convention were an interesting group.

For the record, the 1970 convention was the sixth of its kind in Illinois. The first such gathering was at old Kaskaskia in 1818 when frontier delegates in twenty-three days drew up the constitution with which Illinois moved from territorial status to statehood. Of the five conventions before 1970, voters rejected the work of two, the second of which met in the early 1920s. The last successful convention, obviously, was the one that produced the Illinois Constitution of 1870, the charter under which Illinoisans would live for a century. With each new generation, derision of the 1870 document increased until the belittling of it as an outmoded, horse-and-buggy relic became a cliché—accepted by governors and grade school children alike.

David Kenney of Carbondale, a political science professor at Southern Illinois University for many years and a delegate himself to the 1970 convention, put it more urbanely in underlining in a textbook he authored the need for revision of the 1870 constitution.

"In a static society it might be possible for a state's constitution to continue unchanged for long periods of satisfactory service," wrote Kenney. But, he continued, "when social and economic conditions change rapidly however, as has been the case in the last century, and especially so since World War I, in Illinois, then without adequate constitutional change there is increasing ineffectiveness of performance and disparity between what is expected of government and what it can deliver. Under conditions of rapid social change, piecemeal constitutional amendment occasionally will not suffice and a broader revision of the fundamental law becomes necessary. While constitutions deserve respect they have no claim to immortality. Like records of any sort, they exist in one sense only to be revised periodically in the interest of superior performance."[1]

Still, as much as the impetus for a convention picked up steam in the 1960s, not many individuals really thought it would happen as early as it did. From the start, skeptics regarded the drive for rewriting the constitution as a mission of do-gooders in which the workload fell largely on people uninvolved in the workings of state government. Most leading public officials may have openly supported the call for a convention, but many were surprised when the General Assembly in 1967 authorized a vote on the question by the electorate. Subsequent voter approval of the convention call in the November 1968 election raised even more eyebrows. The next big step was the election of convention delegates, two from each of the fifty-eight state senatorial districts, on November 18, 1969. Contrary to some predictions, independents scored enough victories in the balloting to prevent immediate domination of the gathering by either of the two major parties. This was a welcome development to those who believed that a lopsided majority of Republican delegates was a key factor that led to voter rejection of the product of the last Illinois constitutional convention in the early 1920s.[2]

Although the election of delegates to the 1970 event was officially nonpartisan, the best estimates listed about fifty-five delegates as Republicans, forty-five as Democrats, and the rest, sixteen, independent. Lawyers were most numerous, but other principal segments in Illinois society were represented too. In addition, not many viewpoints were excluded. Albert A. Raby and the Reverend Francis X. Lawlor, both elected as independents from Chicago, were proof of that. Raby was a top civil rights leader in the city, and Father Lawlor was known for his militant opposition to the programs of some civil rights groups. In breaking down the delegates into blocs, the largest was comprised loosely of the forty or so downstate Republicans. Next came the thirty-two Chicago Democrats, supported by Mayor Daley and his machine, a contingent that would be the most cohesive group at the convention. It included one of his honor's sons, Richard M. Daley, later a mayor of Chicago himself. Another member of the Chicago-Daley unit was the same Michael Madigan who would emerge later as a speaker of the Illinois House. A twenty-seven-year-old attorney, Madigan was already a Democratic ward committeeman in his city.

As the convention got under way in December 1969, though, Madigan was only one of many in the sea of fresh faces in the Capitol. It was like a gold rush. Jim Mees was typical of a lot of those who suddenly surfaced. Mees was a twenty-four-year-old Peorian, a bright-eyed history major out of St. Olaf College in Minnesota, who just appeared one day in the Statehouse pressroom, declared himself a freelance reporter, and proceeded to gather news for a weekly column that he offered to small papers around the state for $1 a week.[3] When Mees and more veteran reporters tracked convention events, they frequently turned for assistance to another previously unheard of individual, Caroline Gherardini. She was teamed in the convention's information bureau with James Bradley, a former United Press International correspondent in the Statehouse. As with numerous others, "Con Con" was a coming-out party in the public arena for Gherardini, who went on in later years to edit *Illinois Issues,* the state's respected public affairs magazine.

Yet while the world of the constitutional convention may have been awash with unfamiliar faces, it also featured many familiar ones. Its presiding officer was expected to be one of three quite well-known individuals, all Republicans.

They were former state senator David Davis of Bloomington; Elbert S. Smith of Decatur, a onetime state auditor of public accounts; and Samuel W. Witwer, a lawyer from Kenilworth and an energetic advocate of constitutional revision. Witwer was the favorite to win the top post, and win it he did. From that point on, Witwer—a man who in 1946 chaired the Chicago Bar Association's Committee for Constitutional Revision—was without doubt the single most dominant figure at the convention. The delegates also elected three vice presidents, two of whom were Smith and Chicago Democratic attorney Thomas G. Lyons, a Daley delegate.

The third vice president was John Alexander, a community college government teacher from the small town of Virden, south of Springfield. His role at the convention would be intriguing from start to finish. Witwer did not support Alexander for the third vice presidency, thinking it ought to go to a woman, preferably from downstate. However, a number of delegates felt that the post should be filled by one of the convention's younger members. Alexander, who was twenty-seven, sought it and got it. He had been the downstate field director for the Illinois Committee for Constitutional Convention, which worked successfully for voter approval for the convention. Alexander also had been another one of the Ford Foundation Fellows who served as an Illinois legislative intern, one more Sam Gove trooper. He was assigned to Arrington, an experience that left Alexander an independent Republican instead of the young Democrat he had been back in his Monmouth College days.

Alexander's relationship, or lack of one, with the older Witwer soon became a provocative convention sidelight. They just didn't click. Associates of Witwer said he found Alexander to be an officious upstart, while Alexander professed to "never having the word *pompous* in my vocabulary until I met Witwer." The problem, argued Alexander, "was that Witwer did not want any advice from anybody except for the few people he trusted in the convention's good old boy network of white male attorneys."[4] This may have been stretching it, especially since Alexander came to be regarded by many as a convention renegade. Nevertheless, it was true that women and black delegates were excluded from the convention's twelve committee chairmanships, all of which were held by white males, eleven of them attorneys.

Privately speaking, Witwer's punctiliousness in presiding over the convention with the air of a proper Bostonian precipitated a joke among the delegates. At one point, the convention moved from its first home, the Illinois House chamber, to the newly restored Old Capitol in the center of Springfield, the building that housed the convention that wrote the Constitution of 1870. "Putting the convention in the Old Capitol," so the quip went, "is a dramatic way to put this whole matter into perspective. Now the finishing touch would be to have Sam move into the home of Abraham Lincoln."[5]

Witwer's visibility throughout the convention was in utter contrast to Ogilvie's near invisibility. Few of the delegates had any more personal contact with the governor than Alexander, who remembered "no private conversation of any kind with Ogilvie, nothing beyond him shaking my hand on the day I was sworn in as a delegate."[6] The closest thing to the governor's office that most delegates encountered during the long convention days was Ogilvie's lobbyist, a young woman named Paula Wolff. Ogilvie recognized the importance of not appearing to want to openly stampede anything through the convention—which was not supposed to have the partisan character of a General Assembly session. Diplomacy had to be exercised. For this, Ogilvie turned toward a confidant already by his side, Jerry Marsh.

The title worn by Marsh, special counsel to the governor, seemed to give him freehanded entrée to virtually every matter that drew the attention of the governor's office. If any subject of import escaped the eye of Marsh, it was hard to know. Dissecting the makeup of an Illinois governor's palace guard is always good sport for followers of the state's powerful. With some governors, one person would emerge as the first among equals in a small ring of top advisers. Kerner's top adviser was Christopher Vlahoplus, who before joining Kerner was a wire service reporter in the Statehouse pressroom. Walker made no bones about the person who was his top aide, Chicago political strategist Victor de Grazia. When Jim Edgar served as governor in the 1990s, the assistant on whom he usually relied in a pinch was Michael Lawrence, who like so many other gubernatorial staffers had been a Statehouse newsperson. But with Ogilvie, if there was a preeminent figure among Marsh, Whalen, or Drennan, the members of the elite triumvirate most closely surrounding Ogilvie, it was tough to say—whether during his governorship or decades afterward, when each man still disclaimed any friction or territorial rivalry among themselves.

Many Ogilvie watchers saw Marsh as a blocking back for the governor, who ran interference on major issues and other big doings like the constitutional convention. The description fit because Jeremiah Marsh had been a blocking back, literally, when he was a hefty Minnesota farm kid playing football for Harvard in the mid-1950s. As a blocking back on offense and linebacker on defense, Marsh had the right stuff. He played on teams that beat Yale, Ogilvie's school, and Marsh was named an academic all-American. At Harvard, Marsh received an undergraduate degree in anthropology, and then a law degree. Also at Harvard, he became the friend of another football player, Ted Kennedy. After Harvard, Marsh practiced law in Chicago. Marsh first met Ogilvie while he was prosecuting Accardo. Then Marsh worked under Ogilvie when Ogilvie became a partner in Marsh's law firm, Hackbert, Rooks & Pitts, after the Accardo case. Although the two men got close, their paths separated in the early 1960s. Ogilvie was elected sheriff of Cook County, and Marsh departed for Washington to serve as legislative assistant to a newly elected United States senator from Massachusetts, Democrat Ted Kennedy.

Marsh, who had worked in John Kennedy's 1960 presidential campaign in Illinois, regarded himself as a Democrat of sorts or, to be more precise as he worded it, a "political progressive." One thing for sure, Marsh was brought up in a family that revered Wisconsin governor Robert La Follette, a fiery progenitor of social and economic reforms. The stint with Kennedy did not last that long. Yet it provided fodder later on for certain GOP traditionalists to attribute Ogilvie's perceived liberalism as governor to Marsh, whom they viewed as a closet Democrat.

While this was not a valid assessment, it was fair to note that—after Marsh returned from Washington to the Hackbert law firm in Chicago—his becoming counsel to the Better Government Association had a political motive. Douglas F. Stevenson, a partner in the law firm and member of the BGA governing board, helped engineer that move to counter the contention that the BGA was an arm of the GOP. Marsh's link to the BGA put him in more frequent contact with BGA ally Ogilvie. Then Marsh began advising Ogilvie on legal matters. When Ogilvie served as Cook County board president, Marsh served as Ogilvie's eyes and ears. So it was that Marsh found himself, in his phrasing, "gradually growing into a Republican." However, Marsh never would be considered a doctrinaire Republican, as Brian Whalen was. According to Marsh, "The things I did for Ted Kennedy were not that much ideologically different from the things I did for Ogilvie."[7]

Halfway through the 1990s, Marsh appeared to be a healthy survivor of the Ogilvie experience. As the chairman of Hopkins & Sutter, one of Chicago's larger law firms, Marsh occupied a forty-third floor office in one of those tall buildings that offered a commanding view of the Chicago skyline. At this time and place, decades later and high above Chicago, Marsh could think back on Ogilvie's governorship with a lucidity not possible before.

The constitutional convention came easily to mind for Marsh because it took so much of his time for a year. Marsh believed it to be the Ogilvie administration's premier political success, even more so than the passage of the income tax, which Marsh labeled "a political bloodbath."[8] For months after Ogilvie took office, Marsh recalled that "hardly anybody in the Springfield political apparatus took Con Con seriously." But he added that "at some point it dawned on me and perhaps others that this was a big deal." After being assigned to follow the convention, Marsh boned up on the intricacies of the issues likely to be on the table at the convention. He also had his hands in the tactful effort by Ogilvie's office to encourage certain candidacies for delegate seats, mainly by persons not completely beholden to their parties, Republicans as well as Democrats. Ogilvie favored the election of delegates on an officially nonpartisan basis, superficial as it was in many districts. After the delegates were elected, Marsh gathered every tidbit of information he could about each one, even though he would never meet many of them.

Elaborating, Marsh said: "I read and talked to people and learned all I could. I had a pretty good background brief on essentially everybody. The details came from people in our political apparatus who knew many of them or had party people who knew them. I had a pretty good sense of who the delegates were, what they thought was important, what they didn't care about, whether they would respond, who they would respond to. And that went on for almost the whole year of Con Con."

An experience or two prior to the convention underscored for Marsh the sensitivity of many delegates to any wide-open railroading by Ogilvie on the business of the historic proceeding. At a reception for the delegates at the Governor's Mansion, Marsh noted the testy tone of conversation. As Marsh quickly realized, the delegates "did not view themselves the way legislators do," a reference to the receptivity of most lawmakers to unfettered lobbying as a prelude to give-and-take on issues.

The convention delegates, Marsh felt, "viewed themselves for the most part as being involved in a onetime thing. In many cases, it was going to be the only foray into politics, and they probably didn't even consider it politics, but probably public service. So you had to be very careful in the way you dealt with them." Some convention followers judged more than a few of the delegates to be prima donnas, but Marsh saw them on the whole as "very dedicated people" taking out a healthy part of a year in their lives to carry out what evidently was "a tremendous commitment to making this convention a success."

While Ogilvie's office did not have a formal platform on constitutional revision, it was vitally interested in the degree of changes to be recommended in certain of the charter's fourteen articles, especially those dealing with the executive branch, the judiciary, local government, and revenue. None of the articles in the Constitution of 1870 was blamed for so many of the state's problems as the one on revenue. The main criticism was that the article caused unfair distribution of the tax burden by making property levies and the sales tax the largest sources of revenue. A basic question on that article was whether the convention should recommend giving the General Assembly new taxing powers. Of course, some pressure had been taken off the convention when Ogilvie obtained legislative approval of the state income tax, a significant step toward a more equitable tax structure in Illinois. And the Illinois Supreme Court had upheld the constitutionality of the levy.

Ogilvie also had stolen some thunder from the convention by in effect forcibly resolving ahead of time one of the issues concerning the legislative article. While argument had gone on for years over the constitutionality of annual instead of biennial sessions, the governor already had coerced the legislature to meet yearly by breaking precedent and budgeting for just one year at a time.

The convention's opening day was one of only several occasions when all the delegates saw the governor. In addition to calling the first meeting to order, he outlined his thoughts on the convention in a speech that was a featured part of the first day's program. Outside of calling for reforms in the judicial article, for broader home-rule powers for local governments, and for delegates to protect the rights of individual citizens, Ogilvie put forth few specific suggestions. Instead, he asked the delegates to draw up a brief document, a charter that would not restrain the General Assembly and other governmental units from considerable leeway in coping with issues in the state. If he had his way, Ogilvie made it clear, the convention would produce a document more modest even than the U.S. Constitution.

"The best document we can draw will be simple; the most successful proposals created here are likely to be those which are broadly stated," said Ogilvie. "The more specific the proposal, the more likely will be the kind of controversy and opposition which properly should be resolved in a session of the General Assembly, or in a popular election." Agreeing with the view of many academicians, the governor stated that the authors of the 1870 Constitution "failed not because they did too little, but because they did too much." They were "deeply mistrustful of government and animated by a spirit of frontier independence," Ogilvie said. "Hence, they wrote detailed prohibitions on governmental exercise of power, and tedious and quickly obsolete directions for the conduct of matters now long forgotten."[9]

After the start of the convention, Ogilvie's interaction with it, when not covert or secretive, was certainly subtle. Any remaining doubt about that approach was almost surely erased on the initial day of the convention. After Ogilvie spoke, the opening session was marked by a maneuver, a test balloon said some, intended to embarrass the governor. This occurred when Richard M. Daley suddenly called for consideration of a resolution sharply critical of

Ogilvie for allegedly prejudicial statements on convention issues that the governor was supposed to have made before the convention's start. Daley made his move as his father, Mayor Daley, watched from the back of the crowded House chamber. The Daley maneuver failed, but many observers sensed that the message it sought to convey to Ogilvie reflected the view of more than just the Daley-aligned delegates.

Joining leaders from other walks of life in Illinois, Ogilvie would again appear before the delegates at the ceremony closing the convention on September 3, 1970. On this day, all but a few of the delegates signed the new constitution proposed by the convention. Delegates signed the document on a desk used by Abraham Lincoln when he was a state legislator in Illinois. Afterwards, the document was presented to Illinois Secretary of State Paul Powell—whose office would coordinate arrangements for the upcoming statewide referendum on ratification of the proposed charter.

The nine-month life of the convention was colored by much more raucous wrangling internally than the general public, had it cared to know, might have suspected. However, what came out of it all was something that Ogilvie described in his brief address at the final ceremony as an "organic instrument," a product that in his opinion stood a good chance of receiving public approval. He planned to work for that, and certainly in a more out-front manner than he employed during the convention itself. Much more so.

As for the convention itself, Marsh would never voice any qualm about the way Ogilvie played it. Without question, Marsh was convinced, "one of the reasons we were so successful was that the extent of our involvement was secret, was not well known by the members." The lone Ogilvie agent actually on the convention scene was Paula Wolff, a person who in the words of Marsh many delegates "did not take seriously at all" because "she could not have been more than 25 and was pretty, not what they'd think of as a governor's lobbyist. They just didn't realize how smart she was, that she was 30 seconds away from me and I was 30 seconds away from Ogilvie."[10]

Because so many delegates were young, Marsh observed, Wolff was able "to develop personal friendships with some." With one delegate, thirty-year-old lawyer Wayne Whalen, a Democrat from Hanover, Wolff's relationship turned into something more. On the original Earth Day in April 1970, the two were secretly married by Judge George Coutrakon in Springfield, an event that only became known when several delegates noticed the listing of their marriage license application in the local papers. Paula had met Wayne, who chaired the convention's Style and Drafting Committee, through George Ranney, Ogilvie's deputy budget director. Ranney, who had practiced law with Whalen, also got Wolff involved with the Ogilvie administration. A New Yorker who was president of her senior class at Smith College, Wolff came to Illinois to attend graduate school at the University of Chicago. After Ogilvie became governor, she accepted an invitation from Ranney, a family friend, to work for Ogilvie's budget bureau. Marsh then met her through Ranney, who spent more time assisting Marsh on the convention than any other high-level Ogilvie person.

Impressed with Wolff and "needing somebody" to monitor the convention for the governor's office, Marsh took a chance that she could fill the bill, a move he would not regret. In the twenty-five years following the convention, Paula Wolff spent a good deal of time as a top assistant to Governor Thompson before becoming the president of Governors State University south of Chicago. When contacted in her university office in 1995 and asked to reflect on the convention, she replied that, along with her successful marriage to Whalen, the convention provided her with "a remarkable opportunity for someone like me at the time," in that constitutional law and legal history were areas of vital interest for her. Her role, she said, was "to keep a close eye on things, to listen and learn, to report back to Jerry and George on what I thought was going on, and, as time passed, to suggest where the Governor might inject himself into the issues, into things like the amendatory veto power that he came to want as it was being developed."[11]

The governor's smoke-and-mirrors approach to the convention did not preclude occasional meetings between Marsh and certain delegates (although never at the convention site) nor breakfasts with the governor and a delegate now and then. More likely to occur, though, were other steps that only somebody with Ogilvie's clout could take to either influence a delegate or help one delegate influence others.

As explained by Marsh:

> We had the ability to coordinate—like I mean if a political touch from someone's county chairman was needed, we could do that in five minutes. If you needed to make a deal over a moderate branch banking plank, we were in a position to do that. If you needed to say something that would get media attention in Chicago, you could do that. The governor is a very powerful person.
>
> And yet, things like this were all being done largely by indirection, and much more subtly than in most political ventures, by and large secretly so you weren't tipping your hand, you weren't offending people unnecessarily.

The proper balance between letting it all show as opposed to total secrecy is an art, I guess, in government. But, an important ingredient for us in Con Con, which worked out quite well, was that we were able to keep our confidences and to be secret about our involvement at critical stages.[12]

By whatever means, Ogilvie could take satisfaction in the end that he either helped instigate or at least favored much of the proposed new charter, a document that altered a lot of the Illinois Constitution of 1870 but avoided a drastic overhaul. The output of the convention was characterized by none other than Witwer as "neither reactionary nor radical . . . neither regressive nor visionary. It is practical."[13]

More than forcing a rewriting of textbooks, the proposed charter was tailored to provide a more equitable tax structure, assure greater racial equality, bring about new relationships between state and local governments, and, as expected, eliminate anachronisms in the existing constitution. The recommended new document incorporated in its bill of rights a guarantee against discrimination on the basis of race or creed in employment and in the sale or rental of property. Equal protection of the laws was not to be denied on account of sex, an ironic inclusion in view of the difficulties later encountered by women's rights groups in trying to get the General Assembly to ratify the proposed Equal Rights Amendment to the U.S. Constitution. The bill of rights also was expanded in the rewrite to include an assurance of freedom from unreasonable eavesdropping as well as from other invasions of privacy. Too, the right of individual citizens to keep and bear arms, subject only to the police power, was included—a testament to the sway of the gun lobby at the convention. There were substantial provisions for home rule intended to reverse the old doctrine that made local governments relatively helpless creatures of the state. Broad powers on taxing, borrowing, and regulating were authorized for the first time for cities of more than 25,000 and counties with an elected chief executive officer. Ogilvie was a strong home-rule backer, but all hands recognized that this segment was probably the biggest bonus for Chicago in the proposed charter, enough to ensure Mayor Daley's greatly needed support.

The proposed constitution had a lot of other new provisions. The convention replaced the state auditor of public accounts with a comptroller, still to be elected, while simply eliminating the state superintendent of public instruction as an elected officer. Instead, the chief education officer would be named by a state board of education to be set up under the recommended charter. A state elections board for supervising election code administration throughout Illinois was established, and residency requirements for voting were reduced. The delegates broke new ground by declaring that public transportation was an essential service that the General Assembly could lawfully assist.

In another area ignored by the 1870 Illinois Constitution, its proposed replacement picked up on one of the more recent priorities of society by including a new Article XI on the environment. Credit for this article, which specified that each person had a right to healthful surroundings as well as a duty to provide for such, went to Mary Lee Leahy of Chicago, one of only fifteen women among the 116 delegates. Spunky to say the least, she bucked the Daley machine to win her seat as an independent Democrat. After the constitutional convention, she was frequently a thorn in the side of the political establishment, helping to elect Democratic outsider Walker to the governorship and later, as a Springfield attorney, pushing to the U.S. Supreme Court, and winning, a celebrated case that severely limited traditional political patronage practices.

At least one of the other women delegates also had a great long-range impact on Illinois politics. She was Dawn Clark Netsch, another independent Democrat from Chicago. Following the convention, she served nearly two decades in the state senate before becoming the first woman elected to a state constitutional office, the post of comptroller, in 1990. Four years later, as the unsuccessful Democratic candidate for governor, Netsch broke precedent again by being the first woman nominated for the state's top office by a major party.

Back in the constitutional convention, Dawn Netsch was the vice chair of the Revenue and Finance Committee, a panel to which many delegates wanted to be appointed because of the obvious importance of its subject matter to the success of the convention. Named by Witwer to one of the convention's plums, the chairmanship of that committee, was regular Democrat John M. Karns Jr. of Belleville, a former state's attorney of St. Clair County. While he was a smart fellow, he also had an easygoing manner that, Witwer hoped, would encourage civility by the strong interest groups that would be vigorously lobbying the committee. Out of the revenue committee came the finance article, a totally new one, which spelled out budgeting, appropriations, and accounting procedures geared to permit better management of taxpayers' dollars. It dictated that the General Assembly appoint a new auditor general to examine all aspects of state finances. Drafting an acceptable revenue article in the Karns committee was considerably more difficult, what with corporations, organized labor, farmers, Cook County Democrats, and other powerful groups often at loggerheads over what the proposed constitution should say on the raising of public funds.

The dust never completely settled on the revenue article, which in its final form left many with an uneasy feeling that it not only lacked desired flexibility but also posed problems for the so-called little guys. The main criticism stemmed from the article's prohibition of a graduated income tax. The state AFL-CIO for one still charged that a flat-rate income levy, like the one just enacted in Illinois, weighed most heavily on those least able to pay. It was also pointed out that nothing would prevent the income tax rate for individuals from exceeding that for corporations, although the corporate rate could not exceed the rate on individuals by more than a ratio of eight to five. Revenue article proponents countered, though, that it eliminated any remaining personal property tax by 1979, authorized the legislature to remove the sales tax from food and medicine, and permitted tax relief or credits for elderly men and women who owned or rented homes.

Much of the most heated debate during the writing of the proposed charter centered on two issues: whether to appoint or elect judges and whether to elect state representatives from single-member districts or through the cumulative voting system, then in use, in which three representatives were elected from each district. Since compromises on these two matters could not be reached, the convention decided to let voters decide what they wanted on these issues through a separate submission to the electorate on each, apart from the main body of the proposed constitution. Voters also were asked to decide separately on lowering the voting age from twenty-one to eighteen and on abolishing the death penalty.

The argument over the method of selecting judges was quite acrimonious, not just while the convention was in session but also during the ensuing campaign on adoption of the proposed constitution. The judicial article did encompass changes such as the beefed-up program for disciplining judges, a result of the Solfisburg-Klingbiel scandal. However, Daley's strong insistence on the continued partisan election of judges, a necessity if his organization were to retain control of the judiciary in Cook County, was why it was virtually impossible to get a provision for appointing judges. Ogilvie and others behind the appointive route, popularly termed "merit selection," did what they could to lobby for it during the convention. On this, the visible advocates certainly included Paula Wolff. Nevertheless, in view of the intensity of Daley's stand, merit selection backers regarded it as a victory when the elective-appointive question was approved for a separate submission to voters.

As for other positives for Ogilvie and the executive branch, the legislative article contained the amendatory veto power. This measure would get a lot more attention down the line than it did during the convention. On second thought, though, a number of convention observers did predict that the framers of the

proposed constitution created a little time bomb when they handed this authority to the governor. This provision permitted the chief executive to return a
bill to the General Assembly with "specific recommendations for change."
Ogilvie and his successors interpreted this as a license to rewrite legislation
to reflect their positions. Legislators then could seek to override the amendatory veto, do nothing (in effect killing the measure), or vote to accept the governor's recommendations. If the governor certified that the acceptance conformed to his suggestions, the bill became law. Quickly enough after the Illinois
Constitution of 1970 went into effect, lawmakers would see the amendatory
veto power as a tool for distorting the traditional legislative process by nullify-
ing legislative intent. In Marsh's estimation, little coming out of the convention
was more of a "real thunderbolt." Yet precious few Illinoisans could say they
were even aware of anything called the amendatory veto power either before
or after the adoption of the Constitution of 1970.

December 15, 1970, was the day that voters went to the polls to either ratify
or reject the proposed constitution. Principal figures in both political parties
supported adoption of the proposed new charter, as did leaders of business,
education, agriculture, and other major segments of Illinois society.

With the convention over, Ogilvie did not hesitate to use his office as a bully
pulpit to try to secure backing for the proposed constitution. He sincerely believed that it would improve Illinois government and benefit the state's residents. He also recognized that his association with a drive for a successful referendum might help offset, at least for him personally, the disastrous results
for his GOP in the November 1970 election in Illinois. As the Ogilvie camp
raised money to help finance the adoption effort, the governor himself plugged
away at personal appearances and at other activities intended to draw attention
to the referendum. He proclaimed a seven-day period before the vote as Illinois
Constitution Week. He made Witwer the first recipient of a new state honor,
the Distinguished Service Medal of Illinois, for Witwer's endless toiling for
constitutional revision.

Ogilvie's stumping had its ironic moments, such as his stop at a convention
seminar at Chicago's Temple Sholom. There, after urging support for the proposed constitution, Ogilvie was questioned by a panel of convention delegates,
public officials, and newspeople moderated by another backer of the proposed
charter, none other than Daniel Walker. Just a few days before, on November
18, Walker had stunned the Illinois political galaxy by announcing his intent to
run for governor in 1972. Of course, Walker was viewed almost universally at
the time as hopelessly pursuing a pipe dream because, as almost every person
in his or her right mind knew, nobody got the Democratic nomination for gov-

ernor without the blessing of Mayor Daley. And the mayor had no love for Walker.

Daley did not publicly reveal his support for the proposed constitution until several weeks before the referendum. When he did it, he still expressed serious reservation about the revenue article seeming to favor corporations over individual taxpayers. Nevertheless, Daley's imprimatur produced a huge sigh of relief among the advocates. His approval was expected to ensure a heavily favorable vote for the main package of the proposed charter in Illinois's largest city. The mayor predictably called for the continued partisan election of judges, which placed him directly opposite Ogilvie, a flag bearer for the judicial appointment crowd.

Opposition to the proposed constitution was easy to find, most noticeably in the AFL-CIO, but it was also scattered. Editorially, the situation ranged from the *Chicago Tribune*, which appealed for support of the new constitution, to the *Belleville News-Democrat*, which argued for solid rejection on grounds that the document would give a green light to unbridled taxation. Editorializing to its thirty thousand subscribers that they'd "be sorry" with the proposed charter, the *News-Democrat* averred that "we simply cannot believe that informed citizens of Illinois will voluntarily surrender their heritage of freedom to become slaves of the state."[14]

One of the most visible campaigners against adoption was John Alexander, much to the indignation of many of the other delegates. Going around as a self-described "lone eagle," Alexander hammered away at his contention that the convention failed to do its job by shying from recommending meaningful revision of the General Assembly and other Illinois government institutions. Alexander, who would pursue private business interests after his short fling in the public arena, did his best to persuade whoever would listen that "serious analysis of the proposed constitution reveals that its passage could only stifle real government reform in years ahead."[15] But to no avail.

The product of the Sixth Illinois Constitutional Convention received a thumbs-up from the electorate. By a vote of 1,122,425 to 838,168, the proposed charter was ratified.

Cook countians approved it overwhelmingly, by a margin lopsided enough to readily overcome the negative vote in many parts of downstate. About 40 percent of the electorate went to the polls in Chicago, but the figure was appreciably lower downstate, where predictions of voter apathy came true. Daley's stance was credited for Chicago's support, but the reasons for the downstate opposition were thought to be more complex. To some, it was a resurfacing of an almost traditional aversion to constitutional change. Also, the farther south one went in Illinois, the stronger the feeling that the new constitution was written mainly to assist Chicago. Armchair quarterbacks could hardly be faulted for questioning whether the Illinois Constitution of 1970 would have become a reality without the inclusion of the home-rule provisions, the bait that hooked Daley.

As for the four items submitted separately in the referendum, Daley's influence was prominent here too. Rejecting Ogilvie, the Illinois Bar Association, and a host of others, the voters opted to stick with the Daley-backed partisan election of judges. Daley and many others in the political establishment also got their way when the proposed election of Illinois House members from single-member districts was defeated (although one-member districts for the representatives would go into effect through a constitutional amendment approved in 1980). On the other separate propositions, abolition of the death penalty was soundly rejected and a lowering of the voting age to eighteen from twenty-one was more narrowly defeated, a result that many persons felt was fueled by the disruptive campus protests earlier in 1970. Subsequently, though, the new constitution would be amended to give the vote to eighteen-year-olds.

The adoption of the new constitution made Illinois a leading success story in an era when many were clamoring for constitutional revision in other states. New charters had been approved in some states, but major revisions had been rejected in New York and several other large states. Due to circumstances of time and place, Ogilvie was governor when this happened in Illinois. It was fortuitous for him that the constitutional convention was ordained before he took office. Once the proceeding got rolling, he could have torpedoed it by injudicious intervention. But Ogilvie did not upstage the convention, realizing that the success of this extraordinary undertaking would provide credit enough for all those around. When historians took note of the convention, they would inevitably record that Ogilvie was governor when it transpired. Furthermore, should the convention succeed, it was destined to go down as a hallmark of the Ogilvie governorship.

Back to a more mundane matter, the ratification of a new constitution meant a lot of drudgery lay ahead in implementing it. Statutes needed revision, and a thousand and one other details required attention. To get all this stuff moving, Ogilvie tabbed one of those seeming persons for all seasons, Sam Gove, naming the political science professor the chairman of the Citizens Task Force on Constitutional Implementation. No surprise here, this was perfectly in line with the utility infielder role that Samuel Kimball Gove played for Illinois government off and on for more than four decades. The constitutional implementation assignment Gove accepted without difficulty because he was certain that

Ogilvie, in the words of the professor, "already was one hell of a governor."[16] Ogilvie's calling for the income tax was a key reason for Gove thinking this, but far from the only reason.

Gove was born in 1923, the same year as Ogilvie. Like Ogilvie, Gove was not an Illinois native. He grew up in Walpole, Massachusetts, in an old New England family. Like Ogilvie, Gove saw duty in World War II. He was a young naval officer on a submarine chaser in the South Pacific, but Gove and the crew on *S.C. 1041* never encountered a Japanese sub. Following the war, Gove graduated from the University of Massachusetts and then received a master's degree in political science from Syracuse University in 1949. After that, he surfaced as a research assistant in governmental matters at the University of Illinois. Gove's first taste of Springfield and Illinois government occurred in the early 1950s, when his university loaned him at the beginning of the 1950s to the staff of the Illinois Commission to Study State Government, the state's so-called Little Hoover Commission. There he met Daniel Walker, then a recent graduate of the Northwestern University law school.

Although Gove played no formal role at the constitutional convention, much of the groundwork for it was laid by his university's Institute of Government and Public Affairs, which Gove directed from 1967 to 1985. Gove also was staff director as well as a member of the Illinois Constitution Study Commission created by the General Assembly. In addition, he edited (along with Victoria Ranney, wife of George Ranney) a book of Illinois constitutional issue papers that many delegates and Ogilvie's office used to prepare for the convention. Gove even had a hand in ushering Joseph P. Pisciotte, a constitution study commission staff member, into the executive directorship of the convention.

Long after the Illinois Constitution of 1970 went into effect, Gove would continue to accept special assignments from governors or legislative leaders that would pertain to important, but dry subjects, such as the image of state government or the future of public service. Gove was the first to admit, as he handled a martini or two when relaxing, that sexy matters seldom came his way. But he drew the line on any downgrading of the topic of constitutional revision, to which he gave so much time before and after the convention. The development of the Constitution of 1970 was, Gove insisted, "one of the most significant success stories in modern Illinois government, especially in view of the sharp divisions and partisan nature so prevalent in Illinois public life."[17]

With the constitutional convention receding into the past and no sign of another one coming in the foreseeable future, James Snopko would cherish more and more "an almost certainly once in a lifetime experience for me, my one shot with a big event in public life." Snopko, from little Farmersville, interrupted a career as a high school history teacher in Springfield to serve as the assistant chief clerk of the convention in order "to see government really happening instead of always being on the other side of the table." He would chuckle in time when he looked at pictures of himself at the convention's closing session because of his long sideburns, which were so stylish in 1970. But he would also notice all the delegates and dignitaries in the photographs. And he would say to himself, "I really was part of history in the making."[18]

Political Setbacks

Ogilvie's standing in Illinois history was bolstered by more than the constitutional convention in 1970. He established himself that year as the governor who put Illinois on the pollution-fighting map with a big splash. Launching an all-out assault against polluters, Ogilvie brought to an end years of wheel spinning against the ravagers of the state's air and water.

The governor's political stock was another story. To say his political bubble burst in 1970 was no exaggeration. Those rioting students that year also kept him on edge, forcing him to dispatch national guardsmen to restrict the mayhem in the college towns as the students ran wild, demanding the downfall of Ogilvie and other authorities. The governor was a particular target of their scorn.

Breaks from the pressures of his office were few and far between for Ogilvie in 1970. That was a reason for his obvious pleasure over a June lunch of beef stew and dumplings at the Governor's Mansion with Edwin Rimmel, a St. Louis tavern operator. Rimmel happened to be the driver of the Sherman tank Ogilvie had commanded in 1944. The two men had not seen each other since. Asked what prompted the reunion, Rimmel explained that he had been noticing Ogilvie's picture in the newspapers and on television and that he "remembered the Richard B. part of his name." So, added Rimmel, "I wrote to him, and he answered and here we are."[19]

Even though the still GOP-controlled legislature went along with Ogilvie's antipollution program, his stumbling on other legislative pursuits showed that his magic wand with the lawmakers was losing its luster. This was most evident with downstate Republicans, many of whom felt antagonized by Ogilvie in at least two major confrontations. One was the governor's support of state aid for Catholic and other private schools, a proposal that touched off a bitter fight while failing to pass in 1970. The other imbroglio concerned a state assistance program recommended by Ogilvie for local mass transit systems. His call at one point for another increase in the state gasoline tax to provide dollars for the undertaking ticked off many legislators who complained that voters already were unhappy with the state income tax imposed just a year earlier at Ogilvie's request. Downstate Republicans angrily added that the mass transit initiative, which died, was basically intended to help the fiscally troubled Chicago Transit Authority. Similarly, on Catholic school aid, many of the downstate Republicans contended that Ogilvie was also demonstrating favoritism here for his home base of Cook County, a place loaded with Catholic voters and parochial schools.

Far and away, though, the major political setback for Ogilvie in 1970 came in its general election, a sorry showing for the governor and his party that traced its beginning, if not to the approval of the income levy, then certainly to an occurrence September 7, 1969. Odd as it turned out, that day originally was supposed to be known for, of all things, a picnic—a highly touted rendezvous of Democrats from Illinois and other parts of the Midwest at the old Libertyville farm of the late Governor Adlai E. Stevenson. One of his sons, Illinois Treasurer Adlai E. Stevenson III, the most visible host for the event, was a leader at the time of dissident Illinois Democrats threatening open rebellion against Daley's heavy-handed domination. The expectation of Daley bashing at this event had a lot of folks, including media types, licking their chops. But, lo and behold, Daley himself showed up for the fun, and the picnic ended up being a harmonious and even unifying occasion for the party, which was what the picnic organizers insisted it was supposed to be anyway.

In any case, before that day was over, the impact of the celebrated picnic was eclipsed by another development, the death in Washington of Everett Dirksen, the Republican minority leader in the United States Senate, five days after he underwent surgery for lung cancer. Even before Dirksen was buried at a cemetery outside his central Illinois hometown of Pekin, speculation on his successor was rife.

The task of naming Dirksen's replacement fell to Ogilvie, a ticklish proposition because of the obvious political offshoots involved for both the next occupant of Dirksen's seat and the governor. Ten days after Dirksen's death, Ogilvie ended the suspense by announcing the successor would be Ralph Tyler Smith, the Republican speaker of the Illinois House. The selection was ripe for second-guessing from the start, mainly because of GOP fears that Smith could not hold the seat after he was in it. Smith's appointment was only the first step in filling the post. In the 1970 election, voters would elect the person to serve out the rest of Dirksen's term, which did not expire until 1974. Naturally, it was assumed that the individual whom Ogilvie chose would have an inside track to the Republican nomination for it in the 1970 election. Smith, an Alton attorney, would have that much going for him, but his chance of retaining the seat in the general election, many Republicans conceded, was fraught with question marks.

Betting was heavy, and on target, that Stevenson would be the Democratic nominee. Young Adlai may have been estranged from some regular Democratic leaders, but the bearer of one of Illinois's most prominent political names had a substantial following among uncommitted voters and already had shown he could win statewide office. Moreover, as would be evident soon enough, he had Daley's backing for the U.S. Senate. When in fact the general election contest for the Senate seat did come down to Stevenson versus Smith, Stevenson had the look of a shoo-in.

The rap on Smith that he just did not seem electable in the Senate race did not detract from his record as an accomplished public figure. When named to the Dirksen seat, the silver-haired Smith was fifty-three and a veteran of fifteen years in the Illinois House. As its presiding officer since 1967, he displayed a leadership style both discerning and pragmatic. A middle-of-the-roader who, like Ogilvie, largely had shunned GOP conservative ideologues, Smith was credited with converting the slim, often disunited Republican majority in the House into a unit that pretty much prevailed on major legislative matters. His manner was to proceed adroitly with considerable give-and-take, a far cry from the flamboyance of Arrington, Smith's Republican counterpart in the Senate chamber. Yet Smith achieved a decorum in House operations not obtained by some previous speakers.

As a lawmaker, Smith was a journeyman, associating himself mainly with nuts-and-bolts bills on revenue, appropriations, highways and other basics. It was probably true, as he once said, that "I like to think I know what it takes to run Illinois."[20] Smith did his part in pushing the income tax and much of the rest of Ogilvie's extensive legislative program through the House in 1969. However, at the same time, he was involved in an endeavor or two that may have set him back politically, such as his effort to reduce public aid payments. Even though Smith had supported passage of open-occupancy legislation, he became subject in 1969 to a charge of bias against blacks when he sponsored a bill that would have decreased state welfare payments by 30 percent. Smith tabled the measure after nearly three thousand protesters, mostly blacks, stormed Springfield under the leadership of the Reverend Jesse L. Jackson of Chicago, the national director of the Southern Christian Leadership Conference's Operation Breadbasket. Jackson contended in testimony before the whole House, as his supporters in the gallery noisily agreed, that the Smith bill would be a "murderous" tool for creating a "threat of genocide" throughout Illinois.[21]

If the presence of Jackson and his followers was not enough to convince Smith to ditch the bill, Ogilvie's opposition, spelled out in a letter to the speaker, probably was a sufficient reason. At the time, 500,000 residents in Illinois were receiving one or more types of public assistance. Ogilvie said he believed it was imperative to "maintain the existing level of [public aid] programs in this state" until a time when the federal government bore a greater share of the overall cost. "Our attention should be directed toward reducing the number of people receiving welfare rather than reducing the amount they receive," the governor wrote Smith. "If we are to develop methods to break the welfare cycle and not perpetuate the dole system, we must increase the flexibility in state programs."[22]

Two years later, in 1971, when more and more people had gone on the public aid rolls, Ogilvie would be proposing to the General Assembly a drastic revision of the state welfare system based on what he termed "the old-fashioned notion of working for a living."[23] Even then, though, he still did not favor reducing welfare benefits.

Supporters of Smith's bill in 1969 asserted that Ogilvie backed its concept before the speaker introduced it, but renounced the measure publicly after it incurred the wrath of black legislators. Consequently, it was said, the rapport between Ogilvie and Smith became strained. Nevertheless, later in 1969, when Dirksen passed away, Smith was one of three individuals whom Ogilvie considered for the vacant seat in the United States Senate. Another was John B. Anderson of Rockford, the independent-minded Republican congressman from the Sixteenth District in northern Illinois and the chairman of the House Republican Conference (which made him his party's third-ranking member in the lower chamber). The other person Ogilvie considered was Illinois Attorney General Scott. If most sources in Ogilvie's office were to be believed, the choice would be Scott or Smith.

Smith's ambition to reach the U.S. Senate was no secret. Both Smith and Ogilvie admitted that the subject was discussed in 1968 when Smith played a key role in Ogilvie's downstate campaign. But, both said, no commitment was made. The Ogilvie-Smith relationship also was visible in other ways. Judy Allan, the governor's personal secretary, had been Smith's secretary in the Statehouse. Ogilvie aide Marion Oglesby had been a top assistant to the speaker in the 1967 legislative session. Smith also benefited from a widespread impression that the Dirksen seat should go to a downstater for the sake of traditional balance. The other United States senator from Illinois, Charles Percy, was a Cook countian. Furthermore, Scott's home city of Evanston was part of Cook County.

Nevertheless, those close to Ogilvie thought Scott would be the pick. Ogilvie political operative Jim Mack, one of those in on the discussions with the governor, personally leaned toward Anderson as "probably the strongest appointment," but recognized that "most talking to Ogilvie felt it should go to Scott."[24] The reasons were not hard to see. Scott was the only proven statewide vote-getter among the trio. Too, judging by the course of things, peaceful coexistence in the hierarchy of Illinois government between Scott and Ogilvie was looking more and more doubtful. To anybody with clear vision, Ogilvie's old law school chum had become the governor's biggest rival in the state GOP. Thus, it was reasoned, by packing Scott off to Washington, Ogilvie would be getting him out of his hair. The office of United States senator from Illinois, even with all of its loftiness and prestige, seldom afforded an occupant much of a voice in political or governmental affairs back home.

Since the name of Adlai Stevenson III kept popping up at the time, someone surely must have recalled for Ogilvie a story about Governor Stevenson. He was geared to run for the Senate from Illinois in 1948. Rather suddenly, though, the state Democratic leader at the time, Jacob M. Arvey, told Stevenson that he would have to seek the governorship. The reason was that the other Democrat intended for a top spot on the ticket that year, Paul Douglas, was not acceptable to Chicago Democrats as an aspirant for governor, the office that controlled patronage and other bread-and-butter matters. So Douglas was slated for the Senate, the place that Stevenson really wanted to go, in order to get Douglas out of the state picture.

After thinking it over for about a week, "Ogilvie made up his mind that it was going to be Scott," Jerry Marsh later revealed. What followed was characteristic of the Ogilvie-Scott relationship in those days. Ogilvie was snookered this time. As Marsh told it, Ogilvie went to Scott's office in Chicago and "talked the appointment through with him." Scott said he "was interested," related Marsh, "and would accept, as I understood it, but he wanted to talk to Dorothy Scott, then his wife." Once that happened, Ogilvie and Scott planned to announce several days later, on a Monday, that Scott was going to the Senate, Marsh added. After Ogilvie's visit to Scott, the governor asked Marsh, who spent most of his time in Chicago, to join him for lunch. "We went over to the Bismarck Hotel and had a couple of manhattans," said Marsh. "We had a leisurely lunch, which was very unusual. That just never happened."[25]

After recounting the conversation with Scott, Ogilvie proceeded to stun Marsh by telling him he was going to be the next Illinois attorney general, an appointment that Ogilvie intended to reveal on the coming Monday in Springfield when the naming of Scott to the Senate was announced. Marsh recalled his reaction as being "a little bit thunderstruck and pleased."

Marsh spent the next several days reading all he could about the office of attorney general and "thinking about what the hell I'm going to say when I'm trotted out down in Springfield and that announcement is made." Come Monday, Marsh caught an early plane from Chicago to Springfield while trying to contain the excitement that almost any Illinois lawyer would feel if he knew he was about to be named the chief state legal officer. Arriving at the governor's office in the Statehouse, he found Ogilvie, Drennan, and Whalen awaiting him, sitting as Marsh remembered it "with long faces, looking like somebody had died."

"Well," asked Marsh, "what's the matter?"

Did Jerry not know? Scott, that rascal, had just said at a press conference in Chicago that he had turned down a request by Ogilvie to fill the Dirksen seat. Without saying a word to Ogilvie. His responsibilities as attorney general, Scott said, "could not at this time let me accept such an appointment in good conscience."[26] Scott added that the governor, a close friend of his for two decades, would understand. "So," concluded Marsh, "that was the end of that. We went back to the drawing board, and then the decision was made to appoint Ralph Smith."[27]

When he named Smith, Ogilvie insisted to reporters that the job was "offered to nobody but Ralph Smith." A political fib by the governor perhaps, but a necessary tact in the game of one-upmanship with Scott. And, of course, admitting that Smith was a second fiddle for the appointment would ill serve both Smith and Ogilvie. Whatever, the scribes were left quizzically scratching their heads.

By the time the whole Smith episode was over, Jim Mack would also be scratching his head. At the start, he got stuck with, in his words, "the unenviable task of having to get on a plane and fly to Washington to tell John Anderson that he would not be appointed to the Dirksen seat."[28] Then, Mack served as manager of the doomed Smith campaign to retain the Senate seat. True to all the predictions, Stevenson breezed to victory in the general election in November 1970 by a large margin, 545,000 votes. Democrats also did well most other places on the ballot, leading to inevitable finger pointing within the GOP. More at Ogilvie than Smith. Following his defeat, Smith returned to his law practice and was quickly forgotten politically. Within two years, Smith would be dead, and Ogilvie would praise him as "a politician in the best sense of that much-maligned word."[29]

To his credit, Smith made a hard run at the heavily favored Stevenson. With other Ogilvie people in addition to Mack calling many of the shots, Madison countian Smith tried to paint Stevenson—partly through acerbic television advertisements—as an ultraliberal who was soft on crime; an instigator of campus unrest; a man queasy on defense; a quisling to law enforcement officers; and all the other things that went into being an ultraliberal. Stevenson tried to ignore Smith, concentrating instead on criticisms of the Nixon administration's actions on economic problems and the Vietnam War. Before the race was over, though, the forty-year-old Stevenson slugged back at Smith, referring to his opponent by name as he sought to neutralize the senator by seeking to isolate him as a dupe of the extreme right whose election appeal depended on the stirring of hate and fear. As the Smith-Stevenson contest developed into a free-for-all of rhetorical extremes, the age at hand could not have provided a more appropriate backdrop, what with the radical Weatherman sect and the Black Panthers on the left and the John Birch Society and white citizens councils still visible on the right.

Not much escaped the hail of barbs in that 1970 U.S. Senate race in Illinois, not even W. Clement Stone. Stevenson was better known than Smith, but Smith was believed to have more campaign money, thanks in no small way to Stone, the superrich insurance magnate who happened to be chairman of Illinois Citizens for Smith. Democrats took delight in professing that Stone was out to single-handedly buy Smith's election. Stone himself stoked the fires by saying that, through outright contributions and loan guarantees, he could have been responsible for at least $1 million in assistance for Smith and various other Republican candidates in the state. With a month to go before the general election, and smelling victory, thousands of Democratic workers gleefully parodied Stone at their state party convention in Chicago. To the tune of "Oh, My Darling Clementine," they sang: "Oh, your dollars, all your money, oh, my darling Clement Stone."[30] It was that kind of year in politics.

If the political side of 1970 offered any relief for Ogilvie, it came in the Illinois primary election on a snowy day in March. Smith was facing a challenge from William H. Rentschler for the Republican nomination for Smith's Senate seat. Rentschler, a Lake Forest businessman and former newspaper reporter, was engaged in what many considered a Don Quixote mission in trying to upset Smith. In fact, the senator had just about the entire Illinois Republican leadership armada behind his candidacy. Included were all twenty-four members of the GOP State Central Committee and the bulk of the party's county chairmen—individuals who for the most part had become stalwarts of the Ogilvie political organization. Assorted national party figures, including Vice President Spiro T. Agnew, had even come into the state to endorse Smith.

In reaction, Rentschler aimed his campaign more at Ogilvie than Smith, accusing the governor of political bossism tactics in attempting to stifle open competition within Republican ranks. Wait a minute, some said, the Boss Tweed charge normally was reserved for Daley. No matter, Rentschler tried to play the Ogilvie card to the hilt, and he did it in a bitingly trenchant fashion that left some in the GOP uneasy. Rentschler certainly wasn't all wrong, many in the party agreed privately, when he insisted that Republicans "will never be herded like sheep to the polls to rubber stamp the back room deals of bosses." Rentschler argued that Ogilvie had "summoned the power of his office and, in some cases, applied brutal pressure to extract lukewarm endorsements of Smith from many party leaders who see him as a loser against young Adlai." Rentschler added, "If he had adequate leverage, I have no doubt the Governor would try to wrest an endorsement from the Pope."[31]

Smith defeated Rentschler impressively enough, receiving 60 percent of the GOP vote in the primary contest. This was sufficient to let the Ogilvie organization feel it had performed handsomely. However, the last laugh would be Rentschler's. Besides Stevenson clobbering Smith in the fall, the GOP also lost the two other statewide contests at stake in the general election. State Senator Alan Dixon, the Democratic minority whip in the upper chamber, was elected Illinois treasurer in a relatively close race with Edmund Kucharski, the treasurer of Cook County and also the county's Republican chairman. This was a blow. Hardly anybody was a closer political ally of the governor than Kucharski, the undersheriff of Cook when Ogilvie was its sheriff.

The other statewide race produced the biggest surprise of the election. Republican Ray Page, the state superintendent of public instruction for eight years, was upset in his bid for reelection by a Democratic unknown, Michael J. Bakalis, who was only thirty-two and did not even look that old. While Page's handling of his office had been criticized in the press, particularly because of some office-purchasing procedures and his maintenance of a flower fund fueled by contributions from his employees, his stunning loss still was one of those only-in-America stories. Bakalis, an American history professor and an assistant dean at Northern Illinois University, was a son of a Chicago wholesale baker who had emigrated to this country from Greece. When Daley insisted on slating the clean-cut young professional to run against Page, many viewed it as a whim. His victory made Bakalis the last elected Illinois school chief, but this would not be the last elective state office for Bakalis.

The final *coup de grâce* for the GOP in the November balloting was the loss of control of the Illinois Senate. Democrats picked up ten additional seats in the election to bring about a tie, twenty-nine to twenty-nine, in the Senate. It had been a Republican domain for as long as most in the Statehouse could remember. The even split meant that Lieutenant Governor Simon, the Senate's presiding officer and a Democrat, could cast tie-breaking votes. The election also left the House more narrowly divided with the Republicans' edge reduced to just three seats, ninety to eighty-seven.

After sifting through the GOP wreckage from the 1970 election, analysts predicted difficult days ahead for the Ogilvie governorship in the upcoming third year of his term. As it would happen, the governor adjusted admirably to the altered complexion of the legislature, and more than anyone else, he came out a winner when the new Seventy-seventh General Assembly got down to business in 1971. But that was hard for even Ogilvie partisans to foresee late in 1970. It was no wonder that they put so much emphasis on the governor's part in the successful push for adoption of the Constitution of 1970. It was at least a positive in the political arena for him to latch on to.

As for other landmark developments in 1970, the governor's declaration of war on polluters was sure to ignite fireworks that might or might not help him politically. But nobody downplayed the importance of the antipollution campaign for the future of Illinois.

War on Polluters

*R*ichard Ogilvie, the pollution fighter. Should that have been surprising? No, not at all. The story line was familiar. A problem—shabby treatment of the environment—had long festered in Illinois. State government either had looked the other way or, as in this case, had only danced around the issue, throwing a light punch here and there. Then Ogilvie takes the governor's chair, and once again, the buck-passing stops. Years of playing namby-pamby with polluters suddenly come to an end. Head-on confrontation takes its place. The tank commander charges once more, earning praise and damnation at the same time. It was vintage Ogilvie.

Shortly after Ogilvie named him director of the Illinois Environmental Protection Agency in early 1971, William L. Blaser flew to Chicago with the governor. As the plane circled over the megalopolis prior to landing at Meigs Field, Blaser called attention to the dense clouds of smoke pouring from mills and other industrial sites. "Do you expect me to clean that up?" Blaser asked Ogilvie.

The governor looked Blaser in the eye for what must have been a minute to Blaser before he took his pipe from his mouth and uttered one word. "Yes." Ogilvie then stuck his pipe back in his mouth and peered intently at Blaser. After a few moments of more silence, Blaser met the governor's stare and replied simply, "Okay."[1]

Tall orders were commonplace in the Ogilvie regime, but this one struck many Republicans as unusually curious because a great number of the corporate people owning or managing those factories belching smoke into the air were GOP contributors. Sure, environmentalists would be pleased. However, everybody automatically assumed that most of them voted Democratic, just like all the rest of those in Illinois at the time who were running around seeking radical change in the status quo. So a hefty number of GOP grandees naturally feared that in attacking big-time polluters, Ogilvie was off on another politically no-win mission, much as in his pursuit of the income tax. Did the governor, they had to wonder, ever consider playing it safe?

Predictably so, many of the numerous young aides around the governor's office saw the antipollution offensive as one more adventure, as another justification for their almost zealous belief that the Illinois governorship in the hands of their boss was orbiting toward a higher plain of power and prestige. Too, they recognized that environmental protection was becoming a mainstream issue supported by far more than fringe elements. Even older hands in the Ogilvie troop, many of them not as idealistic as their younger counterparts, joined in the excitement over the drive against pollution. One was Ogilvie's main press person, the often crusty Fred Bird, who would later say in his characteristically blunt manner that "the only thing in government in the Ogilvie years that I personally cared about was our movement on the environmental stuff. That really meant something. I am not sure there was any greater legacy of his governorship."[2]

To get a handle on the evolution of environmental protection in Illinois under Ogilvie, one had to comprehend and fully appreciate the dynamics feeding the situation—the ever present political rivalries and a great cast of supporting actors, honest-to-God characters like Clarence Klassen and the mysterious Fox.

Take the Fox, whoever he was. Individuals who secretly dreamed of wanting to sneak away and plug factory or sewer pipes spitting poisonous wastes into rivers and lakes reveled in the Chicago area exploits of the Fox. He actually did things like that, or tried to, and every guy and his sister would know because the Fox reported his capers to a Chicago newspaper columnist that everyone read, Mike Royko, then of the *Daily News*. The shadowy figure called himself the Fox because he was from the river valley of that name. He would leave behind warnings to his targets with his signature, a sketch of a fox, after each furtive outing to stop up a plant chimney or take some other action sure to infuriate a polluter. His capricious escapades certainly did make for dandy reading. Take the day late in 1970 he suddenly appeared in a Loop office of United States Steel Corporation and dumped on a plush carpet a foul-smelling goo that came, he maintained, from the firm's plant drains. As he nervously spilled the muck over the carpet, some of it splashed on a leg and dress of a startled receptionist. The public just ate it up, and probably accorded this odd sort of vigilante more credit for combating pollution than all of Illinois officialdom. That was not true, although to many it may have seemed so.

Up until 1970, the year that Ogilvie made Illinois a heavyweight in pollution fighting, the state's effort to deal with dirty air and water was largely a one-person show. If Clarence Willard Klassen wasn't a solo act, he was the next thing to it. For as long as anybody could remember, Klassen had been the chief state sanitary engineer, a role entailing the wearing of numerous hats. One was to serve as technical secretary for both the Air Pollution Control Board and the Sanitary Water Board, the state's existing antipollution bodies going into 1970.

Feisty as all get out, Klassen was an internationally recognized engineer whose employment with the state dated back to 1925—which happened to be one year after his memorable first visit to Illinois, a good story in itself and one of many that Klassen, a fine raconteur, loved to tell.

October 18, 1924, was the day Klassen first set foot in Illinois, a clear and unseasonably warm day, the day of the formal dedication of Memorial Stadium at the University of Illinois. It was also a day of ultimate glory for Illini football fans as Illinois routed mighty Michigan, thirty-nine to fourteen, on the unbelievable running legs of Wheaton's Harold (Red) Grange. The Galloping Ghost, as sportswriting dean Grantland Rice called Grange, romped for four touchdowns in the first twelve minutes of the game, and he ran for a fifth in the second half before passing for another. One of the few in Memorial Stadium not wildly cheering Grange that day was a senior engineering major at Michigan, Klassen, who was on the scene because he played a French horn in the Wolverines' marching band. A roommate of Klassen at Michigan, Art Welling, was an end on the football team. Klassen easily believed a dejected Welling's lamentation after the game that "Grange ran with his knees so high in the air that you couldn't tackle him around the legs."[3]

Klassen, son of a hotel manager in Grand Rapids, Michigan, hardly suspected on October 18, 1924, that by the summer of 1925 he would begin a forty-six-year career with Illinois government, during which he would serve ten governors, starting with Len Small and ending with Ogilvie. If he had had his way, there would have been even more. Anything but a faceless bureaucrat, Klassen got to know most of those governors, some well enough that he could regale listeners with anecdotes about the big boys. Democrat Henry Horner, the governor during most of the 1930s, was to Klassen "a great guy." Horner would invite Klassen and others to the Governor's Mansion for Sunday evening meetings, Klassen recalled, adding that "we'd then often quit about 9 P.M. and go to see a movie with the Governor." However, Klassen noted, "I bought my own tickets, as did Horner."

Ogilvie did not escape the repertoire of Klassen, who was Ogilvie's first pick to direct the state EPA after its creation in 1970. Klassen would not forget the time he accompanied Ogilvie to Cincinnati to discuss Ohio River pollution issues at a lunch with Ohio governor James Rhodes. Scurrying along in downtown Cincinnati, Ogilvie, his bodyguard, and Klassen were stopped by a policeman for jaywalking. "This burly cop wanted to ticket the three of us," related Klassen. "But, the Governor's bodyguard finally convinced the cop after some difficulty that Ogilvie really was who he was. So, the cop gives Ogilvie and the bodyguard a pass, and they start to walk off, leaving me standing there with the cop." After Ogilvie proceeded a few steps, Klassen continued, the governor stopped, turned around to look at Klassen, and pronounced with a chuckle: "Clarence, you are on your own." Klassen, who could be very persuasive, also talked the cop out of giving him a citation.

Persuasiveness was at the heart of Klassen's style in trying to bring polluters into compliance with clean water and air dictums. Klassen and the small band of little-known state engineers and technical experts working with him on the environment, people like Robert R. French, Verdun Randolph, and Douglas B. Morton, regarded negotiation and compromise as the best avenues in many cases for dealing with polluters, especially in situations where industries insisted that there was insufficient technology for them to provide the required pollution controls.

Of course, moments arose when they considered hard-line tactics, most obviously when the Air Pollution Control Board decided early in 1969 to seek legislation authorizing temporary state control of facilities that continued to ignore clean air mandates. It may have been a radical idea that understandably went nowhere, but it showed that the board was getting across the message in the early days of the Ogilvie administration that a further conciliatory approach to polluters was frowned upon. Klassen and the members of the board, along with those on the Sanitary Water Board, were also well aware that their world was right in the middle of less-than-cordial competition between the governor and Bill Scott. Debate never ended in some quarters over whether Ogilvie became a strong environmental governor by choice or in response to goading by the attorney general.

Trying to make heads or tails out of the relationship between Ogilvie and Scott was a taxing assignment. Based on conventional thinking, Ogilvie should have had it made with a fellow Republican serving as the state attorney general. It was generally known that Scott and Ogilvie had been close since their law school days together at Kent. Scott himself would remind those questioning his attitude toward the governor that Ogilvie had been a Scott wedding usher. Since the attorney general serves as a lawyer and adviser for other Illinois executive officers and state agencies and represents the state in suits and trials, that officer has the prerogatives and the wherewithal to make life for a governor easier or more complicated. The way it goes normally depends on whether the two officials are political allies. Neither Ogilvie nor Scott would admit openly that they were not political allies, but none of the Democrats on the scene did more to keep Ogilvie on his toes than Mr. Scott. As more than one Ogilvie person sardonically noted, having a compatriot like Scott on his side meant that the governor did not need any Democratic antagonists.

While the pollution issue primarily fanned the hard-to-disguise rivalry between Scott and Ogilvie, other sticking points existed. Scott was angered that Ogilvie wanted the Illinois Constitutional Convention to recommend that Scott's office be an appointive one filled by the governor instead of an elective position. If that came about, Ogilvie felt, the executive branch would be further unified because actions by the attorney general would be fully coordinated with those of the governor. However, Scott argued successfully that the attorney general should remain elected so that he or she could be "a true governmental watchdog and attorney for the people, not a person subject to the pressures, whims and motivations of any governor." To explain his stand, Scott said that in early 1970 the governor-controlled Illinois State Police "wanted to go through every black home in Cairo and search for arms." However, added Scott, "the State Police didn't like it, but we told them they couldn't do this because it surely would violate the civil rights of the persons involved."[4]

The subject of pollution, though, was what Scott preferred to talk about in those days. Scott, who grew up in the shadow of steel mills on the south side of Chicago, called attention to himself in the attorney general's office by filing a large number of unprecedented court suits against allegedly major polluters in Chicago, East St. Louis, and other parts of the state. The defendants, Scott bragged, even included some of his own contributors. Critics of Scott pointed out that many of his petitions, which were aimed at airlines, auto manufacturers, oil refineries, and government agencies, amounted to little more than showboating because they sought only nominal penalties and were based on insufficient technical evidence for obtaining convictions. Nevertheless, even detractors of Scott, a boyish-faced lady-killer whose political career would end like a Shakespearean tragedy, still gave him high marks for seizing on pollution as a front burner issue.

In fairness to Ogilvie, he had made pollution an issue in his gubernatorial campaign, charging that the state under Kerner and Shapiro had failed to combat air and water contamination because of "weakness, confusion and almost total unresponsiveness to the perils we face." A month before the election, in addressing natural resource problems in a speech in the central Illinois town of Shelbyville, Ogilvie said that if elected he would seek creation of a state department of natural resources to supervise all aspects of air, water, and open-space conservation in the state. Under his proposal, the new agency would encompass the Illinois Department of Conservation as well as the Air Pollution Control Board and the Sanitary Water Board, which then were parts of the Illinois Department of Public Health. Insisting that the suggested agency was needed to bring about "order from the present confusion," Ogilvie contended that the alternative was a continuation of official laxity and bureaucratic red tape. This situation had already caused crises in conservation, pollution control, and provision of outdoor recreational facilities. The ineffectiveness of Illinois's antipollution program, Ogilvie argued, encouraged "unprincipled businesses to continue their pollution unabated."[5]

Ogilvie would not end up, as it happened, with the comprehensive natural resources department he wanted. One would be created, but not until 1995 when Governor Jim Edgar would create it by executive order. But Ogilvie certainly got just about everything he sought in upgraded machinery for fighting pollution. During his first year in office, Ogilvie successfully pressed the General Assembly for legislation broadening the authority of the Air Pollution Control Board and virtually doubling the money available to it. By the fall of 1969, Ogilvie also had ordered a state crackdown on water polluters, at just about the time Lieutenant Governor Simon was setting up a special antipollution task force of his own to watchdog what he said was the state's still halfhearted approach to environmental preservation. To many, the pollution control issue was rapidly becoming a political football. They couldn't wait to see what lay ahead in 1970.

It would be plenty. And the governor clearly would be in the driver's seat. In the early stages of 1970, Ogilvie revealed that he planned nothing short of a rebirth for the Illinois antipollution effort. He disclosed plans to ask the legislature for authority to scrap most of the state's existing pollution control machinery and, for all practical purposes, start over. He also revealed that he would ask the lawmakers to submit to voters in the November election a $750 million antipollution bond issue. If approved, it would be used to help communities make sorely needed improvements to their sewage treatment facilities. Many of the details were spelled out in a polished special message on the environment that Ogilvie delivered to the General Assembly April 23, 1970.[6] The timing was perfect for maximum impact, coming the day after the first Earth Day observance.

Few of the activists behind Earth Day would have guessed that it would be the baptism of the 1970s as a decade of intense environmental awareness. Earth Day also presaged the inevitable flood of increased environmental regulation at all levels of government. Two months after Earth Day, President Nixon asked Congress to approve the creation of the Environmental Protection Agency, and by December 1970, it went into business. That also was the year the far-reaching federal *Clean Air Act* came along.

The feds had nothing on Illinois, though. On June 29, 1970, a little more than two months after his environmental message to legislators, Ogilvie signed

House Bill 3788, the *Illinois Environmental Protection Act*. Through it and companion measures passed by lawmakers, Ogilvie declared that Illinois would establish "for the first time anywhere—in any state or in the Federal Government—a comprehensive and unified program of environmental protection."[7]

The signing took place during a convention at Pheasant Run of the National Association of Attorneys General. Seated next to Ogilvie at the signing was Attorney General Scott. Individuals standing with the two included Klassen and David P. Currie, a University of Chicago law professor, the main architect of the legislation setting up the new antipollution machinery. For Klassen and Currie, the day had added importance because Ogilvie used the signing ceremony to announce that they would head the major agencies created by the legislation. Klassen would run the new Illinois EPA, and Currie would chair the infant Illinois Pollution Control Board.

As he applied a pen to HB 3788, Ogilvie predicted that "the signing of this act will be regarded as the turning point in the battle against pollution in our state." Ogilvie told those assembled that from a personal standpoint he had "held three demanding public offices, and in each I encountered what every man in public life faces. And that is, too much of one's time is spent 'putting out fires.' Many of our hours are spent reacting to situations, to the everlasting crises of government, and to events beyond our immediate control. One result is that too little time is left for the achievement of permanent and positive goals. The ceremony today marks the attainment of such a goal, and it is one that gives me great satisfaction."[8]

The governor made sure at the signing to note Scott's assistance in preparing the legislation and in fighting what Ogilvie termed its "strong—even frenzied—opposition." The legislation's most strident opponents, the ones Ogilvie had to have in mind, were industrialists. They battled it tooth and nail but succeeded in eliminating only a few of the facets they found most objectionable, such as the proposal for imposing state charges on emissions of air and water pollutants and the wording intended to give individuals great flexibility in seeking remedies against polluters.

Industry's fear of a new pyramid of bureaucratic agencies coming out of the revised program was on target. Business leaders would decry endlessly the books of tedious but meticulous regulations and the strong-arm tactics used by the fresh new army of eager antipollution officials to reverse decades of environmental neglect. But the army was undeterred, as the clearer water and air in Illinois in future years would prove. The economy was destined to take a hit in areas where businesses cut back operations or canceled expansion plans because of the high costs of complying with the state's antipollution crusade.

Opinion surveys, however, buttressed the belief of leaders like Ogilvie and those to follow that the public's desire for a better environment transcended other considerations.

When the Illinois Environmental Protection Act was passed, David Currie said it would give Illinois the strongest structure against pollution in the country. This was just what it did. Abolishing the Air Pollution Control Board and the Sanitary Water Board, the 1970 legislation set up in their place the agencies steered by Currie and Klassen as well as a third one, the Illinois Institute for Environmental Quality. In addition, the new statutory language on pollution control gave the state so much more latitude and teeth than before. Hardly any despoiler of the environment—factories, garbage dumps, and other refuse disposal sites, even individuals—could escape the tougher antipollution requirements.

The EPA was designed to function as a prosecutor, to investigate and prepare cases against alleged violators of the beefed-up state regulations governing pollution. The Pollution Control Board set control standards for the whole range of known pollutants and considered or heard charges brought by the EPA. The board, in quasi-judicial fashion, then could issue orders against polluters along with the assessment of costly penalties. As for the institute, it was a think tank, an applied research and development body on the environment. Compared to the EPA and the board, the institute was pretty anonymous. On paper, the EPA and the board were supposed to complement one another along functional lines, to cooperate. Nonetheless, the first months under the rejuvenated program were marked by a lack of rapport between the two as confusion and bickering surfaced openly over where the duties of one ended and the responsibility of the other started. The lack of communication and trust between the board and EPA turned into a governmental soap opera complete with personality clashes, most noticeably one involving Klassen and Currie.

In spite of Currie's claim that the differences represented normal growing pains, expectations that Currie and Klassen would work together smoothly were as illogical as mixing oil and water. Klassen was sixty-six years old at the time, nearly twice the age of Currie, who was thirty-four. Most of the key people in Klassen's agency at the start were holdovers, like him, from the previous state antipollution program. Moderation had colored much of their pursuit of polluters through the years because their wrists had been tied from doing their job more stringently. For these old hands, it was not easy adjusting to people on the board and at the institute who were more or less new kids on the block in regard to state pollution control and who, like most new kids, were raring to go. Not that Currie himself was a neophyte on the subject. He was serving as Ogilvie's coordinator for environmental quality when he drew the 1970 legislation, and his law career had covered legal aspects of pollution control.

The philosophical contrast between the Illinois EPA and the board was evident at numerous turns. For instance, against the advice of the EPA, the board approved a late 1973 deadline for the completion of secondary treatment facilities for sewage emissions into the Mississippi River. This drew a howl of protests from local officials who said they could not possibly come up with the money necessary to upgrade their plants in time to meet the deadline. Most of them were counting on financial help from the $750 million water pollution control bond issue that Illinois voters overwhelmingly approved in the 1970 general election. However, Klassen, sympathizing with the locals, asserted that the governor's office either had delayed or prohibited action leading to implementation of the bond issue. Ogilvie apparently intended to do little with it, Klassen said, until the year that the governor faced reelection, 1972.[9]

Countering that contention, Ogilvie pointed out early in 1971 that plans were laid for the sale of $200 million of the bonds right away and that, hopefully, funds from the issue would be reaching local governments by the upcoming summer. Nevertheless, because so much fanfare had greeted the passage of the bond issue, quarreling over its application between Klassen and the governor's office threatened to become a major political embarrassment.

The bond issue flap may have been for Klassen the straw that broke the camel's back. Or it might have been the skirmish between Klassen and Ogilvie's office on top personnel appointments in the EPA. Or it could have come down to aides advising Ogilvie that Klassen just wasn't up to the new get-tough approach to polluters. Whatever, 1971 was only a month old when the ax fell on Klassen. Ogilvie wanted to chop off his head gingerly, to make it less painful politically for both the executioner and the victim. But Klassen was a stubborn man, and he would not play along.

Here is how it went. First, an Ogilvie agent approached Klassen as he was about to board a plane for a hop from Springfield to Chicago. The agent quietly informed Klassen that the governor was beginning to think that a person with Klassen's great qualifications and experience might be better suited for "some other organization that had a wider scope." Klassen could not miss this hint. It was, he said, "as subtle as a train wreck."[10]

"Is the Governor," Klassen asked, "trying to get rid of me?"

"Well, not exactly, but he feels that maybe down the road some changes may be involved, and he just wants to give you this opportunity to expand your professional horizon," Klassen quoted the Ogilvie emissary as saying.

The following day, Klassen was tracked down by several reporters, friends of his, who told him it looked like he was being dumped. Their source was Ogilvie's chief assistant on pollution matters, John Dailey. He was leaking word that the governor pretty much had decided not to rename Klassen, whose term had expired, to the $35,000-a-year EPA directorship. Dailey, a smart fellow, was sure that the scribes would immediately contact Klassen on what they had been told. He was engaging in a ploy to soften up Klassen for his ouster. This particular firing required utmost delicacy because the irrepressible Klassen was quite possibly—except for veteran Illinois public aid director Hap Swank—the state's most popular bureaucrat. This was especially true in the Capitol pressroom, a place where Klassen was feeding stories to numerous reporters before they had ever encountered Richard Ogilvie.

Ogilvie's next step entailed summoning Klassen to a meeting with him. Klassen would not forget what was said in the meeting:

> He indicated he was going to make a change, that I didn't fit into his plans. I told him I agreed if his plans were to make the EPA a political tool. Then he told me there was more. When I asked what, he told me that I was not cooperating with the pollution control board chairman. I told him he was correct. I said, "I am not cooperating with him because he has some policies that I don't believe in and that are not going to work." He also told me I wasn't cooperating with the attorney general. I asked him if Scott had told him that and he replied, "No, but it's obvious." I then agreed that it was obvious and went on to tell Ogilvie that Professor Currie and Bill Scott did differ with me on an important and basic thing. They were criticizing me for not bringing more people into court. But, I told the Governor that I was an engineer and got more done by conciliation, but that the yardstick they wanted me to use for success was the filing of lawsuits. But, I told Ogilvie that I didn't believe in it, that history will show that was not the way to get the job done. Still, I told him I knew he was the boss and that he could get rid of me. But, I also told him I thought I had been used to get the bond issue passed and on other things.[11]

At that, Klassen recalled, "Ogilvie told me to take my time to find something and that he'd accept my resignation." No thanks, Klassen said he responded. "I told the Governor I liked what I was doing, that I was doing a good job and that I didn't intend to resign or retire, even though I'd reached retirement age." The meeting ended.

Several days later, Klassen got a phone call from Bird, who said that out of friendship he was compelled to tell Klassen that the governor planned to announce within a few hours Klassen's "retirement." Subsequently, a state press release did soon come out stating that Klassen was retiring. However, Klassen said publicly it was not true. "You can," he suggested to questioners, "fill in the rest."

Ogilvie had egg on his face. His office was bombarded with telegrams and letters supportive of Klassen from engineering groups and organizations like, for example, the Illinois Association of Sanitary Districts. Newspeople rallied to his defense. Marion (Hap) Lynes, the *St. Louis Globe-Democrat* bureau chief in the Statehouse, opined that the departure of Klassen "throws grave doubt on the future of the state's antipollution control program."[12] Kenneth Watson, the political columnist for the *Illinois State Journal* in Springfield, got more personal, writing that "the Klassen affair" was a "silly sham" even by Ogilvie's "clumsy public relations standards."[13] Nearly a quarter of a century later, when Klassen had turned ninety-one years old and finally was getting close to real retirement from consulting activities, he reminisced that "in those final hectic days with the state the newspaper people were my best friends." Of course, he added, "an enforcer did not make many friends."[14]

Seeking to limit damaging fallout from the admittedly awkward firing of Klassen, John Dailey offered that "Clarence was great at running the EPA out of his hip pocket." But, Dailey allowed, "this could be done at one time when the Illinois antipollution program was small, but not today." Paraphrasing Ogilvie, Dailey said that "we mean to get things done on this program and that requires tougher enforcement of the standards. We are not going to sit around and hold hands with industrialists and others. We are going to produce, even if it means changing some people around and hurting some feelings."[15]

The maladroit manner of Klassen's ouster was further aggravated by his replacement with Bill Blaser, a former Republican state representative from Park Forest who had surveyed a number of state agencies as a consultant on government reorganization for Ogilvie. One agency was the Illinois EPA, which naturally led to suspicion that Blaser may have played a significant part in undercutting Klassen. Questions also were raised over Blaser's lack of background in environmental protection. On that, Blaser answered that "while it is true that I am not an engineer, nor a lawyer for that matter, I am experienced in managing engineers. You don't need a technician to run the agency, to do what the Governor wants."[16]

The same day Ogilvie appointed Blaser, the governor also revealed that he and Scott were forming a special pollution "strike force," not unlike the U.S. Department of Justice's organized crime section. No longer, Ogilvie warned, would the state hesitate to invoke the penalties available in Illinois law against flouters of state antipollution regulations. No quarter, no favoritism were to be shown.

Ogilvie had the person he wanted in Blaser. Nor were environmentalists disappointed by the Illinois EPA's rigorous enforcement policies under Blaser, augmented by the levying of unparalleled penalties by the Pollution Control Board. Manufacturers and other targets of the stepped-up pollution fighting campaign reacted angrily, maintaining that the state was acting beyond reason by restricting its communication with polluters in the main to adversary proceedings. A more disliked state official than Blaser was hard to find. Critics lampooned him, even ridiculing him as a bird-watcher and orchid grower and, God forbid, an Eagle Scout. Advisers were warned that Ogilvie would pay politically for putting Blaser over the EPA. Many amazed by Blaser's gung ho attitude could not fathom the governor giving him such a free hand.

Ogilvie did just that, though, according to St. Louis public relations executive Ronald T. O'Connor. O'Connor, who handled public affairs for the Illinois EPA in Blaser's time, said that "he [Ogilvie] really gave Blaser specific directions to set up an independent organization. Then Ogilvie and his staff kept their hands off. The governor was just very concerned that the new antipollution program get off to the right start. He did not intend to use it for political purposes."[17]

In trying to cover the environmental issues that the Ogilvie administration tackled, one hardly knew where to start. So much ground was broken, often for the first time. No one in Illinois could pick up a paper without reading about the seemingly daily activity to curtail noxious emissions and effluents. But a lot else was brought to the table too: regulation of sanitary landfills; noise control; protection from radiation and hazardous pesticides; dealing with junked automobiles; recycling; helping local governments confront pollution headaches; or, if necessary, kicking local officials in the seat of their pants to get them off dead center on pollution matters. Even shedding light on environment problems was a priority, as was a perceived need to aid Illinoisans to better understand their relationship with their surroundings.

On most of these topics, the environmental quality institute played a leading educational or policy-forming role. Its establishment reflected Ogilvie's belief that Illinois government needed centers for policy planning and useful research in crucial areas. The environmental institute, directed by one more of those energetic individuals in the Ogilvie orbit, Michael Schneiderman, quite likely scored its major achievement in the considerably stiffer regulation of strip or surface mining.

At Ogilvie's request, the General Assembly of Illinois approved in 1971 a new law on strip mining that required much greater restoration of acreage over-turned by the massive mine machinery. Besides imposing stricter reclaiming standards and making the operators post costlier bonds to assure they carried out the reclamation, the new statute dictated for the first time that a complete plan for land restoration had to be filed by a mining firm and approved by the state before any extraction of coal could begin. A great deal of the new law was drafted in the institute. This was done in consultation with certain legislators favoring more extensive reclamation of mined land. One was Representative A. T. (Tom) McMaster, a Republican from Oneida. Another was a twenty-nine-year-old GOP House member who in particular had caught the eye of the Ogilvie camp, James D. Nowlan from Toulon in Stark County. This was the same Jim Nowlan who, as a young political scientist working for GOP interests in Cook County, had directed Ron Michaelson to his first meeting with Sheriff Dick Ogilvie.

The large downstate coal industry got plenty of attention while Ogilvie was governor. After obtaining the new reclamation statute, Ogilvie announced he was setting up another strike force, this one to combat acidic runoff from mined lands—the bulk of them long abandoned—that was polluting streams and lakes. The idea for this came from Schneiderman's shop. Late in 1971, Blaser made public a set of proposed clean-air rules for the state that for the first time would highly limit sulfur dioxide emissions. This created a problem for Illinois coal since much of it was high in sulfur content. When the Pollution Control Board adopted these rules in early 1972, many industries and utilities felt they had no choice but to convert their plants to natural gas or low-sulfur oil or, a little farther down the line, resort to low-sulfur western coal or nuclear power. It fell to Ogilvie's successors, Walker and then Thompson, to channel state re-sources to the large-scale development of technology that would permit the burning of Illinois coal in conformance with environmental standards.

As for the land affected by surface mining, Ogilvie proposed a sort of novel plan in 1972 for restoring some fifty thousand "orphaned" acres, so named be-cause they were the most unsightly acres disturbed by strip mining before Illi-nois's first reclamation law in 1961. The governor wanted the legislature to authorize the state to acquire and reclaim the fifty thousand acres over a ten-year period. However, the proposal died in the House because Democrats be-lieved it was too obviously intended to embellish the legislative record of the House sponsor of the plan, Nowlan. By then, Nowlan was Ogilvie's running mate in the 1972 election. In the years after Ogilvie's governorship, those fifty thousand orphaned acres would be restored under a program directed by the Illinois Abandoned Mined Lands Reclamation Council, a new state agency.

Funding for the work would come from coal companies. Part of the foundation for this successful undertaking, though, was laid by Schneiderman's institute during the Ogilvie era. From compiling a detailed inventory of every Illinois acre touched by surface mining to the devising of reclamation strategies, the institute appeared quite absorbed in the subject—even to the point of fostering a demonstration project here and there.

One involved about fifty state-owned acres in Grundy County near Morris and next to a well-known state recreational area, Goose Lake Prairie. Mining many years earlier had left this area a problem-laden eyesore. Schneiderman wanted to make the tract a model for restoration. Based on the results of the project, completed in 1973 after Ogilvie left office, Schneiderman's goal was reached. An orchestrator of the project was James R. Johnson, a Springfield landscape architect employed at the time by the Illinois Department of Transportation. In 1972, Schneiderman had asked Johnson to direct the reclamation. Johnson considered it "an honor since this was a special project and a challenging one, which I liked." Johnson also recollected that Schneiderman "made it clear there was a real rush on this project because things needed to be done to help Mr. Ogilvie's image for the upcoming election and . . . this project certainly would help his environmental image. No question, an attempt would be made, and was made, to capitalize on the project politically."[18]

When Ogilvie ran for reelection, he banked a lot of his appeal on his environmental record. After all, he had turned Illinois government into a tiger on environmental issues. But his environmental work may have been a Pyrrhic victory. All along, Ogilvie got accustomed as he went throughout the state to being pulled aside by various individuals cautioning him, occasionally in whispered conversation, about a likely backlash on his environmental policies. However, industry moguls were often the ones raising the warning flag. While the governor showed them respect, he also was sure that they didn't influence many votes. If this were the extent of the backlash, Ogilvie felt he could live with it.

But there would be more to the backlash, and it would be insidious. A burning issue it was. Literally. Few may have rebelled against the Pollution Control Board's regulations against big-time polluters, but the panel ignited a tempest by prohibiting the open burning of leaves or fallen branches. Main Street Illinois revolted. Average citizens demanded recrimination against the government officials who had banned leaf burning. Unfortunately, those angry folks could not identify one member of the Pollution Control Board, but they knew the name of the governor.

When the electorate rejected Ogilvie's bid for a second term, ill will over the leaf-burning issue was cited by numerous analysts as a major reason—after the income tax—for his defeat. Ironically, the day after Ogilvie's election loss, the board voted to amend its open-burning rules to permit, under certain circumstances, the burning of leaves and other landscape wastes in some towns with fewer than 2,500 residents. Nevertheless, as Mary Lee Leahy, Governor Walker's choice to run the EPA, would later say, the leaf burning ban "may have done more to harm the environmental movement in this state than anything else we've done."[19]

After Ogilvie, there would be no retreat in Illinois on environmental protection. However, Ogilvie's highly publicized attack mentality would not be repeated by those following him as governor. Yet the antipollution machinery set up by Ogilvie would remain solidly in place and functioning as he envisioned it. Not long after Ogilvie left Springfield, word spread that he was under serious consideration by the Nixon administration for appointment as director of the federal EPA. But it did not happen. Polluters would not have Ogilvie on their tail any longer.

Bill Scott was another matter. Defilers of the environment would continue to have their hands full with him. A phenomenon at the ballot box, he not only won reelection in 1972 but two more times as well. However, his reign as attorney general ended ignominiously. Scott, a onetime GOP golden boy, was forced out of Illinois's top legal office in 1980 following his sentencing to prison for a federal income tax fraud conviction. He was jailed for seven months.

In 1986, at the age of fifty-nine, Scott died of a heart attack. His funeral service at Chicago's Fourth Presbyterian Church drew the who's who of Illinois politics. Scott's son, William G. Scott, used the occasion of the funeral to implore those in attendance to not forsake the environmental cause so militantly espoused by his father. When young Scott did this, applause broke out in the chapel.

Campus Riots and the Guard

It was as if all hell broke loose. Protesters, mostly students, went on a rampage, pelting state and local police with stones, bottles, and bricks and randomly smashing windows of university buildings and businesses on Green Street near the campus. Plenty were arrested on charges ranging from mob action to resisting arrest itself. Anarchy was looming in Champaign and Urbana, the twin towns where the main campus of the University of Illinois sprawls flat as a pancake.

The situation had gotten out of control, forcing university administrators and local officials to request Governor Ogilvie's help. He responded by ordering units of the National Guard to Champaign-Urbana. Order had to be restored, Ogilvie insisted, because in his words "rioting and violence in a tense situation are extremely disruptive of the processes and ideals of our country." While "dissent can be useful and creative," reasoned Ogilvie, "violence is destructive of every legitimate goal. We cannot tolerate it if we want to make progress in America. We will not tolerate it." So, held Ogilvie, "Protest, yes. But violence, no."[1]

The melees that Monday, March 2, 1970, were spurred by the presence on campus of job recruiters for General Electric Company, a major defense contractor. In this era, defense contractors were not very popular with students opposed to the Vietnam War. Fanning the flames further, the university's board of trustees had voted to postpone a campus speaking appearance scheduled for March 3 by radical lawyer William M. Kunstler. Kunstler, an attorney in the Chicago Seven conspiracy trial, had defended antiwar extremists accused of inciting the disorder at the 1968 Democratic convention in Chicago. Most of the trustees thought that delaying the flamboyant Kunstler's appearance was "essential to campus security" because of disturbances at other campuses after his speeches. Reaction to the trustees' decision was mixed. Away from the campus, the trustees' action was widely viewed as necessary for preserving law and order. However, at the university itself, many agreed with the law school students and faculty who wrote to the trustees that their decision was an "arbitrary and capricious" violation of free speech and assembly rights.[2] Even the trustees were not unanimous on the matter. One, Springfield architect Ralph Hahn, said that the banning of Kunstler opened a door "for others to limit our freedom if our position does not coincide with theirs."[3]

And so, on the evening of March 3, a balmy night, students by the thousands streamed across the campus toward the fine large home on Florida Avenue of university president David Dodds Henry. They wanted Henry to tell them first-hand what rights they had. They would then demand Henry to enforce those rights, including an opportunity to hear Kunstler when they desired. Too, they would ask Henry to get rid of the guardsmen, the police, and all the other elements that the protesting students found to be oppressive.

On this night, though, the leaders of the march, some called them ringlead-ers, cautioned against violence or even confrontation. Save for a demonstration of disapproval earlier in the day at a Navy recruiting booth that had closed the Illini Union, Tuesday was peaceful so far in comparison to the tumult of Monday. Before taking off for Henry's house, the protesters, some of whom wore headgear and newspaper padding under their clothes, were warned by one speaker at a rally on the quadrangle south of the union building that "there are thousands of pigs around with dogs, sticks and guns. They're not nice people. Don't provoke them."[4] As others marshaling the crowd also belittled the "pigs," the protesters' derogatory appellation for law enforcement officers, leaflets be-ing circulated contained instructions for dealing with policemen, tear gas, and other threats. One admonishment called for the use of a dry towel instead of a wet rag for protection against tear gas. According to another instruction, "If you are busted, look around for witnesses. . . . at the station, give only your name."

Ogilvie did not escape verbal lambasting. The governor, a fascist dictator in the vernacular of many recruiting for the march, was derided by one rally or-ganizer for "using this university for political purposes." The governor, charged this individual, "has only sent in troops to get votes."

As for the national guardsmen, march leaders told those assembled that, based on reliable sources, the soldiers' weapons would not be loaded. Nervous laughter rippled through the gathering at this, but it was true. Shortly be-fore the rally, Brigadier General Richard Thomas Dunn told reporters exactly that. Dunn was the commanding general of the Emergency Operations Head-quarters of the Illinois National Guard, and he was on the scene in Champaign-Urbana, a veteran of other campus riots and serious disturbances. About 750 guardsmen were on standby duty in the area in response to Ogilvie's order, Dunn noted. Although they would be bearing rifles, ammunition would not be issued to them, Dunn pointed out. But, he added, ammunition was "available" if needed. His soldiers would be carrying bayonets, Dunn said, but sheathed instead of mounted on rifles. The guard also was prepared to use tear gas, the general added, "in event the situation called for it." Dunn, an attorney in private life, had received his undergraduate and law degrees from the University of Illinois. He expressed the hope that the guardsmen would not have to leave their armories that evening. Some did, though.

The protesters' trek to Henry's home was uneventful. On arriving there, the marchers were prevented from entering the grounds by helmeted state police armed with riot sticks. The house was dark. After shouting obscenities at the police and chanting for General Electric to leave the campus, the throng of students, now more unruly, retreated back across the campus and then onto Green Street, where the shops and hangouts comprised a venerable part of the university's campus town. Electricity was in the air as the milling procession slowly made its way, jamming up traffic for blocks. However, tonight would not see a repeat of the random destruction of the previous day. State troopers formed a barricade on Green that budged only so much. The students stamped their feet and clapped tauntingly, and some tossed rocks at the officers—who refused to retaliate. It was a night of confrontation, but not physical clashes. By and by, the students were dispersed by the cops and some three hundred guardsmen dispatched to the scene to help enforce a curfew declared by Mayor Charles Zipprodt of Urbana and his Champaign counterpart, Virgil Wikoff.

The following day, Wednesday, March 4, confrontation resumed, and this time physical altercations ensued when state police forcibly ejected a large number of students participating in a sit-in inside the Illini Union. The sit-in demonstration, a tactic often used by civil rights activists in the 1960s, was intended to protest the continued campus visits by job interviewers for firms tied to the Department of Defense and, assumably through it, to the Vietnam War. The students' militancy also was fed by the university's cooperation with the Defense Department to bring to campus a costly project known as the Illiac IV computer. Critics questioned its educational aspect since much of the computer's time was to be devoted to military use. And the Radical Union, an amorphous campus group recognized as a catalyst of student unrest, charged that Illiac showed that "the university has proven that it is not a neutral institution, but is actively supporting the efforts of the military-industrial complex."[5] Illiac had to go, the Radical Union demanded to Jack W. Peltason, chancellor of the Champaign-Urbana campus.

Guardsmen were ordered into the streets again that Wednesday night to backstop state and local law enforcement officers in controlling disturbances as headstrong protesters numbering up to 1,500 ranged over the campus and into Champaign. Numerous arrests were made for curfew violation. Another day or two of this upheaval still was facing the university community before life quieted down. For a while.

Talk about a difference. Previous protest activity on this campus of more than 30,000 students had followed largely peaceful means. Antiwar activism was visible, of course, but it usually had been carried out through letter writing to the White House, nonviolent rallies, and demure picketing. As the fighting in Vietnam continued to escalate, though, placid styles of protest were being viewed by numerous organizations and individuals as ineffectual. Thus, the violence at Champaign-Urbana in the first week of March 1970 was hardly a surprise to a lot of people. The way many on the faculty and in the student body saw it was echoed by Michael Parenti, a thirty-six-year-old associate professor of political science at the university and a conspicuous protest sympathizer. "Students have become aware that the university is not democratic socially," Parenti said at one of the week's rallies, "but that it is run by a few men servicing decisions of large corporations and the military. Students have found out that the normal communication channels in the system just add up to a runaround." Parenti concluded, "So, direct action is the way to get decision makers to listen. Disruption is the only thing you have left in an authoritarian power structure that responds only to power."[6]

Tumult at the campus would erupt again with a bang the following May, a result of the expansion of the war into Cambodia and the shooting deaths of four students at Kent State University in Ohio. This time, campuses all over Illinois were up in arms, as well as across the nation. State police and the guard soon were back in Champaign-Urbana after thousands of demonstrators went on another reckless spree. And the troops also would be moving, or readily at hand, to preserve order at Northern Illinois University at DeKalb, at Northwestern University in Evanston, and at Southern Illinois University at Carbondale—a place where the unrest really got out of control.

No other Illinois governor in modern history came near having to contend with rebellious, rioting students to the extent that Ogilvie did. Looking back on it, May 1970 was the worst of it for him. Classes were suspended and other regular activities put on hold at numerous institutions. For those accustomed to no more excitement on Illinois campuses than a Saturday afternoon football game or an old-fashioned panty raid, scenes of young men and women running amok, burning American flags, and shouting insults at authorities were hard for many people to stomach, especially in the state's smaller towns where many of those students came from. On the other hand, to those familiar with the bedlam at the Democratic convention in Chicago two years before, the students may not have seemed quite so boisterous.

Of the many reporters covering the Champaign-Urbana demonstrations in 1970, the *Tribune's* pipe-smoking Philip Caputo may have been taking notes with an added depth of feeling. Unlike almost everybody else running around, he actually had been to Vietnam. Caputo had seen action in the war as a Marine infantry officer, an experience he would write about cogently in a widely heralded book published a few years hence, *A Rumor of War*. More than a personal memoir of a young man coming of age in the conflict, Caputo's book brought home the war's horror and futility for those entrapped in it. To read Caputo's depiction of the overpowering malevolence of Vietnam, being there had to be even worse than many back home thought.

Another aside pertains to an unforgettable photograph taken at the Kent State shootings, a picture that became a symbol of the incident, which occurred on May 4, 1970. In time, this photo became as recognizable as the one of the Marines raising the American flag on Iwo Jima. The picture showed a girl screaming with disbelief beside the body of Jeffrey Miller, one of the four student antiwar protesters slain in a hail of bullets from the Ohio National Guard. The picture, destined to be a Pulitzer Prize winner, was snapped by John Filo, then a photo-illustration student at Kent State. In the year to follow, Filo, a gentle giant sort of guy, went to work as the photographer for the Associated Press bureau in the Illinois Statehouse. That was an assignment that had him frequently taking pictures of a governor, Ogilvie, whose national guardsmen were not carrying loaded rifles when they were sent to campuses in 1970.

At times, the Illinois National Guard would be poised not far from a potentially troublesome campus though not called into play. Northwestern was one of those cases. When Nixon sent American troops to Cambodia, Northwestern students took notice, but the killings at Kent State ignited demonstrations. Militancy was suddenly visible at normally staid Northwestern as a large segment of the student body opted to join a nationwide student strike, leading to the virtual closing of the campus for a week as the students turned their attention to things like rallies and a candlelight vigil in Evanston. But guardsmen, ready and waiting, were not summoned, not like they were at other university hot spots, most notably Champaign-Urbana and the campus in Carbondale, where the worst rioting occurred.

Southern Illinois University at Carbondale and its region were viewed as another world by upstaters, including all those Chicago area kids who flocked to the school. A long hike south of Chicago, some 335 miles as the crow flies, Carbondale lay at the upper edge of rugged hill country more scenic than probably any other part of Illinois with the exception of Jo Daviess County, the state's "little Switzerland." In the years since World War II, SIU had grown from a modest teachers' college to a university of prestigious scope. As this evolved, SIU at Carbondale was not known for restraint, whether in academic expansion, in play by students or, as shown during the Ogilvie era, in rioting.

The Carbondale campus garnered a great deal of attention while Ogilvie was governor. In June 1969, the oldest building on campus, Old Main, was destroyed by fire. Arson was blamed. Later that year, controversy erupted over the construction of a new $900,000 home for Delyte W. Morris, the president of SIU. Then there was the aftermath of Cambodia and Kent State in May 1970, when the campus and town came under siege.

Who on the scene at the time could forget it? The wild, compulsive mobs of students and others on Carbondale's Illinois Avenue commercial strip. Beleaguered local police sandbagging their own station. Shopkeepers sitting with guns in their already trampled stores to prevent looting. Other townspeople arming themselves. The fog of tear gas so thick at times over downtown Carbondale that seeing much of anything was difficult. This was Carbondale at the height of the turmoil. Mayor David Keene could only declare in exasperation that "if these are our children, God help us."[7]

Not many liked to think about how far things might have gone if the National Guard had not showed up. Enforcement of the dusk-to-dawn curfew during those days of rage may have been impossible without the guardsmen, hundreds of whom ended up on the campus itself, their rifles not loaded but fixed with bayonets, their belts holding tear gas canisters. Although the conduct of the state police seemed to draw more ire from the students, the guardsmen did not escape the shower of bottles and cans tossed out of high rises on the campus.

Robert W. MacVicar, the chancellor of the Carbondale campus, conceded, "This is the worst crisis that I'm aware the school has had." To MacVicar, who would become president of Oregon State University in several months, "there's been nothing comparable to what has been happening in recent days to higher education in this country."[8]

The final development at Carbondale, deemed inevitable by those witnessing the tumult, was a decision to close the campus for the remainder of the term in progress, ending classes a month before their scheduled windup. That step followed closed-door huddling between Ogilvie and SIU officials at which the governor conveyed his strong impression that it was asking too much, as he succinctly phrased it, to "keep universities open with bayonets."[9]

With the coming of summer, it began to appear that the most violent chapter of Illinois's campus revolution had seen its nadir. Normality was returning to university life in most places. Even in Carbondale, summer school began as usual, and believe it or not, local merchants would throw a dance for students before the end of summer, an event enhanced by a hay wagon loaned by the mayor.

Yet political repercussions from the riots were unavoidable. The General Assembly set up a special joint Senate-House committee to look into the disorders. However, many felt the impartiality of the panel's effort was short-circuited by a statement from the chairman before the first hearing that the rioting had been financed by "Red China, dope racketeers and rich do-gooders." The chairman, Senator G. William Horsley, a Springfield Republican, insisted that the committee was intended not to engage in a witch-hunt but to exert an honest effort to come up with legislative remedies to assist in making "damn sure that the schools keep operating."[10]

The parade of witnesses before the committee did include those who saw a conspiracy behind the campus violence. Others, though, debunked that notion. One was Illinois Treasurer Stevenson, then in the midst of his successful bid for the United States Senate, a race in which he was accused of fostering campus unrest by allegedly encouraging disrespect for authority. To a great extent, Stevenson told the panel, the disaffection of American youth on campuses and elsewhere was a result of the failure of national and state political leaders to address realistically the nation's problems. "What this country needs, and what everyone, including our uneasy students, want most is not more laws but more leadership," argued Stevenson. "It does no good, and it may do harm to panic at the sight of a young man with long hair."[11]

A new era in relationships on Illinois campuses ensued after 1970. For one thing, more democracy was instituted in the governing of universities as both faculty and student groups obtained a greater voice in operation of the schools, sometimes at the expense of traditional university administrators.

Just as 1970 was an incredibly trying year for higher education, the Illinois National Guard would in no way forget the year. Through the decades, the National Guard had been called most often for flooding. In 1993, the men and women of the guard would achieve hero status during the great flood in Illinois, after Governor Edgar diverted them from their normal jobs into active service to protect property and help maintain order in the face of the rampaging waters. Floods did prompt activation of guardsmen more than once when Ogilvie was governor, but civil disturbances triggered most of the mobilizing that occurred with alarming regularity during Ogilvie's first two years in office. The climate could not have seemed more ripe for the guard to get ensnared in firefights. However, nothing of the sort happened, emphasized Major General Harold R. Patton, the state's adjutant general under Ogilvie and later Governor

Walker. In reality, General Dunn told this writer years later, "ammunition was never issued to the individual soldiers" when Ogilvie was governor, whether at campus riots or during several outbreaks of civil unrest in Chicago. Or, Dunn added, "if it ever was issued, it was contrary to my orders."[12]

Contemplating the Ogilvie years, Patton remembered well "the guidelines set down by the Governor, which of course were followed." They were, Patton said, "good common sense instructions on ways to preserve order that did not open a door for any Kent State type of incidents."[13]

In those days, Patton ran the guard out of an office in the northeast corner of the second floor of the State Armory, which occupied much of the block across Monroe Street from the Statehouse. The limestone-faced armory, built to replace the state arsenal on the site that was destroyed by fire in 1934, also housed the headquarters of the Illinois State Police and other state offices (as well as a spacious auditorium and drill hall where Ogilvie and many other state officers were inaugurated). Having the guard and state police operating out of the same building was convenient because, in periods of the guard's mobilization, coordination was vital between Patton and James T. McGuire, Ogilvie's man supervising the state police. At such times, Patton also was in close contact with the one and only person to whom he reported, the governor. Since the process for activating the guardsmen was not always clear-cut to others, Patton always underscored certain points:

> When a situation like a disturbance or natural disaster got critical in some part of the state, local authorities fearful that the situation was getting out of hand could seek the assistance of the National Guard. They could make the request to the Governor directly, to the General Assembly or even to my office.
>
> Whichever, the request was evaluated by the Governor, who approved or did not approve it. He and I would discuss the situation, and the State Police would be in on the discussions. Speaking for my part of it, we [the guard] would know what was going on. We had our own intelligence, and we'd keep our nose to the grindstone. If the Governor approved our going in, he and he alone ordered the mobilization of national guardsmen. When that happened, I'd decide which units to activate. But, and this was important to understand, the National Guard did not go into places to take over the duties of local officials. We went in just to assist them.[14]

The public only may have thought of the guard during emergencies, but for Patton the organization had been an everyday job since he went on full-time duty status in 1953. After Ogilvie became governor, he moved to promote

Patton to major general and elevate him to adjutant general of Illinois, replacing the ailing Leo M. Boyle. In doing so, Ogilvie did more than place two stars on Patton's shoulders. As adjutant general, Patton became the chief administrative officer for a soldierly structure composed of fourteen thousand civilians prepared to don military garb for active duty at a moment's notice. All the tasks entailed in planning and equipping for mobilizations fell to Patton and his staff. Patton's world included the overseeing of forty-eight armories in the state for the guard along with three Air National Guard bases. His command even covered the state's naval militia, which was small and a bit of a mystery since it had no boats anybody knew about and, as far as anyone could recall, hadn't been activated for state duty since the devastating Ohio River flood at Shawneetown in 1937. Actually, Illinoisans in the guard wore two hats. While members of the state's militia under the command of Ogilvie, they also could have a federal role as reservists for the nation's armed forces. Federal funds supported much of the guardsmen's activities, but Patton noted that they were never on federal active duty status while Ogilvie was governor.

Ogilvie was not one to make the rounds of government offices in Springfield, but he did surface now and then in Patton's office. Although insisting that he never was an Ogilvie yes-man, Patton said that a smooth relationship developed quickly with Ogilvie because the governor was "an easy person to listen to" and because of Ogilvie's wartime experience and the fact that Patton once had been an enlisted man like Ogilvie.

Patton, who was born in Virden in 1914, the year World War I started, was a young grocery store manager in Springfield when he enlisted in the army during World War II. Although he started out as a private, Patton was a second lieutenant by the time he was shipped in early 1945 to Europe, where he led a rifle platoon in a division of the Third Army commanded by another Patton, "Old Blood and Guts" himself, General George S. Patton. Lieutenant Patton crammed a lifetime into the final months of the war in Europe as his forty-man platoon crossed Germany by what Patton described as the hard way, "seeing the country by foot and capturing everything in sight—which was not easy since we were after all on German soil, the last place the German soldiers would stop fighting."[15]

Asked to talk about it, Patton would reply that his platoon well could have been the home unit of those mythical GIs Willie and Joe whose miserable existence in the famous World War II cartoons of Bill Mauldin brought about so much empathy for infantrymen. In the admiring eyes of Patton, Mauldin "could not have been more on target." Patton might have found it interesting to know that Ed Pound, that ace investigative reporter in the Statehouse when Ogilvie was governor, had often fetched coffee for Mauldin when Pound was a copyboy and Mauldin the editorial cartoonist at the *Post-Dispatch* in St. Louis early in the 1960s. After World War II and his release from active duty, Patton ran a jewelry and gift shop in Batavia and joined the National Guard. During the Korean War, his division was mobilized, and he ended up serving in Korea as an intelligence officer. Returning to his home state after Korea, Patton embarked on his full-time career with the guard that concluded with his retirement in 1977.

General Dunn, the other major figure tied to the Illinois Army National Guard, as it officially was known, first met Ogilvie after Dunn had directed mobilized guardsmen on the scene in Chicago during rioting that followed the assassination of Martin Luther King Jr. in April 1968. Ogilvie was Cook County board president at the time, and Dunn wanted to assure Ogilvie that he would be included in planning for the use of the guard in any future disturbances in Chicago. Ogilvie appreciated the gesture. Thus, the ice between Dunn and Ogilvie was broken before Ogilvie's governorship. Later, the two worked together easily.

Wherever Dunn stationed himself, be it near a strife-torn campus or in the Chicago Avenue Armory on the lakefront, when guardsmen were called to duty in Chicago, Dunn remembered Ogilvie "always keeping a very close tab on things" through Dunn's friend Patton or through direct contact between the governor and Dunn. Too, an Ogilvie staffer, usually Marsh, was stationed at Dunn's headquarters when the guard was mobilized. For an organization so frequently sitting on a powder keg, Dunn thought the guard "fared well" during the Ogilvie years. The army must have believed so because it wanted Dunn to instruct classes on handling civil disturbances. Ogilvie resisted Dunn's retirement from the guard during his governorship, even to the point of trying to get President Nixon involved in an effort to talk Dunn out of it.[16]

The plaudits for Dunn's performance in the guard seemed endless. In 1993, a letter from John E. Cribbet in support of one more honor for Dunn held that Dunn's command of the guardsmen at Champaign-Urbana twenty-three years earlier could "only be called heroic." Cribbet, a law school classmate of Dunn and dean of the College of Law at the University of Illinois during the 1970 riots, praised Dunn for avoiding "the errors that occurred elsewhere." Dunn was "calm in a turbulent time," wrote Cribbet, and he "understood the students and their concerns about the war in Vietnam." To "this able, courageous man," concluded Cribbet, the university owed a great deal.[17]

In his own field of law, Dunn also made his mark. An initial appointee of Ogilvie to the state's new Judicial Inquiry Board, Dunn steered the early investigative activity of the panel as its first chairman. Years later, Dunn was lauded by Chief Justice Benjamin K. Miller of the Illinois Supreme Court for his service on the court's Committee on Professional Responsibility. As chair of the committee, Dunn guided the drafting of a new professional responsibility code for Illinois lawyers that the court adopted in 1990. If Dunn was not a person for all seasons, he certainly excelled at the solid-citizen business. Practicing law at a family firm in Bloomington, he was a pillar of the Roman Catholic Church and a civic leader in his community. His apple-pie life even included marriage to the girl next door.

Dunn's rapport with Ogilvie was such that the general and his wife, Julienne, dined at the Governor's Mansion several times with Dick and Dorothy. Once, just before Christmas of 1970, the governor and first lady accepted an invitation to dinner with the Dunns in their Northcrest Court home in Bloomington. It was during that occasion that Ogilvie noticed a display case containing the military medals of his host. Back in Springfield, the governor casually mentioned to Dunn's son Dick, a Senate GOP staffer, how much he admired that showcase. This led Dick to pass on the governor's comment to Patton.

What then transpired, in the words of the younger Dunn, was that "General Patton obtained duplicates of Ogilvie's medals from World War II, put them in a display case and gave it to the Governor in a surprise presentation in his State-house office, an event I attended at the request of Patton. I can't tell you how obviously tickled Ogilvie was by that."[18]

Soon after Ogilvie's defeat in 1972, the governor received a letter from the older Dunn offering Ogilvie a position in Dunn's law firm in the event that Ogilvie might not want to return to Chicago. Ogilvie wrote back that he was touched by the offer but that he intended to go back home.

Winning Control of the Budget

*D*on Perkins *often* got calls out of the blue from his pal Dick Ogilvie after he became governor. This time, Ogilvie was telling Perkins he needed somebody to chair the Illinois Board of Higher Education—someone who would not be snowed by the academic jargon from the muck-a-mucks at the universities.

Right off the bat, Perkins knew of the perfect person—George L. Clements, the board chairman of Jewel Tea Company and Perkins's boss. Clements also was the fellow who had given Ogilvie his first political contribution. There was one concern, though. Perkins cautioned Ogilvie that he was pretty sure Clements had only one year of college. No problem, responded the governor. "Ogilvie said Clements was exactly what he had in mind," related Perkins, "a tough-minded businessman to head the higher board, an individual not beholden to academia who could bring the universities' budgets under control."[1]

Clements accepted the appointment, worked hard at it and accomplished what Ogilvie wanted. Ogilvie sought little short of a complete shake-up of higher education, reforms that would achieve his often-stated goal to make the system "more compatible with the state's needs and resources."

Finally, in Ogilvie, critics of higher education appeared to have an ally in the governor's seat, one who thought, as they did, that the university establishment had grown fat, arrogant, and practically unaccountable because of the largely free hand given it for so long to expand virtually at will. The public universities received huge infusions of tax dollars, but numerous observers had an impression that administrators and others in the university network hardly saw themselves as subject to the same scrutiny as regular state workers. Many in public higher education simply did not see themselves as, well, state employees. Ogilvie made it clear that his vision for reshaping Illinois government did not exclude repairs to higher education. When he showed he meant business, he evoked angry and noisy resistance, certainly more so than in other segments of public life where Ogilvie rocked the boat. His governorship brought Illinois academe down to earth, adding one more reason for his unpopularity on some campuses. Ill feeling between Ogilvie and those in higher education grew strong enough that a few persons in academia might have offered a bounty for Ogilvie's hide if they could have gotten away with it. Some would have thought that funny, but not the governor's security detail, which always was on edge when Ogilvie set foot on certain campuses—with good reason.

Ed Heyer, the state policeman in charge of security for Ogilvie, was anything but amused at the governor's hasty exit on one occasion from Champaign-Urbana when University of Illinois students were acting up. Ogilvie was dining in the Illini Union prior to a scheduled speaking appearance when students protesting something or other forced their way into the student union building by pushing through campus security personnel as well as uniformed state troopers stationed at the doors.

"The Governor and I could hear the noise from the students breaking in, could hear glass shattering, and I knew we had to get out of there," said Heyer. "I had to assume, for all we knew, that they were trying to get to the boss." So, recounted Heyer, his crew and "the boss" retreated through a kitchen to escape from the union and reach a plain squad car on the quadrangle behind the building. Nelson Capitano, the young trooper behind the wheel, lost no time whisking Ogilvie away as he sped across the grass of the quad.[2]

On the way to a waiting plane, Heyer received word that two university security persons had been hurt in the scuffling with students at the Illini Union. Hearing this, Ogilvie asked Capitano to turn around the car and drive him back to wherever the injured pair were being treated so he could personally convey his sympathy. But, said Heyer, "I insisted we could not do that. It was just too dangerous. You had to remember what those times were like then. After the boss and I had some direct talk, I prevailed."

In the decades before Ogilvie, the public supported a progressive-expansionist mode for higher education, due in no small part to a wide belief after World War II that college was the preferable course for more and more men and women. SIU provided an easy-to-see scenario of what happened. When the charismatic Delyte Wesley Morris became president of the university in 1948, SIU was still little more than a sleepy teachers' training school that, with a faculty of 250 and a student body of three thousand, had not grown much at all since it first opened for classes in 1874. By the last stage of the twenty-two-year Morris presidency, enrollment had ballooned to well above twenty thousand (making it one of the country's twenty largest universities), the faculty had increased sevenfold, and a major new campus had opened at Edwardsville. While this aptly named "explosive" period of SIU attracted considerable attention because of the construction necessary to accommodate the growth, the boom years also saw the raising of academic standards as curricula were broadened and departments added.

Among the factors that made possible the emergence of SIU was its capability during most of the Morris years to secure almost everything it wanted from the General Assembly. The University of Illinois was never at a loss for a powerful voice in Springfield, but SIU became a strong competitor in the seemingly unlimited funding game. As with most things halcyon, though, the often pell-mell expansion of higher education would end, gradually for a while and then with a hard thud in the Ogilvie years.

Sure enough, just as Ogilvie wished, the clampdown was imposed by the Illinois Board of Higher Education chaired by Clements. As for execution of the panel's policies on a day-to-day basis, the task fell to one of the most controversial figures in the Ogilvie administration, the unrestrained, if not outrageous, James B. Holderman.

The brashness of Holderman, the board's executive director, may have been without equal among all those bright young individuals in Illinois government under Ogilvie. Holderman came to the board in his early thirties from the post of vice chancellor at the University of Illinois Chicago Circle campus. Yet he thought he should have received a bigger job with Ogilvie. He had in mind the state budget directorship held by McCarter, with whom Holderman had a love-hate relationship. Holderman wanted to make a big enough name for himself during the Ogilvie years to garner a Republican nomination in the near future for either governor or United States senator. Big political dreaming by Holderman went back to his days growing up in Grundy County, son of the politically potent S. J. Holderman of Morris. The older Holderman was a GOP leader in northern Illinois, the state's attorney of Grundy for sixteen years, and then chairman of the Illinois Industrial Commission when his friend from Morris, William Stratton, was governor.

At any rate, if Jim Holderman could not land what he perceived to be a more glamorous assignment from Ogilvie, he would have to make the most of what he had. Few thought he would fail. Declaring frequently that "the days of educational empire building in Illinois are over," Holderman quarterbacked the board with the blessing of Clements into a commanding role in higher education that, some observers felt, was pretty much what the General Assembly had in mind when it created the panel in the early 1960s. The board, the majority of the seats on which were filled by the governor, was designed to screen higher education's legislative requests, particularly budgetary, before presentation to the legislature. The panel also was authorized to coordinate development of the public facilities, a function that understandably impinged on the freedom once enjoyed by the individual governing bodies of the institutions.

Predictable carping by education traditionalists about the board in its early years turned into outright verbal warfare when the panel moved decisively, after the arrival of Clements and Holderman, to severely restrict university requests for operating funds and plans for expansion. Proposals for new programs, once routinely approved, had to be scrapped. Many low-priority projects went by the wayside. In short, the day of the big college spender was over, proclaimed Holderman. Critics of the board charged that it was trying to become a dictator of higher education, but the will of the large schools to fight the panel was tempered by the realization that many of its actions conformed to Ogilvie's insistence on a leveling off of appropriations for higher education.

The uproar in 1969 over the building of a new home for Morris at SIU certainly played into the hands of those who believed the time for putting a tight fiscal leash on the universities was long overdue. The $900,000 price tag on the structure, intended to house social functions and guest quarters as well as the residence of the president, prompted an angry Ogilvie to say he characterized "the decision on the house as a very unfortunate one by the administration of the university." The governor voiced agreement with the view of Holderman that "it is very difficult to get public understanding when something like this occurs."[3]

Milking the matter for all it was worth, the higher education board initiated an investigation of the construction of the home on a contention that SIU violated state law and board policy by proceeding with the project without the sanction of the board. The inquiry did trigger a public admission by John S. Rendleman, chancellor of SIU's Edwardsville campus. While in a previous post as the university's vice president for business affairs, he told the SIU trustees that it was all right to go ahead with the project without higher board approval. If he had it to do over again, Rendleman conceded, his advice would be different.

In a dramatic move, W. Clement Stone attempted to defuse the controversy through a $1 million gift of stock, accepted by the SIU trustees, to cover the cost of the house. Still, the higher board sharply assailed the administration and trustees of SIU in a report, stemming from the board's inquiry, that implied strongly that Morris should be stripped of much of his power. In truth, the trustees had already begun doing that before the report came out. However, 1970 would see the finish of the Morris presidency—at just about the time Ogilvie was seriously zeroing in on what he regarded as decades of lavish spending by the state's major universities.

The higher board's parsimonious reaction to many of the universities' spending requests was not the only way the panel irked the tradition-bound institutions. Under Ogilvie, the board did not hesitate to carry out initiatives begun in earlier years to upgrade the community or junior colleges, to further integrate private colleges into the Illinois higher education mainstream, and to establish new public universities, namely Governors State University at Park Forest South and Sangamon State University at Springfield (which eventually would become a branch of the University of Illinois).

The Ogilvie era also was one in which the board tried to go off in various radically new directions. Each time the emphasis was on greater utilization of existing resources instead of on more construction on campuses to accommodate the no longer acceptable proliferation of conventional programs. This was not to say that Holderman, the most forceful advocate for root change, was always successful. He made only marginal headway at best on some of his most far-reaching ventures, such as the establishment of a "collegiate common market"—a complete sharing among public and private schools of students, faculty, programs, equipment, and buildings. Increased state use of private college facilities, Holderman reasoned, was easier on taxpayers than continuous expansion at public campuses.

Because Holderman pursued his objectives with the tenacity of a bulldog, inevitable public spats shook the decorum of higher education that the public was so accustomed to. The most telling confrontation ensued between Holderman and John E. Corbally Jr., a former chief of Syracuse University who became president of the University of Illinois in 1971. They went at each other like opposing generals.

Take the chasing by Holderman of cuts in graduate education. "During the 1960s," said Holderman, "an extremely high demand for PhDs was created by the space program, plentiful foundation and defense funds for basic research . . . and ambitious industrial research programs. Unfortunately, much of the demand has now evaporated, but our massive national capacity for producing graduate degrees remains." Countered Corbally: "Where is the evidence that there is an oversupply of doctoral manpower with doctorates from the University of Illinois? Where is the evidence that in so-called austere times graduate education loses its importance?"[4]

As for the operating budget that the higher board recommended for his university in the fiscal year beginning in 1972, Corbally charged that "survival is the only priority need which can be attained" with the projected funds. "I can find no one who believes that the University of Illinois is unworthy of continued strong support and we cannot understand why other Systems [state universities] continue to receive increased tax support while we receive none," said Corbally. From where he sat, contended Corbally, Holderman was dangerously undermining public confidence in Illinois higher education by insinuating that "a fat and inefficient system of higher education has finally been called to task." If Holderman and his board could not avoid such a "negativistic and self-demeaning approach" to the needs of the institutions, Corbally suggested, his university and the other schools "must look elsewhere than to the Board of Higher Education for representation."[5]

When Corbally got into things like that, hinting at political insurrection, eyebrows went up and Corbally would be forced to explain that "my job is to be an honest and yet realistic advocate of the University of Illinois. Jim Holderman's job is different. It is obvious that the two of us from time to time will clash."

Still, the pungency of Corbally's reactions to Holderman prompted uneasy squirming by some of the university's trustees, who then were elected in partisan contests. One, William D. Forsyth Jr., a Springfield insurance executive and a Democrat with a keen political nose, feared that Corbally may have overreacted at times to a sincere attempt by the Ogilvie administration and legislators from both parties to bring universities out of the doghouse—where they stood with much of the public and state officials—by implementing tighter fiscal controls. He did not truly see, Forsyth said, "any bias against the University of Illinois in the Ogilvie administration or on the higher board."[6]

An irony was that Holderman was catching flak from both sides. From the higher education hierarchy on his left and from certain Ogilvie people on his right, principally McCarter and his budget gang. Corbally, Rendleman, and others in top posts at universities may have found Holderman miserly, but Ogilvie's budget crowd felt that Holderman and the higher board were not doing nearly enough to restrain university spending. Holderman was caught, McCarter knew full well, between a rock and a hard place. As McCarter worded it, Holderman was "in an extremely difficult position" in "trying to walk the line between scarce resources and the Governor's office on one hand and on the other hand the universities to which he wanted to be an advocate and a champion." Holderman just had, concluded McCarter, "a number of fights on his hands."[7]

Squabbles between McCarter's budget bureau and various segments of state government over allocation of tax dollars were not uncommon. With one notable exception, these were what McCarter termed "intramural" or in-house disputes. The exception was the veritable war over money for higher education, which was waged in broad daylight, even publicized. Talented folks were in the trenches on this one. Holderman's team included most capable budgeters like Jerry Porter and Richard D. Wagner, later himself an executive director of the higher board. At the same time, no more erudite staffers in Illinois government were available than McCarter's, including Stephen Phillips, the McCarter budget examiner for education. In dueling with Holderman, Phillips would come to see Jim, according to McCarter, as "a direct conflict" in that, McCarter said, Phillips grew to "regard Jim not as a professional educator but as a politician." Holderman proudly saw himself as both.

Irrespective of their sharp lieutenants, Holderman and McCarter remained at the bottom of it all the main protagonists—two longtime acquaintances who would not or could not get in sync, not even after the much older Clements called the two young men into his office at Jewel and attempted in a fatherly fashion to get them to work out their differences.

Part of the problem lay in Holderman's resentment of McCarter for what Holderman saw as McCarter's unmerited jump over him in the Ogilvie pecking order. Holderman claimed that he brought McCarter into the world of Ogilvie. What Holderman had to be referring to, McCarter assumed, was Holderman contacting him during the 1968 gubernatorial race and informing him that he, Holderman, was campaigning for Ogilvie and that he, Holderman, wanted McCarter to join a support group that Holderman had assembled. This was hardly a surprising request because the two had stayed in touch since their initial meeting in 1960 when both were assistant doorkeepers at the Republican National Convention in Chicago. Their relationship was close enough that McCarter took time during a spring break from Harvard business school to return to Illinois to spend a few days helping Holderman in an unsuccessful bid for a GOP nomination for Congress from northern Illinois in the early 1960s. So, when Holderman reached out to McCarter in 1968, McCarter agreed to assist the Ogilvie campaign. This led to McCarter's preparation of a paper on budget reform, which he said amounted to "the way I did work somewhat on the campaign." But, added McCarter, "I did not meet Richard Ogilvie one-on-one during that time."[8] Later, after Ogilvie won the election, he recruited McCarter to be his top finance person through a proceeding that had nothing to do with Holderman. As trivial as all this may have seemed to most, such little nuances in respect to whether somebody may or may not have lined up another person with a governor usually had a great bearing on the way these individuals regarded each other in the resulting power structure.

In all honesty, while Holderman never ceased blaming McCarter for his absence from Ogilvie's inner circle, Holderman retained unabashed ambition for bigger things. This red-flagged him to most in the governor's palace guard as an individual to be kept at arm's length if possible. After Ogilvie's defeat, when it was quite likely that McCarter's and Holderman's days were numbered, Holderman predicted to this writer that he was "going only one way from here, and that is up, while for many of these other guys [around Ogilvie] it may not be the same story."[9] Speaking for himself, Holderman was on target.

Leaving Illinois, Holderman put in time in a top slot with the Lilly Endowment, a philanthropic organization based in Indianapolis, where he oversaw the disbursement of millions of dollars in grants to education at all levels throughout the country. Following that, Holderman served thirteen years as president of the University of South Carolina, a span in which the school's reputation was greatly broadened through Holderman's successful promotions and fund-raising and by the capital construction accompanying these undertakings. Holderman was widely credited for achieving his goal to put the university on the map, and not just through the increased flow of dollars to the institution and the addition of things like new arts and engineering centers. He was also recognized for having the panache to lure celebrities to the university, ranging from Pope John II to world-famous academics. Holderman became the powerful figure he wanted to be, not in his home state but in South Carolina.

But alas, his presidency crashed in 1990 when he resigned amid mounting criticism of his free-spending style. A year later, Holderman was indicted on charges of having used his public office in South Carolina for illegal personal gain. After plea-bargaining with prosecutors, he was sentenced to five years on probation and ordered to perform five hundred hours of community service. He also had to pay back taxes owed. Holderman's life journey had taken him a long way indeed from Grundy County.

For Holderman and others pursuing success in overdrive, being covetous of McCarter during the Ogilvie governorship was comprehensible. With no pun intended toward Holderman, it was McCarter who truly was a big person on campus.

The takeover of the state budget process, the wresting of it by Ogilvie's executive branch from the General Assembly, was a momentous development. It made the governor the kingpin more than ever in controlling Illinois's purse strings and, consequently, the government of the state—from the big agencies to nickel-and-dime offices. Nothing else did more to ensure that Ogilvie left the governorship a considerably more authoritative office than he found it. For that, Ogilvie's successors had to be grateful, both to Ogilvie and to McCarter for carrying out Ogilvie's directive to get the revolution going.

By the time Ogilvie left office, the Bureau of the Budget was already so penetrative of state government that it was hard to believe it did not exist before the early days of Ogilvie's administration. To fulfill its mission, the bureau was given carte blanche to involve itself in what seemed like everything. Because so much in government was driven by dollars, agencies and their programs never were free of the bureau. Its fingers were visible in the drawing of proposed budgets for every operation, then in obtaining the necessary appropriations, and, finally, in watchdogging the actual release and expenditure of funds. More than a few department directors seldom made it through a day—or were hesitant to go through a day—without getting the bureau's okay on this or that. The bigger the government grew, the more a governor needed centralized control of the fiscal scene, and the bureau provided exactly that. The bureau was the coordinating mechanism that Ogilvie and later governors had to have to avoid political embarrassment from unmonitored pushing and shoving over state dollars, whether from the public or private sectors.

Many in state government thought the bureau's often cold-eyed analysts were too pervasive, too heavy-handed in using the necessity for fiscal responsibility as an excuse to poke their noses into every nook and cranny. After the creation of the bureau in 1969, a great deal of the fun and spontaneity disappeared from budgeting. Gone was the freedom and freewheeling so many had enjoyed.

Before Ogilvie, budgeting for the state was a balkanized affair, more resembling the concocting of mulligan stew than any particularly discernible process. The governor was responsible for preparing and submitting the state spending plan to the General Assembly. After that, the situation was up for grabs. About the only thing for sure was that the final product coming back to the governor's desk would cover, and generously so, the favorite programs or projects of the principal legislative power brokers, individuals personified to a tee by Senator Everett R. Peters from St. Joseph and by Paul Powell. A main tool used by Powell, Peters, and certain other lawmakers to work their will with the budget was the old Illinois Budgetary Commission, which since the Great Depression had provided its legislative members with just about unlimited license to greatly shape if not dictate state expenditures. All of it was aboveboard in that the commission had the duty to investigate budget requests from the agencies and then to make recommendations based on its findings to not only the legislature but also to the governor. While the governor may or may not have listened to the commission as he prepared his proposed budget every other year, it was certain that the General Assembly paid heed because the commission's membership was dominated by folks like Powell or Peters who could pull or control a lot of votes between the two houses. It was no wonder that the legislative elite identified with the commission had so much to say about the budget in its final form.

Since the mid-1940s, when Dwight Green was governor, "Nubby" Peters, a coal dealer when he took time away from the Senate, had served more terms as chairman of the budgetary commission than anybody could remember. The biggest, but by no means only, beneficiary of this was the Champaign-Urbana campus of the University of Illinois, which was in Peters's district. The commission's equivalent to Peters on the Democratic side was his de facto political ally Representative Powell, who served on the panel from 1945 until he was elected secretary of state in 1964. That gave Powell a strong hand. With it, he built his reputation for bringing home the bacon for his southern Illinois constituents while, in the process, increasing the number of state jobholders loyal to him.

Making it even easier for master legislative craftsmen like Powell and Peters to exercise such fiscal sway was the skimpiness of the governor's own budgetary operation. Right up to the moment Ogilvie took office, the Department of Finance was the executive branch's budgeting agency. As bureaucracies go, this one wasn't much.

Under Kerner in the 1960s, the finance department was directed by James A. Ronan, a Chicago lawyer and a live-and-let-live gentleman who was not disposed to butt heads with major political counterparts on the budget. A Dick Daley fellow, Ronan had other matters on his mind besides state finances. Ronan served as chairman of the Illinois Democratic Party. And he operated a wholesale meat business in Chicago established by his father. Ronan certainly was accessible enough, but when questioned to any degree about the state budget, he would quickly summon to his office T. R. (Ted) Leth. Leth was the department's budget superintendent and about the only person in the executive branch able to address in detail the allocation of state funds—besides Jerome mayor Vernon Shontz or one or two other veteran officials. Why? Well, since leaving his post as comptroller of Oak Park in 1943, Leth had supervised the drawing of each two-year budget and then, after some version of his handiwork was appropriated, watched to see that spending from the appropriations was suitably carried out. For more than a generation, Leth and the state budget were synonymous.

When Ogilvie was persuading McCarter to join him in Springfield, he accented his distaste for another political party chief like Ronan serving as the top state finance officer. As for Leth, Ogilvie announced his resignation two weeks after Ogilvie became governor. The terse press release on Leth's departure noted he was seventy-six years old. Wisecracking reporters said this explained Leth's occasional grouchiness when bombarded with questions about the parceling of state dough.

McCarter replaced Leth, but the only resemblance between the two was that McCarter, like Leth, was from Oak Park. John Wilbur McCarter Jr. brought superior credentials to his preeminent role in the Ogilvie administration. In the thirteen years since his graduation from Oak Park High School, McCarter had graduated from the Woodrow Wilson School of Public and International Affairs at Princeton University, spent time at the London School of Economics, and received a master's degree in business administration from Harvard. He served as a White House Fellow while Lyndon Johnson was president. That experience exposed him to the inner workings of the federal budget. It also allowed him to observe Johnson up close in the oval office, direct contact that left McCarter "enormously impressed" with the president, even though he was a Democrat and McCarter considered himself a Republican.

Johnson was not the only top Democrat that McCarter saw firsthand. While a Princeton student, McCarter was granted something not many journalists could get, an hour-long interview with Mayor Daley in his city hall office. McCarter used the information from the meeting in a senior thesis on the skillful manner in which Daley merged his governing and political responsibilities. The interview was arranged by John Dreiske, the political editor of the *Sun-Times* and a friend of McCarter's parents. With occasions like this and the White House stop in his background, McCarter could not resist being "fascinated by politics." Nevertheless, at a breakfast with this writer in 1994 at Chicago's Union League Club, he stressed that Ogilvie "had positioned me as a numbers guy, not a political operative."[10]

While old Ted Leth never seemed to have much help, McCarter surrounded himself in the new budget bureau with a large cadre of individuals like himself—meaning most were young and largely apolitical. To critics in the old-boy network, who lamented the demise of the budgetary commission, the bulk of those in McCarter's crew would be seen as austere technocrats trying to go too much by the book in budgeting. It may have been an exaggeration to say, as did some, that everybody in the Bureau of the Budget had the same mind-set. However, McCarter did personally recruit just about every one of his troops, and a large number of them had budget experience in Washington. This helped to explain why the Illinois budget bureau, in starting from scratch, essentially installed in the state a simplified model of the federal budget structure.

The Bureau of the Budget may have been on paper just a part of the governor's executive office organization, but it stood out like a sore thumb. From its start under McCarter, the bureau operated like an elite unit managing to live in a world of its own. Detractors said it constituted a governmental ivory tower. Even though staffers in governmental operations generally as a rule remain anonymous, the names of many with the bureau in its early days would come to mind years later because they literally forged the radical update of the Illinois budgetary system that, in turn, so strengthened the potency of the governor. After McCarter, there was Ranney of course and Steve Phillips, the jouster with Holderman. Others who made names for themselves were John Cotton, Paul Kerz, James Bankard, Lester Munson, Troy Murray, David Rinker, Richard Kolhauser, Jeffrey Miller, Floyd Skloot, Craig Bazzani, Bob Taft, and Robert Mandeville. Taft's father and grandfather served in the United States Senate from Ohio and his great-grandfather was President William Howard Taft. Mandeville would become much better known down the line as the director of the Bureau of the Budget during the fourteen-year retention of the governor's office by Jim Thompson.

For those seeking historical comparison, McCarter and his key assistants may have furnished Ogilvie with a touch of Franklin Delano Roosevelt's brain trust, the politically popular name given to Columbia University's Raymond Moley and other university professors who served FDR during his campaign for president in 1932. Most were relatively young and intent on shaking up the status quo, and they were respected more for their particular knowledge than for any official title or political standing. McCarter's people were cast a lot like that. And, like Roosevelt's "brain trusters," they sported an abundance of degrees from the finer schools.

Hardly a day passed when Ogilvie was governor without a reminder that his budget shop represented the state's passing from one governmental era to another. There were those who might argue that the death of Powell while Ogilvie was in office could not have more symbolized the fade from the old to the new. But the omnipotence of the budget bureau was apparent on a daily basis.

John W. Lewis was a veteran of twenty-six years in the General Assembly and a former speaker of the House when Ogilvie named Lewis, a farmer and auctioneer, to direct the Illinois Department of Agriculture. Lewis, who was voting on state spending when some of the Ogilvie budget bureau kids were still in diapers, was incensed when the budget examiner assigned to his agency, James Elsass, heavily cut Lewis's budget. Later, when Lewis found himself sitting in front of an appropriations committee including a number of his old legislative pals, Lewis made it unmistakably clear that he did not recommend the agriculture budget proposed by Ogilvie.

"This is the budget of a man by the name of Elsass in the budget bureau," Lewis testified. "If you want to hear it defended, talk to Elsass. Elsass does not know the difference between a gilt and a boar, but this is Elsass's budget."[11] Thereafter, in a meeting with McCarter, Lewis signaled an intent to resign. However, Ogilvie liked Lewis. So, after Ogilvie, Lewis, and McCarter all talked it over, Lewis stayed on. In fact, he was destined, as it happened, for a bigger role.

Far from simply pumping up his own world, McCarter was quite apropos when he stressed the importance of the budget among the various avenues open to a governor to spell out his priorities. Said McCarter: "One [avenue] is clearly a state of the state message. Others are discrete or individual messages or pieces of legislation that he might propose. But the one that is central, that integrates it all, is the budget process. When you get somebody like Ogilvie who was interested in government, and who is committed and has opinions on programs, you can make that [budget] document very, very responsive to his interests."[12] In addition to underscoring the intentions of a governor, the annual state budget provided the easiest guide for tracing the destinations of taxpayers' dollars.

The second budget proposed by Ogilvie while he was governor contained little of the drama of his first—the one in 1969 calling for enactment of the state income tax and umpteen hikes in already existing state levies. His second budget, for fiscal year 1971 (beginning July 1, 1970), predictably sought no new or increased taxes. It did incorporate record state expenditures of $4,947,682,000, which encompassed more state funds for schools and governing bodies in local communities while reducing appropriations for some state agencies. The major budgetary hikes were ticketed for welfare and social service programs in addition to education, particularly in state aid to elementary and secondary schools. To be specific, 58 percent of the projected revenue for that budget was reserved for education costs, including the budgets of the public universities and colleges.

The dispute over higher education funding really hit the fan in Ogilvie's presentation of his third budget, his spending plan for the 1972 fiscal year. In that budget Ogilvie called for the state to expend $5,662,000,000 in the twelve-month fiscal period beginning July 1, 1971, some $715 million more than he sought to shell out in his previous budget. To meet the spending targets in his third budget, he said the state would have to drain its general revenue coffer or raise taxes, something he was not about to try to do. Also, in a bit of a bombshell, Ogilvie revealed that he had taken the unusual step of returning the proposed budgets for the public universities to the Illinois Board of Higher Education—on a ground that they were outlandish. Otherwise, the governor warned, there would not be enough money for a number of other state operations to maintain even survival-level funding.

When Ogilvie addressed this subject in delivering his third budget message to a joint session of the House and Senate on March 3, 1971, he spared few words in voicing a belief that "we must take a hard look at our commitment to higher education in Illinois. It is essential that we begin asking whether this system which has doubled its expenditures in the past four years has produced corresponding results. In the face of widespread student dissatisfaction and public impatience with the quality of higher education, it is essential that we ask why the system has failed to satisfy the very people it exists to serve."[13]

Along with higher education, Ogilvie emphasized in his budget presentation that welfare was the other in the "pair of almost insatiable demands so overwhelming as to threaten the very solvency of our state." While the bulk of the proposed budget was unavoidably earmarked for education, welfare, and highways, Ogilvie noted pointedly that the $1,119,600,000 budget for public aid alone would consume more than 80 percent of the increase expected in fiscal year 1972 from state revenue sources. While Ogilvie asserted that getting a handle on higher education ought to be doable, he warned that the 700,000-plus people on public assistance in the state were creating a social and financial disaster for Illinois. Judging by the fourth Ogilvie budget, which would be his last, the public aid funding predicament was only accelerating. The governor called for another new high in state expenditures of $6,040,000,000 in the 1973 fiscal year, of which $1,451,000,000 was budgeted for welfare, an increase of more than $230 million above the amount needed the previous year.

Ogilvie's final spending plan, outlined to the public March 1, 1972, reflected his desire to complete or further implement many of the governmental revisions he had initiated, such as the transfer of a great number of mental health patients from large institutions to the more personalized atmosphere of community-based facilities. For the third straight year, no tax hike was requested in the budget. Instead, he unexpectedly asked the General Assembly to approve a program—to cost the state $16 million a year at first by his calculation—that would provide special relief from excessive property taxes for many low-income persons over sixty-five years old who either owned a home or still paid such levies indirectly through rental payments. Consequently, lawmakers passed a measure, Senate Bill 1363, approved by Ogilvie in July 1972, that authorized individual cash grants of up to $500 to offset the property taxes or rents owed by certain elderly or disabled Illinoisans. At the same time, Ogilvie signed another bill that exempted qualified pension plan payments to retired persons from the Illinois income tax. These bills were the main components of an Ogilvie effort to provide tax relief to needy individuals in his last year in office—the year of his unsuccessful bid for reelection.

Under his final budget, just about every state activity was scheduled to receive more money than in the preceding fiscal year, which Ogilvie said was possible without a tax increase because of growing yields from state levies and federal aid. A notable feature of Ogilvie's last budget was its inclusion of

$1,454,000,000 from the federal government, making those dollars a greater source of revenue for Illinois than the state's income tax, sales levy, or any other Illinois tax or revenue source. Federal money was counted on to pay for about 25 percent of Ogilvie's spending proposals in his concluding budget go-around.

The federal contribution resulted at least in part from intense lobbying in Washington for federal dollars—at McCarter's direction. When the stakes were high, McCarter himself would fly to Washington. "We used to go," he said, "to the Roger Smith Hotel [in Washington], which was a cheap hotel, and I would be with ten or twelve budget examiners, and we'd just stay and blanket the town."[14] Those were still the early years in the political career of Senator Charles Percy, a period when he was considered a rising GOP star, and he proved to be a clever tactician in helping McCarter in his quest for federal funds. McCarter had another ace in the hole with debonair Tom Corcoran, whose effectual managing of the Illinois office in the nation's capital set a tough example for his successors to match.

Ogilvie also went to Washington frequently. The exposure he got there was important if he was to fulfill any political ambition beyond the borders of Illinois. The governor also realized that the severity of the public aid funding crisis in Illinois demanded his personal attention in Washington. Here, firepower was necessary beyond what could be mustered by handsome young fellows like McCarter and Corcoran.

The Illinois chief executive was in the vanguard of those seeking to drum up support for the federal revenue sharing and welfare revisions pushed by President Nixon. Whether confronting congressional committees or federal bureaucrats, Ogilvie portrayed a dark vision for his state if more federal money for public aid was not forthcoming. In the absence of such dollars, Ogilvie warned, his state's other vital responsibilities were being short-circuited by the burgeoning costs of welfare.

Governor Nelson A. Rockefeller of New York attracted national attention in 1971 when he reversed an earlier position by taking a hard-line approach to welfare problems. But for Ogilvie, a natural would-be competitor to Rockefeller for prominence among the governors, this was already a *fait accompli*. Before Rockefeller, Ogilvie was calling for philosophical and operational alterations in a welfare system that he labeled "a human outrage and fiscal monster." It was then that Ogilvie launched his drive to require able-bodied recipients to accept employment or be denied benefits. Attainment of part of that goal under Ogilvie's plan involved the creation of thousands of public service jobs. To help make that happen, federal funds were solicited. Getting them, though, was not easy.

Ogilvie also ignited inevitable protest marches and rallies by attempting to not only bring under control but actually lower Medicaid and general assistance payments. He was gambling in doing so that the move would ingratiate him with middle-class wage earners who themselves were being pinched by the country's economic slump at the beginning of the 1970s. Yet he risked alienating many poor Illinoisans. So Ogilvie nixed lowering grants to the huge number of Illinoisans—nearly 650,000—receiving Aid to Families with Dependent Children.

Medicaid was another story. Presaging a subject that would give governors after him more gray hair, Ogilvie classified Medicaid as "the most demanding and difficult item in the financing of state government" since the program's enactment by Congress in the mid-1960s.[15] From early 1966 to mid-1971, Ogilvie pointed out, Illinoisans eligible for Medicaid increased to 850,000, from 250,000. In order to begin bringing the program within reasonable bounds, Ogilvie favored a freeze on hospital and other rates, token payments by recipients for requested assistance, and elimination of "certain marginal services."

Precious few jobs in Illinois government were viewed as frustrating as that of director of the Department of Public Aid. Since volunteers for this position were hard to find, Ogilvie kept in that spot Harold (Hap) Swank, the department's only director since it became a code agency in 1963. Much like Clarence Klassen, Swank was one of Illinois's bureaucratic legends, a person who had worked his way up the ladder, after starting as a public assistance caseworker in Vermilion County in the 1930s. A skilled and affable technician, Swank benefited from the widely held impression that not many other capable individuals were available for this less-than-attractive directorship. After a while, though, Swank's perceived reluctance to join in the hunt for federal funds or to embrace operational changes encouraged by McCarter and other Ogilvie "brain trusters" led to his departure. His eventual replacement was Edward T. Weaver, the initial director of the Department of Children and Family Services under Ogilvie. Considerably younger than Swank, Weaver was more receptive to the administration's desire for a fresh approach in tackling the challenges in public aid that seemed to do nothing but grow and grow.

The moves by the Ogilvie administration for innovations in government fell short more than once. Although Ogilvie's Institute for Environmental Quality accomplished many of its goals, its sister operation, the Institute for Social Policy, did not live up to expectation. Modeled to some degree after the Rand Corporation, the social policy institute was designed to foster research into ways to make public assistance outlays more meaningful and to upgrade the handling of divisive social issues. However, McCarter and others felt it bogged down in the same morass that impeded so many other efforts aimed at solving problems involving minorities and the poor.

Still, after all was said and done, the bottom line in McCarter's mind was that "we were not afraid to do or try things that had never been done before." The Ogilvie team went up to bat a lot, he felt, and it was impossible to get a hit every time.

As the 1990s moved on, and McCarter found himself back in Chicago as a management consultant and then as president of the Field Museum of Natural History, he could not resist observing in retrospect that "people on the outside of large institutions, be they state government, universities or businesses, tend to look with awe at the people who are in those institutions. But, when you are one of those insiders, you know they are just a lot of fallible people making a lot of decisions that are good, bad or indifferent," said McCarter. "I hoped that most of ours were good ones. I believe they were."[16]

Ogilvie in Person and in the Press

Ogilvie, One Leg at a Time

The sorts who snuggle close to officialdom—reporters, lobbyists, holders of government contracts—knew John McCarter was right. Individuals in important positions of public trust were fallible all right, leading them to many decisions that were neither good nor indifferent but simply bungled. During Ogilvie's time, cynicism about government ran rampant, thanks to Vietnam and the Watergate scandal.

In Illinois, though, the governor somehow remained bigger than life. Maybe it came with the office. Perhaps, too, a lot of people wanted it that way. But those men who attained the governorship had to watch how they handled this image. If the governor did not portray a little humility, an earthiness now and then for all to witness, he might breed resentment. The populace loved to see such a powerful person putting on his pants one leg at a time.

Otto Kerner was more than a tad stuffy, but he could get away with it because of his regal look and the prim fit of his vested suits. And what a smile he had in those canned pictures. Unfortunately, the war wound to Ogilvie's face deprived him of a photogenic smile. Ogilvie also was no clotheshorse. By Brooks Brothers' standards, he wasn't even a good dresser.

Dan Walker was hardly an average Joe, even though he went to incredible lengths—walking the entire state on bloody feet and shunning many of the perquisites of the office after becoming governor—to depict a common touch. After Walker came Big Jim Thompson. Thompson was a public relations practitioner's delight, a charming figure who packed personally appealing qualities into the majesty of the governorship. Approving heartily, voters might have kept him in office for the rest of his life if he had not quit on his own.

The trouble with Dick Ogilvie was that he just did not come off very well in any of these areas, as cosmetic as they may have seemed to some of the more serious students of the governing process. The outwardly bland Ogilvie was simply the governor who forged the overhaul that dictated the quality and agenda of his state's government for decades to follow, a framework tinkered with only slightly by his successors. However, many Illinoisans either failed to grasp that he did all this or they cared hardly at all. It was bad enough for Ogilvie that he did not endear himself to those he governed. It was a political tragedy for him that they never got to know him. To believe those familiar with Ogilvie, he did happen to be an occupant of the governor's chair who put on his pants one leg at a time.

Ogilvie even stated so himself. Ed Heyer heard him say it after the governor spent the good part of a day hunting and dining with a number of the state's leading corporate executives at Nilo Farms, a private preserve near Brighton owned by the Olin Corporation of East Alton, an explosives manufacturer. As the governor's black Lincoln departed from the preserve, Ogilvie remarked to Heyer that he found the business bigwigs with whom he had just rubbed shoulders to be "really regular guys." "You know, Ed," Heyer quoted Ogilvie as saying, "they put their pants on one leg at a time, just like you and me." Hearing this, Ogilvie's security chief quickly shot back, "Hey, Boss, come on now. I'm just a trooper. You are the Governor."[1]

Charles N. Wheeler III, a Statehouse scribe for the *Sun-Times* for more than two decades, saw great irony in the way the personality factor played out in Ogilvie's 1972 race with Walker. The impression most widespread, observed Wheeler, was that Ogilvie was cold and distant while Walker was down-to-earth. But, Wheeler held, "Walker always struck a lot of us as uptight, with little personality, while Ogilvie actually was charming in person . . . really quite personable."[2]

As implausible as it would have seemed for a politician reaching the office of governor, Ogilvie came across to some who met him as almost shy. Dorothy Ogilvie found him quite reserved when they met. As for Paul Simon, the lieutenant governor saw "early on" after he and Ogilvie were sworn into office that "Ogilvie was a laid-back figure who did not have a political type personality." Ogilvie never would exhibit "the flamboyance of Walker," Simon said, or "the backslapping ability of Jim Thompson and some others."[3]

To assistants who spent long hours with him in the governor's office, Ogilvie was, more than anything, very subtle, even unassuming—a radical departure from the whiz-bang mentality of so many in Illinois public life. He had that extra-dry wit, and he had that stolid manner that people meeting him for the first time found hard to penetrate.

Arthur (Ron) Swanson, an Ogilvie staffer brought in late term to assist on legislative relations, could not erase the memory of Ogilvie "sitting relaxed in his chair, puffing on his pipe, listening to gripes, complaints and screwball recommendations. He looked and listened silently, barely nodding his head occasionally, and the visitor would leave thinking he or she had won an enormous victory."[4]

The governor was not above altering his style, though, to fit the occasion. Russ Adams, an assistant director of the Illinois Department of Labor under Ogilvie, would remember getting a kick out of one such deviation. Said Adams: "The Governor was always a gentleman, but he had a little technique he used when we met with labor leaders which made my job a lot easier. He would be sipping a Scotch and soda and, in the midst of the conversation, he would drop a few swear words. The labor people were amazed that such a regular guy could be governor."[5]

To gain an appreciation of Ogilvie, his adherents insisted that one had to watch for the small things, the nuances he displayed. A lot of the old school was visible in Ogilvie. It went beyond his rapid rise to his feet when a woman entered his office and his hesitation to be seated until she was. More revealing was the experience of Julie Cellini.

Cellini, whose husband Bill was running the state highway network, went to a party at the mansion in the wake of a difficult pregnancy. Although Ogilvie "kept reminding me to sit down," she said, "I wanted to mix and mingle. Finally, out of the corner of my eye, I saw the Governor headed toward me carrying two little gold chairs. And there we sat, the Governor of Illinois and I, in the center of a cocktail party. It was one of the nicest things anyone ever did for me."[6] It was as if everyone walking the Illinois corridors of power had a story to counter the negative tag of impersonality routinely affixed to Ogilvie.

After Ogilvie placed him in charge of the Illinois Housing Development Authority, young Daniel Kearney worked day and night to get the fledgling agency off the ground, a task that permitted Kearney precious little time with his new wife. As a consequence, Kearney was most thankful when the governor approached Kearney's wife at a black-tie dinner to tell her what a great job her husband was doing. "He knew he didn't have to say that to me," remarked Kearney, "but that my wife had paid the more extensive sacrifice. It was evident he had that special touch."[7]

A few even found Ogilvie exciting, or at least hair-raising to be with. Bill Hanley, the governor's legislative counsel, remembered the adrenaline flowing when Ogilvie spotted a purse snatcher in action as he and Hanley were being driven one day through Chicago's Loop. Hanley braced himself as Ogilvie ordered the trooper behind the wheel to give chase. Then when the car got snarled in traffic, Ogilvie chased the man on foot. The thief escaped, leaving

Hanley shaking his head in amazement that neither the snatcher nor the victim "knew the Governor had taken after the snatcher."[8]

Interrupting his schedule for a brief game of cops and robbers may have made Ogilvie's day. If only part of what was said was true, Ogilvie bonded strongly with the field of law enforcement. The governor assumed he shared a camaraderie with any person wearing a peace officer's badge. Close to home, it was easy for Ogilvie's followers to detect his obvious affinity for his own security detail. And if Fred Bird knew what he was talking about, "the coppers" in the security unit "adored the Governor because he was one of them, and a fellow who had no airs whatever."[9]

However, traipsing around with bodyguards could be a mixed blessing for a governor already saddled, fairly or not, with an image of aloofness. One of the knocks against Ogilvie was that he was too security conscious, an observation voiced not just by his detractors. Yet Bird, a man who hated pretentiousness, saw no iota of it in the security for Ogilvie because, said Bird, "it was a great convenience that made things function a lot easier for the Governor."

Heyer cited other reasons for protecting the governor. Threats. Threats through the mail and threats delivered in other ways. "We had to take the threats seriously because those were really wild and dangerous times," insisted Heyer. "I didn't think he [Ogilvie] cared much about the threats himself, but he was concerned about Liz and the Missus [Dorothy Ogilvie]. As for the man himself, he did not scare easily. Take my word for it. He was a two-fisted guy."[10]

Heyer, who ended a twenty-six-year career with the Illinois State Police in 1982, seldom veered far from the tough-guy characterization of Ogilvie. In a 1995 interview one warm evening at his home in Jacksonville, Heyer hashed over his days with Ogilvie. The former trooper recalled with uncloaked affection what he said was "Ogilvie's frequent reminder that he'd help me and my guys if we needed it. If it ever hit the fan, Ogilvie told us he'd be there. No doubt he meant it. He'd have been right there."

Did Heyer ever fire his gun while guarding Ogilvie? No. Did he ever draw it? He would not say. However, Heyer did reveal an arrangement concerning guns that, he contended, "was never known by anybody except for the Governor and myself." It grew out of Ogilvie's resolution, according to Heyer, that "there was no place in Illinois that as governor he was afraid to go to." But when Ogilvie's destination was an obviously violence-prone place, such as Cairo, Heyer took an added precaution with the secret concurrence of Ogilvie.

On certain occasions when Ogilvie ventured into unpredictable terrain, Heyer said he carried an extra gun in addition to the state-issued Smith and

Wesson pistol he wore on his hip. The second weapon was a three-inch barrel .357 Magnum revolver belonging to Ogilvie, since his stint as sheriff. Heyer said he would stick the weapon in the back of his trousers hidden under his suit coat. One reason Heyer and Ogilvie did not let on about the extra weapon, explained Heyer, was that "a state trooper was only supposed to carry the weapon issued to him or her. Our thinking," Heyer said, "was that if trouble came up and I got hit and went down, he [Ogilvie] would grab that second gun if he could and help. Believe me, he could use it. He was a good shot."

Heyer took note of Ogilvie's marksmanship when the governor accompanied Heyer now and then to a firing range. Ogilvie's love of hunting may have equaled his passion for golf and Chicago's football Bears, his favorite team. Dorothy Ogilvie swore her husband once told her he had killed two wild turkeys with one shot on a hunting trip to Texas. Although she could not remember if that outing took place during or after the governorship, she had no doubt the two-for-one actually happened since she never knew Dick Ogilvie to tell tall tales.

Sharing Ogilvie's yen for golf, Heyer relished the governor's persistence in getting out to the links whenever possible. Heyer discovered no part of his job more rewarding than the governor's annual excursion, along with Perkins and several others, to the Augusta National Golf Course in Georgia, the home of the Masters tournament.

With the possible exception of Ogilvie's wife and daughter, no individual spent more hours at Ogilvie's side when he was governor than Edmund Lawrence Heyer, a coal miner's son raised in the German settlements of Breese and Carlyle in Clinton County. Heyer came to know Ogilvie so well that the trooper even carried an extra one of the blue pouches of the mild tobacco that Ogilvie smoked in his pipe because, as Heyer put it, "he was always running out."

When Ogilvie roamed outside his office, downstate at least, Heyer was that solemn-faced guy without a name seldom more than a few feet from the governor. At receptions and other gatherings, Heyer stationed himself on Ogilvie's "right hip pocket." If Ogilvie took off walking, Heyer tried to stride in front of him. The trooper always preceded his boss through doors and into elevators. In cars transporting the governor, Heyer occupied the right front seat, the "command seat" for the security detail. In the beginning, Ogilvie wanted to roost in that seat, and he and Heyer quarreled about it until Heyer convinced the governor that the right back rear seat was the appropriate place for the "commander in chief."

Ogilvie's designation of Heyer to direct his security was an egalitarian move since Heyer was only a corporal in rank in the state police. As if that was not enough to annoy higher ranking officers, some noses really got out of joint when Ogilvie made it clear that Heyer was not to be countermanded from above on any matter involving protection of the governor. The higher-ups would have to wait until Ogilvie was no longer around to give Heyer his come-uppance, which they did.

For most of the Ogilvie governorship, Heyer ran a detail comprised of thir-teen persons assigned out of the state police operation known as District 25, the plainclothes detective section. Members of the security detail continued to shun uniforms except for the driver of the vehicle carrying Ogilvie, a task nor-mally given to a trooper aptly named Bill Dragoo. To those in the know, a tip-off to Ogilvie's approach was the appearance of the detail's advance person, which in Heyer's gang happened to be a quite thorough chap, Robert Bower-sock, a trooper from Mason City. When Bowersock surfaced, that four-door black Lincoln often conveying the governor would not be far behind. (Ogilvie also had a black Cadillac limousine at his disposal along with a Chrysler Impe-rial in Chicago, also black.) Heyer routinely had a car with several troopers tailing the governor's unless he was in always potentially explosive East St. Louis. There, more than one security car accompanied Ogilvie's vehicle.

Up to and continuing through the Ogilvie years, those almost intimidating black limousines were a traditional mode of transportation for the governor and other Illinois constitutional officers. After replacing Ogilvie, Dan Walker ditched the limousine image by riding in ordinary Chevrolets. Walker also cut back on security, at least the visible segment of it, by settling much of the time for just one trooper in his car, a driver out of uniform, with no lead or trailing vehicles. Walker hoped to gain politically through steps like these, thinking the public had more than its fill of what Walker saw as top officials flaunting the trappings of office.

Analogous to Ogilvie, though, Walker became very close to the state police-man heading his security, Pete Wilkes. Were guys like Heyer or Wilkes ever to spill the beans on their bosses, many persons conjectured, gossip columnists would have had a field day. To this, Heyer had a simple comeback. Speaking for Ogilvie, he laughingly maintained, "The juiciest tidbit I could have divulged was that he and Dorothy escaped from time to time to share a bourbon, or he'd have a martini, or maybe two . . . but always in moderation."[11]

Oh sure, there were humorous happenings. On one visit to Chicago by Presi-dent Nixon when Ogilvie was governor, Nixon and his staffers were chauf-feured around in limousines while the governor of Illinois and another gover-nor or two on hand were relegated to a common bus for lesser lights. Ogilvie himself was not amused by the insult. Or there was the day at the White House when Ogilvie, confronted by security personnel wanting to know who he was, flashed his Illinois hunting or fishing license to identify himself.

But in Washington, as Heyer witnessed for himself, unexpected turns were the norm. A perfect example was the night Heyer escorted Ogilvie and his wife to a get-together at the apartment of an assistant to Vice President Agnew. When the Ogilvies went into the apartment, Heyer remained outside with their automobile. Pretty soon, though, Ogilvie came out of the apartment and approached Heyer at a fast pace.

"Ed, you've got to come inside and hear this," Heyer quoted the governor as saying in an unusually excitable tone. So Heyer followed Ogilvie back inside to discover Dinah Shore singing a tune being played on a piano by Agnew. After a moment or two, Heyer related, Agnew turned toward the trooper while still hitting the keys and asked Heyer if he "had ever had cheap entertainment before." Looking at Agnew, who was smiling, Heyer remembered replying, "No sir, not involving the Vice President and Dinah Shore."[12]

Maybe, just maybe, had word circulated through Illinois about the human side of Ogilvie, about the Good Samaritan chasing purse snatchers and doing other fine deeds, the state income tax that he pushed may have been easier for some to swallow. But the prevalent notion about Ogilvie in many places was that he was nigh invisible, the next thing to a stranger. Southern Illinois always came to mind.

One individual definitely no stranger to southern Illinois was Samuel O. Hancock of UPI, who spent nearly forty years covering the region as a reporter before his retirement in 1987. Hancock may have been low-keyed, but he knew visceral politicians when he saw them, the Powells, the Walkers, the Choates. Hancock did not put Ogilvie in this league. Ogilvie did not openly appeal to the emotions of southern Illinoisans as did more gregarious political figures, surmised Hancock. There was no pulling at heartstrings. In a 1994 interview at his home in Herrin, Hancock was asked about Ogilvie. He discovered it was difficult to get beyond "a lingering impression that Ogilvie, who seemed pretty much of an all business kind of person, never got that well known in southern Illinois. He just didn't appear to make that many trips down here into this part of the state, which was basically Democratic anyway." Compared to "certain others through the years," suggested Hancock, "Ogilvie was really not a publicity hound."[13]

Nevertheless, while not arguing with Hancock's perception, another southern Illinoisan, C. Dayton McReaken, was very aware of Ogilvie's painstaking attentiveness to matters of importance in southern Illinois. McReaken, a Democrat, served as the acting director of the Department of Mines and Minerals late in Ogilvie's governorship. For McReaken, this was a high point in a lifetime in coal, in which McReaken had been a union miner, a company man, and a federal as well as state mine inspector. McReaken happened to be the state inspector at large in April 1971 when seven men in an underground fluorspar mine near the Ohio River town of Golconda died from exposure to hydrogen sulfide gas. McReaken recalled Ogilvie joining David L. Gulley, the mining department director, at the scene of the disaster. McReaken also was impressed that Ogilvie attended a wake at a Golconda funeral home for one of the victims and that Richard Mathias, an Ogilvie aide, went to wakes for the other victims as the governor's representative.

Ogilvie's concern over the incident led him to take steps to establish a state mine rescue station at Elizabethtown, not far from Golconda. The governor also made sure the state got five new mine rescue team trucks as soon as possible. In the summer of 1971, Ogilvie signed legislation prompted by the Golconda disaster that increased the state's regulation of metal mines. At the same time he approved a measure that got the state much more involved in the control of explosives, a dangerous element of mining.

Another thing McReaken noticed, out of the ordinary and unknown to the public, was the periodic breakfast that Ogilvie would share with state mine inspectors at a motel in Benton. On these occasions, he would receive direct reports on a crackdown he had instigated on unsafe mine conditions. As a result, there were far fewer state-directed shutdowns of collieries for weak roofs, inadequate ventilation, and other hazardous situations in 1972 than in 1971. The effort entailed greater attention to safety by the more than eleven thousand working miners, by mine operators themselves, and state officials.

Governors could be haunted by fears of a recurrence of one of the major disasters that had marked the history of coal mining in Illinois. When Ogilvie took office, the last governor to go through a mining disaster was Adlai Stevenson in 1951. A few days before Christmas that year, 119 men died in an explosion at the Orient No. 2 underground mine at West Frankfort. McReaken, a resident of West Frankfort, was on the Benton state mine rescue team when the disaster occurred. He became involved in recovering the bodies of the victims, most of whom he knew. He would later describe the experience to Ogilvie, who asked many questions about it. In turn, the governor told McReaken that he had read as much as he could about the coal mine explosion near Centralia in 1947 that killed 111 miners.

When Ogilvie named McReaken acting Illinois mining director late in 1971, McReaken said the governor "emphasized in the strongest possible terms that he wanted no part of a Centralia or West Frankfort situation."[14]

Since McReaken, or "Wormy" as he was known in the coal fields, was a Democrat, GOP county chairmen in southern Illinois objected to McReaken's appointment. However, McReaken noted, "Ogilvie made it clear to me that he did not want political considerations to be a factor in choosing the head regulator of mining safety." Furthermore, McReaken said Ogilvie gave him a green light to select his own key personnel. But, when McReaken proceeded to do this, a nasty spat ensued.

It concerned McReaken's hiring of Thomas Pinnell of Farmersville to be a mine inspector. Pinnell had been a Democrat. When Ogilvie patronage chief Donald Udstuen got word of this, he called McReaken in anger and demanded that Pinnell be fired. When McReaken told the often acerbic Udstuen he could not comply, McReaken quoted Udstuen as saying he would be coming to see McReaken "to show me how to fire two people, Pinnell and myself." As fast as he could, McReaken placed a call to Judy Allan, Ogilvie's personal secretary, and informed her of Udstuen's threat. Within minutes, McReaken was in the governor's Statehouse office explaining the matter to Ogilvie himself. Based on McReaken's version of what followed, he became one of the small number of persons to ever see Ogilvie lose his temper.

"After I laid it out," related McReaken, "the Governor got Udstuen on the phone while I was still sitting there and just ate him out. In language that could not be mistook, curse words and all, he told Udstuen that he [Ogilvie] had told me I could pick my own key people. He finished by telling Udstuen, 'Now, goddamn it, you stay out of it. I don't want you on this man's back.' "

McReaken was relieved to have Ogilvie's backing. Still Dayton could not help but be startled by the governor's tartness with Udstuen. Maybe not at McReaken's small department, but in certain other governmental sectors, the governor's administration was quite forceful in moving Republicans and other supporters into as many positions as possible, policy making and clerical, high level and low level. Ogilvie may have been the last in a long string of Illinois governors with considerable flexibility in handing out jobs. The traditional patronage system was not served well in the last part of the twentieth century by increasingly cumbersome civil service regulations, the growth of public employee unions, and court decisions inimical to political hiring and firing.

Nevertheless, Ogilvie and his main factotum in this area, Udstuen, never could do enough to quench the insatiable demand for jobs. Swarming over the governor's office like locusts, some people even pushed for whole families to get on the public payroll. For many of the Republican county chairmen, obtaining jobs for themselves and their local cronies appeared to be all that mattered. Ogilvie staffers new to the Statehouse swore that chairmen of some of the smaller counties would cut a throat to land just one job.

Especially to the young Ogilvie aides, most of the county chairmen were anachronisms, relics of an earlier time when candidates had to rely on party organizations instead of the mass media for reaching the electorate. Dealing with the county chairmen and other job seekers as Udstuen did, his compatriots thought, was a thankless if not impossible assignment. It was hard to tell who ticked off the other the most, Udstuen or those pounding on his door.

When Ogilvie failed to win reelection, it became almost *pro forma* to try to finger his young aides, the ones tabbed whiz kids, for part of the blame. Too many of them were said to be overbearing, and none more so than the diminutive Udstuen. He was just twenty-five when he became the governor's patronage boss, no more than a few years removed from the campus of Northern Illinois University where he had been president of the Illinois Young Republican College Federation.

Some people who failed to get jobs dispensed by the governor's office were left with hard feelings and a frequent inclination to complain to reporters. Ogilvie was asked sometimes at press conferences if he found having to deal with patronage one gigantic sore spot. Once when the question was popped by William O'Connell of the *Peoria Journal Star*, Ogilvie responded, "The only trouble with patronage is there is not enough of it." Because a number of the reporters present had found some other governors very evasive at the mention of patronage, that answer by Ogilvie was taken as one more example of the candor that they had seen and come to expect from this particular governor. When O'Connell heard Ogilvie's reply, the wiry little reporter turned to his colleagues and asked a question of his own. "How can you hate a guy like that?"[15]

Ogilvie and the Fourth Estate

Ogilvie did not swig beer in the Statehouse pressroom. He did not fraternize with reporters. He did not even personally leak any of the thousand and one stories being played out at any given time in the broad domain he ruled. And with the press, Ogilvie came out smelling like a rose.

It easily could have been a different story, given the untamed nature of the Statehouse press corps. A unique assortment of individuals, with its share of zany characters, the corps was very much a part of Ogilvie's world—yet quite apart from the rest of it.

Like a lot of other things around, the pressroom went through a radical metamorphosis while Ogilvie sat in the Statehouse. To call it drowsy in the era before Ogilvie would be neither accurate nor fair to those pecking day and night at the keys of the old typewriters in the cramped and smoky press lodging on the third floor of the Capitol. However, Ogilvie had hardly settled into the Statehouse before the pressroom turned into a beehive or worse—a repository of a new wave of stinging muckrakers. Since their unabashed goal was to expose corruption in Illinois public life, reporters found the governor their most desirable target. But the incessant investigations never ensnared Ogilvie, not like they did a number of the other governmental big shots. Certainly, traps were laid for Ogilvie but to no avail.

He would leave the governorship about as personally clean as a hound's tooth. He would receive the highest accolade that the men and a woman or two in the Statehouse media ever would bestow. They would call him a good guy.

Before coming to the Illinois capital, Ogilvie had a good run with Chicago's fourth estate during his public office days in Cook County. Since he welcomed coverage by radio and television in those years, some Statehouse traditions would have to fall. Radio newsman Bill Miller called the traditions a "horse-and-buggy situation."[16] The radio people, still dubbed "dry cell boys" by some bystanders back then, were prevented by a long-standing practice from bringing recorders into press conferences with the governor. The same prohibition applied to television reporters bringing in cameras. This allowed the more numerous newspaper and wire service reporters based in the Capitol to have a competitive leg up and maintain an air of superiority over the electronic journalists.

Miller, whose real name was Alvin Pistorius, was a pioneer in radio coverage of Illinois state government. Prior to Ogilvie's election, Miller was feeding stories to numerous stations in Illinois and bordering states through his Capital Information Bureau. However, he recalled with irritation that "the radio and TV reporters could only sit in on gubernatorial news conferences with a pad and pencil. Our equipment had to be left outside the governor's office. After a press conference was over, a governor might consent to an interview with me outside his office unless something embarrassing or unpleasant had come up during the news conference. Then the governor would duck out or just refuse to talk to the broadcast reporters. Our association [the Illinois News Broadcasters Association] complained continuously about this matter."[17]

With the approach of Ogilvie, Miller and his brethren were prepared to show up at the door of the new governor's first press conference with their equipment in hand. They would see in a quick test what Ogilvie's policy would be. No test was necessary. Reaching a decision to end that particular tradition took "all of two seconds," Fred Bird remembered. "I never knew or would have guessed that broadcast people were not allowed to record or film or tape at the press conferences. It was absurd to even think we'd continue that exclusion. Ogilvie fully understood the impact of the broadcast media. And, besides, Joe Mathewson was still there at the start."[18]

Mathewson, Governor Ogilvie's first press secretary, was previously in television news reporting in Chicago. Had any argument ensued over the snap decision to permit electronic equipment in the governor's press confabs, the broadcasters assumed with good reason that Mathewson would have been in their corner.

While Ogilvie was in the Statehouse, the broadcast reporters also made headway on another front. Paul Simon, not Ogilvie, was involved on this one. This time a test did occur. Bill Miller brought it about. Sitting in the Senate press box one day, Miller decided to record a debate, even though it was prohibited by the Senate's rules. Spying what Miller was doing, a senator rose to object. Lieutenant Governor Simon, presiding over the Senate, determined right then that a reconsideration of the taping ban was in order. He called for a vote on the matter, and a majority of the solons favored elimination of the prohibition. The incident paved the way for widespread taping by radio and television in both chambers.

Allowing recorders and television camera crews into the governor's meetings with the press was momentous at the time, though. Ogilvie not only held far more press conferences than predecessor Kerner, but the sessions soon were dominated by, really geared toward, TV and radio. As a result, Ogilvie became what Miller termed "a champion of broadcast media."[19] This left the once paramount newspaper correspondents no choice but to take it, knowing full well that reaching the mass markets of the broadcast outlets was the primary objective normally behind the summoning of reporters to Ogilvie's office. Chalk up another major departure from the past by Ogilvie.

Still, while not ignoring the broad audience appeal of electronic journalism, Ogilvie's office was anything but derelict in its attentiveness to the print reporters covering the administration in the Statehouse and from Chicago. Putting it diplomatically, they still presented far more danger for the administration than the television and radio reporters, who gleaned most of their hard-hitting or disclosure pieces from the larger daily papers just like everybody else. No, the print journalists still were the diggers, the ones going beyond the press releases to get to the possibly dirty roots of an issue; to penetrate the camouflage of so many governmental actions and pinpoint the underlying motives or beneficiaries; to discover the actual costs or implications for taxpayers of this or that undertaking.

Years in the future, when the Statehouse pressroom no longer was a hotbed of investigative journalism, the eight-year period in which Ogilvie and Walker occupied the governorship would stand out as the modern-era apex of gumshoe and advocacy reporting in the Capitol.

The kickoff for this chapter in pressroom history was Ed Pound's 1969 disclosure of the Solfisburg and Klingbiel stock dealings that forced their departure from the Illinois Supreme Court. An even more explosive development was the revelation of Secretary of State Paul Powell's cash stash of $800,000 after his death in 1970. As reporters scurried frantically to try to determine the origins of the money, their efforts produced spin-off disclosures of shady holdings of racing stocks and of other questionable activities that buried or blemished the careers of a number of Illinois officials. On and on it went. From exposing clever money-raising schemes by politicians to the uncovering of scams in many other parts of public life, investigative reporters were having a field day. It is interesting to note that Illinois officials were subject to such feverishly investigative reporting at least two years before it became a national craze in the wake of the 1972 Watergate burglary.

When Ogilvie was governor, the makeup of the Statehouse press corps consisted of about thirty newspaper, television, and radio reporters and photographers. However, the number would magnify when the legislature was in session or a major newsworthy event was occurring. Another big source of information for Illinoisans about their state's government came from the state itself, through the Illinois Information Service. The Ogilvie administration brought in a former executive editor of the Pioneer Newspapers, John O. Mongoven, to turn this once sleepy shop into a bustling tax-supported operation putting out thousands of written press releases and radio and television tapes on the activities in state agencies seldom covered by the media. Since the output of the IIS went directly to loads of newspapers and stations, in addition to the Statehouse pressroom, many of the news outlets that could not afford firsthand coverage at the Capitol relied heavily on the IIS for government data. Naturally, because the agency never cast the governor and his programs in a negative light, many in the pressroom regarded it as little more than a propaganda arm of the administration.

But then, cynicism was a staple of the pressroom psyche in that era. It may have been faint praise for Ogilvie when he was characterized by Henry Hanson of the *Chicago Daily News* as the "good one" of the three governors he wrote about extensively—in that, as Hanson framed it, "the other two [Kerner and Walker] went to prison."[20]

The *Daily News* was one of four major dailies still being published in Chicago while Ogilvie was governor. Each maintained a bureau in the Statehouse. Virtually every day the bureau reporters jostled with each other for exclusive stories. This meant plowing deeply and sometimes resorting to reportorial extremes. Chicago editors pushed their bureau personnel very hard for scoops, as did the home offices of the *St. Louis Post-Dispatch* and some other newspapers with Capitol bureaus. Throw in the presence of a BGA investigator in the pressroom, and one could see why few weeks passed without one or more exposés about alleged wrongdoing by elected or appointed officials.

Some of the older denizens of the pressroom still reporting when Ogilvie arrived, reporters like Charles Whalen of the Associated Press and the *Chicago Tribune* bureau's Bob Howard, had a tough time countenancing the fervor or tactics of the young reporters bursting into the pressroom in the late 1960s and early 1970s. The older hands lamented the transformation of the pressroom from a comfortable nest of congeniality to an accursed place where many state officials hesitated to tread or be seen. They feared being branded informants for the zealous reporters hell-bent on ferreting out crooks in government. Gone were the days when bureaucrats would loll around the pressroom watching the veteran reporters match wits in rummy or other card games with the state-paid pressroom secretary, Shelby Vasconcelles. On the other hand, some of the newer reporters would later find a respite from the pressures of investigative reporting through long hours of dice baseball in an out-of-the-way corner of the pressroom.

Every major elected official needed a savvy press secretary or other emissary capable of dealing with the press. Without one, and if the officeholder seemed vulnerable, the sharklike reporters could attack quickly. The most sensible tact for a governor, attorney general, or secretary of state to take with the press was to sign up a former reporter or two to parley with the media. Former reporters did not break out in sweat when the press called, had insights into the workings of the real world, and were not likely to be pushed around by their former colleagues.

Keeping a onetime reporter at his right hand often paid dividends for a governor, but not always. It worked for Kerner. Kerner may have seemed tense around reporters, even defensive at times, but he had an effective buffer in his press secretary, Christopher Vlahoplus, who came to Kerner from the UPI bureau in Springfield. But then there was the case of Walker, whose disastrous relationship with the Statehouse media contributed to his political undoing. It mattered not that his main press aide, Norty Kay, had been a respected political editor in Chicago and former Statehouse reporter.

After observing the hostility between Walker and much of the fourth estate, Ogilvie's rapport with the press probably merited in retrospect an A plus. His press agents also could not have been much more fascinating. The Ogilvie press office literally was not a button-down part of the administration. That is, it was not button-down after Mathewson departed and Bird became press secretary.

Mathewson, the initial press secretary, was a suave fellow, an Ivy Leaguer, thirty-five years old when Ogilvie took office, a person who dressed well and was not easily shaken. He impressed some of the print reporters as a little stiff-necked, but they suspected that might change as Mathewson got more familiar with the lay of the land in Springfield. They would not find out, though, because Mathewson abruptly left the administration in May of Ogilvie's first year in office to make an unsuccessful bid for Congress in the Chicago area. His departure opened the gate for Bird to advance from assistant press secretary to the top spot.

Bird and Mathewson could not have had less in common, except that they once were neighbors in Winnetka, and Bird, like Mathewson, was an Ivy Leaguer, having attended Cornell. When Bird was made, they threw away the mold. Quick-tempered. Even impetuous. Honest himself and intolerant of those who were not. Never one to mince words. Hardly an exponent of sartorial splendor either.

Frederick Huey Bird Jr. showed signs early on that he would fit well into Windy City journalism. Prior to his graduation from New Trier Township High School in 1938, where he was editor of the student newspaper, Bird got into a censorship dispute with the paper's faculty sponsor because, Bird said, "I wouldn't let him read the copy ahead of time." At Cornell, where he spent more time on the *Cornell Daily Sun* than studies, Bird displayed "muckraking tendencies." He did not become the top editor because, he felt, "the powers that be thought I was too abrasive."[21]

Bird seemed to experience little smooth sailing in life. Few persons survive one midair collision, let alone two. But Bird did. While Bird was serving as a World War II flying instructor in Alabama, his AT-6 training aircraft was rammed by another plane, in two separate incidents. Neither was his fault. In the first encounter, Bird and his student pilot bailed to safety while the student aviator in the other plane was killed. Bird managed to land his damaged aircraft after the second collision, and nobody was injured. Then Bird became a "tow target pilot." This entailed, he explained, "the pulling of targets through the sky for other people to shoot at." Finally, his itching for combat zone duty was realized right before the end of the war when Bird, piloting a P-47N fighter plane, flew six strafing and bomber escort missions over the southern part of Japan.

Bird took his fighter-pilot vitality into his Chicago newspaper career—which he had begun earlier with stints at the City News Bureau, *Tribune*, and old *Chicago Sun*. Not long after his military days, Bird was back at the City News Bureau, a proving ground for young reporters that supplied police, fire, and other news stories to the Chicago papers and broadcast media. Bird's second stay at the bureau was followed by years with the *Chicago Daily News* and *Chicago's American* in which he was an investigative reporter, rewrite man, feature writer, and editor, everything except copyboy. Bird earned credentials as a top-notch reporter and as a tough one too, especially when he poked his nose into matters involving the mob or politicians. While he described himself as "the kind of reporter some persons took a swing at," Bird's peers never doubted he'd attack anybody giving him too much lip.

For what it was worth, Jim McCaffrey tells of Bird, as Ogilvie's press secretary, shoving Malden Jones, the Statehouse reporter for *Chicago's American*, across a room. Jones and McCaffrey, still a BGA investigator, went one night to Bird's Springfield residence to discuss a story Jones and McCaffrey were doing. The two had detected a possible conflict of interest involving Dan Malkovich, acting director of the Department of Conservation, and a magazine that he published. Bird did not think it was much of a story, and according to McCaffrey, Bird angrily shoved Jones. But, Bird insisted, "I didn't lay a glove on him [Jones]."[22]

Bird possibly leaped to defend Malkovich because Malkovich was overseeing a part of government, environmental preservation, closest to Bird's heart. Bird held the highest regard for Malkovich, even visited Malkovich's home at Benton and met the family (including a son, John, destined for acting stardom). Malkovich had no stronger defender. Those Bird disdained would be told so to their face. As a result, Bird was depicted in a bit of an understatement by John Kolbe as "something of a controversial figure in the administration."[23] Kolbe became the assistant press secretary to Ogilvie after Bird replaced Mathewson.

Normally, the opinions of one staffer in a governor's administration may not have been of great import to the outside world. Bird's impressions, though, could not be readily discarded because he talked to the press. A few other administration figures secretly fed certain reporters on specific items, but Bird's door was open to any person with a question about anything the administration was doing. Bird had his own private list of good people in the governor's circle, and he would subtly boost their stock with just a word here or there. Folks like McCarter, Ranney, Hanley, Michaelson, and George Mahin topped Bird's chart—along with Jay Bryant, the governor's scheduler. In Bird's eyes, Bryant "was such a crackerjack at what he did that you could always pick Ogilvie out of thin air at any moment because of the precise detailing with Jay's schedules."[24]

Bird knew better than to openly bad-mouth those around the governor. Still, he could hardly hide his frequent displeasure with a few like Marianne Quinn, the governor's appointments secretary. More than once Bird got caught calling her the "abominable no woman" because he felt that she ran a ship so tight that it countered efforts to favorably promote Ogilvie. Likewise, the press secretary may have been the only one in Ogilvie's office to privately get testy with Marsh or Drennan. No question they were astute fellows, Bird conceded, but he would get nervous feelings that the two heavy hitters could be too smart from time to time, or even conspiratorial, in laying or suggesting strategy for the administration on big-picture issues.

Bird went way back with Drennan. They met in the early 1950s when both were covering Chicago's city hall, Bird for the *Daily News* and Drennan for the *Sun-Times*. Bird was impressed with Drennan's "fierce competitiveness" and, even more, with "his great connections." Later, in the mid-1960s, when Bird had joined the ranks of ex-reporters in political public relations, Drennan enlisted Bird in various undertakings intended to enhance the image of Ogilvie when he was Cook County board president. Bird worked in the Ogilvie campaign for governor, penning position papers and handling sundry other tasks delegated by Drennan.

Friction between Drennan and Bird during Ogilvie's governorship was not picked up by the Statehouse press. Drennan, and Marsh too, were warned by some other staff members that Bird's blunt manner could backfire on the administration, but each denied Bird's contention years afterward that they had asked Ogilvie to fire Bird.

Drennan had this to say about it. "We didn't try to get Fred fired, although Jerry and I did try to keep him in focus. He was a great mechanic, but his political judgment could be terrible on what to say or not say. He sometimes forgot the difference between working for the city desk and the other side of the fence. Still, Fred did a good job."[25] Echoing Drennan, Marsh added with a straight face, "Fred was the Ogilvie team's lonesome end."[26]

Besides playing the curmudgeon, Bird also stood out as the worst dresser in the office. Marilyn Willey, Brian Whalen's secretary, would not soon forget "Fred running around in his house slippers with no tie, and keeping booze and carrots and celery in his desk." She recalled "more than a few being scared to death of him because he could be so grouchy," but she added that "we also knew he was the office character and, under it all, a fine guy."[27]

Bird's dislike of neckties came up when Ogilvie discussed the press secretary post with Bird, and in a matter of profound importance to the citizens of Illinois, the governor agreed that Bird would have to slip on a tie only for press conferences. It was not known whether Ogilvie signed off on Bird's "moccasins" or if he sanctioned the bottle of bourbon that Bird kept within reach in a drawer of his desk.

Crabby as Bird was on occasion, the pressroom types found visits to his office rewarding for a number of reasons. They included his willingness to offer a shot of whiskey to offset long evenings in the Statehouse; his truthful answers to questions; the unexplainable string of beautiful young women (Mary Cavanagh, for one) serving as secretaries to Bird; and finally, the location of his office. For a while, Bird was located just down a corridor from a private back door to the governor's second-floor office in the Statehouse. To use the private entrance, one had to walk by Bird's office, giving Bird and any reporter there a clear view of Ogilvie's unannounced visitors. However, Whalen eventually would end that situation, in the words of Bird, "by kicking me out of that office and into another one that took me out of the flow of things."[28]

Bird's detractors whispered that he leaked to reporters like a sieve. Actually, he did not. But Bird's penchant for accuracy and his refusal to equivocate often propelled him to steer a reporter to sources where the reporter could get correct information on a story he or she was following, regardless of the story's impact on the administration. Bird also might frame the right questions to be asked by a reporter. Bird felt comfortable proceeding like this because, he explained, "I had only one really serious condition in working for Ogilvie. It was that he be an honest man. And, he never disappointed me."

Certain people in the media knew they also could go to Drennan. To Charles Nicodemus of the Daily News, Drennan was the "eminence grise" of the Ogilvie administration even though he was not a state employee. "In oversimplified terms," wrote Nicodemus, "Ogilvie provides the ideals and fiber for his administration, and Drennan provides the canniness and compromise."[29] Chicago Today's Joel Weisman claimed that Drennan was the governor's alter ego and, Weisman added, probably "the only person who can reach Ogilvie at any hour of any day or night" outside of Ogilvie's wife and daughter.[30]

Drennan may not have been exaggerating when he said that he could not "think of any major Ogilvie decision made through all the years that I wasn't involved in."[31] There also were few potential flaps in which Drennan was not summoned to maneuver openly or covertly to protect Ogilvie. Since leaving reporting in 1954 to open his business, Chicago Public Relations, Drennan's already considerable contacts and his insights into Chicago's inner world had only broadened. He could not always get an unfavorable story about a client spiked, but he was one of those who could get at least fair treatment for a target.

Thomas Joseph Drennan, who still sported an outmoded crew cut along with a surprisingly mild manner, came out of Chicago's west side Austin neighborhood. A son of a shipping clerk, he was a graduate of St. Ignatius High School and Loyola University. He was a Democrat at first, which may not have hurt him. As a young reporter, he would sometimes accompany Cook County Clerk Richard J. Daley to White Sox games. However, Drennan became a Republican primary voter before he quit reporting, and his public relations firm would be employed against Daley, both before and after Daley became mayor.

Although Drennan was riding high, the era of Ogilvie's governorship was bittersweet for him. In May 1971, one of his nine children, Ray Drennan, a twenty-six-year-old state helicopter pilot, was killed when his helicopter crashed at Rockford. It was a sad irony that Ray had survived combat as a Marine helicopter pilot in Vietnam only a few years earlier. In addition, Tom Drennan's business interests came under scrutiny during the Ogilvie years as a result of certain state publicity contracts. Early in Ogilvie's governorship, it was revealed that Chicago Public Relations held publicity contracts for the Illinois Toll Highway Authority and for the Chicago area state highway operations. The biggest controversy ignited, though, when the administration awarded a contract for a more than $1 million state promotion program to a Chicago advertising agency, James & Thomas, a firm that Drennan helped establish and one in which he remained an officer. Drennan steadfastly insisted that he was not active in the firm and did not "expect to profit in any way" from the agency's work for the state. Nevertheless, no incident provided more fodder for those contending that Ogilvie could invoke the old spoils system as well as anyone.

When Nicodemus of the *Daily News* was pursuing the James & Thomas contract story, he asked Bird to comment. Bird asked Ogilvie what to say. The governor replied, Bird said, that "I should tell him [Nicodemus] the truth." Ogilvie was not one to complain about press coverage, Bird professed. "I'd squawk, but the Governor did not. He looked at it this way. You put a ship in the water, he'd say, and pretty soon it starts gathering barnacles. That was politics and government."[32]

Bird was sure, he said, that "Ogilvie actually enjoyed reporters, something that a lot of people would find hard to understand." Unlike many others high up in Illinois politics, Ogilvie's hands did not tremble in the morning as he waited to read what the *Tribune's* George Tagge and the other Chicago political writers had to say about him. Ogilvie did not shy away from face-to-face meetings with the Chicago papers' editorial boards when he felt a need to personally explain what he was trying to accomplish in a particular area. He was well informed about internal doings in the Chicago media because he was acquainted with many of its top figures and, also, because he was constantly fed by Drennan.

Ogilvie tried to bone up on the background and idiosyncrasies of the working stiffs in the Statehouse pressroom who had frontline responsibility for reporting the daily political happenings. Ogilvie's own track record in Cook County prepared him for the Ed Pounds, the crusaders categorized by Bird as "natural sin fighters who came with the territory." The governor also could not be oblivious to the quintessential pressroom performers—people like Peoria's O'Connell, *Rockford Morning Star* correspondent Jim Williams, and Edward Nash of the *Waukegan News-Sun*—who put in grueling hours compiling stories. Nothing could be taken for granted with any of the reporters, some of whom were as eccentric as Bird. The pressroom had yet to reach the stage when most media spouses, it seemed, would surface sooner or later on the state payroll. It was quite a break from tradition when John Dreiske Jr., whose father was political editor of the *Sun-Times*, turned up as administrative assistant to Herbert Brown during the Ogilvie years. Brown, a former Winnebago County sheriff, was director of the Department of Law Enforcement.

The wild period in the pressroom would outlive Ogilvie in the Statehouse by half a decade. By the late 1970s, only a few reporters from the Ogilvie days would be left. The *American* and its successor, the tabloid *Chicago Today*, would be gone as would the *Daily News*, which folded in 1978. Fading fast were the days when certain reporters might capture as much attention as those they covered. The Henry Hansons were being supplanted by much more subdued individuals.

If the pressroom was as outrageous as some pictured it, Hanson was its epitome. Hanson was an aggressive reporter and a witty writer, an unusual combination. An artist. An authority on alcoholic beverages. And a balloonist too. He once survived a dunk in cold Lake Michigan when a hot-air balloon carrying him aloft for a *Daily News* story crashed. There were times when politicians in Springfield wished they could have dunked him, too—when he wrote investigative pieces that hit where it hurt.

Hanson created an uproar when he got his hands on Paul Powell's income tax returns while gathering information about the finances of the secretary of state. Powell claimed that Hanson somehow stole a copy of the returns off his Statehouse desk. Not true, Hanson countered many years later, saying he secured the returns out of Powell's mailbox at the St. Nicholas Hotel in Springfield, made a copy, and then put them back in the box.[33] Perhaps not Powell, but many of those stung by Hanson's articles could not stay mad at him very long. He was an endearing person with an elfin grin and the manner to go with it. Hanson may have loved art more than reporting, and people he wrote about, among others, often bought his paintings and offbeat collages.

A year before his death in 1995, Hanson took a break from his duties as a senior editor at *Chicago* magazine to huddle with an old Springfield press colleague at Riccardo's, a restaurant at the corner of Rush and Hubbard streets in Chicago. It was a favorite hangout for journalists, artists, and bon vivants. Ric's featured sketches of leading patrons on its walls, and Hanson was up there. He recalled with great satisfaction the days when many people, including a tavern owner or two, "thought it a badge of distinction to have one of my works on the wall." Hanson was not drinking any more, not like in his Springfield period when he regularly made the rounds of the watering holes, picking up tips on stories as he himself tippled. After all, Hanson reminded his friend, "reporters in those days were supposed to be hard drinkers."

For Hanson, though, it led to some embarrassing moments. One of the more vivid occurred at the Governor's Mansion on a night that the press was present with Governor and Mrs. Ogilvie. Hanson was in his cups, and before the evening was over, several troopers were seen gently ushering him from the premise. The cops said only that Henry had gotten overbearing.

To clear the air, Hanson was asked about that night, as he sat at Ric's. "I got smashed," Hanson replied. "And all I remember was that I told the Governor to his face he was lackluster. He didn't like it one bit. He was really very good, you know, but it was just that he didn't have much dash. And I told him so."

Prisons, Highways,
and Other Ventures

"*There are no* neat, well-adjusted or humble leaders," lamented *Life* magazine in an essay on the "dramatic lack of great political figures on the world scene" in its October 8, 1971, issue. As for the United States, essayist Brock Brower stated, "We in this country, with far more expansive political hopes," have not "escaped this sense of departed, perhaps even lost, leadership. On the contrary, those who aspire to lead us seem increasingly, sometimes desperately devoid of the necessary stature, and public response to their rallyings has grown unaccustomedly cynical." And then the essay broached "that much misunderstood concept of charisma—'the gift of grace' in a leader, as the sociologist Max Weber rightly defined it, not mere political sex appeal."[1]

"Of late," Brower continued, "there has been much vociferous demand for 'somebody with charisma,' but very little attention has been paid to the conditions necessary for his possible arrival. Historians refer to a 'charismatic situation,' a moment when the people are ready to believe in the possibility of grace, and are willing to sacrifice something of themselves to receive it from a gifted leader." However, the essay concluded, "such moments . . . seldom occur during periods of social stalemate such as we are experiencing now in this country."[2]

Nine years earlier, *Life* magazine had singled out Ogilvie as one of the future leaders of the nation, but that 1971 essay made no mention of Ogilvie or hardly anyone else for that matter. Was Ogilvie's candle already burning low? Could it be that Ogilvie's stewardship of Illinois was being conducted in a political and cultural milieu too unstable and fractious to permit anyone to sense an emerging leader of any stature? Was Ogilvie simply out of vogue in the maelstrom?

After all, in this age, some revered rock stars and even professional athletes in an uncertain if not blind search for leadership, not war heroes or a plain, unassuming governor holding his state together in a most difficult time. Illinoisans were still on the covers of popular publications in 1971—not Governor

Ogilvie, but celebrities like Ann-Margret, the curvaceous actress and nightclub performer out of New Trier High School.

At this juncture, a governor had not advanced to the White House for years, not since Franklin Roosevelt. Analysts who viewed governorships as political dead ends made this point clear. This notion would soon fade, with the election of three governors or former governors to the presidency between 1976 and 1992, Jimmy Carter, Ronald Reagan, and Bill Clinton. All were individuals with infectious smiles that could charm the pants off voters.

Back to Ogilvie, expecting him to be measured by traditional yardsticks in 1971 may have been asking too much. As with the first two years of his governorship, great change was ongoing everywhere, and with it, life as many persons had known it was gone. In Illinois as elsewhere, the exodus from the farms continued. Yet, when many of those leaving rural areas arrived in the cities, they found life different than expected. The once familiar downtown commercial centers were deteriorating as people flocked to the new shopping centers proliferating on the outskirts of towns. Inflation was rampant, or seemed so at the time. Serious crimes were way up, along with venereal disease. No end appeared in sight to the Vietnam War. However, campuses were calmer in 1971, a break for Ogilvie and some other governors. Activists were directing antiwar protests pretty much toward Washington.

For many persons, an upshot was withdrawal. As historian William Manchester framed it, "Americans were yearning for the past because they were fed up with the present."[3] Thus, the wave of nostalgia sweeping the land should have been no surprise. Americans sought solace by discovering old movie ads, comic books, and pulp magazine stories and revivals of Broadway plays and hits from the big-band era. Sears, Roebuck reissued an 1897 catalogue, which was a big hit. Hardy Boys books and other old mysteries came off the shelf, and Mickey Mouse watches were seen even on the wrists of hippies. Steel-rimmed granny glasses were in.

Not many politicians were in, that was for sure. Many who did buck the tide of antipathy for officeholders managed to be seen as hip, or were blessed with catchy styles. All too often, political substance took a backseat. Late in 1971, Walter Jacobson, then a news analyst for NBC television in Chicago, may have pinpointed the essential predicament of the Ogilvie governorship when he surmised in a *Tribune* magazine piece that "what makes him [Ogilvie] unusual in Illinois politics is that his substance transcends his form. Fancy a politician," wrote Jacobson, "who has to worry about making himself look as good as he is."[4]

The gist of Jacobson's assessment was that there "has never been anything theatrical about the man. In fact, Richard Ogilvie is very likely one of the most all-business-no-froth governors ever to occupy the mansion in Springfield." Yet, added Jacobson, "most of his business most of the time has been good. Even the critics who denounce the Ogilvie administration in public candidly, if grudgingly, admit in private that he is an extraordinarily effective governor." Perhaps even more telling, Jacobson went to great length to point out that "what Richard Ogilvie is all about" was "being like the rest of us. A classic example of the traditional middle class. He looks, sounds, and acts like the great majority of everybody else. His values and his motivations, his attitudes and most of his likes and dislikes, are distinctly American-from-the-Midwest. Gov. Ogilvie is a staunchly conservative meat-and-potatoes, love-thy-country exponent of the philosophy that some good, hard work and a lot of commitment to the American dream will serve any man well."[5]

By the dusk of 1971, little ambiguity remained about Ogilvie's design for Illinois government. Not much of anything that significantly affected Illinoisans had gone unchanged. There were the increased taxes, the radical revision of state budgeting and other fiscal policies, and the zealous war against polluters on one hand. Another hand held the numerous new directions in the state's operation of prisons and the launching of a massive program of highway improvements. Even in areas in which the state did not have a historically grandiose presence, such as in attention to human relations problems, there was no standstill. Some of the administration's initiatives may have gone awry, but Illinois under Ogilvie certainly avoided many of the pitfalls entrapping officials in other large states.

When the nightmarishly bloody riot at Attica prison in rural western New York erupted in September 1971, claiming the lives of more than forty inmates and guards, speculation abounded about ripeness in Illinois for a similar insurrection. The biggest ingredient in the Attica revolt—nonwhite extremist inmates and white guards—was just as evident in Illinois, where close to 70 percent of the state prison system's nearly eight thousand inmates were black and the bulk of the guards were white. Many feared that Illinois might be next.

However, Ogilvie was no neophyte on penal administration problems, thanks in large measure to his experience in running the Cook County Jail. Ogilvie had not even warmed the seat in the governor's office before he pushed the buttons for an overhaul of the state's prison administrative policies because his political sixth sense warned him that Illinois's penitentiaries were tinderboxes.

Consequently, the Ogilvie years saw a revamping of the correctional system from the top on down, ranging from operating-rules revisions intended to make inmates' existence more humane to the laying down of statewide standards for county and municipal jails. A cornerstone of the overhaul was Ogilvie's successful call at the beginning of his governorship for legislative approval to create a new agency, the Department of Corrections, to centralize control over the state's twenty-four adult and youth correctional facilities. Ogilvie's signing of the requested legislation on July 18, 1969, would lead to his pronouncement of the birth of a "whole new philosophical framework" on corrections in Illinois, one placing much greater emphasis on vocational training, therapy, and other rehabilitative aspects.[6] Much of this would be authorized by other measures passed by the General Assembly at Ogilvie's urging. In the end, many would view the corrections legislation approved during Ogilvie's one term as the most far-reaching in the field in Illinois since the passage of the *Juvenile Court Act* in 1899.

Attica prison's location may have seemed placid, but the world inside its gray concrete walls had been administered in a forbidding manner that raised howls from civil libertarians. It was perfect for firebrands. In Illinois before Ogilvie, there too were large gray-walled prisons governed by rigid discipline under iron-willed wardens. However, changes in the rules under Ogilvie, some sanctioned by the legislation passed at his bidding, did much to more humanize the oppressive life of those behind bars. Selected inmates within a year of eligibility for parole were permitted to visit families and friends for short periods. The department was authorized to grant educational furloughs to some qualified prisoners and to allow others to volunteer for work on outside conservation projects. Evening recreation periods in the yards were initiated at some prisons and lengthened at others in an attempt to reduce the time inmates spent in their cells. In response to a desire of many prisoners, new privileges on mailing authorized an inmate to send an unlimited number of letters each week to individuals on his or her "approved correspondence list." Outgoing mail no longer was to be censored, although the rules still provided that such correspondence could be "opened and 'spot-inspected' for contraband."[7] Other clarifications intended to bolster inmates' morale ensured regular meals, showers, and bed linen changes and gave inmates more latitude in airing grievances and defending themselves in disciplinary procedures.

The arrival of such liberalized policies triggered predictions by skeptics of a backlash. They were right. Hard-liners, some of whom had helped to run Illinois prisons before Ogilvie's reforms, blamed the permissiveness in Ogilvie's policies for what they perceived to be the virtual loss of control at several prisons. Just maybe, the critics contended, the old order was being broken down too quickly. Even some Ogilvie people felt betrayed by disruptive incidents tied to malcontents in the prisons who were exploiting the effort to make the penal system more endurable.

At the Pontiac Penitentiary, a maximum-security facility in Livingston County where the average age of the inmates was nineteen, Warden John J. Petrilli had to backtrack somewhat on concessions he had made because so many of the inmates belonged to outside youth gangs. After a fight between gang factions caused a riot at Pontiac, permission given the largely Chicago gang members to hold meetings inside the prison was revoked. A similar situation occurred at Stateville, the prison at Joliet that had been the Illinois version of a movie big house with its authoritarian administration and infamous Chicago gangsters as inmates. There, Warden John J. Twomey, a sociologist in his early thirties, had tried a new approach that included decentralization of authority and other alterations intended in his words to "recognize individual human dignity." However, after a rise in disciplinary problems, Twomey issued a directive that strongly reversed a number of his earlier actions by imposing tough penalties on prisoners who refused a direct order, orally abused an employee, or participated in a group action, or "crowding around," in support of other inmates. His order, Twomey acknowledged, was necessary to respond "to our problems in social control."[8]

Nonetheless, Twomey and Petrilli would not escape rebuke by the hard-handed penologists for allegedly undercutting the basic purpose of the penal system by catering to the inmates. The hard-liners much preferred the response of Warden Elza Brantley at Menard Penitentiary along the Mississippi River at Chester when three hundred inmates complaining of bad food engaged in a sit-down. Brantley, a twenty-eight-year veteran of the state police, fired a shotgun over the heads of the balking prisoners, and presto, the strike ended. While insisting afterward that he was "not a tough cop," Brantley nevertheless attributed his shotgun approach to "a firmness that the inmates want to see because they really don't want to run the prison."[9]

Still, in spite of the retreat from some reforms, Peter Bensinger, the state corrections director, insisted that a throwback to "the old ways" was out of the question. As Bensinger saw it, "We've made changes that have opened up our prisons a little bit, and they're not so mysterious any more. But of course, this also makes it easier for the problems to be noticed."[10]

Ogilvie himself addressed the matter when he spoke at a ceremony October 8, 1971, at the minimum-security state prison by Vienna. The Attica outbreak was still fresh on everybody's mind, prompting the governor to blame it for having "galvanized public doubts" about the changes in the Illinois system. "The coincidence of tragedy with the growing movement toward a system

based on rehabilitation rather than repression has raised understandable questions about the wisdom of our course," Ogilvie said. "But we will not let the
frustrations raised by tragedy and violence deter us from the course we have
charted in Illinois."[11]

Ogilvie's selection of Bensinger to direct the state prisons was in itself
enough to irk the old-timers in the system. Unlike the hardfisted Joseph E.
Ragen and Ross V. Randolph, penal directors under Kerner, the considerably
younger Bensinger did not have a storied history in the corrections network.
Furthermore, Bensinger being an Ivy Leaguer from a well-to-do family prominent in Chicago society set him apart. Bensinger and his squad of mostly young
assistants and wardens were well aware of the hostility they engendered in
some places. "We knew," conceded Joseph McFadden, an administrative assistant to Bensinger, "that a number of individuals saw us as super liberal reformers. But, we were there to do what the Governor wanted, and that was a different approach in corrections."[12]

The appointment of Bensinger also served Ogilvie's strategy to invigorate
Illinois government with a gubernatorial cabinet of fresh faces not shackled
by past state practices. In doing so, he was not always playing it safe. He did
succeed with Bensinger, though, who went on after his Illinois penal years to
run the federal Drug Enforcement Administration. But Ogilvie didn't always
luck out.

William L. Rutherford was a case in point. In the decades after the Ogilvie
governorship, wealthy Peoria attorney Rutherford was renowned for his cru-
sading efforts to protect the environment and wildlife in Illinois and abroad.
Rutherford's nonprofit Forest Park Foundation was an originator of the practice of private procurement of land for public use. Many people regarded his
grandest achievement to be the opening in 1978 of his Wildlife Prairie Park, a
two-thousand-acre attraction on a former surface mine site and farmland west
of Peoria. A favorite destination of families, it featured log cabins, lakes, a train,
and most exciting of all, a menagerie of wolves, bears, bobcats, and other wild
animals in natural settings.

Besides watching the wildlife, visitors to Rutherford's park could not miss
the visible evidence of his detestation for bureaucrats. His fling with the
Ogilvie administration surely had a lot to do with that. In a stormy stint as
Ogilvie's first director of the Department of Conservation, Rutherford was
often at odds with the Ogilvie crew. Rutherford was credited in the year or so
he was director with a successful push for the acquisition of about 27,000 acres
for public use. This seemed to far surpass any comparable effort in Illinois in
preceding years. Nevertheless, the administration found him to be a thorn in

the side. Rutherford had the temerity to insist that the department grant no special favors in the handling of hunting licenses, dispensing of jobs, or anything else. Then he ordered a halt to the special availability to high public officials during goose hunting season of a small lodge at the Horseshoe Lake conservation area in Alexander County. As for the patronage structure, Rutherford considered it a danger to the public welfare. And bureaucratic inefficiencies? They drove the man wild.

Fielding complaints about Rutherford became a daily chore in the governor's office. Ogilvie's aides said they never saw anybody as inflexible and unrealistic in his demands. Calling Rutherford bullheaded was an understatement in the eyes of Flora native Marion Oglesby, the very politically astute Ogilvie assistant who probably most frequently butted heads with Rutherford over jobs and other matters. Early in 1970, Rutherford was "elevated" by Ogilvie from the department directorship to a newly created post, state coordinator of environmental quality. This may have been a promotion on paper, but in reality it took Rutherford from a position with hands-on responsibility to a vague policy role. Rutherford would quickly figure this out, saying he had been turned into "a toothless tomcat sending memos that get no response."[13] After a few months, he walked away in frustration from the coordinative slot.

Mitchell Ware became a bigger headache for the administration, and in an area very close to Ogilvie's heart. Ware was picked by Ogilvie to be the first superintendent of the state's "Little FBI," the street name for the Illinois Bureau of Investigation. Ogilvie wanted the IBI to be a marquee operation. Official news releases billed it as the state's "elite crime-fighting agency." From day one, the IBI seemed hell-bent to live up to this expectation.

Moving with the flare of old-time gangbusters, IBI agents soon were capturing headlines with far-flung raids on drugs and weapons stocks that appeared to overshadow previous undertakings in this field by other law enforcement officials. Television crews accompanied agents on some of the raids, and press conferences were an integral segment of almost every large-scale action. Such matters were easily finessed by Ware, an attorney and former state narcotics inspector who also had been a television news reporter in Chicago. Almost overnight, it seemed, Ware succeeded in putting the IBI on the law enforcement map. Its impact was glamorized even more by his flamboyance in taking on anybody and everybody, including judges and other elected officials. For a while, no state official outside of Ogilvie was more in demand as a public speaker than Ware. Ware's performance reminded some of J. Edgar Hoover's early years with the Federal Bureau of Investigation.

As things go, though, a backlash against the IBI was inevitable. Just as Ware and the IBI had not hesitated to step on toes, their critics in turn sought to make sitting ducks out of Ware and his agents. Some detractors had real gripes, others had axes to grind. The latter groups included bureaucrats in the Ogilvie administration who envied the unusually free hand the governor had given Ware to make the most of his infant agency. "You'd think," Ware remarked at the time to this writer, "the IBI was the worst thing to ever happen to Illinois."[14]

Little argument greeted the IBI's contention that it seized during its first year in operation, 1970, more than forty times as much drugs as state authorities confiscated the previous year. More than a few persons did question whether the bureau was overemphasizing its fight against drugs at the expense of another key part of its duties, combating organized crime. The assertion that his agents ignored major hoodlums and focused on pot smokers irked Ware and prompted him to remind the gallery that the IBI's organized crime division drew attention early on by playing a role in the indictments of a number of underworld figures. None of the carping touched Ware more personally than the insinuation that he grandstanded in leading the IBI, most obviously through his ability to obtain the utmost publicity for the bureau. Other law enforcement officials—jealous plainclothes detectives in the state police in addition to sheriffs and local police chiefs—resented Ware's showmanship.

However, not until early 1971 did criticism of the IBI turn full-blown. First, Democratic leaders complained that the bureau acted like it was on a political witch-hunt in assisting Illinois officials investigating the late Paul Powell's estate and financial dealings. In April, Ware was criticized more strongly after the IBI coordinated raids on weapon and drug sellers in southern Illinois. The magnitude of the raids was intentionally misconstrued by the IBI, it was charged, to assure broad coverage. At this juncture, Ogilvie for the first time took Ware to task for letting television crews participate in those and previous IBI raids. Opining that it was "not a good practice," the governor said he felt it placed the fledgling agency under unnecessary pressure.[15]

The turbulence was not about to end, though. The IBI received considerable attention by reporting after a raid at Champaign that it had made a record seizure of LSD. However, it was later disclosed that the substance was not LSD. Another negative was an unsuccessful attempt by Democratic legislators to pass a bill abolishing the IBI. A number of politicians, primarily Democrats, went around whispering that they feared the IBI under the freewheeling Ware might be employed in partisan situations to harass Ogilvie opponents, a thought pooh-poohed by Ogilvie. Ware, who said he was not a Republican, denied he would be a party to that. Nevertheless, all these matters served to undermine the IBI superintendent.

Seven months into 1971, Ware resigned his post, a development many came to see as inevitable. His exit came on the heels of his acceptance of a controversial appointment by a Cook County circuit judge loyal to Mayor Daley. Ware was named to investigate the activities earlier that year of a special grand jury in the Black Panther case. This case arose out of a 1969 raid by the Cook County state's attorney's police on a Chicago apartment in which two Panther leaders were killed. Ware, a black, was asked to determine whether special prosecutor Barnabas Sears tried to improperly coerce the jury. The Daley machine thought that Sears did, to the possible detriment of the mayor's organization.

When Ogilvie's office learned that Ware had accepted this appointment, Ogilvie people saw it as a conflict with Ware's administration position. Ware was informed that one of the roles had to go. An assistant to Herbert Brown explained that Ware could not "do Daley's dirty work and work for a Republican governor at the same time."[16] As director of the Department of Law Enforcement, which included the IBI, Brown was Ware's boss. Few individuals outside of government realized that fact, though, in view of Ware's continued upstaging of Brown and others.

Ware's resignation from the IBI had more than one upshot. Without him, the agency entered a more placid period under the direction of Richard F. Gliebe, a former FBI agent. This phase continued until late in 1972, when the IBI found itself back on the front page with the brutal slaying of one of its undercover agents, thirty-year-old Peter E. Lackey of Winchester, during a drug-dealing investigation. Ware's departure also deprived the Ogilvie administration of one of the relatively few African-Americans filling a highly visible slot. Not many blacks were with the administration for the long haul like William H. Robinson, the former Cook County public aid chief who was Ogilvie's director of the Department of Registration and Education, which licensed and policed various trades and professions.

The few blacks in Ogilvie's immediate orbit did not signify that he was inattentive to areas of crucial concern for African-Americans and other minority groups in Illinois. Ogilvie and his administration threw convention out the window in their extraordinary efforts to rescue East St. Louis from its severe social and economic ills. In 1971, East St. Louisans pulled off a political shocker by electing a black mayor, James E. Williams, who was not aligned with the city's old power structure. Williams found access to Ogilvie available anytime he wanted it. They would consult so frequently that the two came to be seen as unlikely political allies. Yet many Republicans thought Ogilvie was risking too much on a place that, in the mind of some extremists, could be renewed literally only through a complete razing before any rebuilding.

Donald Bourgeois may not have lasted long with the Governor's Office of Human Resources, but Bourgeois made it clear in his short stay that Ogilvie meant to back up his promises on East St. Louis. Ogilvie's successful push for establishment of the State Community College in East St. Louis spoke for itself. Yet it was only one example of the numerous ways in which Ogilvie circumvented normal channels to make sure East St. Louis got priority treatment among the cities in the allocation of state resources for capital projects and other programs. All buttons were pushed, from Ogilvie's support for plant expansion loans in the city to the governor's insistence that East St. Louis be given every break possible by Frank Resnik, the Ogilvie person running the Illinois Department of General Services, the housekeeping agency for state government.

No individual could have done more than Ogilvie to bring about construction of a new major airport for the St. Louis area at a site in Illinois near East St. Louis. The economic benefits from the project would have been incalculable. Ogilvie had the support of Mayor Alfonso J. Cervantes of St. Louis along with the backing of Democratic and other public officials and civic leaders in southern Illinois. As with certain other matters affecting East St. Louis, Ogilvie saw to it that all steps to land the airport in Illinois emanated from his own office. In the end, the governor had top lieutenant Whalen coordinating the undertaking, a sure sign of the project's importance. When Ogilvie left office, the groundwork was firmly laid for a go-ahead on the airport in Illinois. But it would not happen. Opposition to the Illinois site would mount from some major Missouri politicians as well as from numerous landowners in the vicinity of the proposed location. Too, Governors Walker and Thompson would not pursue the project with the energy of Ogilvie, and finally, the necessary cooperation of federal officials would wane.

Speaking of federal officials, the East St. Louis area was a target while Ogilvie was governor of a freeze on federal highway funds as a result of what federal policymakers contended was discrimination against blacks on highway construction jobs in St. Clair and Madison counties. The embargo was lifted after Ogilvie instituted a minority employment program for road building in the two counties, a delicate assignment carried out by Paul J. Wisner, the subsequent director of the governor's human resources office. Wisner's effort resulted in what was known as the Ogilvie Plan.

The Illinois Commission on Human Relations was one in the long list of often nondescript commissions or boards that even many followers of Illinois government could not keep straight. This commission was important to blacks and other minorities, though, because it implemented programs aimed at easing racial and other intergroup tensions in Illinois cities. Still, if any state commission had no claim to pomposity, it was the human relations commission. In spite of the greatly heightened racial unrest in Illinois in the 1960s, the commission staff remained a subject of rebuke and ridicule when it went before the legislature's budgetary commission to plead for funds. Ivan R. Levin, the human relations commission's downstate director, would dread the insults from the elderly old liners on the legislative panel, calling them "troglodytes with no sympathy whatsoever for our mission."[17] Unlike many state officials, Levin did not operate out of sumptuous surroundings. His office was across Monroe Street from the Capitol in a dilapidated frame house that the state would in later years tear down for a parking lot. As tough as life seemed for the commission, those who cared assumed it might get even worse with the coming of Republican Ogilvie.

Levin, a liberal Democrat from St. Louis, found just the opposite to be the case. To be honest, the governor was not a complete unknown to Levin because he once had an opportunity to have lunch with Sheriff Ogilvie. Levin's recollection of Ogilvie from that occasion was as "a quiet, conservative and thoughtful man." Ogilvie's governorship would leave Levin with an even more positive impression of the man, especially since, said Levin, "many Republicans cared so little about human relations problems." However, Levin noted, "he [Ogilvie] knew this was an area that couldn't be ignored." Moreover, added Levin, "Ogilvie happened to be a decent person, not a phony, and he had a modern outlook on how to govern a big state. As a result, he never interfered with the commission and staff in doing their job. He knew he had to support us, and he did."

The commission, one of three state operations merged in later years to become the Illinois Department of Human Rights, proceeded at full tilt in the Ogilvie years. In Levin's opinion, Ogilvie made prestigious appointments to the panel, starting with the chairman, Byron DeHaan of Peoria, public affairs manager for Caterpillar Tractor Company. The commission's executive director during most of Ogilvie's time in office was Beatrice Young, a striking white woman and authority on African-American history who once had been jailed in Mississippi for assisting in the development of so-called freedom schools for blacks.

Levin also could breathe a sigh of relief over Ogilvie's capture of control of the state budgeting process from the General Assembly. To Levin, "Illinois government took a gigantic step forward when Ogilvie put the budgeting power in the hands of the state's elected chief executive, where it belonged. It not only instilled fiscal integrity into the process, but was a godsend to little places like ours that had no defense against the whims of legislative bullying."[18]

The Ogilvie era also would prove to be progressive for many other state-related programs largely unnoticed by the public. A prime example was the Illinois Housing Development Authority, whose acronym was pronounced like the name Ida. IHDA was created through enabling legislation passed by the General Assembly in 1967, two years before Ogilvie took office. But it was under Ogilvie and Dan Kearney, Ogilvie's IHDA director, that the authority flowered.

In brief, IHDA was set up as an independent state operation to spur an increase in the supply of reasonably priced housing for moderate and middle-income Illinoisans through the provision of low-interest financing and technical aid to developers. The agency sold tax-exempt securities to private investors to raise the funds ultimately made available for construction or mortgage programs. IHDA became an important tool for fighting urban decay, although housing coming out of the program, instead of being public housing, was privately owned for rent or sale. Before the end of Ogilvie's final year in office, around four thousand new residential units financed with IHDA building and mortgage loans were under construction in the state. Legislation hiking IHDA's bonding power to $500 million while Ogilvie was governor would lead to many more thousands of new dwellings.

Pictured frequently in that period were Ogilvie and Kearney with shovels in hand at groundbreaking ceremonies for IHDA-assisted projects in Rockford and other cities. It was a way for the governor to get political mileage out of a program with low visibility. Much more bountiful political gain was expected for Ogilvie from another program involving construction, the overhaul of the highway network in Illinois that he fervently pushed.

Just as it was true that Ogilvie fathered more reshaping of Illinois government than any chief executive since Governor Lowden, Ogilvie also stood to be his state's biggest road builder since Len Small, a Republican governor in the 1920s. In a book on Illinois governors, Robert Howard labeled Small the "good roads governor." Small "pulled Illinois out of the mud" early in the automobile age by giving the state "one of the nation's best hard road systems." Added Howard: "The 7,000 miles of 18-foot pavement he constructed in eight years were badly needed, well-engineered, economically built, and highly political. Each county got its share of the pavement if it voted for Small and his legislative candidates."[19]

The political overtones of road building also would be a fact of life in succeeding decades as other administrations found highway construction contracts an easy reward for supporters, meaning individual contractors as well as specific regions. Small was governor in the decade following the passage of the *Federal Aid Road Act*, a major road-building package. Parallel to that, Ogilvie was elected governor late in the decade following Congress's biggest road-building program in history, the transcontinental interstate system. The construction of the Illinois segments of the interstate system, 90 percent of which was financed by federal dollars, was well on the way to completion while Ogilvie was governor. However, the smoothness of the interstate roads underscored even more graphically the poor condition of many of the other highways in Illinois, a situation that Ogilvie milked heavily in his campaign for governor.

Consequently, Ogilvie was determined to revitalize the older state highway system and, along with it, to upgrade mass transportation and airports in the state. Many suspected that, along with his other hats, Ogilvie also wanted to be recognized as Illinois's modern-era transportation governor. He took a route that attained this goal, but it had its share of potholes.

In 1969, as part of his blitzkrieg of successful initiatives, Ogilvie persuaded the General Assembly to approve a plan for the initiation of a massive emergency road rebuilding program. The heart of it was the establishment of the Illinois Highway Trust Authority with power to issue $2 billion in bonds without referendum to pay for construction of a new supplementary freeway system of nearly two thousand miles throughout the state. The Illinois gasoline tax and vehicle registration fees also were hiked. The following year, though, the Illinois Supreme Court ruled that the legislation permitting the authority to issue the bonds violated the Illinois Constitution of 1870, then still in effect. In an opinion written by Justice John T. Culbertson Jr. of Delavan, the court ruled that the charter placed a $250,000 limit on state indebtedness unless bonds were approved at a referendum. Therefore, the opinion concluded, issuing bonds without a popular vote was illegal in that the highway authority was in reality only an arm of the state.

Disappointed but undaunted, Ogilvie bounced back on this issue in 1971. That year, the newly ratified Illinois Constitution of 1970, with its modernized and less-restrictive state debt limits, went into effect. Ogilvie cast the need for action on transportation problems as the top challenge facing the state that year. He delivered a missive on the subject to the General Assembly February 17, 1971. In it, Ogilvie said that "our transportation capabilities are the foundation of our prosperity. Opportunities for jobs and business exist in direct relationship to our ability to get people to and from their place of work, to bring new materials to industry, and to deliver finished products to consumers."[20]

Consequently, Ogilvie attained his top objective that year when lawmakers approved $900 million in bond issues for improving highways, urban transit systems, and aviation facilities. Of the total, $600 million was designated for the governor's supplementary freeway network, $200 million for capital improvements for mass transit, and the rest for new and existing airport development. Ogilvie sought no new or increased levies to retire the bonds. The Ogilvie legislative package also created the Illinois Department of Transportation (IDOT) to unify under one roof the state's administration of road construction, maintenance, and other conveyance-related programs. The first IDOT chief was Bill Cellini, who had been director of the old Department of Public Works and Buildings, the main agency replaced by IDOT. Few more enduring figures would come out of the Ogilvie administration than Cellini.

Ogilvie's impact on the Illinois transportation picture also had to take into account William Robert Blair II. The revenue raising and other aspects of Ogilvie's first road improvement program, the one he pushed in 1969, were based heavily on the work of the Illinois Highway Study Commission. Blair, a Republican representative from Park Forest, chaired the commission. In 1971, when Ogilvie returned to the General Assembly to seek approval of his revised transportation program, Blair was in his first year as speaker of the House. This permitted him to exercise a big hand in steering the governor's legislation through the lower chamber, a tricky task because the 1970 election had left the GOP with only a narrow edge in the House.

On many issues besides transportation, Blair proved during Ogilvie's last two years in office to be an effective steward of legislation favored by the governor. An attorney and real estate businessman, Blair had won the top post in the House in the eyes of many observers as a compromise candidate capable of unifying the GOP factions in the chamber. His path would be a rocky one, though. Although praised in many quarters for firmness and efficiency in running the House, a number of its Republicans complained bitterly that W. Robert Blair, as he was known, excluded them from policy deliberations. Their anger especially was piqued when Blair worked with Democratic leader Clyde Choate, and not always behind the scenes, to resolve controversies. However, Blair, a self-described political pragmatist, felt he had little choice in the matter because of his party's narrow majority.[21] Some of the dissatisfaction with Blair also stemmed from his frequently high-handed response to criticism and from his involvement in personality conflicts. Too, he had a sometimes tempestuous relationship with reporters, some of whom took to calling him "Bulletproof Bob." This grew out of his link to an attempt to enclose the House chamber in bulletproof glass, a move that could have denied the press easy access to the House floor.

A sharp split with his own GOP floor leader, Representative Henry J. Hyde, a Park Ridge lawyer, later a congressman from Illinois, almost prevented Blair's reelection as speaker in the Seventy-eighth General Assembly that convened in 1973. Blair did retain the post, though, and went on to function as a major Republican power broker in 1973 and 1974, so much so that he was viewed as a serious possibility for the GOP nomination for governor in the near future. For a fellow from West Virginia, in Illinois only since 1955, Blair had come a good distance in public life.

However, his political career came crashing down in the general election late in 1974 with his stunning failure to win reelection to a seat in the House. Blair, forty-four years old at the time, did not argue with those who attributed his defeat mainly to his strong push for a regional transportation authority for the Chicago area. It had been a successful drive, though not popular with voters in his suburban Chicago legislative district. It was ironic that Blair would come to such an ignominious end politically on the transportation issue.

Of course, much of the groundwork for what would become Chicago's Regional Transportation Authority (RTA), from fiscal and planning standpoints as well as politically, was laid by the Ogilvie administration. Blair had considered himself a political ally of Ogilvie since the 1968 primary fight for the Republican nomination for governor when Blair backed Ogilvie. As Blair recalled, he and Ogilvie were both "coming along as party moderates and, besides that, we talked in 1968 about the road situation, about his much needed heavy stress in the campaign on the sad condition of so many of the highways."[22]

Illinoisans always had abundant reasons for considering their state the transportation hub of the nation, but they also had become accustomed in the years before Ogilvie was elected governor to sniping by national publications at the dangers presented by many primary routes in the state, especially away from Chicago.

Richard Adorjan for one would not forget, in his words, "the designation of some of our roads as 'killer highways,' criticism that was not far off target." Adorjan left a job as UPI bureau chief in the Statehouse early in 1970 to become a public information specialist for the public works agency and then its successor, IDOT. It was a role that Adorjan would continue to play for decades, but few of the later years would be as exciting as those first ones working for William Cellini and experiencing the frenetic pace of everything the Ogilvie administration was doing on roads and other transportation fronts. "There was a lot of turmoil," said Adorjan. "But it was inevitable because we were doing so much, carrying out improvements everywhere, overseeing the birth of a major new department and having to explain it all to the public."[23]

A go-ahead on Ogilvie's supplemental freeways may not have come as quickly as he desired, but the administration's offensive against the so-called killer highways was in full swing in 1969 under what the administration called its "immediate action program." Almost overnight, it seemed, more than three thousand miles of pavement and 160 narrow bridges were widened and resurfaced at the direction of Cellini and Richard H. Golterman, the chief state highway engineer. And that was only a start.

A truism of Illinois government was that department heads often achieved their greatest recognition on the day of their appointment by a governor. It was downhill for most of them after that as they melted into the bureaucracy on a day-to-day basis, soon to be forgotten after their departure. William F. Cellini Jr. proved to be a fascinating exception.

First off, he was not a run-of-the-mill member of Ogilvie's cabinet. Cellini was certainly qualified for the key assignment Ogilvie gave him, having served as Springfield's streets commissioner. Beyond that he became what Robert S. Cohen saw as "one of the real movers in the Ogilvie administration."[24] And Springfield attorney Cohen was in a position to know, as a close friend of Cellini and a legal beagle for IDOT while Cellini was its secretary. Cellini may have been only thirty-four when Ogilvie anointed him, but he was in many ways a throwback to an earlier era in the state when most department directors were not politically antiseptic. Cellini had the managerial skills to get IDOT off to a very credible start, Adorjan observed, and in addition, Adorjan said, "Bill became quite important to Ogilvie politically."[25] For one thing, Cellini had a large hand in patronage because many of IDOT's ten thousand employees were not extensively covered by the state personnel code.

Cellini and top assistants Peter F. Dunne and E. Allen Bernardi also were adept at raising political funds for Ogilvie, a chore shunned by many in the administration but absolutely necessary for the governor to launch a strong campaign for reelection. In the years following Ogilvie, Cellini would continue to be a significant fund-raiser for the Illinois GOP and a figure with considerable influence in the administrations of later Republican governors. Although Cellini was a private developer, some of his projects—such as his engineering of the building of a new hotel in Springfield—would project him into the news as a result of the projects' reliance on a mixture of public money with private dollars. Cellini also was a pioneer investor in the riverboat casino industry in Illinois that boomed in the 1990s.

As the years passed, Cellini would find himself categorized as many things by the media in Chicago and other places: Republican power broker. Downstate political boss. Reclusive. Intriguing even. What it all meant, observers would conclude, was that perhaps no figure from the Ogilvie administration would engender more mystique down the line than Cellini. Not bad, his pals would say. Not bad for a likable piano-playing son of a policeman out of the decidedly unaffluent north end of Springfield.

Back in the Ogilvie era, all of those roads that Cellini's agency was improving were supposed to play a big part in furthering the political career of Ogilvie. By the summer of 1971, a chap trying to short-circuit Ogilvie's career also was seeking to work the state's roads to his advantage—in a quite unorthodox manner. Dan Walker, in pursuit of the Democratic nomination for governor the following year, had undertaken a walk along various highways that would take him from the bottom of Illinois to the top of the state. The trek was intended to draw attention to Walker's long-shot candidacy, but most in his own party as well as in Ogilvie's saw it as folly born out of desperation. Most political insiders just could not take Walker seriously. A few still didn't even recognize him.

Several months before Walker started walking, House Speaker Blair was waiting to board a plane in Springfield for Chicago when Norton Kay, whom Blair had known as a reporter, approached with another fellow. Kay asked Blair to shake hands with Dan Walker. Kay informed Blair that he was meeting the next governor of Illinois. A handshake did ensue, and Walker and Kay moved on. After they did so, Blair turned to an associate with a quizzical look.

"Tell me," said Blair, "who that was."[26]

Dorothy Ogilvie

N*o matter how* far her husband's political career might take them, Dorothy Ogilvie was determined to keep her feet on the ground. She also knew she had to be prepared to face anything at anytime. But did she foresee being stuck in an elevator at the Vatican? She definitely had not anticipated that.

The first lady, the governor, and their daughter Elizabeth visited Rome late in March 1972 on one leg of a trip abroad that began in Israel. A large contingent of Chicagoans had flown with the Ogilvies to Israel, many of them contributors to a library project near Jerusalem in honor of Ogilvie and his support for the sale of State of Israel bonds. While in Israel, the governor and his wife met with a number of the republic's luminaries, including Prime Minister Golda Meir. From Israel, the Ogilvie family and a handful of others flew to Italy for the start of a largely nonofficial jaunt through Europe. In Rome, the major destination of the group was the papal headquarters, where a private audience with Pope Paul VI was arranged.

Dorothy Ogilvie relished retracing the literal ups and downs of that visit as she relaxed in Chicago's Tavern Club on an early spring day in 1994. For one thing, the very short skirts that sixteen-year-old Liz had been wearing on the trip just would not do for meeting the Pope. So Liz had to quickly scurry about in Rome to find a long dress for the occasion.

The visit started off smoothly enough as the small Ogilvie party was ushered to St. Peter's Square in two limousines. After getting a glimpse of some of the Vatican's art treasures, the group was greeted by Bishop Paul C. Marcinkus, the contact person for the audience with the Pope. A tall and husky man a year older than Ogilvie, Marcinkus was a major leaguer at the Vatican. A native of Cicero, Illinois, Marcinkus was a talented linguist who had risen to become Vatican treasury minister and then head of the Vatican bank. Ironically, the Vatican elevator carrying these heavyweights—the bishop, the governor of Illinois, and his party—malfunctioned. It got stuck between floors.

What happened, as Dorothy Ogilvie told it, was that "the bishop pressed up, but we went slowly down. Then it stalled between floors and there we were, stuck and going nowhere. Dick took it lightly. He said to everybody, and he was chuckling, that we were stuck in the bowels of the Vatican. But I was getting nervous that we were going to be late for the audience with the Pope."[1]

Swinging into action, Bishop Marcinkus picked up the phone in the elevator, imploring for help. Ogilvie staffer Jay Bryant, who was present, noticed that "the bishop was conversing on the phone a bit of a while, but we could not understand what he was saying because he was speaking in Italian. When he hung up, he was laughing. He told us that most of the time on the phone was spent trying to convince the little nun at the switchboard that it was really him she was talking to and that he really was stuck on this elevator. She apparently had to be convinced it wasn't a prank."[2]

But the bishop got his message across because, in Mrs. Ogilvie's words, "we were cranked down" to a lower level and then led briskly by foot up to the Pope's receiving room in the nick of time. The audience went well, although Liz's nervousness was recorded in her scrapbook when she wrote that the Pope "kept holding my hand and asked me about school. . . . I trembled the whole time."[3]

On the subject of schools, Bryant recalled the slender white-robed Paul VI expressing to the governor through an interpreter "the Holy Father's aware-ness and appreciation of the Governor's effort to improve education." This prompted a knowing look from Bryant to Tom Drennan and his wife Lorraine, who were the only two Catholics in the Ogilvie group. "Tom and I understood, of course," said Bryant, "that the Pope was referring to Ogilvie's strong support back home for providing state aid to Catholic schools."[4]

All in all, Rome and the other European stops provided a welcome respite for the Ogilvies, away from the glare of the public spotlight. All of them were under the lights, not just the governor. Dorothy Ogilvie realized the pressure on her family would be greater than ever after this trip because her husband was heading into the meaty stages of his campaign for reelection. Demanding months lay ahead, she knew, quite likely the most challenging of Dick's political career. Whatever, for her part, she would remain composed. That was clear to those who had watched her blossom as the first lady of Illinois.

At first, in her early speaking appearances as the governor's wife, she came across to observers as reticent, a little bashful. However, as she grew more com-fortable with her role, that would change—certainly not to the surprise of close friends who knew her as a feisty and intelligent dynamo with a great sense of humor and an enthusiasm for life.

Unlike some of the state's other first ladies, Mrs. Ogilvie would maintain high visibility. She was assured of that alone by the renovation the Governor's

Mansion was undergoing. However, she herself attracted attention. Her choice of gowns, evening suits, and other apparel were lauded by Chicago columnists and fashion writers. She once even modeled jewelry, conveying a glamorous side of the Ogilvie family. One thing for sure, the need for decorum could never be out of the first lady's mind, particularly at the countless dinners, ceremonies, and other formal occasions to which she accompanied her husband. She could maintain a stiff upper lip when she had to, especially around the press because she realized that one word out of place could undermine the man at her side who had shaken up so much.

If Dorothy Ogilvie had a signature, some persons would have said it was her hair. Those who watched her were fascinated that she wore her long brown hair in a bun, never down. Elegant but restrained, not carefree like the tendency of the time back then. Yet there was plenty of free spirit in the first lady, who had started life as Dorothy Louise Shriver, born in Carlisle, Pennsylvania, one of six children of Jesse Shriver, a sales representative.

No way was she going to be imprisoned by the trappings of her husband's office. Sooner or later, she and Dick would return to a life without a chef, body-guards, or a chauffeured limousine. Anything but wealthy, the Ogilvies were not facing a cushy retirement after his days in public office. Dorothy Ogilvie insisted on preparing Sunday meals herself for the governor and Elizabeth. She'd serve one of his favorites, steak cooked medium well, pork chops, or beef stew. Dorothy would insist too on walking alone to shop in downtown Springfield, ditching the security that many felt to be an ingrained part of her husband's image.

Elizabeth had few opportunities to leave behind the state police. A trooper drove her to and from Sacred Heart Academy, a Catholic girls' high school in Springfield. When she got a driver's license, Liz drove around Springfield in the white Vega that her mom and dad bought for her. On the rare occasions when she was alone, she took along a walkie-talkie. She never used it, even though the vehicle stood out like a sore thumb because of the number on its license plate, 1.

Vanity plates have stories behind them, and that one was no exception. The plate had been held by John Cardinal Cody, the Catholic archbishop of Chicago. However, he had surrendered it to Paul Powell when he was secretary of state. After Powell died and the plate fell into the hands of John Lewis, Powell's successor, Lewis gave the plate to Dorothy Ogilvie at the urging of her husband.

A life in the public eye had to be a far cry from the mind of Dorothy Shriver Ogilvie during her modest upbringing. Her family moved a lot. When she was about ten years old, she and her family lived in Oak Park, where Dorothy would attend public schools and graduate from Oak Park High School. By June 29, 1948, her parents were living near the city of McHenry northwest of Chicago. The date would have special meaning for Dorothy Shriver because it was the day she met a pipe-smoking, twenty-five-year-old law student named Dick Ogilvie. Dorothy had a houseguest at the time who was engaged to a relative of Ogilvie. When the Ogilvie relative came calling to Dorothy's home, brown-haired, blue-eyed Dick Ogilvie, all 5 feet 8 inches of him, tagged along.

"He [Dick] just showed up that day," recalled Dorothy Ogilvie. She would accompany him before the day was over to boat races on the Fox River and find him to be "pleasant and polite and, while reserved, full of a bunch of questions."[5] Dating followed, not "every week at first" as Dorothy explained it, but soon enough for two persons getting serious about each other. There was so much that Dorothy admired about Dick. She refused to get married, though, until he had graduated from Chicago-Kent College of Law and was admitted to the bar in Illinois. Dick was admitted in January 1950, and the two exchanged vows the following month before members of their families in the First Presbyterian Church of Oak Park. The groom was an Episcopalian at the time, and the bride had been raised Presbyterian, the religion with which they affiliated during their life together.

Their marriage lasted thirty-eight years until his death in 1988. Afterward, Dorothy Ogilvie evinced special pride that in her husband she had a man who refused to duck any issue that needed to be dealt with. And if he happened to be swamped with a preponderance of such matters at certain stages, there were times when she could fill his shoes. The Governor's Mansion illustrated her expertise.

The dismal condition of the mansion, over a century old and one of the state's most prominent historical structures, was amply documented by the time the Ogilvie family moved in. In addition to the notoriously weak floors, reports by experts and firsthand observation attested to termite damage, paint problems, rat infestation under ground-level sections, and woefully inadequate heating, plumbing, air conditioning, and electrical systems, including wiring best described as a "patchwork affair." Much of the plumbing was said to fail to meet sanitary code requirements, which probably explained Governor Kerner's complaint that "you've got to step back at first when the showers are turned on because rust has come out of the pipe."[6] As far back as 1954, state engineers recommended that dancing be prohibited on the first and second floors of the building and that large gatherings be distributed as much as possible and held to a minimum. Put simply, the Governor's Mansion, which housed official state social functions as well as Illinois's first families, was not safe. Nevertheless, in the pre-Ogilvie era, few concrete steps to correct the problems had been taken—in part because some groups wanted to renovate and enlarge the mansion while another contingent in Springfield favored the building of a new one.

The inertia ended with the Ogilvies' arrival. Quickly deciding that further delay was out of the question, the governor and his wife would come down on the side of restoration, were determined to see that it got done, and would insist that it be carried out in a historically proper fashion. "If it wasn't done right," said Dorothy Ogilvie, "Dick and I would have gotten the blame."[7] To accomplish this, they felt they had to scrap or largely ignore earlier proposals for rescuing the mansion. They would start from ground zero, surreptitiously in the early going, and proceed with their own people to spearhead the project under the ultimate boss, the first lady.

The individuals collaborating with Dick and Dorothy on this task were James T. Hickey and Lowell Anderson. Impressed with the Old Capitol restoration in the center of Springfield, the Ogilvies had learned that Hickey headed the historical research for the project and that Anderson, the state's curator of historic sites, was the main expert responsible for securing period furnishings and artifacts for it. Both men would carry out similar roles in the renovation of the mansion.

Hickey had an unusual background for a person with his title—Lincoln collection curator at the State Historical Library. He personified a kind of homespun success story. Still living in the house in which he was born near Elkhart, Hickey was a self-made historian who became a nationally recognized expert on Abraham Lincoln through relentless exploration into the life of the Civil War president. Governor Stratton selected Hickey for the curatorship in 1958, a new position at the time, and Hickey held the job for nearly thirty years. Visiting scholars were often surprised to find that Hickey was not a college graduate. But that had been precluded by service in the army air force in World War II and then, after the military, by a need to run the family farm after his father's death.

Anderson was a different sort from Hickey. He was a college man, a decorative arts graduate of the University of California who taught interior design at the University of Illinois prior to his days in Springfield. Like Hickey, Anderson was a World War II veteran. Anderson was wounded twice while serving overseas with an armored division. Unlike Hickey, Anderson was shy, a person seemingly most comfortable in "Lowell's mole hole," a hideaway office beneath the Old Capitol, near a storeroom filled with antiques, paintings, and other objects. Anderson and Hickey complemented each other quite well.

At the behest of the Ogilvies, Hickey labored clandestinely on the research and other actions necessary to lay solid footing for renovation of the mansion in the manner the Ogilvies desired. Hickey had his hands full because the building was not orthodox architecturally, in that it had an exterior of one design and an interior of another. This had caused confusion in the past when improvements were made or contemplated. The mansion was, in Hickey's phrase, "a bastard building."[8]

By the end of Ogilvie's initial year in office, Hickey had privately come up with a scheme for complete renovation of the structure that would reconcile its incongruous elements while preserving historical integrity. Approving Hickey's plan, the Ogilvies moved to implement it publicly. For his part, the governor pushed successfully for an appropriation by the General Assembly in 1970 to finance a good deal of the restoration. Ogilvie left no doubt about the say-so of Hickey and also Anderson as the renovation progressed. Hickey was free to select architects of his choice for designing the project, and he got one he wanted, August P. Wisnosky of Springfield, as well as his associate, Carl Fischer.

The tax dollars appropriated for the restoration covered only structural work, not decoration and furnishings. It fell upon the first lady to marshal the necessary effort, which amounted to a campaign, needed to secure the resources for the refurnishing. To ensure historical correctness, Dorothy and her husband had agreed with Hickey that the Greek Revival interior design of the mansion had to be maintained in the renovation and that, furthermore, the new furnishings and decor in the mansion's public rooms had to follow the English Regency style in order to be compatible with the Greek Revival architecture. Such harmony was not always considered in the past when things were brought into the mansion.

Spurred by public interest in the renovation, the first lady agreed to numerous appearances throughout the state to explain the project and solicit support for it. The governor did not accompany her on what he called her "road show," but she usually had Hickey and Anderson on hand. This also was the time of the establishment of the Illinois Executive Mansion Association, a private nonprofit organization intended to locate and help purchase appropriate furnishings for the building. Dorothy Ogilvie would develop a close working relationship with Margaret Van Meter, an energetic Springfield community leader heading the association.

In view of the first lady's preoccupation with the mansion restoration, a conspicuous irony would occur. Because of the construction activity generated by the project, the Ogilvie family was forced to move out of the mansion for part of the governorship and into an apartment in Springfield's Lincoln Tower. Unlike other wives of governors, the first lady, who was a driving force for turning the mansion into a showcase, lived in the building for only several somewhat limited periods.

Supervision of activities in the mansion was a main duty for most first ladies. Dorothy Ogilvie supervised as well, operating during the time she spent in the mansion out of a lower-level office, where she might be found orchestrating a function or conferring with Kathy Kolbe. Kolbe, a volunteer assistant and scheduler for the first lady, was the wife of John Kolbe, the governor's assistant press secretary. Dorothy Ogilvie had to take care to avoid showing favoritism among her husband's staff members, but she could not hide her fondness for John and Kathy Kolbe. Nobody was surprised when John Kolbe joined the Ogilvies on their visit to Europe in 1970. Besides wanting the pleasure of John Kolbe's company, Dick and Dorothy seemed to be rewarding the assistant press aide, some thought, for the job he was doing as the governor's principal speech writer.

The 1970 European visit, in contrast to the visit two years later, was officially intended to promote business for Illinois interests in Europe. However, the segment of the trip that would be most memorable was Ogilvie's stop on a gray day in France at the site where he was wounded in World War II. The visit had both light and poignant moments.

This time, Ogilvie was driven toward the town of Bitche with a motorcycle escort and a helicopter hovering overhead, thanks to some pulling of strings by French president Georges Pompidou. After bestowing a hero's welcome on Ogilvie, the dignitaries of Bitche treated the governor, the first lady, and Kolbe to a feast. At its conclusion, the chef himself brought out the dessert for the honored guests. As a stuffed and very appreciative governor took notice of the ruddy-cheeked cook, Ogilvie asked a person near him to convey in French their gratitude for the meal. However, Ogilvie had no sooner gotten the request out of his mouth than the chef looked at the governor and posed a question in plain old English without the slightest hint of an accent.

"Are you all from Illinois?"

"Why, yes we are," answered a stunned Ogilvie.

"Well good," replied the cook. "I am from Waukegan."[9]

After that, the Ogilvie group took off to try to find the exact place outside town where Ogilvie had been wounded. The Pentagon had supplied the governor with topographical maps of the region at the time of the war. During the meal, the maps were spread out on a table, allowing everybody a chance to help point Ogilvie in the right direction.

Kolbe was riding with Ogilvie in the caravan of vehicles that headed out of

Bitche. Years later, when contacted at the *Phoenix Gazette*, where he was a political columnist, Kolbe would remember that ride as "perhaps the neatest experience I got to share with the Governor. We were driving out on these hilly dirt roads when we came to a bend in one of them that looked maybe like the place where he got hit," related Kolbe. "I asked him if that was it. After a bit, he said he doubted it. But he added that he would say that was the place if we could not find anything closer to it."[10]

Even though time was running out, the caravan pressed forward for a few more minutes. "We had gotten onto another dirt road and then, all of a sudden, there it was," said Kolbe. "Ogilvie said we were at the exact spot where he got it. You just knew that was it from the way he said it. He was touched, and I got to be there with him at the moment."

Powell's Cash and Racetracks: Public Anger Boils

The political climate in Illinois was poisoned, pure and simple, by the disclosure that Paul Powell left an $800,000 cash hoard. This occurred halfway
through Ogilvie's term as governor, triggering public indignation that spared
few persons in office, justified or not. The resulting climate could not have been
more perfect for outsiders trying to get a foot in the political door, especially
the hard-driving fellow seeking to unseat Ogilvie. Streetwise folks, people with
a real nose for such matters, guessed very quickly that Powell's stash was going to cause a big stink. A degree in political science was not needed to figure
that out.

Pete Romanotto, an Italian immigrant coal miner's son, had been operating a
shoe repair shop for decades on Monroe Street a short hike from the Statehouse.
He knew exactly what to expect. Wiping his hands on his apron as he took a
break from his shoe-stitching machine, Romanotto predicted to his chums passing time in his place that "this one is going to hurt some of the boys, maybe
even some of my customers."[1] It was a safe assumption that Romanotto had in
mind the Statehouse bigwigs who would have their flunkies run shoes over to
Pete's shop for sole and heel work.

"Once the Powell thing hit the street," Romanotto observed later in his un-
derstated manner, "it was all anybody would talk about. Everybody was asking
where the dough came from." As hard as official investigators and reporters
tried to trace the $800,000, though, no surefire answer to its origins ever was
reached, then or in later years. The mystery surrounding Powell's secret hoard
would only deepen, feeding the Powell legend more and more with each passing
year.

For a fact, Powell was already a political legend before his death on October
10, 1970, and the subsequent revelation of the $800,000. He was a legend long
before he was first elected secretary of state in 1964, having built a reputation
for himself during a three-decade career in the Illinois House, beginning in
1934. Powell was elected speaker of the House in 1949, 1959, and, incredible
though it was, in 1961. The 1961 approbation was surprising because members

of Powell's Democratic Party actually held one less seat in the House than the GOP. Then again, the 1961 speakership was the kind of coup that legislators and others had come to expect of Powell. Whether his party was in the majority or minority in the House, Powell made himself a player in significant General Assembly doings, because of his mastery of the legislative process, his inclusion on the budgetary commission and the other important panels, and the nearly blind loyalty accorded him by so many other downstate lawmakers. As Powell's years in public office mounted, his admirers as well as his critics saw him as a canny old fox. There were plenty of people in each category—although detractors were fewer and far between downstate. Southern Illinois may have been in many ways the stepchild of Illinois, but the region fared exceptionally well when the pie of state resources was divvied up during the era Powell sat in a catbird seat. Powell was in truth a one-person public works department for much of Illinois south of Springfield, a shrewd operator who never helped deliver the votes needed for grandiose projects up north, such as Chicago's huge McCormick Place convention center, without a quid pro quo for downstate. Powell also happened to be a major legislative benefactor of certain big interests. Some of them, the horse racing industry being one for sure, made certain his palms were thickly greased in return.

The extent to which Powell profited privately from his public life did not become abundantly clear until the hullabaloo over his financial affairs in the wake of his death. Even then his reputation below Springfield appeared to slip nary a bit. His home in quaint Vienna, the house in which he was born and lived until his death, was maintained as a museum by the Johnson County Historical Society. His nearby grave—with the hard to miss wording, "Here Lies A Life Long Democrat," on the gravestone—became a tourist attraction.

A person only had to wander south in Illinois, especially off the beaten path, to gain an appreciation of Powell's standing. For years on end, prominent politicians and other folks would head as if on a pilgrimage for Sunday dinner to the rambling old red-brick hotel owned and run by Carl Wittmond down in Brussels, in Calhoun County. Long after Powell was gone, hotel visitors could still see two vintage pictures on a wall. President Kennedy was in one, and the other was of Powell. He and Wittmond became friends when Wittmond served as a Democratic state representative with Powell.

Robert Charles Winchester of southern Illinois knew the inside dope about many people in the area, including Powell. Nightclub owner Lester (Shot) Winchester and his wife, Cora, lived in Vienna when their son Bob was born in 1945. The Winchesters were friends of Powell and his wife, Daisy. Powell and other political figures often frequented the best known of Shot Winchester's nightspots, the Club of Distinction, a gambling hotbed near Olmsted in Pulaski County where little Bob was free to peddle his tricycle around the slot machines and blackjack and craps tables. The years after World War II were a heyday for gaming in southern Illinois and certain other places in the state where authorities winked at the gambling in spite of its illegality. Money and patrons flowed freely at spots like the Club of Distinction, which brought in big-name bands and strip shows to complement the wagering. The days of wide-open gambling were numbered, though, after a crackdown ordered by Governor Stevenson.

It was Powell who gave Bob Winchester the nickname Butch. Powell also got Bob a scholarship to SIU, where Bob was an active young Democrat. When Ogilvie was governor, Winchester wound up in Springfield working for state purchasing agent Thomas B. Blanco and socializing with a clique of those gung ho young Ogilvie Republicans in government. Winchester would become a Republican himself and a successful one at that, getting elected to the House in 1974 from southern Illinois. But Winchester never lost his admiration for Powell, insisting that "anybody who knew anything realized how tough it was in Springfield for southern Illinois. So it was easy to see why Powell was so appreciated. He showed that he could stand up to Chicago and all the rest and not let our part of the state just get steamrolled."[2]

Powell savored recognition in his own backyard, but he often was not around to receive it. The salty-tongued Daisy Powell was a good surrogate, though. On nights when Paul's duties as secretary of state kept him away from home, onetime court reporter Daisy would herself hold court over a few beers at Big Boy's tavern in Vienna. The routine was pretty much the same every night, Winchester remembered, even the rough-around-the-edge part. As Winchester told it, "Daisy would sit at Big Boy's, or preside I guess you could say, exchanging praise with Paul's supporters as they came in. But she'd also loudly berate those who hadn't helped Paul or had been heard to criticize him. She knew how to use profanity and, believe me, she'd use it to tear apart those people. It was okay for her to blast Paul, but God help anyone else who did it."

Daisy's funeral service in 1967 drew Governor Kerner and thousands of other mourners to Vienna, which made it quite an event for the area. The town went through it all again three years later when Powell died. Paul Powell's funeral was even a memorable spectacle for Mike McCormick and other kids in Vienna at the time. Mike was the son of C. L. McCormick, a Republican in the Illinois House and a general store operator on the square in Vienna. Mike recalled the funeral being "one very big deal in Vienna because of all the important people coming to town, especially this one person, Mayor Daley."[3]

Prior to his funeral in Vienna, Powell already had been eulogized by Governor Ogilvie and other state political heavies as his body lay in state in the Capitol rotunda in Springfield. There, Powell's casket rested on the same bier used to transport President Lincoln's body from Washington to Springfield after his assassination. Powell was lauded by his long-standing political compatriot and former business associate Clyde Choate as "the most unforgettable man to ever walk these [Statehouse] halls." Ogilvie did not go so far. The governor depicted Powell as "a master politician" who "fought for southern Illinois, for the land that he loved and represented so long." Ogilvie linked Powell's political success to "fair dealing, according to clearly understood rules, which his allies and opponents alike could respect." Since Powell was "a man of his word," Ogilvie said, "no handshake was necessary; only his plain statement of his intentions."[4]

When Ogilvie assistant Jay Bryant wrote the eulogy the governor read, he was cautioned by Ogilvie, Bryant later revealed, "not to include any praise about Powell that could come back to haunt the Governor. We had all been hearing things, but I assumed the Governor probably knew more than the rest of us."[5]

Rumors implying Powell's finances were clouded by dark secrets circulated in the weeks after his death. However, because nobody came forward with concrete information, the speculation was treated as just that, hearsay. Ogilvie and others did know that in the hours after Powell's death, his closest aides were very busy removing documents and belongings from his Statehouse office. Bill Hanley, one of the governor's trusted lieutenants, observed some of this activity firsthand after he received a phone call from Whalen late on the night of October 10, 1970.

"Brian told me that Powell had died," Hanley said. "He also said that materials were being removed from the Statehouse, and that I should get on down there to see what was going on." Arriving at the Capitol not long after midnight, Hanley did observe what to him seemed "like a lot of activity in Powell's office at that late hour." But, he added, "I wasn't really sure what was going on." Before leaving the scene, Hanley did offer to Nicholas D. Ciaccio, Powell's chief assistant, "the condolences of the Governor's office and any assistance that might be needed." Ciaccio "was very polite," Hanley said, "but he was obviously emotionally upset. It was also apparent that Nick and the others there were not ready for visitors."[6]

An accurate account of the actions of Ciaccio in connection with Powell's death would not surface until nearly three months after the death, not before the discovery of the $800,000 was made public. This account would conflict with the original story. Originally, Ciaccio had said he was the one who found

Powell dead in a hotel suite in Rochester, Minnesota, where Powell had gone for medical tests. The true story, when it finally surfaced, bolstered the contention that nothing about Powell was ever simple, not even his death and its aftermath. The emergence of the truth left Ciaccio, a very capable fellow in his own right, wounded. As many saw it, he ended up a major casualty of the Powell affair.

Ciaccio, who died in 1987, related to this writer on January 7, 1971, in Springfield, what he said really transpired after Powell's death. He said he was trying to set the record straight at a point when daily disclosures about Powell's life, dealings, and money were only whetting the manic public appetite for information of any kind about the late secretary of state.

Ciaccio maintained that he deliberately created a wrong impression about the circumstances of Powell's death to protect Powell. Ciaccio admitted that he was not in Rochester with Powell, when the secretary of state died. Instead, the sixty-eight-year-old Powell was accompanied by his private secretary, Margaret (Marge) Hensey.

"I'm not the stupidest guy in the world; I knew hotel and other records could be checked," Ciaccio said. "Still, I didn't think it would be good reading for 11,000,000 Illinoisans that he was up there with his personal secretary." Hensey was the person who discovered that Powell had died, Ciaccio said. This occurred late in the morning of October 10, he explained, when she was unable to rouse Powell in their two-bedroom suite in response to a phone call from Ciaccio. Ciaccio was in Springfield at the time. "I created an impression that I was in Minnesota at the time of the death with my wife, Marilyn Towle [another Powell secretary], and Marge Hensey out of a sense of human charity for a public official," said Ciaccio. He was trying to prevent, he asserted, possibly scandalous insinuations of a secret tryst between widower Powell and Mrs. Hensey, who was divorced.[7]

After learning of Powell's death, Ciaccio said he went to Powell's suite of offices in the Statehouse. At first he denied carrying anything away on that visit but later admitted to removing various contents of a private safe in the office. Following that, Ciaccio, his wife, and Marilyn Towle flew that same day to Rochester to make arrangements for returning Powell's body to Illinois. Late that night, Ciaccio and the others, including Marge Hensey, flew back to Springfield and immediately proceeded to Powell's office in the Statehouse. There, joined by some of the office's division heads, a search of records and other documents ensued. Some of these materials, along with pictures and other personal effects of Powell, then were removed from the office in the early morning hours of October 11 and taken to Hensey's home in Springfield. After leaving the Statehouse, Ciaccio, Hensey, and one or two others, including Emil Saccaro, a Powell chauffeur, paid a visit to the St. Nicholas Hotel suite where Powell stayed when in Springfield. Entering the apartment with a key produced by Hensey, the visitors proceeded to remove various items, just as in the Statehouse. They would then take these to Hensey's residence. Neither Ciaccio nor the others said they saw any money in the apartment.

Two days later, on October 13, the day Powell was eulogized in the Capitol, John S. Rendleman said he made the most amazing discovery of his life. Rendleman, executor of Powell's estate, was going through the speaker's effects at his St. Nicholas suite. There, he stumbled on the stash of cash. Most of it was found in shoe boxes, briefcases, and strongboxes in a closet. All counted, the money was reported to total about $750,000. The other fifty grand or so in the Powell hoard was said to have been found in the secretary of state's Capitol office.

Rendleman, a Powell friend and chancellor of SIU at Edwardsville, would wait until the following December 30, two-and-a-half months later, to reveal his discovery in a story in Carbondale's *Southern Illinoisan* newspaper. As word of the find spread like a wildfire through Illinois and beyond, Rendleman would be quoted as saying that the discovery left him "naturally . . . frightened" and feeling as if "I'd been caught in the tower with the crown jewels in my pocket."[8] Seriously, he said that he delayed public disclosure of the cache to give himself time to search for more hidden Powell money, to try to figure out the source of the $800,000 and to get some idea of what tax liabilities might be involved. But, he added, he struck out in his effort to learn where the money originated, and he found no more dough in searches of Powell's home and other places.

Rendleman's hesitation to go public right away, or at least much earlier than he did, was the first thing about the Powell case to openly anger Ogilvie. The governor, who maintained that he found out about the $800,000 only hours before it became public, pushed without success for Rendleman to resign from the university post because of his involvement in "an uncomfortable secret." In fact, a main pastime in Illinois, after the story broke, was establishing the time when each of the state's major officials learned of the hoard. Many concluded that the public was kept in the dark about it for too long.

It surfaced, for instance, that Attorney General Scott was informed of Powell's money stash a month after the discovery. Scott did not tell Ogilvie about it, both said later, but Ogilvie staffers said that Scott's silence was appropriate, considering the statutory duties the attorney general had to carry out in the disposition of an estate.

Lieutenant Governor Simon also got word of it early—on November 3, the day of the 1970 general election. Rendleman visited Simon that day, and the gist of the meeting Simon reconstructed nearly a quarter of a century later when he was a United States senator from Illinois. He said,

> John asked me if I remembered some years previously when we had been together in Carbondale and I told him I thought Paul Powell, then a powerful legislator, was a crook. I said I did remember, and then John reminded me that he had told me he didn't think that was true. And I told John I remembered that, too.
>
> But then I told John on that day in 1970 that I thought Powell had straightened up quite a bit as secretary of state. At this, John said to me that he was wrong in that conversation a long time ago in Carbondale and that in this latest discussion I was wrong. John then mentioned the $800,000, but swore me to secrecy about it. John said there was a strong feeling that Powell had stashed more cash other places, and he wanted to know if I could suggest some spots to look. The only thing I replied was that I thought he should go through Powell's house in Vienna. John also said that day that he was going to inform Scott, but also ask him not to say anything about it.[9]

Powell might have turned over in his grave had he known the executor of his estate was confiding in Simon, a man Powell disliked, even though Simon was a fellow Democrat. Simon's independence as a state representative had made him a thorn in Powell's side. And Simon had not hesitated through the years to camouflage his negative opinion of Powell's manipulations on behalf of various special interests.

The death of Powell, Simon would say years later, "ended a period when the crude kind of corruption was practiced blatantly." From that point on, added Simon, "corruption was more sophisticated."[10]

Powell also had little use for Simon's Democratic ally, Adlai E. Stevenson III. Powell was House speaker part of the time that Adlai's father was governor, but the urbanely sophisticated Governor Stevenson and earthy Powell had a strained relationship. Powell considered the politically successful son of Governor Stevenson to be just as pretentious as his father seemed. For his part, Adlai III was more outspoken than most political leaders about the Powell affair.

A month after Rendleman's public revelation of the $800,000, Stevenson came to Springfield to address Democrats at a fund-raiser, the Franklin Delano Roosevelt dinner. "Recent events in Illinois," U.S. Senator Stevenson told the crowd, "have done little to sustain . . . hopes or encourage renewed faith in our government. They have stained the reputation of conscientious and conscionable public officials." Yet Stevenson added that "it is unfair to single out Paul

Powell. He was not a hypocrite. He made few bones about his conflicting interests. He never was guilty of self-righteousness."[11]

With interest focused on the Powell case in the first months of 1971, some analysts predicted that the General Assembly might give in to those pushing for income disclosure requirements for public officials and for a law requiring public listing of campaign contributors. Ogilvie went on the initiative early. A few days after the Powell cash furor erupted, he called for legislation requiring full disclosure of income and assets by all public officials. The governor also requested certain rules governing political spending, saying that in his judgment "certain events of recent days demand action to restore public confidence in government and in those who administer it."[12]

In a special message to the legislature on February 2, 1971, Ogilvie called for passage of a law that would require for the first time in Illinois disclosure of the sources of campaign dollars and of amounts of political expenditures. The day before, Ogilvie made public his own income tax returns for the three previous years as well as a listing of the assets of himself and his wife (a disclosure showing they had a net worth of $91,328 as of February 1, 1971).[13] He also ordered more than a thousand appointed state department heads, their deputies, and major assistants to report sources of income, including capital gains of $1,000 or more.

Numerous so-called ethics measures would be introduced in 1971 and afterward, leading eventually to new or more stringent economic interest or financial disclosure requirements intended to curtail conflicts of interest by public officials. The long-sought public disclosure of campaign contributors—considered the keystone of reform in this area—finally was required by legislation that went into effect late in 1974, about a year and a half after the end of the Ogilvie governorship.

The opportunity to make political hay out of the Powell matter was not overlooked. Dissident Democrats popping up all over the state were expected to try to capitalize by picturing Powell as an outgrowth of machine domination of a political party, their own. Some more regular Democrats like Simon who had been openly mistrustful of Powell felt vindicated by all the commotion. As for Ogilvie, the Illinois political world anticipated that he would move to drum up the Powell issue at a strategic time in his race for reelection in 1972. Powell would come up all right, again and again through the 1972 election, but not with the result envisioned or desired by some, most notably Ogilvie. Earlier, at the Roosevelt dinner, Stevenson had noted prophetically how someone like Powell could stain the reputations of all public officials. The brush of Powell's hoard would have a wide sweep.

The disclosure of Powell's stash ignited the steamiest chapter in the time of great trouble. It began with the Illinois Supreme Court scandal in 1969 and continued on through much of Ogilvie's governorship. One reason the Powell affair so magnified the time was that when reporters and others began to dig for the source of Powell's cash, their investigations produced other disclosures, mainly about politicians linked to horse racing, that shed a number of other officials in an unfavorable light. Yet the probing did not solve the mystery of the Powell money. The public would be reminded of that with regularity, such as in Bernard Schoenburg's 1990 look back on Powell in Springfield's *State Journal-Register*.

"It's been two decades since Paul Powell made 'shoe box' part of the political vocabulary of Illinois," wrote Schoenburg, "but the mystery of how the popular legislator and secretary of state secreted away more than $800,000 in cash remains. To some, especially in his Southern Illinois home town of Vienna, Powell is still a political hero tarnished by bad press that he could have explained away—if only he had been alive when the money was found. But he is still widely viewed as the epitome of an official who used his public office for private gain."[14]

Many theories about the money were put forward over the years, including some crackpot ideas. Only days after word about the $800,000 got out, a seasoned Powell watcher then running the BGA, George Bliss, flatly asserted that much of the hoard came from payoffs by Illinois trucking firms grateful for Powell's permission for them to use cheaper out-of-state license plates. Other persons, like Springfield attorney Melvin N. Routman, simply figured that the bulk of the money well may have been an accumulation of contributions in cash received and saved by Powell throughout his long public career. Routman, a House parliamentarian and assistant to Powell in his speakership days, felt strongly that "Powell never stole a dime in taxpayers' money."[15]

According to Illinois political tradition, many people owed Powell. In fact, Powell ushered a countless number of southern Illinoisans into state jobs. And later, thousands served in the patronage army of the secretary of state, individuals on whom Powell never hesitated to put the arm. Lobbyists also stood in line to reward Powell, a rare individual in his legislative days because he delivered on his promises.

Ultimately, the Powell matter was investigated inside out, or so Illinoisans were led to believe, by state and federal grand juries and a host of agencies. There would be indictments, even prison sentences, for several individuals accused of extorting contributions or arranging bribes for Powell. The sums involved in their cases, though, hardly added up to the Powell hoard amount, leaving many Illinoisans convinced that the only person with an answer to the riddle of the money lay in a grave at Vienna.

The size of Powell's estate, which had grown with interest to $4.6 million by the time it was closed in 1978, also raised eyebrows. On one hand, newspapers like the *Wall Street Journal* figured out that Powell's total remuneration during his long public service career, his only job in those years, came to no more than $300,000. On the other hand, an old Powell legislative crony expressed surprise that Powell "didn't leave a hell of a lot more." In the early going, the state and federal governments sought to claim Powell's whole estate because of the questions over how he amassed his fortune. In the end, the feds claimed $1.8 million, the state's general revenue fund got $100,000, and an Illinois inheritance tax payment of $222,215 was approved. All told, Powell's will named 136 beneficiaries, a number of worthy causes included.

Like the estate of many wealthy persons, Powell's estate included ample stocks and holdings in businesses and a number of corporations. Jumping out among his assets, though, were substantial interests in horse-racing organizations, usually obtained at cheap insider prices while he was fronting in the General Assembly for the racing folks. His holdings in at least five harness-racing groups included 15,800 shares alone in the Chicago Downs Association—shares willed to Margaret Hensey that were valued at about $700,000. Actually, many of Powell's racing investments were no secret while he was alive, partly because he could not resist boasting of things like his Chicago Downs stock turning into a fortune. He had purchased it at ten cents a share back in his early days of power in the House. In truth, other Illinois political figures had revealed, or at least not denied, their racing holdings.

However, until Powell's death, the public had scant notion of the great extent to which many leading Illinois politicians had cozied up to the racing world. Not that some observers had not pointed it out. As early as February 1963, journalist Thomas B. Littlewood, a keen analyst of Illinois politics, wrote about it in a story on Powell in *Chicago Scene* magazine: "For reasons not altogether clear, the passions of the ordinary legislator are aroused by the vision of closely bunched pacers, their hooves flashing in unison, their coats glistening in the sunlight, rounding the stretch turn on a dirt track."[16]

But it took the inquiries triggered by the uproar over Powell's estate to finally flush out the full story. The unraveling of these relationships—long obscured by mysterious trusts, straw parties, and a dearth of official records—showed why track operators did not have to blanket the General Assembly with lobbyists to get what they wanted. No wonder well-known lawmakers frequently were at the tracks as special guests.

In the view of many observers, the investigation of Powell's estate turned into nothing short of a Pandora's box. Numerous leading Republicans and Democrats apparently realized large profits rather quickly in racing stock transactions. The most prominent in the group was Otto Kerner, who ended up in a federal prison, convicted of conspiracy, mail fraud, and tax evasion in connection with a shielded racing stock deal in the 1960s when he was governor. In Kerner's case, the prosecution contended that in exchange for stock made available to him by Marjorie Everett, certain interests in her Illinois racing empire at the time received favored treatment by the state. The state maintained its influence over racing through the Illinois Racing Board. Through its allocation of racing dates to racing groups and its other regulatory powers, the board had much say over the profits of racing organizations. Furthermore, members of the board were appointed by the governor. During Kerner's years in office, the federal government argued, Everett's racing associations repeatedly were awarded lucrative racing dates, leading to skyrocketing profits for her interests. William S. Miller, racing board chairman under Kerner, was among others indicted for alleged complicity in the stock case involving Kerner. However, Miller escaped prosecution by agreeing to testify for the government. Everett herself was not a target of the investigation.

As for legislators with extensive stock holdings in tracks or racing associations, some had been quite instrumental in assuring that wagering on horse racing was just about immune to the rising trend of taxation that had hit individuals and most other businesses. Although Illinois enacted its income tax in 1969 and had increased levies like the sales tax, the tax on wagering as of 1971 had changed little since 1946.

For Ogilvie, the seemingly unending disclosures linking Illinois officialdom to racing diverted attention from the main event, his desire to make Illinois government a model for the nation. Unfortunately, this long brewing tempest in a teapot exploded during Ogilvie's "watch." The public seemed galvanized by the situation, and it was an angry fixation. The governor knew that Stevenson had been right. The Powell mess was staining the image of the whole political crowd.

As for the tarnished image of racing and what to do about it, some pretty far-reaching suggestions were floated in the Ogilvie years. One came from a blue-ribbon member of the racing board itself, Palatine banker Gerald F. Fitzgerald. He recommended that Illinois should follow the lead of New York and set up a nonprofit corporation to operate all or most of racing in the state. There were others who just wanted a complete takeover by the state, period.

While nothing so extreme would occur, the racing board under Ogilvie did move to address a number of the issues giving the industry a black eye. Alexander MacArthur, named by Ogilvie to chair the racing board, proceeded to insist that tracks, racing associations, and related organizations identify stockholders and other beneficiaries—revelations that uncovered some of the politicians tied financially to racing. MacArthur also backed numerous steps designed to tighten state regulation of racing and bring about improvements at deteriorating track facilities. Much of what MacArthur and the board were trying to do on their own was put into the statutes when Ogilvie signed a series of bills in 1972. The laws made it more difficult to conceal the identities of individuals seeking state approval to conduct harness and thoroughbred racing. The measures also required the Department of Law Enforcement to provide security personnel and investigative services at racetracks. And the legislation prohibited associations and other racing interests from making political donations.

Getting ahead on racing issues was not easy for Ogilvie, though. For all his good intentions, MacArthur irritated many important people who had been quite satisfied with the status of racing in Illinois. The racing panel chairman was a cattle farmer from Algonquin and a nephew of philanthropist John D. MacArthur. He was also one of the more colorful characters of the Ogilvie era. Recognized by his wide-brimmed hats, string ties, and cowboy boots, he became known for his often earthy responses at stormy board sessions to racing interest lawyers and others seen as antagonistic to MacArthur's goal to make racing as open as a fishbowl.

Political enemies of Ogilvie also would take interest in a disclosure in 1971 that the late Philip J. Levin, who headed a firm controlling two racetracks in the Chicago area, contributed $100,000 to Illinois Republicans in the summer of 1970. At the time, the racing board was questioning Levin's fitness for participating in the state's racing industry. However, he eventually was permitted to pursue his interests by the board.

Ironically, even John W. Lewis, whom Ogilvie appointed secretary of state after Powell's death, turned out to have had extensive racing holdings. Lewis, a onetime GOP power broker in the House from Marshall, acknowledged that he was among major politicians who participated in the original investment in the old Cahokia Downs Race Track by East St. Louis. Lewis was also, among other things, on the ground floor at the founding of the Egyptian Trotting Association. His wife, Mahala, paid $3,000 for three thousand shares of stock in the Washington Park Trotting Association in 1964. She sold the stock three years later for $18,000.

As he trekked from hamlet to hamlet on his 1971 walk through Illinois, Dan

Walker contended to anyone who would listen that only a political iconoclast like himself—one not part of the establishment in his own Democratic Party or the GOP—could clean up the "racetrack politics" that, he argued, had made a travesty of Illinois governmental integrity. He was running for governor, Walker maintained, because the Paul Powell scandal showed convincingly that only fresh blood at the top in Illinois could cut entrenched and nefarious interests down to size. Walker did not hesitate to charge that Ogilvie and Simon were culprits in the system failing to deal forcefully with the scandal. Defenders of Ogilvie and of Simon countered that Walker was a demagogue. Ogilvie, his friends said, had no connection to Powell's doings, and the governor hardly even knew the late secretary of state. As for the lieutenant governor, his often adversarial relationship with Powell in past years was a matter of record, Simon supporters noted.

Of course, neither Ogilvie nor Simon was particularly worried about Walker at that juncture in 1971. The two were pretty sure they would be facing each other in the election for governor in 1972.

Political Death

*T*he 1972 election year was one for the book in Illinois. Dan Walker's success could not have been more sweet for him. By early 1972, the political establishment had rated his chance of winning the governorship still as zilch.

As for Ogilvie? Well, he conceded early on in the election cycle that he was an underdog in his bid for reelection. Nevertheless, he also believed in the early days of 1972 that he had the record in office and the political muscle to prevail in the end against Paul Simon. Ogilvie thought for sure Simon would be his Democratic opponent. But Ogilvie would be wrong on all counts. Simon was not his opponent in the general election in November, and Ogilvie did not make up enough politically lost ground to retain Illinois's highest office. He came close to doing it, but he fell short.

For Richard Buell Ogilvie, 1972 was the year of his political obituary. He recognized he was losing the race as he sat sipping liquor late on the night of November 7, 1972, staring at a television screen in Room 1831 of the Bismarck Hotel. Ringing phones would bring reports that eleventh-hour tallying of votes from this or that part of the state gave at least slim hope that Ogilvie still might squeeze out a narrow victory. But the governor had seen enough to know that no last-minute triumph would materialize. He was already resigned to his fate when a reporter notified an Ogilvie aide about an hour after midnight that his newspaper was declaring Walker the winner.

At one point late on election night, Ogilvie had a surprise visitor, none other than Lieutenant Governor Simon. "Yes, I did pay a visit to Ogilvie in his election night roost in the Bismarck," Simon recollected decades later to this writer. "When I saw him, he knew he was going to lose. I'm sure I consoled him. He was just very stoic. He wasn't showing much emotion at all."[1]

Even after allowing for all the uncertainty of politics, precious few soothsayers foresaw the outcome of the 1972 gubernatorial race. A flashback to the start of the race revealed just how improbable the ending would be. By every reading imaginable, Simon appeared to be the most highly regarded political figure in the state. As Ogilvie's popularity dropped while he was governor, the political stock of the forty-three-year-old lieutenant governor, who looked like a choirboy, had soared as he deftly staked out his own stands on issues and developments, positions sometimes counter to what Ogilvie was doing. Simon was well suited for the ombudsman role that he carried out so effectively as lieutenant governor. In his earlier days as newspaper publisher and legislator, he always had shown concern with unresponsive pomposity in government as well as in the private sector.

At no time, though, was Simon's second-guessing of Ogilvie anything but civil or par for the course. From the day Ogilvie and Simon were sworn into the state's two highest offices, their mutual respect ruled out the playing of any political dirty tricks. Simon would see much that he liked in Ogilvie's government revamping. Yet Simon would note that "Ogilvie and I were not close personally and we never socialized." Simon could not remember "ever once having dinner with him."[2]

Trying to relax with Simon might have been especially inconvenient for Ogilvie at the approach of the 1972 election season since every known poll or other sounding had Simon trouncing him. The possibility that Simon might not be the Democratic candidate for governor was hardly considered. Besides the across-the-board approval that Simon seemed to have going, he had locked in the support of the Illinois Democratic leadership through the party hierarchy's so-called slatemaking process. Such a political blessing at that time virtually guaranteed victory for a Democrat in a primary election.

For that reason alone, the primary of March 21, 1972, would evermore remain a stunner. Walker, the Chicago corporate lawyer, had been an unknown south of Chicago when he announced for governor. Yet in the primary, he outpolled Simon, 735,193 to 694,900, to capture the Democratic nomination for the state's highest office. Walker pulled it off with a masterful grassroots campaign in which the impact of his statewide walk could not be overestimated.

Tapping into the discontent of so many people with the established order, Walker molded his candidacy into a referendum on bossism in both parties, racetrack politics, and on an often-voiced contention—really pushed by Walker—that the average person no longer had a voice in the decisions governing the lives of everyone. The candidacy of Walker was a political revolution, an insurrection attracting an incredibly ragtag army of political have-nots. Its success was like an earthquake hitting Illinois politics.

If a figure with the demonstrated appeal of Simon could be overcome by the Walker surge, then surely Walker posed big trouble for Ogilvie in the general election. With regard to Simon, his political mettle would be proven again through a subsequent twenty-two-year career in Congress and a serious bid for his party's nomination for president in 1988.

After the unexpected conclusion of the Walker-Simon primary contest, many predicted the Walker-Ogilvie race would be anticlimactic. Writing off Ogilvie became *pro forma*. It was amazing how Walker, who had been taken so lightly by so many right up to the primary election, was suddenly a heavy favorite to unseat the incumbent governor of Illinois. Before it was over, though, Walker would know he was in a horse race.

Just as he was against Simon, Walker was a flamboyant aggressor against Ogilvie, at least in the initial stages of their race. Ogilvie strategists vowed that their man would avoid Simon's apparent mistake in not vigorously responding to Walker's attacks. But Ogilvie's early showing in the general election contest offered no proof that he had gotten the message. In his first early campaign debate with Walker and in the weeks that followed, Ogilvie was sleepwalking, acting as if he was unaware that he had an opponent who pulled no punches in bringing out skeletons in the closet—bar none. Reporters and others eagerly anticipating that Ogilvie would slug it out with Walker toe to toe were rather disappointed to see that Ogilvie seemed intent to try to win reelection essentially on his record as governor. Recitations by Ogilvie of his numerous reforms and new programs could be cures for insomnia, many Ogilvie partisans even agreed.

Having no record in public office to defend nor any governing duties to tie him down, Walker was free to continue plying without baggage the main streets and byways of Illinois, always building on the bedrock of support established by his intensive face-to-face campaigning since the announcement of his candidacy. National analysts called the race the country's most interesting contest for governor, primarily because of Walker's perceived evolvement in the eyes of some into the most exciting new populist in the United States. Of course, Walker seldom missed an opportunity to emphasize his line that Illinoisans needed and deserved a visible governor—something he preached that Ogilvie was not. Walker was not just throwing wild punches on this one. They were measured jabs at Ogilvie's underbelly, the widely accepted notion that he was too wrapped up in a gubernatorial cocoon. That it might not have been true did not dispel the image.

A close study of the ways Ogilvie used time as governor, which was exactly what veteran Ogilvie staffer Ron Michaelson did during the month of June 1971, revealed that Ogilvie spent many more hours on public relations events, such as the daily speeches, receptions, and ground-breaking ceremonies, than on the actual management of state government. Moreover, Michaelson found, the largest segment of the public relations activities involved travel to Illinois communities, an excellent way to attract local media attention. Nevertheless, when Ogilvie hit the campaign trail hard in the last months of the contest with

Walker, a lot of folks in more than just out-of-the-way places asked him to his face, many with utmost sincerity, why he had not been a more visible state chief executive.

A part of the problem for Ogilvie, numerous observers concluded, was that the governor, by deliberately eschewing dramatics, had just come across as vapid to many of those he encountered. In an interesting effort at reverse psychology, Ogilvie tried to score points on Walker by suggesting to voters that personal magnetism was not everything. Ogilvie even had a campaign poster plugging that theory. Too, Ogilvie would not hesitate to tell crowds that "this is a race between our good record and his good looks."[3] But in a rapidly developing world of image-dominated politics, Ogilvie's deficiencies on this matter were tough to overcome. Worse for Ogilvie, the only picture many Illinoisans did hold of the governor was that he was the one who called for approval of the state income tax.

Still, even after taking all this into account, hardly any of those whiz-bang young Republicans and government technocrats around Ogilvie really saw him losing—not to Walker, not to that master of campaign gimmickry, not to an opponent disparaged by the Illinois smart set as having all the makings of a political flash in the pan. All would end well, Ogilvie partisans liked to think, if a fire just could be lit under the governor. He had to seem less wooden and more humane. With that, his followers reasoned, the situation could be salvaged. After all, Ogilvie was thought to have ample campaign funds, at least in comparison to Walker's dollars. Ogilvie certainly was not saddled with a second-class political organization or prevented from seizing the bully pulpit—thanks to the advantages of incumbency. And Ogilvie certainly had had no trouble dispatching a nominal 1972 primary opponent of his own, Dr. John H. Mathis, a urologist from Peoria. The governor got 442,323 GOP primary votes to 143,053 for Mathis.

However, getting a revamped Ogilvie out on the hustings for the general election was not easy. While Ogilvie had won his share of elections, the governor's running mate in the 1972 contest, young Illinois House Republican James Nowlan, probably sized up the situation as well as anyone. Nowlan, on the verge at the time of getting a doctorate in political science from the University of Illinois, would be qualified in the future to comment that GOP Governor Jim Thompson, who won election to the office four times in the late 1970s and 1980s, "governed so he could campaign." In contrast, Nowlan said, "Ogilvie campaigned so he could govern."[4]

The newest version of Ogilvie that anybody would see in the governor's race appeared after the beginning of September, the traditional start of the final crucial stage of an Illinois political campaign. In a swing through rural western Illinois, Ogilvie's stop in Pittsfield, the seat of pig-raising Pike County, said it all. There, lifting a page from Walker's book, Ogilvie wiled away an hour in Lindsay's tavern, a popular blue-collar bar right off the town square that was filled with Democrats hoisting beers to mark the end of the workday. Walking in unannounced, the governor plunked down $16 to buy the house a round of drinks, then shot the bull with guys leaning on the bar. At first, the tavern's patrons weren't convinced Ogilvie was who he said he was because the two plainclothes troopers accompanying Ogilvie on this tour stayed outside Lindsay's. Campaign aide Jim Harry, a onetime high school football star in Pittsfield, did follow Ogilvie into the tavern, but several tipplers recognizing Harry did not connect him to Ogilvie.

In one of the great events in the history of the Illinois governorship, Ogilvie challenged some of the watering hole's regulars at the shuffleboard in the rear of the place. Ogilvie won every game, leaving the overall-clad onlookers with their mouths hanging open in disbelief. This did not jibe with what they had heard about Ogilvie.

Moments afterward outside the tavern, a chuckling Ogilvie predicted that this was only a first step "to show people that I am not a stuffed shirt. It is unavoidable that, when you're governor, you get an aloof reputation. You just can't talk to everybody if you're going to be a good governor. But, I can have fun too, and match Walker stride for stride at this game."[5]

There would be plenty of similar stops by Ogilvie in following days, which were smart on his part because that particular campaign swing through western Illinois—which should have been friendly terrain for the governor—showed how far he had to go in cultivating rank-and-file voters. Repeatedly, as Ogilvie strolled through Jacksonville, Beardstown, Mount Sterling, Macomb, and even Quincy, people that he stopped simply did not recognize him. Of course, one reason may have been that they were seeing a more sleek Ogilvie (his weight had dropped to 180 pounds from 235 a year and a half earlier).

As the campaign entered its homestretch, nobody doubted that Ogilvie had narrowed Walker's lead. By the end of October, a week before the election, a lot of analysts saw the race as too close to call. An irony was that a major boost for Ogilvie was thought to be surfacing in Democratic Chicago. Canvasses were showing Ogilvie running ahead of his 1968 campaign pace in both Chicago and its Cook County suburbs. The only slight edge reported for Walker in Cook was not an encouraging sign for him since most Democratic candidates trying to win statewide normally needed big pluralities in Cook. If the polls were accurate, Walker apparently was suffering from the hostility many Chicago Democrats harbored toward his candidacy.

On the other side of the coin, voter surveys in traditionally Republican sections of downstate were giving Ogilvie only a slim lead over Walker. One person not surprised by this had to be Nowlan, who spent much of the campaign courting votes at county fairs, small-town dinners, and other rural area doings that time constraints prohibited Ogilvie from attending.

Nowlan was well suited for this role since he epitomized small-town Illinois, going back to his football and basketball playing days as a high schooler in rustic Toulon (population 1,200 in 1972). In fact, all the residents of Stark, the county of which Toulon was the seat, would not have filled more than a few blocks in some parts of Chicago. Nowlan, a moderate Republican like Ogilvie as well as editor of the weekly *Stark County News*, actively lobbied Ogilvie for support for the GOP nomination for lieutenant governor. Nowlan may have assumed that the Ogilvie campaign wanted a running mate for the governor better known across the state than Nowlan, but Nowlan also had an impression, as he put it, that "some of the potential running mates with considerable stature were not interested since Ogilvie was not considered a sure bet for re-election."[6] Whatever, Nowlan, barely thirty years old, was summoned to a meeting with Ogilvie in Springfield late in 1971, a confab at which the governor informed Nowlan that he was endorsing him for their party's nod for the state's second highest office.

Ogilvie's open backing for Nowlan was intended to discourage primary opposition for Nowlan, which it did since he had none. Even better for Nowlan, Ogilvie insisted that Nowlan not spend time soliciting money for the campaign, taking Nowlan off the hook on what most Illinois office seekers view as their most onerous task. Nowlan still raised close to $20,000 for the race, but in the main, he noted, "his [Ogilvie's] campaign paid for mine."

Of course, the contest for lieutenant governor in 1972, pitting Nowlan against thirty-four-year-old Democratic attorney Neil F. Hartigan of Chicago, was quite different from the past. Under the new Illinois Constitution of 1970, each party's candidates for governor and lieutenant governor were running as an official team for the first time. This meant that a person no longer could vote for the gubernatorial candidate of one party and the nominee for lieutenant governor of another party. The framers of the new charter wanted to avoid what they considered the obviously awkward situation that came out of the 1968 election when Republican Ogilvie was elected governor and Democrat Simon, lieutenant governor.

Back on the matter of money. One reason Nowlan was told not to go after any was that he probably would have been hitting many of the same sources of dollars for Ogilvie, which the governor's crew sought to avoid. This would be the last gubernatorial race in Illinois in which contenders still did not have to publicly disclose contributors, meaning only very few persons were privy to the inside stories of the candidates' campaign finances.

Victor de Grazia, the Chicago political guru masterminding much of Walker's campaign, replied when asked about the subject many years later that Walker spent more than $2 million in the race with Ogilvie—a good portion of which predictably went for television ads. Many observers at the time would not have hesitated to bet that Ogilvie spent three times as much.

However, in a 1994 interview with Donald Sheldon Perkins at his Winnetka home, Perkins contended otherwise. By then, Perkins had long since retired from Jewel Companies, the business empire he had such a large hand in building. As for the 1972 campaign, which found Perkins in his customary role as Ogilvie's finance chairman, Perkins recollected that about $2.5 million was raised directly for the governor's reelection bid—roughly the same amount that Perkins remembered being garnered for Ogilvie in the 1968 gubernatorial contest. Unlike Walker, Ogilvie did not emerge from the 1972 race saddled with a burdensome campaign debt. "As always, if we didn't have the money," related Perkins, "Dick said we wouldn't spend it."[7]

An irony of Ogilvie's 1972 campaign was that many insiders regarded it as a model effort, even though it was not successful. Campaign director Jim Mack was one of them. Going on the campaign payroll the day the governor announced for reelection, Mack would be left after the conclusion of the race with memories of unending hours in his campaign office in Chicago's floodlit Wrigley Building, of too many burgers in the hurly-burly of nearby Billy Goat's bar, and with a feeling that not much more could have been done from a campaign organizational viewpoint to save the Ogilvie governorship.

On those occasions when Mack replayed the campaign in his mind, the same things always came to mind.

That was a textbook campaign, at least in terms of organization. We recognized early on that you could not rely entirely on the local party apparatus outside of selected areas. So, in many downstate communities, we started putting together our own local groups. We had many business people and other volunteers for Ogilvie in 1972 besides those in regular party organizations and those already in Ogilvie citizens groups. We had thousands in our campaign, just like he [Walker] had many thousands out working for him.

That 1972 campaign for governor was really one of the last in Illinois with major grass roots involvement on both sides.

In many places, the best thing Ogilvie had going economically was his extensive road building program. Overall, though, the economy was in the doldrums during the last part of the Ogilvie governorship, especially in certain sections of Illinois.

Our whole 1972 campaign was aimed at the guy in Skokie who was asking what did Ogilvie do with the money from the [Illinois] income tax. We knew that a bottom line of our organizational effort, actually of our entire campaign, was to provide a means for getting across or showing what we did with the money from the increased taxation [under Ogilvie]. Out of the 10,000 or so precincts in the state in 1972, we must have hit 7,000 door-to-door on the weekends before the election, telling people what we did with those dollars from the income tax.[8]

Ogilvie supporters were not alone in seeking to spread word about the governor's accomplishments. Newspapers were quite helpful, particularly editorial writers, a great number of whom loved his record. If the press could have decided the election, Ogilvie would have won in a breeze. Paper after paper, including the Chicago majors, endorsed his reelection. Over in Missouri, the *St. Louis Post-Dispatch*, which usually endorsed Illinois Democrats, did an about-face from its opposition to the election of Ogilvie in 1968. Now, four years later, the Pulitzer family newspaper editorially concluded that Illinoisans would be foolish to give Ogilvie the boot. Most working reporters covering the campaign could not camouflage their preference for Ogilvie, in part because of the fourth estate's growing dislike for Walker that would erupt in outright antagonism after he became governor.

The avalanche of newspaper editorial endorsements for Ogilvie understandably rankled the Walker campaign hierarchy, and the Ogilvie crowd tried to exploit the situation whenever and wherever it could. Any occasion would do, such as a campaign visit by Walker to Illinois State University at Normal, a stop that began well with students and friendly faculty members. However, someone in the crowd tried to spoil the day by asking Walker why all the newspapers wanted Ogilvie to win. Walker did not know that the smart-aleck questioner was Robert Charles Maple, an ISU graduate student in political science from Alton and, hardly coincidentally, a state leader of Young Republicans for Ogilvie. He was also a son of Ivan F. Maple, the executive director of the Illinois Liquor Control Commission in the Ogilvie administration. "Why may I ask,"

Walker shot back in annoyance at the query, "would you let newspapers tell you how to vote?"[9]

Walker had good reason for not wanting anyone to pay heed to the editorials. The *Chicago Sun-Times* summarized the way many papers regarded Ogilvie. The paper urged his retention in office, editorializing that the governor "has brought about great changes for the better in Illinois. He has brought the state government from near-bankruptcy to a point where it has doubled state aid to schools; rebuilt highways that were death traps; modernized the penal system, crime-fighting agencies and mental hospitals, and written the toughest anti-pollution laws in the nation."[10]

The *Chicago Tribune* was even more grandiloquent in asking the electorate to "keep Ogilvie," a politician who had displayed "skill, courage, and common sense" in meeting Illinois's problems. The state's largest newspaper could not have gone much further in its Ogilvie endorsement editorial than in saying that "to describe his record as superior is understatement; he may well go down in history as the best governor the state has ever had."[11] This was not exactly faint praise, coming at a time when public officials above so much else were targets of undisguised cynicism in America.

Those hoping for an Ogilvie victory also had to be encouraged by the general outlook for the election in Illinois. Except for the gubernatorial contest, a GOP elephant stampede appeared likely in most of the top races. In his bid for reelection as president, Richard Nixon surely was going to blow away his Democratic opponent, Senator George S. McGovern of South Dakota, in the balloting in Illinois. Charles Percy looked like a hands-down favorite to retain his seat in the United States Senate against Democratic Congressman Roman C. Pucinski of Chicago. In the contest for attorney general, Bill Scott was expected to handily whip Democratic state senator Thomas Lyons, who had been a vice president of the state constitutional convention in 1970. Yes, based on the forecast for Nixon, Percy, and Scott, Republican landslides were shaping up in Illinois. If they occurred, many supposed, the tide might be strong enough to nudge Ogilvie to victory—a Republican version of 1964, the year that President Lyndon Johnson swept the state and helped many Illinois Democrats gain or retain office, including incumbent Governor Kerner.

As the campaign neared an end in Illinois, the Ogilvie-Walker race seemed to be virtually monopolizing statewide attention, creating without question the most suspense. Nixon, given little reason to worry about Illinois, made only a few brief campaign appearances in the state. This opened him to post-election criticism by some Ogilvie partisans that the president could have visited Illinois more often to try to help an important state Republican governor obviously in trouble. Percy and Scott ended up maintaining relatively low profiles in an attempt to avoid numerous confrontations with their opponents.

With regard to interest and drama, the Illinois election came down to the two intense and gutty men vying for the state's most coveted political prize, a contest made all the more vivid by the continual juxtaposition of the short, stocky Ogilvie with the taller, good-looking Walker. When both men turned to rapid-fire television commercials to try to win final points near the end of the campaign, observers still could not help but notice Ogilvie's shortcomings in the personal magnetism game, even in video productions of his own doing.

In any event, for a candidate believed to be so many miles behind early in the race, Ogilvie was upbeat at the end. When Ron Michaelson encountered the governor the day before the election at the Decatur airport, he said his spirits soared as Ogilvie took him to the side and told him that "he just wanted to let me know that he thought we had caught him [Walker] and that, as a result, it was looking good for tomorrow."[12]

Nowlan also found Ogilvie quite optimistic in the hours before the election, but Nowlan did not share the mood. "In all those hours I had spent in little towns and other places in the campaign," Nowlan remembered, "I never did find a lot of enthusiasm for our ticket. Even when Ogilvie himself might be present, I didn't see any sparks."[13]

Nevertheless, as a large number of the state's 6,215,331 registered voters filed into voting booths on November 7, the governor's race was seen by most as a toss-up. Regardless of the winner, most analysts agreed, the race would be decided by fewer than 100,000 votes.

It was. Walker defeated Ogilvie by 77,494 votes, making it one of the closer contests for governor of Illinois in the twentieth century. The team of Walker and Hartigan, carrying Cook and 54 of the state's other 101 counties, received 2,371,303 votes—50.7 percent of the vote for governor. The tally for Ogilvie and Nowlan was 2,293,809. The Socialist Labor and Communist parties also had candidates on the ballot for governor and lieutenant governor, but they got only a handful of votes.

Ogilvie did indeed run better in Cook County this time than four years earlier, when he lost the county by 169,657 votes to Shapiro. Walker only carried Cook by 99,411 votes against Ogilvie, 1,178,446 to 1,079,035. The rest of the state killed Ogilvie. Walker held Ogilvie to a 21,917-vote plurality outside of Cook, as Ogilvie received 1,214,774 and Walker 1,192,857. In comparison, Ogilvie carried downstate by 297,451 votes in getting elected governor in 1968. The forty-seven downstate counties Ogilvie won in 1972 seemed like a small number in contrast to the eighty-three he had carried in 1968. For a Republican governor at that time in Illinois, Ogilvie's 1972 downstate showing was a political disaster. Unfortunately for the Ogilvie-Nowlan ticket, young Jim was reading it accurately when in his downstate campaign appearances he failed to detect the ticket generating "sparks."

To his credit, Ogilvie did capture, and quite readily in most cases, DuPage, Kane, McHenry, Will, Sangamon, Champaign, McLean, and Walker's home county of Lake, all places where Ogilvie should have done well. For instance, Ogilvie ran away with GOP stronghold DuPage, outpolling Walker, 142,805 to 87,056, a tally giving the governor more than 62 percent of the DuPage vote. However, Walker either beat Ogilvie or cut into his anticipated victory margin in numerous other counties that would have been solid Republican territory in an era not that long ago. For example, Walker won in populous Winnebago County in normally Republican northern Illinois by 52,566 votes to 40,922.

Ogilvie also was hurt by his failure to repeat in 1972 his stellar performance in 1968 in certain traditionally strong Democratic counties downstate. He carried Madison and Rock Island and made a surprise showing in St. Clair in 1968. These were far cries from the wide margins for Walker in each of those counties in 1972. In sum, Ogilvie lost St. Clair, Madison, and Rock Island to Walker by 52,928 votes, a significant figure in that he only lost the entire state by 77,494. To Ogilvie's disappointment, but as expected by many observers, the governor carried only a handful of counties south of Springfield, most of them small ones.

Ogilvie's defeat was especially hard for Illinois Republicans to accept because, as anticipated, Nixon, Percy, and Scott all won by lopsided margins in the state. While their triumphs were significant, GOP professionals—the ones dealing in public jobs and other outgrowths of political clout—knew that the loss of the governorship signaled tough times ahead for the party.

To make matters even worse for the Illinois GOP, the only other statewide race won by a Democrat was in the contest for secretary of state. In that one, Michael Howlett, the outgoing state auditor of public accounts, defeated Edmund Kucharski, the Republican chairman of Cook County and veteran Ogilvie political ally. Kucharski's defeat meant the Republicans faced surrender of a goodly number of the nearly 4,200 jobs in the patronage-rich secretary of state office, the second most important political base in state government besides the governorship. There was one other statewide contest, for the new office of Illinois comptroller, and it was won by Representative George W. Lindberg, a Crystal Lake Republican, over Democrat Dean Barringer of Anna. However, the Republican pros knew that all their statewide victories put together amounted to small consolation politically for the losses in the governor and secretary of state races.

As it turned out, the Republican hiatus from the governor's office lasted only for the four years of Walker's term. After that, the GOP had a lock on the top Illinois post for decades. Republicans could not foresee this, though, in their days of gloom following Ogilvie's defeat. Anyway, they and others were busy pointing fingers at the perceived causes of Ogilvie's demise.

The main reason, most of the Illinois political world quickly concluded, was not hard to figure—the state income tax. Nobody had forgotten the warnings to Ogilvie that he was committing political hari-kari by demanding the levy. After his defeat, even his antagonists were pegging him as a martyr for ignoring political expediency and taking an action widely considered unavoidable. Bite the bullet Ogilvie did. And he paid the price.

Plenty of other developments also were cited as contributors to the downfall of Ogilvie. Ogilvie himself confided to more than a few persons his belief that the strong backlash against the leaf-burning ban may have greatly spurred his defeat. Of course, industrialists and others had cautioned him frequently during the campaign that the aggressive enforcement policies of the governor's antipollution officials had hurt his chances for reelection.

Actually, there was no end to the list of factors blamed for Ogilvie's defeat. Bill Harris, one of those long-standing Republican stalwarts in the Illinois Senate, was told that Ogilvie may have hurt himself seriously downstate with his 1969 veto of a bill that would have exempted firearm owners in downstate counties from having to register under the Illinois gun owners identification law. Southern Illinois legislators behind the measure argued that the 1967 law was ineffective nuisance legislation never accepted by most Illinoisans.

When the exemption bill was nixed by Ogilvie, its main sponsor, Representative Gale Williams of Murphysboro, a Republican no less, had some words at the time for the governor that would be somewhat prophetic in view of the 1972 election outcome. Contended an angry Williams, the veto by Ogilvie "showed that the Governor forgot it was downstate that elected him. This was a very popular bill downstate, and I told him [Ogilvie] that. To me, his veto means he is done downstate, and the three years left in his administration aren't going to be enough for people to forget."[14]

Another matter that may have been more politically harmful to Ogilvie than helpful, an issue as volatile in parts of downstate as gun owner registration, was his vigorous pitch for state assistance for cash-strapped Catholic and other private schools. Going to the wall on this one, Ogilvie finally received from the General Assembly and signed in 1971 a legislative package providing grants to cover the cost of some textbooks in nonpublic schools as well as the cost of certain services, such as health care, guidance programs, and remedial reading courses. Public school advocates fought the enactment of so-called parochiaid, and a dandy fight it was, leading among other things to the embroiling of Protestant and Jewish groups in heated clashes with Catholic leaders over church and state issues. Although most of the aid program was declared unconstitutional by the Illinois Supreme Court in 1973, the emotional strain from its enactment still lingered during the 1972 campaign. In the state Senate especially, a number of the veteran GOP members never forgave Ogilvie for putting them on the spot on this pressure-cooker issue. Chicagoan John Lanigan, who lost his Senate seat to a Democrat the year before parochiaid passed, still felt years later that "this issue contributed more to Ogilvie's defeat than many people may have thought because of the alienation it caused."[15]

Just the opposite was intended. Noting that Drennan was a "major player" with Ogilvie on the parochiaid issue, Jerry Marsh said that he "agreed with Tom that aiding Catholic schools was an effort at broadening the base of the Republican Party." The traditional image of the party "as a mainly WASP organization was already changing back then," said Marsh. "We thought this could help that trend along. Also, from a policy standpoint, we could see that Catholic schools were better in some places than public schools. For one thing, they were more cost efficient. We just felt a lot of interests would be served by keeping the Catholic schools going."[16]

However, when Drennan looked back on the "parochiaid" fight, he seemed to take little issue with Lanigan's perspective. "I did recommend to Ogilvie that he support parochiaid because I thought it was a good idea and an appropriate move for state government," said Drennan. "But politically, just looking at it from a cold political viewpoint, it did not turn out to be a good move by him."[17]

And so they would go on and on, the postmortems on the defeat of Richard Ogilvie. As for Ogilvie himself, life had to continue.

Walter (Bud) Lohman, board chairman of the First National Bank in Springfield, was surprised on the day after the 1972 election when he got a call at his office from his friend Governor Ogilvie. Lohman had not anticipated that Ogilvie would be back in his Springfield office so soon after the election, tending to daily details of the governorship.

Ogilvie asked Lohman if he would mind a visit by the governor, who as Lohman remembered it "just wanted to get out of the Statehouse for a while." Shortly thereafter, the state's newest lame-duck governor was sitting in Lohman's office. "Both of us passed time," recalled Lohman, "trying to be pleasant in a sad moment." Lohman did utilize the occasion to tell Ogilvie that "in my opinion you've got to be the best or second best governor in Illinois history, right up there with Henry Horner." Lohman admired Democrat Horner for forcing a radical revision of the state's revenue system, including institution of the sales tax, to permit the state to cover chronic unemployment relief costs and other emergencies resulting from the Depression. "I told Ogilvie that he, like Horner, acted like a statesman and not a politician in doing what had to be done in a most difficult time for our state," Lohman said. Ogilvie accepted the compliment passively, Lohman observed, so that Lohman almost felt as if he were more upset than Ogilvie. That had to be, Lohman thought, "the side of Ogilvie that was a hardened politician."[18]

Ogilvie would be in a much lighter mood when Lohman saw him again on New Year's Eve, a little more than a week before Ogilvie would relinquish his office to Walker. The governor and first lady had decided to usher in the New Year surrounded by a handful of friends at the mansion. This was not another pressure occasion, just an evening with people with whom Dick and Dorothy could relax: Lohman and his wife, Carol; Margaret Van Meter and her husband, A. D. Van Meter Jr.; Judy Allan and her husband, Harper, a Springfield insurance executive; Springfield newspaper publisher John (Jack) Clarke; and a few other folks.

After a casual dinner, all on hand went upstairs to the Ogilvies' private living quarters. Some of the men played cards up to midnight. Earlier in the evening, Dick and Dorothy and their guests had huddled around the piano in the mansion, singing old songs. The Ogilvies really loved that. It was their thing.

Afterward

On January 7, 1973, the last full day of his governorship, Ogilvie bade farewell to Illinoisans with a communique that was Ogilvie to a tee. The mechanism was a constitutionally required State of the State message, an epistle formally penned for the General Assembly that would have to serve as Ogilvie's official parting words. It could have been a flowery outpouring. But since this was Ogilvie, it read like business as usual with its unadorned prose going straight to the point, so much like his outgoing administration.

In assessing his four years as governor, keeping in mind that no one in that office ever gave himself a failing grade, Ogilvie concluded that the "successes far outnumbered the failures, and the state of the state is good." Moreover, he contended, "in many areas that are critical, it is excellent." With minimal verbiage, Ogilvie rehashed the positives, not the least of which he reasoned was his rescue of the state from financial chaos. He also owned up to the unmet challenges, most notably in combating the "racial and economic deprivations" continuing "to plague us all." In an especially providential admission, Ogilvie granted that "we must count among our failures the lack of any sizable improvement in the human aspects of what all concede is the 'welfare mess.' " Nevertheless, Ogilvie did maintain—and this was about as far as he ventured in forecasting a historical niche for himself—that in numerous areas a "solid base" had been created for "future progress."[1]

But yet, as for credit for the accomplishments that might be ascribed to his governorship, Ogilvie emphasized that the "one element that seems to be common to the successes of the last few years was the spirit of bi-partisan cooperation that was achieved. We surmounted more often than not the differences between the parties, the rivalries of Chicago and downstate, and the personal bickering and cross-accusations which frequently are the substitutes for action."

Ogilvie's final message didn't stir much interest. He was already categorized as yesterday's news, a casualty of the attention showered on Walker. For a person who so recently had been a king of the hill, Ogilvie appeared for a while after his loss to be on a fast track to oblivion. There seemed to be little he could or would do about it, disdaining jeremiads as he did and ducking interviews or even extensive comment on the doings of his successor.

Ogilvie would not be forgotten, though, and as the years increased since his departure from office an outright hankering for Ogilvie and his brand of leadership gradually surfaced. Ogilvie—the man himself and what he fashioned as governor—would be resurrected with regularity as pundits and others sought to set out the standard by which to judge other individuals and events shaping public life. The revival of Ogilvie would come in bits and pieces, each contributing to a public consciousness, a growing recognition of the uniqueness of Ogilvie.

None other than Mayor Daley of all people helped to get the ball rolling. Throughout his political career, Ogilvie was the mayor's rival. Even after entering the governor's office, Ogilvie intended to oversee the disassembling of Daley's machine. But Ogilvie got nowhere with that. The reality of it was a state of coexistence between the governor and the mayor that permitted the domain of each to prosper. Ogilvie never brought the Chicago Democratic machine to heel as did Walker in winning the Democratic nomination for governor in 1972. Walker then persisted in inflicting further misery on Daley after becoming governor. Even so, onlookers still could hardly believe their ears when an angry Daley declared before lawmakers and others during a visit to Springfield while Walker was governor that darn few folks did not rue the day that a good governor, Richard Ogilvie, was replaced by Walker. Of all things, that unlikely pronouncement was judged by some in later years to have signaled the birth of renewed appreciation for Ogilvie. The admiration would only grow.

Robert D. Reid, a widely traveled public affairs journalist in Illinois, seemed to almost wax sentimentally when he wrote in *Illinois Issues* magazine in September 1994 that Ogilvie's time as governor "was the golden era of Republican and Democratic competition and cooperation in Illinois," an observation Ogilvie himself appeared to have tried to make in his farewell message twenty-one years earlier. While the Ogilvie era "smelled at times like sausage being made," said Reid, "in retrospect it was more the essence of statesmanship, seasoned with pork and patronage, but more idealistic than cynical, more responsible, on balance, than exploitive." Reid admitted finding the central figure of the era, Ogilvie, "one of the least charismatic politicians in the history of the United States." Nonetheless, Reid wrote, "in just four years [Ogilvie] laid the groundwork for modern Illinois state government."[2]

One of Ogilvie's successors, Governor Jim Edgar, did not hesitate to note in a 1996 interview that Ogilvie used old-fashioned tools to lead Illinois into a new era of state government. To Edgar, Ogilvie "was the last governor to enjoy the full powers of patronage and party discipline—powers that have been significantly diminished by court decisions and other changes. He was not a great communicator. He did not achieve his goals by using the bully pulpit. He used the institutional powers that were available to him to advance the governmental programs that mark his stewardship as historic and truly outstanding."[3]

Putting it as simply as possible, Ogilvie was, in the estimation of Phillip M. Gonet, the "father of modern Illinois government."[4] Gonet was qualified to make that observation. As a deputy chief of staff for Governor Thompson and an administrator in various Illinois agencies through the years, Gonet exemplified the often faceless managers of the programs established by governors and other elected officials.

Paul Simon may have once set his sight on defeating Ogilvie, but that did not subtract from the high esteem that Simon too expressed for Ogilvie in later years. History buff Simon was not of the opinion that Illinois "has had a number of really outstanding governors." He could not think of one, he said, who dominated the history of his state like Wisconsin's Robert La Follette—whose Progressive movement favored greatly increased action by government to improve the lives of ordinary citizens. Still, held Simon, "Ogilvie was clearly one of the superior governors of Illinois. I'd think there would be no question about that." Facing up to the state's severe need for revenue as Ogilvie did, noted Simon, "had to be done . . . but it really hurt him."[5]

Simon stopped short of calling Ogilvie a political martyr for pushing the income tax, but some others have not hesitated to do so. One was Mike Lawrence, who was still an active Statehouse reporter when he obtained a rare interview with Ogilvie for an article on the former governor in the December 1982 edition of *Illinois Issues*. In the piece, Lawrence depicted Ogilvie as "Illinois' first martyred governor since John Altgeld," who was cast by liberals as a martyr for pardoning some of the Haymarket bombing defendants.[6]

Reflecting on the passage of the income tax, Ogilvie was quoted in Lawrence's story as saying the following about himself. "I've described myself, and I really mean this, as an optimistic fatalist. It was something I had to do. I was fatalistic as to what was going to happen. I was hopeful, of course, that I could overcome it. In fact, I damned near did."[7]

Other comments in that interview clearly illustrated that the principled Ogilvie of old was still around, that he had not retreated from his convictions on strong leadership. "I think you're elected to lead," said Ogilvie. "Remember my inaugural address? I really laid it out there for everybody to see: I was going to lead this state and, for better or worse, I was going to do it. . . . I don't want to be critical of anybody using devices that I didn't use, but I just happen to think being re-elected is not the goal of public service or public opportunity. That sounds a little bit, I suppose, like an afterthought. But I was elected to be governor, and I was going to govern and not just occupy the office."[8]

As Jim Nowlan saw it, Ogilvie was a vigorous practitioner of the school of political thought—which was riding a crest in Ogilvie's time—that "felt deeply that government could be applied to the solving of problems." By this reckoning, Ogilvie was to Nowlan "a man of action," which Nowlan in turn found to be "the reason that so many sharp people from all over were attracted to Ogilvie's administration."[9]

The alumni of the Ogilvie administration would prove to be, all considered, a fascinating lot, real go-getters. Bob Taft was not atypical. By 1995, he had risen through the political ranks in Ohio to become its secretary of state and an individual with an eye on the governorship. However, his days as a whiz kid in Ogilvie's budget bureau were not forgotten.

For Taft, Ogilvie was "kind of a mentor," the Ohioan said, "particularly in his tough no-nonsense approach to government, in the way he was a doer, in the way he supported the bright young people that seemed magnetically drawn to his administration. After all," Taft added, "we were in the main just young guys being given a chance to be part of something very important at the time."[10]

For many of the whiz kids, landing with Ogilvie was an incredible change of pace. Take Bill Hanley for instance. Hanley, a person who could lighten up the oh-so-serious nature of the Ogilvie crew, knew the feeling of being rescued when he secured the research directorship for Ogilvie's first campaign for governor. As a young attorney in a Chicago law firm, Hanley was tied down, as he explained it, to "product liability defense for Sears, which meant I pretty much defended Sears on matters like suits related to wringer washing machines. I was getting disenchanted, wondering if this was the way it was going to be. So, for me, getting to join Ogilvie and staying on board for his governorship was like a new lease on life."[11]

For James R. Helm, being with Ogilvie had to be a culture shock. Helm was a naive kid from rural Clinton, the DeWitt County seat, when he suddenly found himself looking upon Ogilvie as his "surrogate father." Anybody in Helm's shoes would have felt the same way. After gaining experience as an advance person for Ogilvie, Helm spent much of the last two years of the Ogilvie governorship as a staffer often on the road with the governor. This was an enormously educational assignment that allowed Helm to observe Ogilvie "dealing with anything and anyone" coming to his attention while out of the Statehouse. But the really indelible part of it for Helm was what he described as "the open give-and-take I got to have with Ogilvie." Calling himself "a pretty young guy at the time needing a lot of advice," Helm remembered the governor "just counseling me on a lot of subjects." Above all, offered Helm, "the thing about Ogilvie that I'll never forget was how, regardless of the situation, he was a remarkable gentleman first and a politician second. He was a rarity for an individual in high office in that his ego did not take priority. We should have done a lot better job of marketing him in that 1972 race. It was a shame that we were not more creative, a shame for him and for the state."[12]

Richard Ogilvie would live for a little more than fifteen years after leaving Illinois's highest office. He would not again seek elective public office even though his name would crop up now and then as a possible candidate for mayor of Chicago or some other high office, speculation fueled at times by Ogilvie's own show of interest. Since Ogilvie was only forty-nine years old when he lost the governorship, many analysts thought it safe to assume that Ogilvie would take a shot at a political comeback sooner or later.

However, the abrupt end to his governorship left Ogilvie with other matters with which to concern himself. Financial security for himself and his family had to top the list because, unlike Paul Powell and numerous other major figures of his era, Ogilvie had not enriched himself while in public office. Right after Ogilvie's defeat in 1972, Don Perkins broached the subject of finances with Ogilvie.

"Because Dick was an incredibly honest public official, I was sure his financial situation wasn't real great and that it had to be on his mind. I asked him to sit down and talk, wanting to get into what was involved for him in reentering civilian life. He told me that his net worth was less than $100,000 [which had been revealed by his public disclosure of his personal finances in 1971]. I told him that since he no longer was going to be governor that I would like him to go on the Jewel board as a director."[13]

Ogilvie would serve on the board of Jewel Companies as well as on the boards of numerous other businesses. Chicago civic groups and benevolent undertakings, like the Gateway Foundation, also would receive much of his time. He and Dorothy would not return to their home in Northfield but would live most of their remaining years together in an apartment building on a stretch of North Lake Shore Drive, one of the city's finest neighborhoods.

There was no better example than Gateway to show the tireless support Ogilvie would give to an endeavor he considered worthy. Ogilvie was a major player in the progression of Gateway. Founded in the year before Ogilvie became governor, the Chicago-based organization would be providing within decades innovative and comprehensive programs in Illinois and other states for the prevention and treatment of alcohol and drug addiction. Besides recruiting many of his influential friends to assist the foundation, Ogilvie raised big dollars for it from the private sector, an important source of funding for the nongovernmental operation.

As a result of Ogilvie's involvement, the foundation established, after Ogilvie's death, the Richard B. Ogilvie Society to anchor Gateway's endowment program and to recognize Ogilvie's legacy in helping substance abuse victims. Many of Ogilvie's friends along with others "found contributing to Gateway through the society just one more way of honoring Governor Ogilvie," explained Michael J. Darcy, the president of the foundation.[14] By the mid-1990s, the society's honorary committee members included numerous widely known individuals, persons such as Eppie Lederer (columnist Ann Landers), news commentator Bill Ḳurtis, and jazz pianist Ramsey Lewis.

When he left the governorship, Ogilvie returned to the Chicago legal world, joining the venerable law firm of Isham, Lincoln & Beale—a founder of which was Robert Todd Lincoln, the oldest son of President Lincoln. This time Ogilvie's practice of law would be more financially rewarding.

The former governor would earn millions of dollars alone as trustee for the bankrupt Chicago, Milwaukee, St. Paul and Pacific Railroad Company. In this role, Ogilvie won wide praise for guiding a reorganization of the railroad that saved more than a thousand rail workers' jobs while turning the former transcontinental line into an attractive regional operation prior to a merger. Later on, not long before his death, he was chosen to become trustee for the bankrupt Chicago Missouri & Western Railway Company.

In one other development shortly before he died, Ogilvie had affiliated with another law firm, Wildman, Harrold, Allen & Dixon. This followed the dissolution of Isham, Lincoln & Beale amid heavily publicized conflict several years after it merged with the firm of Reuben & Proctor. Ogilvie had a lead role in arranging the marriage of the two firms, as had Don Reuben, a personification of Chicago legal clout in his time.

Besides facing adjustment to a new law firm, Ogilvie was looking at another significant challenge in the days before his death. He had been slated to become chairman of the board of the troubled Chicago Housing Authority as part of a reform effort being pushed by the mayor at the time, Eugene Sawyer. It would have been a role similar to one Ogilvie had handled quite well a few years before when Governor Thompson and then Chicago Mayor Harold Washington placed Ogilvie in charge of overseeing the finish of a McCormick Place annex project hampered by construction problems and cost overruns.

Ogilvie, it seemed, never could say no. In a written tribute to Ogilvie after his death, George Ranney Jr. reminded Chicagoans that Ogilvie energetically campaigned after losing the governor's office for approval of the referendum on the Regional Transportation Authority "when his successor as governor refused to surface because the referendum authorized a tax." Without Ogilvie, contended Ranney, "the RTA referendum, and public transportation in Chicago, would have failed."[15]

Ducking a challenge, any challenge, went against the grain of Ogilvie's ultimate nature. Here went an individual whose life was governed by an unflinching tenacity to take on any job that needed to be done if the world as Ogilvie saw it was to be a better place. The gritty determination so evident in the young tank commander in France in 1944 was like a fire inside Ogilvie that did not burn out until the end of his life's journey.

The journey concluded May 10, 1988, the date of his death. The day before, Dorothy Ogilvie had just arrived in Bradenton, Florida, for a visit with her mother-in-law when Dorothy was notified that her husband had been rushed to Northwestern Memorial Hospital in Chicago, where he was in very serious condition. Without unpacking her bags, Dorothy immediately flew back to Chicago.

She arrived to find that the sixty-five-year-old former governor, who had put on much more weight since his days in office, had suffered a massive heart attack at his downtown law office. After being quickly taken to Northwestern Memorial, Ogilvie underwent emergency quadruple coronary bypass surgery lasting five hours. He died the following day, having never regained consciousness after the operation. His body was cremated, and his ashes were placed in a mausoleum at Rosehill Cemetery in Chicago.

A memorial service for Ogilvie was held at the old English Gothic-styled Fourth Presbyterian Church along North Michigan Avenue. From the lectern, the Reverend John Buchanan saw a sea of well-known faces that brought to mind every chapter of Ogilvie's public career. Up front, of course, were Dorothy and the other family members, including Elizabeth and her husband, Timothy Scott Simer, the minister's son she had met at DePauw University.

Nobody budged when Reverend Buchanan allowed that "when it comes to politics, good decisions are not always easy decisions; the right choices are not always popular choices." Yet, he said, "this experiment in self-determination and representative government depends absolutely on leaders with strength and character, the courage to make right but unpopular decisions."[16] In Ogilvie, there was such a courageous person, Reverend Buchanan said.

He then saw fit to add, "Our city, our state, our nation need that courage today."

NOTES

SELECT BIBLIOGRAPHY

INDEX

Notes

1. Turning Points: 1944 and 1969

1. Much of the information in the chapter on the 781st Tank Battalion is from "Up from Marseille," a history of the unit obtained from the U.S. Army Military History Institute at Carlisle, Pennsylvania. Background also was provided by the U.S. Army Armor School Library at Fort Knox, Kentucky.

2. A copy of Ogilvie's official army discharge record and reports on the 781st Tank Battalion at the Army Armor School Library list December 14, 1944, as the date that Sergeant Ogilvie was wounded in action. However, Ogilvie himself gave the date of his wounding as December 13, 1944, in an interview with the author prior to his inauguration as governor and also in several later conversations. In addition, Dorothy Ogilvie said during interviews for the book that her husband was wounded on December 13, not the following day. The source for most of the information on the wounding of Ogilvie and its aftermath is a transcript of a conversation that Elizabeth Ogilvie Simer taped in 1987 with her father, Richard Ogilvie; her mother, Dorothy Ogilvie; and her grandmother, Edna Ogilvie, mother of the former governor.

3. "The Take-over Generation," *Life*, Sept. 14, 1962, pp. 2–7.

4. "A Searching Look at Big Crime," *Life*, Feb. 23, 1959, pp. 19–27.

5. Mike Royko, "Ogilvie Too Good for Us," *Chicago Daily News*, Nov. 9, 1972, p. 3.

6. "A Good Man Leaves Office," editorial, *Chicago Tribune*, Jan. 9, 1973, sec. 1, p. 10.

7. Most of the information on Ogilvie's roots is based on six interviews with Dorothy Ogilvie covering more than twenty hours, as well as information taken from yearbooks and other personal memorabilia of Richard Ogilvie and his family, an Ogilvie family tree compiled by Elizabeth Simer, and the previously cited transcript of a conversation taped in 1987. (See chap. 1, n. 2.)

8. Glenn D. Bradley, "Builders of the Santa Fe—Captain R. M. Spivey—a Grand Old Man," *Santa Fe Magazine*, June 1914, pp. 23–27.

9. Quotes here and in the following paragraph are taken from Tim Thoelecke, telephone conversation with author, July 18, 1994.

2. Inauguration and Transition:
The Early Days of Ogilvie's Governorship

1. Dorothy Ogilvie, interview by author, Chicago, Ill., May 7, 1994. Hereafter, each interview cited in these notes was conducted by the author on the date indicated.

2. Governor Richard B. Ogilvie, Inaugural Address, Springfield, Ill., Jan. 13, 1969, Institute of Government and Public Affairs, University of Illinois.

3. Ogilvie, Inaugural Address.

4. Ogilvie, Inaugural Address, here and in following paragraph.

5. Taylor Pensoneau, "Illinois Legislature Votes for Pay Hike," *St. Louis Post-Dispatch*, Jan. 8, 1969, p. 6A.

6. Governor Ogilvie, Executive Order No. 1, Jan. 29, 1969, Institute of Government and Public Affairs, University of Illinois.

7. Governor Ogilvie, message to the General Assembly of Illinois, on law enforcement, Springfield, Ill., Feb. 19, 1969, Institute of Government and Public Affairs, University of Illinois. Quotes here and in the following paragraph are taken from the February 19, 1969, message.

8. Governor Ogilvie, Executive Order No. 2, Jan. 31, 1969, Institute of Government and Public Affairs, University of Illinois.

9. Governor Ogilvie, letter to A. Donald Bourgeois, n.d., from author's personal file.

10. Governor Ogilvie, message to the General Assembly of Illinois, on local government, Springfield, Ill., Mar. 26, 1969, Institute of Government and Public Affairs, University of Illinois.

11. Jeremiah Marsh, interview by author, Chicago, Ill., June 10, 1994.

12. Taylor Pensoneau, "Government Reform: BGA's Controversial Crusade," *Illinois Issues*, Mar. 1976, pp. 7–9.

13. Transition Plan of incoming Ogilvie administration, Nov. 5, 1968, Institute of Government and Public Affairs, University of Illinois.

14. Taylor Pensoneau, "Officials Asking Whom Ogilvie Will Retain," *St. Louis Post-Dispatch*, Nov. 10, 1968, p. 31A.

15. See Ogilvie Administration, Allerton Park Conference file, Feb. 1969, Institute of Government and Public Affairs, University of Illinois, for texts of presentations by Governor Ogilvie, Brian B. Whalen, George E. Mahin, and other key members of the administration. Quotes from Whalen here and in following paragraph are taken from the Allerton Park Conference file.

16. George E. Mahin, Allerton Park Conference, Feb. 1969, cited here and in following paragraphs.

17. Samuel K. Gove, interview by author, Urbana, Ill., May 21, 1994.

18. Governor Ogilvie, Allerton Park Conference, Feb. 1969.

3. A Political Career on the Line

1. John W. McCarter Jr., interview by author, Chicago, Ill., July 8, 1994.

2. Jeremiah Marsh, interview by author, Chicago, Ill., June 10, 1994.

3. Quotes here and in following paragraph are taken from Governor Ogilvie, message to the General Assembly of Illinois, on fiscal matters, Springfield, Ill., Feb. 5, 1969. Available at the Institute of Government and Public Affairs, University of Illinois.

4. George A. Ranney Jr., interview by author, Chicago, Ill., May 6, 1994.

5. From notes of interview by author with a Republican state senator, Springfield, Ill., Apr. 1, 1969.

6. Governor Ogilvie, budget message to the General Assembly of Illinois, Apr. 1, 1969, Springfield, Ill., Institute of Government and Public Affairs, University of Illinois. Quotes here and following are from the budget message.

7. Governor Ogilvie, interview by author, Springfield, Ill., Feb. 5, 1969.

8. Maurice W. Scott, comments to author, Springfield, Ill., Apr. 1, 1969.

9. W. Russell Arrington, interview by author, Springfield, Ill., July 1, 1969. Quotes here and in following paragraph are taken from the Arrington interview.

4. From Sheriff to Cook County Board President

1. Brian B. Whalen, interview by author, Chicago, Ill., Mar. 26, 1994.

2. Quotes here and in following paragraph are taken from the Whalen interview.

3. Whalen, interview.

4. Whalen, interview.

5. Dorothy Ogilvie, interview by author, Chicago, Ill., Feb. 26, 1994.

6. Thomas J. Drennan, interview by author, Chicago, Ill., Sept. 2, 1994.

7. Drennan, interview.

8. Donald S. Perkins, interview by author, Winnetka, Ill., Sept. 2, 1994. Quotes here and in following paragraphs are taken from the Perkins interview.

9. Perkins, interview.

10. Louis J. Kasper, interview by author, Chicago, Ill., June 10, 1994.

11. George Tagge, "G.O.P. Sees County Sweep," Chicago Daily Tribune, Nov. 4, 1962, part 1, p. 1.

12. Thomas Fitzpatrick, "Workers Hail a Weary but Happy Ogilvie," Chicago Daily Tribune, Nov. 7, 1962, part 1, p. 9, cited here and in following paragraph.

13. Willard Hansen, "Top Aide Describes How Ogilvie Cleaned Up Sheriff's Department," (Champaign-Urbana) News-Gazette, Aug. 14, 1968, sec. 2, p. 14. Quotes here and in following paragraph are from the News-Gazette.

14. Whalen, interview.

15. From notes taken by author during interviews with Ogilvie during 1968 election campaign.

16. William F. Roemer Jr., telephone conversation with author, Oct. 25, 1994.

17. Kasper, interview.

18. Kasper, interview.

19. Ronald D. Michaelson, interview by author, Springfield, Ill., Feb. 24, 1994.

20. Perkins, interview.

21. Drennan, interview.

22. "The County Races," editorial, *Chicago Tribune*, Nov. 6, 1966, sec. 1, p. 16.

23. Jeb Stuart Magruder, *Jeb Stuart Magruder, an American Life: One Man's Road to Watergate* (New York: Atheneum, 1974), pp. 40–41, 45–47.

24. Drennan, interview.

25. John Oswald, "G.O.P. Faithful Enjoy a New Experience—Victory Party," *Chicago Tribune*, Nov. 9, 1966, sec. 1, p. 3.

26. "Chief of County Board Looks to Future," *Chicago Tribune*, Nov. 10, 1966, sec. 1, p. 1.

27. Whalen, interview.

28. Michaelson, interview.

29. Quotes here and in the following paragraph are taken from the Whalen interview.

30. Whalen, interview.

5. The Accardo Case: Taking on the Big Tuna

1. Donald S. Perkins, interview by author, Winnetka, Ill., Sept. 2, 1994.

2. Dorothy Ogilvie, interview by author, Chicago, Ill., May 7, 1994.

3. Ronald Koziol and John O'Brien, "Reputed Mob Boss Accardo Dies at 86," *Chicago Tribune*, May 22, 1992.

4. Perkins, interview.

5. William F. Roemer Jr., telephone conversation with author, Oct. 25, 1994.

6. Quotes from Ogilvie here and in following paragraph are taken from "Prosecutor, Judges Assail Court Ruling," *Chicago Daily Tribune*, Jan. 6, 1962, part 1, p. 2.

6. The 1968 Campaign and Vote

1. James (Pate) Philip, conversation with author, Springfield, Ill., May 13, 1994.

2. Taylor Pensoneau, "Illinois Strikes, Riot Affect Governor Race," *St. Louis Post-Dispatch*, Apr. 27, 1968, p. 27A.

3. Michael J. Lawrence, interview by author, Springfield, Ill., Feb. 13, 1994.

4. Thomas J. Drennan, interview by author, Chicago, Ill., Sept. 2, 1994.

5. Quotes from Joseph L. Harris here and in following paragraph are taken from an interview by the author, Springfield, Ill., Oct. 14, 1994.

6. Results of the 1968 primary election were provided by the Illinois Board of Elections at Springfield.

7. Quotes from Joseph D. Mathewson here and in following paragraph are taken from an interview by the author, Chicago, Ill., Sept. 29, 1994.

8. William S. Hanley, interview by author, Springfield, Ill., June 7, 1994.

9. Taylor Pensoneau, "Law, Order Issue Reflected in Illinois," St. Louis Post-Dispatch, Oct. 16, 1968.

10. Jeremiah Marsh, interview by author, Chicago, Ill., Sept. 3, 1994.

11. Quotes from Donald S. Perkins here and following are taken from an interview by the author, Winnetka, Ill., Sept. 2, 1994.

12. James H. Mack, telephone conversation with author, Oct. 24, 1994.

13. Victor L. Smith, interview by author, Robinson, Ill., Oct. 13, 1968.

14. "Shapiro and Simon in Illinois," editorial, St. Louis Post-Dispatch, Oct. 23, 1968, p. 2E.

15. "For Governor: Ogilvie," editorial, Chicago's American, Oct. 29, 1968, p. 8.

16. Mack, interview.

17. Mack, interview.

18. A major part of this section is based on the conversation at a breakfast at the Governor's Mansion during the week of November 24, 1968, to which Governor Shapiro invited the author and a small number of other reporters from the pressroom in the Illinois Statehouse.

19. The results of the 1968 general election cited here and elsewhere in this section were provided by the Illinois Board of Elections at Springfield.

20. Taylor Pensoneau, "Defeat of Shapiro Laid to E. Side Vote," St. Louis Post-Dispatch, Nov. 24, 1968, p. 13A.

7. Bourbons in the Senate, Scandal in the High Court

1. Paul Simon, interview by author, Effingham, Ill., July 23, 1994.

2. Richard W. Carlson, interview by author, Springfield, Ill., June 17, 1994.

3. Carlson, interview.

4. The relating of this incident is based in part on a conversation by the author with W. Russell Arrington and also in part on later corroboration of the incident by an individual who witnessed it but asked to remain anonymous.

5. John J. Lanigan, interview by author, Springfield, Ill., June 15, 1967.

6. W. Russell Arrington, conversation with author, Springfield, Ill., June 16, 1967.

7. Donald Tolva, telephone conversation with author, May 19, 1994, cited here and in the following paragraph.

8. William C. Harris, interview by author, Chicago, Ill., Sept. 29, 1994.

9. Edward T. Pound, telephone conversation with author, Feb. 17, 1994.

8. Proposed, Debated, Passed: The State Income Tax

1. Taylor Pensoneau, "Illinois 3 Per Cent Income Tax in Doubt after Rebellion Against Daley," *St. Louis Post-Dispatch*, June 15, 1969, p. 6F.

2. Mike Lawrence, "Ogilvie Revisited," *Illinois Issues*, Dec. 1982, p. 26.

3. This description is taken verbatim from the segment on Clyde L. Choate in a document, "The Medal of Honor of the United States Army," on file at the Illinois State Library at Springfield, pp. 301–2.

4. Taylor Pensoneau and Bob Ellis, *Dan Walker: The Glory and the Tragedy* (Evansville, Ind.: Smith-Collins, 1993), p. 319.

5. "Text of Ogilvie's Statement Appealing for Income Tax Bill," *St. Louis Post-Dispatch*, June 17, 1969.

6. John G. Gilbert, *Memoir* (Springfield: Sangamon State Univ., Oral History Office, 1985), p. 126.

7. Quotes here and in following paragraph are taken from John W. McCarter Jr., *Memoir* (Springfield: Sangamon State Univ., Oral History Office, 1984), p. 57.

8. Quotes from John J. Lanigan here and following are taken from an interview by the author, Chicago, Ill., Feb. 27, 1994.

9. Lanigan, interview.

10. Donald Tolva, telephone conversation with author, May 19, 1994.

11. Lanigan, interview.

12. Lanigan, interview.

13. *Journal of the Senate (Illinois)*, June 27, 1969, p. 3190.

14. Taylor Pensoneau, "Income Tax Bill Passed and Signed by Ogilvie," *St. Louis Post-Dispatch*, July 1, 1969, p. 7A.

15. Comments of Governor Ogilvie to the author and other reporters during the signing of the Illinois state income tax bill, Springfield, Ill., July 1, 1969.

16. Ogilvie's comments, signing of Illinois state income tax bill.

17. Pensoneau and Ellis, *Dan Walker*, p. 174.

18. McCarter, *Memoir*, p. 59.

19. Quotes from Jeremiah Marsh here and in following paragraph are taken from an interview by the author, Chicago, Ill., Sept. 3, 1994.

20. Clifford B. Latherow, obituary, *Chicago Tribune*, Oct. 28, 1994, sec. 2, p. 11.

9. More Ogilvie Coups

1. William C. Harris, interview by author, Chicago, Ill., Sept. 29, 1994.

2. Norton Kay, "Ogilvie Gains National Attention," *Chicago Today*, July 3, 1969, p. 5.

3. James T. Hickey, interview by author, Springfield, Ill., Mar. 15, 1994.

4. Taylor Pensoneau, "Ogilvie Pushed Through Most of His Big Program," *St. Louis Post-Dispatch*, July 6, 1969, p. 3B.

5. Governor Ogilvie, speech delivered to the Mental Health Association of Greater Chicago, May 9, 1969.

6. Brian B. Whalen, interview by author, Chicago, Ill., Mar. 26, 1994.

7. Taylor Pensoneau, "Ogilvie Says Fraud Cost State Fair $500,000," *St. Louis Post-Dispatch*, Aug. 19, 1969, p. 7A.

8. Taylor Pensoneau, "Court Inquiry Shakes Public's Confidence," *St. Louis Post-Dispatch*, July 19, 1969.

9. Pensoneau, "Court Inquiry."

10. "Ogilvie Removes Perbohner from Post on Illinois Commerce Commission," *St. Louis Post-Dispatch*, Aug. 15, 1969, p. 3A.

11. Address by Ogilvie at opening of the Sixth Illinois Constitutional Convention, Dec. 8, 1969.

10. *The Constitutional Convention: A Triumph amid Setbacks*

1. David Kenney, *Basic Illinois Government: A Systematic Explanation* (Carbondale: Southern Illinois Univ. Press, 1974), p. 391.

2. Taylor Pensoneau, "New Constitution Is Goal in Illinois," *St. Louis Post-Dispatch*, Dec. 7, 1969, p. 3B.

3. James O. Mees, interview by author, Springfield, Ill., Nov. 19, 1993.

4. John Alexander, interview by author, Springfield, Ill., Mar. 17, 1995.

5. Taylor Pensoneau, "Storm over Constitution Brewing," *St. Louis Post-Dispatch*, Jan. 25, 1970, p. 3C.

6. Alexander, interview.

7. Jeremiah Marsh, interview by author, Chicago, Ill., Nov. 18, 1994.

8. Quotes here and following are taken from the Marsh interview.

9. Governor Ogilvie, address at opening of Sixth Illinois Constitutional Convention, Springfield, Ill., Dec. 8, 1969.

10. Marsh, interview.

11. Paula Wolff, telephone conversation with author, Mar. 27, 1995.

12. Marsh, interview.

13. Taylor Pensoneau, "Constitution Drafter Warns of Extremists," *St Louis Post-Dispatch*, Sept. 3, 1970, p. 4A.

14. "You'll Be Sorry," editorial, *Belleville News-Democrat*, Nov. 30, 1970.

15. Alexander, interview.

16. Samuel K. Gove, interview by author, Urbana, Ill., May 21, 1994.

17. Gove, interview.

18. James Snopko, interview by author, Springfield, Ill., Apr. 16, 1995.

19. Rimmel is quoted from "Traces Old Army Buddy: He's Governor of Illinois," *St. Louis Post-Dispatch*, June 10, 1970, p. 24A.

20. Ralph T. Smith, interview by author, Springfield, Ill., May 14, 1969.

21. Taylor Pensoneau, "Aid-Cut Move Dropped in Illinois Assembly," *St. Louis Post-Dispatch*, May 15, 1969, p. 6D.

22. Pensoneau, "Aid-Cut Move Dropped."

23. Taylor Pensoneau, "Ogilvie Proposes Welfare Revision Based on Work," *St. Louis Post-Dispatch*, May 20, 1971, p. 3C.

24. James H. Mack, telephone conversation with author, Oct. 24, 1994.

25. Quotes from Jerry Marsh here and following are taken from the Marsh interview.

26. Taylor Pensoneau, "Rejects Dirksen Seat," *St. Louis Post-Dispatch*, Sept. 16, 1969.

27. Marsh, interview.

28. Mack, interview.

29. Governor Ogilvie, statement in response to death of Ralph T. Smith, Aug. 14, 1972.

30. Taylor Pensoneau, "Democrats Satirize GOP Financial Angel," *St. Louis Post-Dispatch*, Oct. 4, 1970, p. 20A.

31. William H. Rentschler, interview by author, Mar. 10, 1970.

11. War on Polluters

1. The exchange between Blaser and Ogilvie is taken from "Memories of Richard B. Ogilvie," edited by Frederick H. Bird Jr. for a reunion of members of the Ogilvie administration after Ogilvie's death in 1988.

2. Frederick H. Bird Jr., interview by author, Springfield, Ill., May 2, 1994.

3. Quotes from Clarence W. Klassen here and following are taken from an interview by the author, Springfield, Ill., Apr. 8, 1994.

4. William J. Scott, interview by author, Springfield, Ill., Nov. 4, 1970.

5. Taylor Pensoneau, "Ogilvie Discusses Pollution," *St. Louis Post-Dispatch*, Oct. 3, 1968, p. 8D.

6. Governor Ogilvie, special message to the Illinois General Assembly on the environment, Springfield, Ill., Apr. 23, 1970.

7. Governor Ogilvie, statement at the signing of House Bill 3788, June 29, 1970, at St. Charles, Ill.

8. Quotes from Governor Ogilvie here and in the following paragraph are from Ogilvie's statement at the signing of HB 3788.

9. Klassen, interview.

10. Quotes here and following are from the Klassen interview.

11. Quotes here and following are from the Klassen interview.

12. Marion Lynes, "Illinois Program in Doubt," *St. Louis Globe-Democrat*, Feb. 6, 1971.

13. Kenneth Watson, " 'Klassen Affair' Rocks the Boat," *Illinois State Journal,* Mar. 18, 1971, p. 3.

14. Klassen, interview.

15. Taylor Pensoneau, "Ogilvie Aid Explains Ouster of Klassen," *St. Louis Post-Dispatch,* Feb. 4, 1971, p. 8A.

16. William L. Blaser, interview by author, Springfield, Ill., Apr. 4, 1971.

17. Ronald T. O'Connor, telephone conversation with author, Apr. 6, 1995.

18. James R. Johnson, interview by author, Springfield, Ill., Aug. 18, 1994.

19. Mary Lee Leahy, interview by author, Springfield, Ill., July 6, 1995.

12. Campus Riots and the Guard

1. Taylor Pensoneau, "National Guard Goes on Alert at Illinois U.," *St. Louis Post-Dispatch,* Mar. 3, 1970.

2. Patrick D. Kennedy, "Reactions Against the Vietnam War and Military-Related Targets on Campus: The University of Illinois as a Case Study, 1965–1972," *Illinois Historical Journal,* vol. 84, no. 2 (1991): p. 111.

3. Kennedy, "Reactions Against the Vietnam War."

4. Quotes here and following are based on notes from the author's coverage of student protest activities during the week beginning March 1, 1970, at the University of Illinois at Champaign-Urbana.

5. Quote from the Radical Union is taken from the author's notes, Mar. 4, 1970.

6. Parenti is quoted from the author's notes, Mar. 4, 1970.

7. Tracy James, "Crisis in Carbondale," *Southern Illinoisan,* May 14, 1995, p. 1D.

8. Taylor Pensoneau, "Tear Gas Used on Crowd at Carbondale," *St. Louis Post-Dispatch,* May 10, 1970, p. 24A.

9. Lawrence E. Taylor, "Closing Brings Quiet to Carbondale Campus," *St. Louis Post-Dispatch,* May 17, 1970, p. 9A.

10. Taylor Pensoneau, "Hearing on College Unrest," *St. Louis Post-Dispatch,* Sept. 17, 1970, p. 4B.

11. Taylor Pensoneau, "Stevenson Links Campus Turmoil to Radicals, Not Red Conspiracy," *St. Louis Post-Dispatch,* Sept. 17, 1970.

12. Richard T. Dunn, telephone conversation with author, Apr. 21, 1994.

13. Harold R. Patton, interview by author, Springfield, Ill., Mar. 19, 1994.

14. Patton, interview.

15. Quotes here and in the following paragraph are taken from the Patton interview.

16. Dunn, interview.

17. John E. Cribbet letter to the College of Liberal Arts and Sciences, University of Illinois, Apr. 12, 1993.

18. Richard E. Dunn, interview by author, Springfield, Ill., Apr. 15, 1994.

13. Winning Control of the Budget

1. Donald S. Perkins, interview by author, Winnetka, Ill., Sept. 2, 1994.

2. Quotes from Edmund L. Heyer here and in the following paragraph are taken from an interview by the author, Jacksonville, Ill., Apr. 10, 1995.

3. Taylor Pensoneau, "Ogilvie Assails SIU Building," *St. Louis Post-Dispatch*, Nov. 5, 1969, p. 3A.

4. Quotes from John E. Corbally Jr., statement released Jan. 4, 1972, in Chicago in response to Report No. 103 of the executive director of the Illinois Board of Higher Education.

5. Corbally, statement.

6. William D. Forsyth Jr., interview by author, Springfield, Ill., Jan. 11, 1972.

7. Quotes from John W. McCarter Jr. here and in the following paragraph are taken from an interview by the author, Chicago, Ill., July 8, 1994.

8. McCarter, interview.

9. James B. Holderman, interview by author, Springfield, Ill., Nov. 16, 1972.

10. McCarter, interview.

11. John W. McCarter Jr., *Memoir* (Springfield: Sangamon State Univ., Oral History Office, 1984), p. 24.

12. McCarter, interview.

13. Quotes here and in the following paragraph are taken from the Ogilvie budget message to the General Assembly of Illinois, Springfield, Ill., Mar. 3, 1971.

14. McCarter, interview.

15. Taylor Pensoneau, "Illinois Welfare Deficit Gives Political Leverage to Ogilvie," *St. Louis Post-Dispatch*, Nov. 11, 1971, p. 4E.

16. McCarter, interview.

14. Ogilvie in Person and in the Press

1. Edmund L. Heyer, interview by author, Jacksonville, Ill. Apr. 10, 1995.

2. Taylor Pensoneau and Bob Ellis, *Dan Walker: The Glory and the Tragedy* (Evansville, Ind.: Smith-Collins, 1993) p. 171.

3. Paul Simon, interview by author, Effingham, Ill., July 23, 1994.

4. From "Memories of Richard B. Ogilvie," edited by Frederick H. Bird Jr., p. 2. (See chap. 11, note 1.)

5. "Memories of Richard B. Ogilvie," p. 5.

6. "Memories," p. 1.

7. "Memories," p. 8.

8. "Memories," p. 7.

9. Quotes from Frederick H. Bird Jr. here and in the following paragraph are taken from an interview by the author, Springfield, Ill., May 2, 1994.

10. Quotes here and following are taken from the Heyer interview.

11. Heyer, interview.

12. Heyer, interview.

13. Samuel O. Hancock, interview by author, Herrin, Ill., Mar. 30, 1994.

14. Quotes from C. Dayton McReaken here and following are taken from an interview by the author, West Frankfort, Ill., Mar. 6, 1995.

15. Quotes from Ogilvie and O'Connell are taken from the author's notes of a Governor Ogilvie press conference, Springfield, Ill., n.d.

16. Alvin Pistorious (Bill Miller), interview by author, Springfield, Ill., June 16, 1995.

17. Pistorious (Miller), interview.

18. Frederick H. Bird Jr., interview by author, Springfield, Ill., July 12, 1995.

19. Pistorious (Miller), interview.

20. Henry Hanson, interview by author, Chicago, Ill., July 8, 1994.

21. Quotes here and following are taken from the Bird interview, July 12, 1995.

22. Bird, interview, July 12, 1995.

23. John W. Kolbe, telephone conversation with author, Sept. 8, 1995.

24. Quotes here and following are from the Bird interview, July 12, 1995.

25. Thomas J. Drennan, interview by author, Chicago, Ill., Sept. 2, 1994.

26. Jeremiah Marsh, interview by author, Chicago, Ill., Nov. 18, 1994.

27. Marilyn Willey Cohen, interview by author, Springfield, Ill., May 24, 1995.

28. Quotes here and following are from the Bird interview, July 12, 1995.

29. Charles Nicodemus, "Ogilvie's Reward to Close Adviser," *Chicago Daily News*, Feb. 2, 1970.

30. Joel Weisman, "Drennan Denies 'Kingmaker' Role," *Chicago Today*, Feb. 3, 1971, p. 5.

31. Drennan, interview.

32. Quotes here and following are from the Bird interview, July 12, 1995.

33. Hanson, interview, cited here and following.

15. Prisons, Highways, and Other Ventures

1. Brock Brower, "Where Have All the Leaders Gone?" *Life*, Oct. 8, 1971, p. 74.

2. Brower, "Where Have All the Leaders Gone?" p. 74.

3. William Manchester, *The Glory and the Dream* (New York: Bantam, 1975), p. 1225.

4. Walter Jacobson, "Ogilvie: Rock at the Top," *Chicago Tribune Magazine*, Nov. 28, 1971, p. 56.

5. Jacobson, "Ogilvie: Rock at the Top," p. 47.

6. Governor Ogilvie, statement distributed in Springfield, Ill., July 18, 1969, the day he signed legislation creating the Illinois Department of Corrections.

7. Taylor Pensoneau, "Illinois Loosens Its Grip on Inmates," *St. Louis Post-Dispatch*, Mar. 11, 1972.

8. Taylor Pensoneau, "Illinois Rethinks Prison Policies," *St. Louis Post-Dispatch*, Oct. 17, 1971, p. 1C.

9. Pensoneau, "Illinois Rethinks Prison Policies."

10. Pensoneau, "Illinois Rethinks Prison Policies."

11. Governor Ogilvie, text of speech given at the state prison at Vienna, Ill., Oct. 8, 1971.

12. Joseph McFadden, interview by author, Springfield, Ill., June 3, 1995.

13. Pensoneau, "Illinois Rethinks Prison Policies."

14. Mitchell Ware, interview by author, Springfield, Ill., Feb. 15, 1971.

15. Taylor Pensoneau, "Publicity for Head of IBI Incited Officers' Jealousy," *St. Louis Post-Dispatch*, Aug. 8, 1971, p. 3A.

16. Conversation by author with an assistant to Herbert Brown, director of the Illinois Department of Law Enforcement, Springfield, Ill., Aug. 15, 1971.

17. Quotes from Ivan R. Levin here and in the following paragraph are taken from an interview by the author, Springfield, Ill., Mar. 8, 1994.

18. Levin, interview.

19. Robert P. Howard, *Mostly Good and Competent Men* (Springfield: *Illinois Issues*, Sangamon State Univ., and Illinois State Historical Society, 1988), p. 237.

20. Governor Ogilvie, special message to the General Assembly of Illinois, on transportation, Springfield, Ill., Feb. 17, 1971.

21. W. Robert Blair, interview by author, Chicago, Ill., Mar. 25, 1994.

22. Blair, interview.

23. Richard Adorjan, interview by author, Springfield, Ill., Oct. 5, 1994.

24. Robert S. Cohen, interview by author, Springfield, Ill., May 24, 1995.

25. Adorjan, interview.

26. Blair, interview.

16. Dorothy Ogilvie

1. Dorothy Ogilvie, interview by author, Chicago, Ill., May 12, 1995.

2. Jay P. Bryant, interview by author, Springfield, Ill., Sept. 13, 1995.

3. Dorothy Ogilvie, interview.

4. Bryant, interview.

5. Dorothy Ogilvie, interview.

6. "Damage Found in Governor's Home in Illinois," *St. Louis Post-Dispatch*, Feb. 27, 1966, p. 2-I.

7. Dorothy Ogilvie, interview.

8. James T. Hickey, interview by author, Springfield, Ill., Mar. 15, 1994.

9. John W. Kolbe, telephone conversation with author, Sept. 8, 1995.

10. Quotes here and in following paragraph are from John W. Kolbe, telephone conversation, Sept. 8, 1995.

17. Powell's Cash and Racetracks: Public Anger Boils

1. Quotes from Pete Romanotto here and in following paragraph are taken from an interview by the author, Springfield, Ill., July 6, 1994.

2. Quotes from Robert C. Winchester here and in following paragraph are taken from an interview by the author, Springfield, Ill., Apr. 20, 1994.

3. Mike McCormick, conversation with author, Springfield, Ill., June 5, 1995.

4. "Powell 'Master Politician . . . Fighter': Ogilvie," *Quincy Herald-Whig*, Oct. 13, 1970, p. 1.

5. Jay P. Bryant, interview by author, Springfield, Ill., Sept. 13, 1995.

6. William S. Hanley, interview by author, Springfield, Ill., June 7, 1994.

7. Nicholas D. Ciaccio, interview by author, Springfield, Ill., Jan. 7, 1971.

8. "Executor Tells of Finding $800,000 in Paul Powell's Apartment," *(Springfield) Illinois State Register*, Dec. 31, 1970, p. 1.

9. Paul Simon, interview by author, Mattoon, Ill., July 23, 1994.

10. Simon, interview.

11. "Powell Case Shaping Illinois Political Future," *St. Louis Post-Dispatch*, Jan. 31, 1971, p. 20A.

12. Taylor Pensoneau, "New Move in Illinois for Disclosure Law," *St. Louis Post-Dispatch*, Jan. 9, 1971.

13. Listed as major assets of Richard and Dorothy Ogilvie as of February 1, 1971, the date of the public disclosure of their holdings, were the couple's home in Northfield, valued at about $35,000, and 864 shares in W. Clement Stone's Combined Insurance Company of America valued at $38,880. According to the disclosure, the stock was purchased in 1968. The disclosure also listed an outstanding mortgage of $20,096 on the Ogilvie home.

14. Bernard Schoenburg, "The Mystery Remains," *State Journal-Register*, Oct. 7, 1990, p. 21.

15. Melvin N. Routman, interview by author, Springfield, Ill., Oct. 12, 1994.

16. Thomas B. Littlewood, "The Political Prowess of Paul Powell," *Chicago Scene*, Feb. 1963, p. 18.

18. Political Death

The 1972 election results cited in the chapter were provided by the Illinois Board of Elections.

1. Paul Simon, interview by author, Mattoon, Ill., July 23, 1994.

2. Simon, interview.

3. Governor Ogilvie, quote heard by author numerous times during Ogilvie campaign for reelection in October and November 1972.

4. James D. Nowlan, interview by author, Springfield, Ill., Dec. 19, 1995.

5. Governor Ogilvie, comment to author during a reelection campaign stop in Pittsfield, Ill., in early September 1972.

6. Quotes here and in following paragraph are taken from the Nowlan interview.

7. Donald S. Perkins, interview by author, Winnetka, Ill., Sept. 2, 1994.

8. James H. Mack, telephone conversation with author, Oct. 24, 1994.

9. Robert C. Maple, interview by author, Springfield, Ill., Sept. 16, 1995. Walker was quoted in the Maple interview.

10. Taylor Pensoneau and Bob Ellis, *Dan Walker: The Glory and the Tragedy,* (Evansville, Ind.: Smith-Collins, 1993), p. 172.

11. "We Must Keep Ogilvie," editorial, *Chicago Tribune,* Oct. 1, 1972, sec. 1A, p. 4.

12. Ronald D. Michaelson, interview by author, Springfield, Ill., Feb. 24, 1994.

13. Nowlan, interview.

14. Gale Williams, interview by author, Springfield, Ill., Oct. 14, 1969.

15. John J. Lanigan, interview by author, Chicago, Ill., Feb. 27, 1994.

16. Jeremiah Marsh, interview by author, Chicago, Ill., Sept. 3, 1994.

17. Thomas J. Drennan, interview by author, Chicago, Ill., Sept. 2, 1994.

18. Walter R. (Bud) Lohman, interview by author, Springfield, Ill., Aug. 3, 1994.

19. Afterward

1. Quotes here and in following paragraph are taken from Governor Ogilvie, special message to the General Assembly of Illinois, on the state of the state, Springfield, Ill., Jan. 7, 1973, Institute of Government and Public Affairs, University of Illinois.

2. Robert D. Reid, "Whither the Democrats?" *Illinois Issues,* Sept. 1994, pp. 12–14.

3. Response of Governor Edgar pursuant to author's request for an Edgar assessment of Governor Ogilvie, Jan. 18, 1996.

4. Phillip M. Gonet, interview by author, Springfield, Ill., Oct. 11, 1995.

5. Paul Simon, interview by author, Effingham, Ill., July 23, 1994.

6. Mike Lawrence, "Ogilvie Revisited," *Illinois Issues,* Dec. 1982, p. 27.

7. Lawrence, "Ogilvie Revisited," p. 27.

8. Lawrence, "Ogilvie Revisited," p. 28.

9. James D. Nowlan, interview by author, Springfield, Ill., Dec. 19, 1995.

10. Bob Taft, telephone conversation with author, Sept. 20, 1995.

11. William S. Hanley, interview by author, Springfield, Ill., June 7, 1994.

12. James R. Helm, interview by author, Springfield, Ill., Feb. 5, 1996.

13. Donald S. Perkins, interview by author, Winnetka, Ill., Sept. 2, 1994.

14. Michael J. Darcy, telephone conversation with author, Feb. 23, 1996.

15. George A. Ranney Jr., "Richard Ogilvie: He Took the Risks and Did Much Good," *Chicago Tribune,* May 18, 1988, sec. 1, p. 23.

16. Thomas Hardy, "Friends Eulogize ex-Gov. Ogilvie," *Chicago Tribune,* May 17, 1988, sec. 3, p. 16.

Select Bibliography

Anton, Thomas J. *The Politics of State Expenditure in Illinois.* Urbana: Univ. of Illinois Press, 1966.

Bird, Fred. *Memoir.* Springfield: Sangamon State Univ., Oral History Office, 1984.

Gertz, Elmer, and Joseph P. Pisciotte. *Charter for a New Age: An Inside View of the Sixth Illinois Constitutional Convention.* Urbana: Univ. of Illinois Press, 1980.

Gilbert, John G. *Memoir.* Springfield: Sangamon State Univ., Oral History Office, 1985.

Howard, Robert P. *Illinois: A History of the Prairie State.* Grand Rapids, Mich.: Eerdmans, 1972.

——. *Mostly Good and Competent Men.* Springfield: *Illinois Issues,* Sangamon State Univ., and Illinois State Historical Society, 1988.

Keegan, John. *The Face of Battle.* New York: Viking, 1976.

Kenney, David. *Basic Illinois Government: A Systematic Explanation.* Carbondale: Southern Illinois Univ. Press, 1974.

——. *A Political Passage: The Career of Stratton of Illinois.* Carbondale: Southern Illinois Univ. Press, 1990.

Kilian, Michael, Connie Fletcher, and F. Richard Ciccone. *Who Runs Chicago?* New York: St. Martin's, 1979.

Klassen, Clarence W. *Memoir.* Springfield: Sangamon State Univ., Oral History Office, 1984.

Littlewood, Thomas B. *Horner of Illinois.* Evanston: Northwestern Univ. Press, 1969.

Magruder, Jeb Stuart. *Jeb Stuart Magruder, an American Life: One Man's Road to Watergate.* New York: Atheneum, 1974.

Major Legislation, 1969–1972. Springfield, Ill.: Governor Richard B. Ogilvie, n.d.

Manchester, William. *The Glory and the Dream: A Narrative History of America, 1932–1972.* New York: Bantam, 1975.

Martin, John Bartlow. *Adlai Stevenson of Illinois.* New York: Doubleday, 1976.

McCarter, John W., Jr. *Memoir.* Springfield: Sangamon State Univ., Oral History Office, 1984.

Michaelson, Ron. *Memoir.* Springfield: Sangamon State Univ., Oral History Office, 1984.

Nowlan, James D., ed. *Inside State Government in Illinois.* Chicago: Neltnor House, 1991.

O'Neill, William L. *Coming Apart: An Informal History of America in the 1960's*. New York: Quadrangle, 1971.

Papers in Public Finance: The Ogilvie Years. Springfield: Illinois Bureau of the Budget, n.d.

Pensoneau, Taylor, and Bob Ellis. *Dan Walker: The Glory and the Tragedy*. Evansville, Ind.: Smith-Collins, 1993.

Wittmond, Carl. *Memoir*. Springfield: Sangamon State Univ., Oral History Office, 1988.

Index

Accardo, Tony, 4, 42, 49, 59–63
Adamowski, Benjamin S., 51–52, 70
Adorjan, Richard, 223–24
Agnew, Spiro T., 143, 194
Agriculture, Department of, 182
Air Pollution Control Board, 146, 148, 149, 150, 152
Alexander, John, 122–23, 133
Allan, Judy, 139, 196
Altgeld, John Peter, 29, 263
Alton Evening Telegraph, 92–94, 113–14
Altorfer, John Henry, 67–68, 69, 70
Anderson, John B., 139–40, 141
Anderson, Lowell, 230–31
Arrington, W. Russell, 12, 36, 82–83, 96, 99, 103, 122; early life, 83–84; expansion of General Assembly and, 85–86; housing initiative and, 88–90; interns and, 86–87; Ogilvie and, 90–91; personality, 84–85, 99–100

Bakalis, Michael J., 143
Bensinger, Peter, 18, 213–14
Better Government Association (BGA), 21–23, 53, 111, 124, 201
Bilek, Arthur J., 46–47
Bird, Frederick Huey, Jr., 108, 146, 154–55, 191, 199, 206–7; image of, 204–5; press releases, 203–4; World War II service, 202–3
Blair, William Robert, II, 222–23, 225
Blaser, William L., 145, 155–56, 157
Bourgeois, A. Donald, 18–19, 218
Brady, James S., 39, 121
Brantley, Elza, 213
Brown, Herbert, 207, 217
Broz, Elmer, 93
Bryant, Jay, 204, 227, 237
Buchanan, John, 267–68
budget (*see also* tax, state income), 16–17, 91–92; annual, 34–35; Constitutional Convention and, 125–26; executive takeover, 178–79, 181–82, 219–20; federal contribution, 184–85; higher education and, 183–84; mental health and, 184; revenue, 20, 23, 27, 31, 125–26; welfare and, 184, 185–87
Budget, Bureau of, 178–79, 181–82
Budgetary Commission, 91, 179
Buell family, 8–9

Cain, Richard, 48–49, 75
Cairo (Illinois), 15, 111
Capitano, Nelson, 172
Capone, Al, 52, 59, 60, 62, 64
Caputo, Philip, 164
Carey, William, 61
Carlson, Richard W., 86, 87
Catholic school aid, 136–37, 258–59
Cellini, Julie, 190
Cellini, William F., Jr., 24, 25, 71, 222–25
cement bill case, 88
Chew, Charles, 104
Chicago Crime Commission, 45, 48, 59, 62, 88
Chicago Daily News, 6, 45, 146, 200–201, 203, 205, 207
Chicago Housing Authority, 266–67
Chicago Public Relations, 42, 206
Chicago's American, 78, 203, 207
Chicago Scene, 243
Chicago Sun-Times, 41, 93, 181, 189, 255
Chicago Today, 108, 111, 133, 207
Chicago Transit Authority, 137
Chicago Tribune, 6, 50, 52, 70, 107, 164, 201, 207, 210, 255
Choate, Clyde L., 32, 33, 83, 95–98, 105, 222, 237
Ciaccio, Nicholas D., 237–39
Cicero (Illinois), 49–50
Civic Center Bank and Trust, 113–16
Civil Administrative Code of 1917, 14

Clark, William G., 65
Clements, George L., 42, 171, 173–74, 177
coal mining, 156–58, 195–96
Cohen, Robert S., 224
Combined Insurance Company of America, 84
Commerce Commission, 113
Con Con. (*see* Constitutional Convention)
Conservation, Department of, 149, 203, 214–15
Constitutional Convention (*see also* Illinois Constitution of 1970), 14, 36, 117–18; delegates, 120–23, 125, 133; environment (Article XI) and, 130; executive power and, 131–32; Illinois Constitution Week, 132; impetus for, 120–21; implementation of, 134–35; judiciary and, 117–18, 133, 134; lobbyists and, 130; provisions of, 129–30; ratification of, 132, 133–34; revenue and, 125–26, 130; signing of, 127
Constitution Study Commission, 135
Cook County Jail, 47, 211
Cook County Young Republican Movement, 41, 43
Corbally, John E., Jr., 175–76
Corcoran, Tom, 39–40, 87, 185
Corrections, Department of, 17, 212
Coulson, Robert, 90, 91
Courts Commission, 117
Cribbet, John E., 169
crime syndicate, 48–49, 52, 59–63
Currie, David P., 151, 152–54

Dailey, John P., 25, 87, 90, 154
Daley, Richard J., 13, 21, 57–58, 181, 206, 217; candidates for office and, 40, 67, 117, 137, 138, 143; Constitutional Convention and, 121, 127, 133; elections and, 41, 44; on Ogilvie, 262; state income tax and, 72, 83, 96, 98–99; voting patterns and, 77, 78; Walker and, 262; West Side bloc, 40
Daley, Richard M., 126–27
Darcy, Michael J., 266
Davis, Charles W., 32
de Grazia, Victor, 123, 253
Democratic National Convention, 66, 72, 160
Democratic Party, 13, 44, 65, 180; Illinois Senate and, 144; primary of 1972 and, 248; racial issues and, 15; sheriff's race and, 44; tax proposal and, 96–97

Dirksen, Everett McKinley, 12, 39, 40, 44–45, 65, 68, 81, 137
Dixon, Alan J., 104, 143
Dolph, Robert, 115
Douglas, Paul H., 54–55, 140
Dreiske, John, Jr., 181, 207
Drennan, Thomas, 25, 41–42, 51–53, 69–70, 76–77, 103, 227; early career, 206; parochiaid issue and, 259; press and, 204, 205–6
Dunn, Richard Edward (Dick), 87–88, 170
Dunn, Richard Thomas, 87, 118, 161–62, 167, 169–70
Dunne, George W., 57–58
Dwyer, Robert A., 78

Earth Day, 150
East St. Louis (Illinois), 15, 19, 80, 110, 217–18
Edgar, Jim, 86, 123, 150, 166, 262–63
education: community/junior colleges, 110, 174; construction projects, 172, 174; graduate, 175; private, 34–35, 136, 174, 227, 258–59; public support for, 172; revenues for, 34–35, 183–84; state aid, 109, 136; university budgets, 171–78
Education, Illinois Board of Higher, 171, 173–74, 183
Eisenhower, Earl D., 56
Elsass, James, 182
environment, 16, 109, 136, 144; acid runoff, 157; acquisition of land, 214; agencies, 149–50; bond issue, 150; coal mining, 156–58, 195; Constitutional Convention and, 130; industry response, 151–52, 156, 158; leaf burning, 158–59, 258; public opinion, 152, 158–59, 258; sewage emissions, 153; strike forces, 155–56, 157
Environmental Protection Agency (EPA), 150
Environmental Protection Agency, Illinois, 145
Everett, Marjorie, 244

Fair Employment Practices Commission, 104
Federal Aid Road Act, 221
Federal Bureau of Investigation (FBI), 63
Filo, John, 164
Finance, Department of, 180
Fitzgerald, Gerald F., 244
floods, 166, 168
Ford Foundation Fellows, 86, 90, 122
Forsyth, William D., Jr., 176

Gateway Foundation, 265–66
General Assembly: annual sessions, 126; auditor general, 130; crime agencies and, 17; expansion of, 85–86; higher education and, 173; legislative interns, 86–88; Republican domination of, 82–83; Senate seats, 84; support for Ogilvie, 36; taxing powers of, 126
Giancana, Sam, 49, 59
Gilbert, John G., 99
Gonet, Phillip M., 263
Gove, Samuel Kimball, 27–28, 86, 134–35
governor: budget process and, 179, 183; National Guard and, 167; power of, 14
Governor's Committee on Criminal Justice, 17
Governor's Mansion, 109, 227–28, 229–32
Governor's Revenue Study Committee, 32–33
Grange, Harold (Red), 147
Great Depression, 9, 19, 82
Green, Dwight H., 64, 179
Greenberg, Frank, 114, 116, 118
Groen, Egbert B., 104
gun control, 88, 129, 258

Hahn, Ralph, 160–61
Hancock, Samuel O., 194
Hanley, William S., 24, 74, 190–91, 237, 264
Hansen, Willard, 46
Hanson, Henry, 200–201, 207–8
Harris, Joseph L., 70
Harris, William C., 90, 91–92, 108, 258
Helm, James R., 264–65
Henry, David Dodds, 161–62
Hensey, Margaret, 238–39, 243
Heyer, Edmund Lawrence, 172, 189, 191–93
Hickey, James T., 109, 230–31
Highway Study Commission, 20, 222
Highway Trust Authority, 221
Hoffman, Julius J., 59, 62, 63
Holderman, James B., 173–78
Holderman, S. J., 173
home rule, 129, 134
Horner, Henry, 147, 260
Horsley, G. William, 166
Housing Development Authority, Illinois (IDHA), 190, 220
Howard, Robert P., 66, 201, 220
Howlett, Michael, 13, 81, 257

Human Relations, Illinois Commission on, 218–19
Human Resources, Office of, 18
Human Rights, Department of, 219

IBI. (*see* Illinois Bureau of Investigation)
IDHA. (*see* Housing Development Authority, Illinois)
Illinois: as bellwether state, 72; criminal charges against officials, 112–13; downstate, 16, 133–34, 136–37, 194–96, 235–36, 256–59; farm exodus, 210; restructuring of government, 13–14, 16–17, 56–57; voting patterns, 71, 79–81, 256–57
Illinois Bureau of Investigation (IBI), 18, 215–16
Illinois Commission to Study State Government, 135
Illinois Committee for Constitutional Convention, 122
Illinois Constitution of 1870, 14, 16, 95, 129, 130, 221; tax proposals and, 95, 102, 106, 125
Illinois Constitution of 1970 (*see also* Constitutional Convention), 51, 84, 86, 132
Illinois Environmental Protection Act (HB 3788), 151, 152–53, 155
Illinois Information Service (IIS), 200
Illinois Issues, 121, 262, 263
Illinois State Journal, 70, 155
Illinois Supreme Court, 48, 170, 259; scandal, 36, 92–94, 113–16, 131, 200, 242; special commission, 114–15; tax reform and, 126
income disclosure, 241, 265–66, 283n. 13
Institute for Environmental Quality, 152, 156, 186
Institute for Social Policy, 186–87
Internal Security and Fraud Investigation, Division of, 27
Isaacs, Theodore J., 94, 113–17

Jackson, Jesse L., 138–39
Jacobson, Walter, 210–11
Jewel Tea Company, 42, 53, 171, 265
Johnson, James R., 158
Johnson, Lyndon, 19, 65, 181, 255
Judicial Inquiry Board, 117, 169
judiciary, Constitutional Convention and (*see also* Illinois Supreme Court), 117–18, 133, 134
Justice Department, 60, 61, 112

Karns, John M., Jr., 130
Kasper, Louis J., 43, 47–50
Kay, Norton, 108, 111, 202, 225
Kearney, Daniel, 190, 220
Keene, David, 165
Kennedy, Edward (Ted), 37, 67, 123, 124
Kennedy, John F., 39, 79, 124
Kent State University, 163, 164
Kerner, Otto, 5, 64, 80, 82, 94, 180, 229, 236, 255; illicit transactions and, 112, 116–17, 244; media and, 188, 199, 201
Klassen, Clarence Willard, 146–48, 151–55
Klingbiel, Ray I., 113, 115, 131, 200
Kolbe, John, 203, 232–33
Kolbe, Kathy, 232
Kucharski, Edmund J., 43, 48, 53, 71, 101, 143, 257
Kunstler, William M., 160–61

Lanigan, John Joseph (Jack), 89, 100–101, 104, 259
Latherow, Clifford B., 107
Law Enforcement, Department of, 17, 207, 217, 245
Law Enforcement Commission, 46
Lawrence, Michael, 69, 123, 263
Leahy, Mary Lee, 130, 159
Legislative Audit Commission, 85
Lehnhausen, Robert J., 19–20
Leth, T. R. (Ted), 180, 181
Levin, Ivan R., 219–20
Levin, Philip J., 245
Lewis, John W., 182, 245
lieutenant governor, 12–13, 33, 84, 85
Life, 4–5, 59, 209
Lincoln, Abraham, 127, 230, 237, 266
Little FBI. (see Illinois Bureau of Investigation)
Little Hoover Commission, 56–57, 135
Littlewood, Thomas B., 243
Local Government Affairs, Department of, 19–20, 109
local governments: agencies, 19–20, 109; home rule, 129, 134
Lohman, Walter (Bud), 259–60
Loukas, James P., 90–91
Lowden, Frank, 14–15, 220
Lynes, Marion (Hap), 155
Lyons, Thomas G., 122, 255

MacArthur, Alexander, 245
Mack, James H., 76, 77, 79, 140–42, 253–54
MacVicar, Robert W., 165
Madigan, Edward, 105
Madigan, Michael, 100
Magruder, Jeb Stuart, 53–54
Mahin, George E., 21–23, 26–27, 111
Malkovich, Dan, 203
Manchester, William, 210
Mandeville, Robert, 182
Maple, Robert Charles, 254–55
Marcinkus, Paul C., 226–27
Marsh, Curtis, 111–12
Marsh, Jeremiah, 21, 24, 25, 75, 169, 204; on amendatory veto, 132; as attorney, 123–24; attorney general appointment and, 140–41; Constitutional Convention and, 123–25, 128; tax proposal and, 30–31, 103, 106–7
Mathewson, Joseph D., 25, 72–73, 199, 202
Mauldin, Bill, 93, 168–69
McCaffrey, James F., 23, 203
McCarter, John Wilbur, Jr., 23, 24, 27, 99–100, 106; early career, 180–81; as finance director, 30, 180–83, 185–87; higher education and, 173, 176–78
McCormick, Mike, 236
McFadden, Joseph, 214
McGloon, Thomas (Art), 84, 95, 103
McReaken, Dayton, 194–96
media: Accardo case and, 63; on Constitution, 133; downstate, 73; election of 1968 and, 73, 78, 79; election of 1972 and, 254–55; fickleness of, 110–11; investigative journalism, 22, 93; Klassen firing and, 154–55; newspapers, 201; print journalists, 199–200; radio and television coverage, 198–99; Statehouse pressroom, 197–200; student protests and, 164; support for Ogilvie, 11–12, 41–42, 45, 57, 73, 78, 254–55; tax proposal and, 33–34, 108; television commercials, 52, 256
Medicaid, 186
Mees, Jim, 121
mental hospitals, 16, 67, 109–10, 184
Michaelson, Ronald Dwight, 50, 56–57, 58, 157, 249, 256
Miller, Jeffrey, 164
Miller, William S., 198–99, 244
Mines and Minerals Department, 195

Mississippi River, sewage emissions into, 153
Mitchell, John, 78–79
Mongoven, John O., 200
Morris, Delyte Wesley, 165, 172–73, 174
Municipal League, 74

National Guard, 15, 50, 73, 160–62, 165; Air National Guard, 168; flooding and, 166; governor's role, 167
Ness, Eliot, 52, 63
Netsch, Dawn Clark, 130
Newhouse, Richard, 104
News-Gazette, The, 46
Nicodemus, Charles, 205, 206
Nixon, Richard, 24, 39, 53, 54, 72, 76, 78–79, 119, 150, 159, 169, 185, 193–94, 255–56
Northern Illinois University, 163
Northwestern University, 135, 163, 164
Nowlan, James D., 51, 157, 250, 252–53, 256, 264

O'Connell, William, 197, 207
O'Connor, Ronald T., 156
Ogilvie, Dorothy Shriver, 8, 12, 41, 60–62, 108–9, 189, 192, 267; childhood, 228–29; European visits, 226–27, 232–33; marriage, 229; personality, 227–28; restoration of Governor's Mansion, 229–32
Ogilvie, Elizabeth, 61, 108–9, 226, 228, 267
Ogilvie, Kenneth Spivey, 7–9
Ogilvie, Ralph, 7
Ogilvie, Richard Buell: on Accardo, 63–64; advisors to, 123; as assistant to attorney general, 40, 46, 60–61; Board of Cook County Commissioners race and, 51–55; budget proposals, 183–85; confidence, 72–73, 78; Constitutional Convention, approach to, 123, 125–29, 132; Constitutional Convention address, 126–27; death, 267; downstate image of, 194–96; early career, 10, 41; fearlessness, 5, 29, 190–92, 267; finances, 265–66, 283n. 13; on fiscal crisis, 30–31, 34; ideals, 13, 61, 106–7; inaugural speech, 13–14, 15–16; IRS investigation and, 75–76; as law-and-order candidate, 73–74; leadership, 56, 106–7, 136, 263–64; media support for, 11–12, 40, 41–42, 45, 52, 57, 73, 78, 106–7, 254–55; organized crime and, 4–5; on penal system, 213–14; personal life, 60–61, 108–9, 170, 192, 260; political astute-

ness of, 41, 43–44, 69; polls and, 251–52; on pollution, 149, 150–51; as president of Cook County board, 55–58, 68; public image of, 126, 188–90, 210–11, 249–50; purse snatcher and, 190–91; realism of, 110–11; revival of, 262–64; scandal and, 112; Scott, rivalry with, 148–49; security detail, 192–93; as sheriff, 4, 21, 45–50; sheriff's office race, 38–45; on spending by public officials, 241; State of the State message, 261; student protesters' view of, 161; tax proposal speech, 33; time, use of, 249; on transportation, 221; veto power, 57–58, 131–32; on violence, 160; Washington visits, 185, 194; welfare and, 185–86; World War II and, 1–4, 9, 232–33, 271n. 2
Ogilvie, Robert Spivey, 8
Oglesby, Marion, 24–25, 27, 139, 215
open-housing initiative, 88–89
opinion polls, 70, 106, 251–52
Owens, Lina, 7
Ozinga, Frank, 89

Page, Ray, 44, 55, 143
Parenti, Michael, 163
patronage, 25–27, 196–97, 215, 224, 242, 262, 263; prison jobs and, 47–48
Patton, Harold R., 166–70
Paul VI, 226, 227
penal system: Attica riot, 211, 212; Cook County Jail, 47, 211; humanization of, 212–13; racial makeup of prisons, 211; rehabilitation programs, 16–17, 212; restructuring, 17, 109; youth gangs and, 213
pension plans, 184
Perbohner, Robert M., 113, 115, 117
Percy, Charles, 12, 54–55, 139, 185, 255, 256
Perkins, Donald Sheldon, 53, 60–61, 171, 265; on Accardo prosecution, 63; as fundraiser, 25, 42–43, 51, 70, 76–77; on reelection campaign, 253
Peters, Everett R., 179–80
Philip, James (Pate), 68
Phillips, Stephen, 176–77, 181–82
Phipps, Raymond W., 111–12
Pinnell, Thomas, 196
police: Chicago, 46; Illinois State, 18, 149; increase in force, 18; merit program, 46; sheriff's force, 45–46

Pollution Control Board, 151, 152–53, 156, 158
Pound, Edward Thomas, 92–94, 113, 168–69, 200, 207
Powell, Daisy, 236
Powell, Paul, 13, 67, 81, 117, 127, 179–80, 200; career of, 234–35; death, 236–39; estate, size of, 243; financial dealings, 207–8, 216, 234, 242; indictments and, 242–43 press conferences, 198–99
Public Aid Department, 186
Public Health, Department of, 149

racetrack stock scandal, 117, 235–36, 242, 243–46
racial issues, 15, 18, 49–50, 54, 111; administration posts and, 217; Illinois Commission on Human Relations, 218–19; open-housing initiative, 88–90; welfare and, 138–39
Racing Board, 244
Radical Union, 162
Ranney, George A., Jr., 31–32, 127–28, 181, 267
Regional Transportation Authority (RTA), 223, 267
Registration and Education, Department of, 217
Registration and Miscellany Committee, 89
Reid, Robert D., 262
Rendleman, John S., 174, 239–40
Rentschler, William H., 142–43
Republican National Convention, 177
Republican Party: Better Government Association and, 21; Illinois legislature and, 12, 54–55, 82–83, 144; patronage and, 25–27; racial issues and, 15; tax proposal and, 34, 35–36; train tour, 65; Watergate scandal and, 54; Young Republicans, 39, 41, 43
Revenue, Illinois Department of, 20
Revenue Committee, 96
Richard B. Ogilvie Society, 266
Rimmel, Edwin, 136
Robinson, William H., 217
Robson, John E., 110
Rockford Morning Star, 207
Roemer, William F., Jr., 49, 62, 63
Rogers, William, 60
Romanotto, Pete, 234
Ronan, James A., 180
Roosevelt, Franklin D., 19, 182
Routman, Melvin N., 242

Rovere, Richard, 119
Royko, Mike, 6, 146
Rumor of War, A (Caputo), 164
Rust, Franklin H., 112
Rutherford, William L., 214

Saccaro, Emil, 239
Sanitary Water Board, 146, 148, 149, 152
Schneiderman, Michael, 156–58
Schoenburg, Bernard, 242
Scott, Maurice W., 35
Scott, William G., 159
Scott, William J. (Bill), 12, 41, 44, 55, 81, 109, 239; campaign of 1972 and, 255, 256; environment and, 148–49, 151, 154, 159; Senate appointment, 139–41
Sears, Barnabas, 217
Semrow, Harry H., 52, 55
Senate, United States, 137–40
Senate Bill 1150. (see tax, state income)
Senate Rackets Committee, 62
Shapiro, Samuel Harvey, 5, 16, 32, 48, 64, 71–72, 74, 77–78, 82, 275n. 18; defeat of, 79–81; public image of, 65–66
Sheehan, Timothy P., 52–53, 68, 69, 71
sheriff's office: crime, connections to, 40; intelligence personnel, 47; payroll, 45; police force, 45–46; vice raids, 46–47
Shriver, R. Sargent, 67
Simon, Paul, 13, 33, 77–78, 79–81, 85, 109, 144, 189, 199, 239–40, 246; election of 1972 and, 247–49; environment and, 150; as lieutenant governor, 248; on Ogilvie, 263
Skolnick, Sherman, 92, 93–94, 113–14, 116
Small, Len, 220
Smith, Ralph Tyler, 24, 81, 83, 103, 137–39, 141–43
Smith, Victor L., 77
Snopko, James, 135–36
Solfisburg, Roy J., Jr., 5, 114–16, 131, 200
Sours, Hudson Ralph, 99, 104
Southern Illinois University, 163, 164–66, 172–73
Spencer, Roswell T., 21, 40, 44
Spivey, Alta, 7
Spivey, Reuben M., 6–7, 47
State Community College, 110, 218
State Fair, 36, 106, 111–13
State Journal-Register, 242

Stevens, John Paul, 115–16
Stevenson, Adlai E., III, 13, 55, 67, 137–38, 140, 141, 142, 166, 240–41
Stevenson, Adlai Ewing, 13, 137, 140, 195, 236
Stevenson, Douglas F., 124
St. Louis Globe-Democrat, 155
St. Louis Model City Agency, 18
St. Louis Post-Dispatch, 78, 93, 108, 169, 201, 254
Stone, W. Clement, 84, 142, 174
Stratton, William G., 5, 67, 173, 230
student protests, 136, 169; conspiracy theories, 166; curfew violations, 162–63; faculty support for, 163; Illini Union sit-in, 162; media response, 164; political repercussions, 166; strike, 164
Swank, Harold (Hap), 186
Swanson, Arthur (Ron), 189–90

Taft, Robert A., 39, 182, 264
tax: budget process and, 184–85; gasoline, 136–37, 221; personal property, 106, 131, 184; relief/credit, 131; sales, 32, 33, 103, 131; vehicle registration, 221; on wagering, 424
tax, state income, 138; compromise legislation, 103–5; design of bill, 32; election and, 29–30, 258; expenditure proposals, 34–35; flat-rate income levy, 32–33, 95, 131; flat-rate income levy proposal, 32–33, 95; passage of, 105; rebates, 103; Senate passage of, 92, 104; sponsors of bill, 90–92; unpopularity of, 30–32, 105–6; validity, challenge to, 106; variable rate of taxation, 96–99, 102–3
Taxpayers' Federation of Illinois, 21, 35
Thoelcke, Tim, 8
Thompson, James, 64, 128, 182, 188, 189, 250
Times-Democrat, 69
Tolva, Donald, 90, 102
Touhy, John P., 96, 103
transition plan, 21, 24–25; communications, 25; personnel recruitment, 25–27; retreat conference, 27–28; team, 24–25
transportation, 25, 223; airport proposals, 110, 218, 221, 222; emergency rebuilding program, 221; highway system, 20, 35, 57, 73, 103–4, 220–21, 223–24; mass transit, 136–37; railroads, 266
Transportation, Illinois Department of (IDOT), 25, 222

Udstuen, Donald, 196–97
United Republican Fund (URF), 50–51
United States Court of Appeals, 59, 63, 66
University of Illinois (*see also* student protests), 27, 169, 172; freedom of speech issue and, 160–61
Untouchables, 52, 64

veto, 57–58, 131–32
Vietnam War (*see also* student protests), 5, 54, 66, 119, 142, 210
Vlahoplus, Christopher, 123, 201
voting, 71, 77–81, 134, 256–57

Walker, Dan, 6, 10, 111, 130, 135, 159; Constitutional Convention and, 132–33; grassroots campaign of, 225, 248; media and, 201–2, 254–55; polls and, 251–52; populism of, 193, 249; public image of, 188, 189; on racetrack politics, 245–46; scandal and, 112
Wall Street Journal, 24, 73, 243
Ware, Mitchell, 215–17
Watson, Kenneth, 155
Weaver, Edward T., 186
Weisman, Joel, 205
welfare, 35, 138–39, 184, 185–87, 261
Whalen, Brian, 20–21, 26, 51, 56, 78, 103, 124, 218, 237; early career, 39–40; and sheriff candidacy, 38–40, 47
Whalen, Charles, 39, 201
Whalen, Wayne W., 118, 127–28
Wheeler, Charles N., III, 189
White, Alexander, 57
Willey, Marion, 204–5
Williams, Gale, 258
Williams, James E., 207, 217
Winchester, Lester (Shot), 235–36
Winchester, Robert Charles, 235–36
Wittmond, Carl, 235
Witwer, Samuel W., 122–23, 129, 130, 132
Wolff, Paula, 123, 127–28
Woods, Joseph I., 53
Woods, Rosemary, 53
World War II, 1–4, 232–33

Yakstis, Ande, 94, 113
Young, Beatrice, 219
Young Republican Federation, 39

Taylor Pensoneau, the vice president of the Illinois Coal Association, was formerly the Illinois political correspondent of the *St. Louis Post-Dispatch*. He is the coauthor (along with Bob Ellis) of *Dan Walker: The Glory and the Tragedy*, which was awarded the Illinois State Historical Society's Certificate of Excellence in 1994.